INSIDERS' GUIDE® TO

PORTLAND, OREGON

8/11

HELP US KEEP THIS GUIDE UP TO DATE

We would love to hear from you concerning your experiences with this guide and how you feel it could be improved and kept up to date. Please send your comments and suggestions to:

editorial@GlobePequot.com

Thanks for your input, and happy travels!

INSIDERS' GUIDE® TO
PORTLAND, OREGON

SEVENTH EDITION

RACHEL DRESBECK

INSIDERS' GUIDE

GUILFORD, CONNECTICUT
AN IMPRINT OF GLOBE PEQUOT PRESS

All the information in this guidebook is subject to change. We recommend that you call ahead to obtain current information before traveling.

INSIDERS' GUIDE ®

Editor: Kevin Sirois
Project Editor: Heather Santiago
Layout Artist: Kevin Mak
Text Design: Sheryl Kober
Maps: XNR Productions, Inc. © Morris Book Publishing, LLC

ISSN 1541-7921
ISBN 978-0-7627-6475-4

Printed in the United States of America
10 9 8 7 6 5 4 3 2 1

CONTENTS

CONTENTS

Directory of Maps

ABOUT THE AUTHOR

Rachel Dresbeck, a writer and editor, has observed and written about Portland for a variety of publications. She's also an author of the first edition of the *Insiders' Guide to the Oregon Coast*. She was educated at Whitman College and the University of Oregon, has taught writing and literature at Portland Community College and the University of Oregon, and now teaches writing and writes about research at Oregon Health and Science University. She lives with her husband and daughters in the Richmond neighborhood of Portland, where she studies ways in which citizens sustain their civility and community spirit against all odds.

ACKNOWLEDGMENTS

Portland is a city of neighborhoods, so first I would like to thank my neighbors for their insight, witticisms, and generosity over the years. As always, the Banchero, Allison-Brown, Frost, Forrest, Bolles, Thomas, and Colwell-Averett families have been especially generous with their time, knowledge, and hospitality. I am especially grateful for the time shared in the meadow at the Old Ranch.

Thanks also to my ever-patient husband, Tom, and my daughters, Flannery and Cleo, who make writing anything a more interesting experience, who are my favorite companions for exploration, and who had to make a lot of dinners as I was completing this volume. This book is dedicated to them.

Portland

Downtown Portland

Portland Neighborhoods

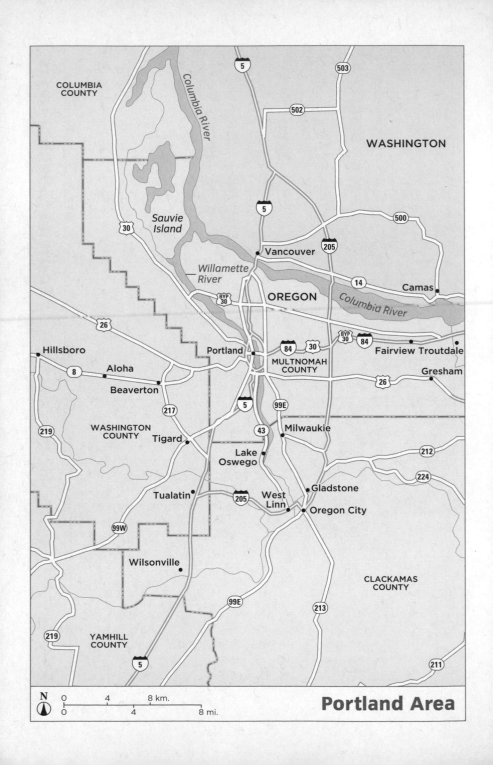

Portland Area

INTRODUCTION

Compared with cities such as Los Angeles, San Francisco, or even Seattle, Portland is small. But we like it that way. Though Portland contributes its share to cyberspace, it is also concerned with human space. Portland is the home of groundbreaking biomedical research and world-class firms for animation, advertising, and athletic wear. Yet it is also renowned for its amiable, everyday civility, for its dedication to wise planning and public transportation, for its charming neighborhoods, for its bookstores, sidewalk cafes, and pubs. The parks contain more forest than any city in the nation. People ride their bikes or walk to work. The library serves coffee. Portland is a city where the fire department will still come to your block party.

Portland is an attractive city with a friendly skyline in a beautiful region of the country. Its setting, in a fertile valley ringed by mountains and bordered by the Columbia and Willamette Rivers, shapes the character of the city in ways that residents tend to take for granted. But the beautiful country surrounding us and within the city itself commands great loyalty—a loyalty that extends to the way we live and work. Many local businesses, for example, are consciously devoted to growing and creating products that draw from our regional abundance, and many others are devoted to using and promoting these products. We work hard to maintain our quality of life.

But we are also a playful city. Citizens prize their parks and libraries. Neighborhood coffee shops and brewpubs are busy long into the night. Workers may leave the downtown area at 5 p.m., but they are soon replaced by recreators attending the theater, the movies, the ballet, the symphony, or the opera, strolling the boulevards, stopping for dinner or a glass of wine. On the weekends, crowds gather at the Saturday Market, at the Farmers' Market, at the river. Or people head up to the mountains or to the coast. We know how to have a good time.

Sometimes we lose our way. But when that happens, Portland rises to the challenge. When our downtown area was dying in the 1970s, the community—the residents, businesses, government—came up with a plan to save it. When sprawl began to threaten farms and forests, we created an innovative regional government to coordinate growth, create places where people want to live, preserve green spaces, and organize public transportation. This feature of Portland life extends to the entire state. When beaches were under siege by acquisitive developers, Republican governor Tom McCall insisted that we keep the entire coastline open to the public, up to the high tide line, resulting in higher property values for owners and sublime beaches for everyone. We have our share of problems, but we do not feel helpless before them, and our efforts to solve them represent an enormous amount of creativity and goodwill on the part of our citizens to try to work things out.

As a result, we have a clean, safe, interesting city. We have a city where you can still send your kids to public schools. We have a city where you can sit on a downtown park bench in peace. We have a city where you can talk to the farmer who grew your vegetables and the brewer who made your beer. We have the largest independent bookstore in the nation and one of the most well-read populations. We have a city where you can escape to the forest on your lunch break. We have space to dream and plan and hope and the resources to make those dreams, plans, and hopes come true.

These are the reasons we love our city, and we think you will love it too. This appealing mixture of nature and culture, of sophistication and friendliness, draws people from all over the world to visit, and sometimes when they have visited, they want to stay. Who can blame them? The population gets bigger, but we retain the small-city values that define us. There's room for everyone.

HOW TO USE THIS BOOK

Insiders' Guide to Portland, Oregon is designed to allow you to make the most of your time here, however long it is. Our guide is organized into thematic chapters that cover everything from accommodations to well-being. The internal organization of chapters will vary depending on their content. For example, the Festivals and Annual Events chapter is sorted chronologically, but the Recreation chapter is set up alphabetically by topic. Many chapters, such as Accommodations, Restaurants, or Attractions, may be additionally organized into geographic areas for easier navigation.

Portland is divided into eastern and western halves by the Willamette River. It is further divided by Burnside Street, which runs east and west, into four quadrants: **Southwest, Northwest, Southeast,** and **Northeast.** A fifth "quadrant," North Portland, the portion west of Williams Avenue, extends from the Broadway Bridge to the Columbia River; however, for the purposes of this book, listings in North Portland and Northeast Portland have been kept together. Vancouver, which is immediately north of Portland just across the Columbia River in the state of Washington, is also mentioned frequently in our book, as are the towns that surround the city. Thus you will also find sections for **Vancouver** and for **Outlying Areas,** for a total of six basic geographical divisions.

The first chapters are designed to help you orient yourself to the Portland Metro area by giving you information about transportation and history. The next several chapters concern the exigencies of daily living—where to eat and sleep. Then we devote a large number of chapters to various forms of recreation; these range from telling you how to find a nearby brewpub, antiques shop, or climbing park to securing Blazers tickets. We also include a chapter on Day Trips, should you want to go exploring the innumerable attractions of the region beyond the city limits.

Moving to the Portland Metro area or already live here? Be sure to check out the blue-tabbed pages at the back of the book, where you will find the **Living Here** appendix that offers sections on relocation, child care, education, health care, retirement, and media.

Within all chapters, you will find frequent cross-references and even, for the sake of convenience, some cross-listings.

Throughout this book you'll find **Insider's Tips** (indicated by an **i**), which offer quick insights, and **Close-ups,** which provide in-depth information on topics that are particularly interesting, unusual, or distinctly Portland.

You'll also find listings accompanied by the ✳ symbol—these are our top picks for attractions, restaurants, accommodations, and everything in between that you shouldn't miss while you're in the area. You want the best this region has to offer? Go with our **Insiders' Choice.**

A few basic maps are included in the guide, but you may also want to purchase a more detailed map of the city and surrounding areas in order to prevent those interesting discussions between driver and navigator about which way to turn.

The Greater Portland Metro area comprises Multnomah, Washington, and Clackamas Counties. You won't notice when you cross from one county into another, but you will need to know which county you are dealing with for the sake of real estate, schools, and government. Where necessary, then, we will point out these distinctions.

Don't just take our word for it: Use this guide to explore for yourself the charms of Portland. Our dynamic city is always changing, adding new attractions and business, and closing others down. You may discover some of these changes in your own travels.

AREA OVERVIEW

The Portland Metropolitan area comprises Multnomah, Washington, and Clackamas Counties, as well as the southern edge of Clark County in Washington State across the Columbia River to the north. The area is home to nearly two million people, who live, work, and play in one of the most beautiful urban areas in the country—at least, that's what we think.

Portland sits just to the south of the confluence of the Willamette and Columbia Rivers; it is indeed a port city. It is situated approximately 70 miles from the Pacific Ocean and connects to the Pacific via the Columbia River. Its busy shipping schedule makes it the third-leading commercial maritime center on the West Coast. A significant portion of its freight is eastern Oregon grain, barged down the Columbia, loaded into huge grain elevators, and poured into freighters heading for Asia. On the receiving end, Portland is the third-largest West Coast port for ships bringing Japanese cars into the United States.

ECONOMIC DEVELOPMENT

Like many American cities, after the world wars Portland thrived during the 1950s, but by the late '60s the city was faced with serious economic problems. Due to environmental concerns and international competition, its economy, dependent on timber and Pacific fisheries, spiraled downward. The decline of these two major industries affected secondary service and retail businesses. But the city rose to the challenge: In 1973 the city council and planners came up with the Downtown Plan, a vision that reinvigorated local retail, housing, entertainment, and government. A westside freeway was torn down and redirected around town, and the Tom McCall Waterfront Park, named after a popular Oregon governor, was built along the edge of the Willamette River. Another major change that dynamically rearranged Portland was comprehensive transportation planning, including investing in light rail and reestablishing a streetcar line. And key to all has been a commitment to a lively downtown area, anchored by Pioneer Courthouse Square, a central open space for community events.

This commitment to infrastructure has been complemented by robust land-use planning. An urban-growth boundary was designed as an outer edge for housing developments within the city limits of Portland and its neighboring towns. This strategy, combined with tax breaks and grants for low-income housing, encouraged contractors to "in-fill" within the growth boundary. This plan has worked well—though not without grumbling by some who complain that it's too strict and others who think it's not strict enough. On the whole, however, the urban growth boundary has allowed Portland to become a vibrant city filled with high-density vertical shops, apartments, and other mercantile and living spaces. The result: Portland regularly earns high praise as an exemplar of a city that is planned with the future in mind—a future that offers its residents alternatives to reliance on oil.

> **i** The official state website is a rich and exhaustive resource for information on all things Oregon. Here you'll discover the market conditions for starting a business, profiles on communities, details on state historic sites, the locations of good cross-country ski trails, and anything else you might want to know about our beautiful state. You'll find it at www.oregon.gov.

Unsurprisingly, then, economic growth areas include green building and sustainable energy. Another major facet of the local economy is the high-tech sector. Beginning in the 1980s, microchip makers flocked to the area, attracted by cheap electricity generated by dams on the Columbia River, lots of clean water, and tax incentives offered by city and county governments. Activewear is also important. Nike has its world headquarters here, and inspired by its rival, Adidas moved its American headquarters here as well—and so did outdoor footwear maker Keen. Columbia Sportswear is a locally grown outfit, and Portland is also the home of Langlitz Leather, which supplies Harley gear for anyone willing to pay top dollar for the coveted handmade jackets. And Portland's DIY atmosphere has nurtured dozens of local clothing designers beyond the activewear sector, including Nau, a local firm that combines activewear fabrics with chic urban design, so that you can ride your bike to work and arrive looking stylish.

Portland's strongest industry at present is health care, and the areas forecast to grow the most are the service and trade sectors, with slight dips in manufacturing. But that just describes the large employer sectors. Portland's entrepreneurial culture is thriving, and more than 8 percent of area workers are self-employed. It costs as little as $50 to incorporate a business. While our state income taxes look high, there is no sales tax, and commercial property taxes are among the lowest in the US.

THE CITY OF ROSES

But there is more to living in a city than making a living. Portland is known as the "City of Roses," and it possesses the ideal climate in which to grow these lovely flowers. Each June, they are celebrated with a party called the Rose Festival, an event that includes three parades, a carnival, the crowning of a queen, and a visit from a dozen ships from the US Navy, US Coast Guard, and the Canadian Navy and Coast Guard.

Part of what makes those roses grow, of course, is rain. While Portland has 82 days per year when the sky is blue and the sun is shining, it also has, on the average, 82 partly cloudy days and 220 cloudy days per year, with 165 of those coming with at least some precipitation.

Then there are the wonders of nature surrounding the city: the Columbia Gorge; Mount Hood, one of the crown jewels of the Oregon Cascades; and the North Coast, with beaches, jutting capes, and art colonies. (Read more about these in our Day Trips chapter.)

Few things define Portland as much as its neighborhoods, however, and so to these we now turn.

SOUTHWEST PORTLAND

Southwest Portland encompasses the **downtown area,** stretching west beyond Washington Park and south along the Willamette River. The result is an urban village cradled by a friendly wilderness. The downtown area is composed of short blocks, platted in the 19th century to contain lots of little stores and cross streets, thus limiting the size and height of new construction. Above downtown are affluent neighborhoods with lovely houses lining hillside streets. Down on the plains of the Willamette River, the area has undergone vibrant renewal as new condominiums and businesses are built along the river.

A good place to start a tour of the Southwest is **Pioneer Courthouse Square** (www.pioneercourthousesquare.org), which is bordered by Yamhill Street, Morrison Street, 6th Avenue, and Broadway. This piazza anchors the city; it is full of tourists, office workers eating lunch, teenagers expressing themselves, families with children, and all the characters that city plazas attract. It is also noted for its waterfall fountain, its imaginative sculpture, and an echo chamber—if you face the steps of the small amphitheater while standing on the round marble stone, you can create a cascade of sound by just saying hello.

Depending on the time of year, Pioneer Courthouse Square is also the site of sandcastle contests, cultural festivals, flower gardens, and a huge Christmas tree. The Tri-Met bus information and tickets office is found here, as is **Travel Portland,** the official visitor center run by the Portland Visitors Association (POVA), with info and tickets to special events (www.travelportland.com). The center features, in addition to a superabundance of information, a small theater that shows short films about Portland.

Portland Index

- The Portland Metropolitan area has more than 2 million people.
- The city of Portland covers 134 square miles.
- The average rainfall in Portland is 36 inches per year.
- Portland residents enjoy an average of 128,618 minutes of sunshine per year.
- Portland has nearly 13,000 acres of parks and open space—15 percent of its land area.
- The number of hens a Portland household may keep without a permit: 3. No roosters, please.
- The median age in the metro area is 37.5.
- The mean time for commuting to work is 24.5 minutes.
- The largest private employers in the Portland area are Intel (15,000), Providence Health System (13,000), Oregon Health and Science University (13,000), Fred Meyer Stores (9,600), and Kaiser Foundation Health Plan (8,700).
- Portland-area residents drink more microbrewed beer than anyone in the nation.
- Portland has 28 coffeeshops for every 100,000 inhabitants.
- Portland is the home of Powell's City of Books, the largest independent bookstore in the world.

Tom McCall Waterfront Park borders the west bank of the Willamette. Here, you'll find the Salmon Springs Fountain, children's play areas, a monument to the battleship *Oregon,* and a sculpture garden dedicated to the World War II relocation trauma of Oregon's Japanese-American community (see Portland's Parks).

The Park Blocks run from Portland State University to West Burnside and beyond, providing a beautiful backdrop for a number of the city's performing arts venues, shops, restaurants, and museums. Across the South Park Blocks is the Portland Art Museum, with European paintings, an exciting Native American art wing, and blockbuster touring exhibits. The Park Blocks are also the home of Portland's cutting-edge farmers' market, from Feb through Nov.

Other highlights of Southwest Portland are Washington Park, nestled on the east side of the long ridge called Forest Park, the International Rose Test Garden, the Japanese Garden, and the Washington Park Zoo.

The newest neighborhood in Southwest Portland is the South Waterfront area, a district rising atop old shipbuilding yards along the banks of the Willamette. This neighborhood features sleek high-rises built alongside a verdant greenway. It is the home of one of the campuses of Oregon Health and Science University and the lower landing dock of the Portland Aerial Tram (see the Getting Here, Getting Around chapter for more information on this unique transportation alternative, and see the Relocation chapter for more information about Southwest Portland's neighborhoods).

NORTHWEST PORTLAND

Northwest Portland is characterized by its creative energy, both in its industrially chic Pearl District and in its beautiful Victorian district, Nob Hill. Northwest Portland is also the home of Old Town on the north side of Burnside Street and Chinatown and the Skidmore District.

Chinatown, with its entrance at 4th Avenue and Burnside Street, is an Asian-American neighborhood with grocery stores, restaurants, and art galleries. This small neighborhood was once home to the West Coast's largest population of Chinese Americans, immigrants who mined for gold here and built the railroad. The Portland Classical Chinese Garden, a standout in the district, is one of the few authentic classical-style Chinese gardens in the United States.

Nearby is the Skidmore Historic District, north of West Burnside Street and between Front and 4th Avenues. Once the hangout of unemployed loggers and sailors, this riverside cluster of streets led to the term "Skid Row," borrowed from "Skid Road," a muddy path of logs leading down from the forests to the river. You may still see folks down on their luck lining up for a Salvation Army lunch here. But this sad reality aside, Skidmore is worth a visit for its charming old buildings and its colorful history.

i Portland has a number of colorful nicknames: the City of Roses, Puddletown, and Bridgetown, as well as PDX, our airport code. And we are still known as Stumptown, from the hundreds of fir stumps left in the streets by hasty 19th-century builders. Hinting at our future commitment to good public transportation, early city officials painted them white to warn wagoneers out after dark.

Northwest Portland is the site of Powell's Books, one of the largest bookstores in the world. Powell's marks the outer edge of the Pearl District, a reclaimed industrial area that is now home to art galleries, luxury condos, upscale shops, art schools, and fine restaurants. Across from Powell's is the historic **Blitz-Weinhard Brewery,** which is now part of the **Brewery Blocks** development and home to swanky shops and condominiums. First-Thursday gallery walks turn the neighborhood into one big open house.

The Pearl also hosts the **Weiden & Kennedy Advertising Agency** (they do ads for Nike, Old Spice, and Coca-Cola) and **Laika,** the animation studio that produced the films *Coraline* and *Corpse Bride,* among other things. Other film, video, mixed-media companies, and recording studios inhabit this neighborhood as well. The streetcar system links the Pearl to the rest of Northwest Portland, including the excellent **shopping districts** along Northwest 21st and 23rd Avenues, before it heads back downtown.

Along 21st and 23rd Avenues, you'll find boutiques, antiques shops, and bookstores in renovated Victorian houses. The street life along both avenues is bustling and vibrant, and it's a city favorite for window-shopping and people-watching. The district is also home to some of the city's best restaurants. After exploring the neighborhood at ground level, it's fun to head up to the **Pittock Mansion** and its 46-acre site, 3229 Northwest Pittock Dr., to capture the bird's-eye view. See the Relocation chapter for more information on this neighborhood.

SOUTHEAST PORTLAND

Southeast Portland is a sprawling district characterized by parks, funky residential neighborhoods, indie businesses, Reed College, a riverfront industrial area, and an emerging indie business scene. **Lower**

Area Codes & 10-Digit Dialing

Due to a proliferation of telephone numbers, Portland, like most metropolitan areas, has added area codes in recent years. The area codes that serve Portland are (503) and (971). These are also codes for Salem and northern coastal towns. Area codes (541) and (458) will give you access to southern, central, and eastern Oregon, including the central and southern coasts.

When you make a call in the Portland area, you will need to dial the area code first—all 10 digits. (It won't be a long-distance call unless you dial a "1" first, which would make 11 digits.) Area code (360) serves Vancouver; calls from Portland to Vancouver, however, are long-distance calls.

Burnside is the epicenter of new urban energy and its attendant development. The **Hawthorne, Belmont, Division,** and **Clinton Districts** are filled with single-family homes and apartment buildings mixed with shops, music stores and bookstores, coffeehouses, microbrew pubs, and restaurants geared to every palate. It's a delightful area for shopping and browsing

Further south, **Sellwood,** a historic district annexed to Portland in 1893, features **Antique Row,** more than 50 antiques stores tucked into the neighborhood of Victorian homes and turn-of-the-20th-century architecture (see Shopping). Sellwood is south of the **Oaks Bottom Wildlife Refuge** (see our Recreation chapter), a refuge for herons, beavers, ducks, and other marsh animals and birds. Here, the neighborhood floats in houseboats along the river's edge.

Westmoreland, north of Sellwood, has its share of fine restaurants and unique shops, as well one of the city's most beautiful parks—a haven for picnickers, joggers, basketball players, and duck feeders. Across McLoughlin Avenue, **Eastmoreland**'s residential neighborhood is tranquil, bordered by the public **Eastmoreland Golf Course,** the brick campus of **Reed College,** and **Crystal Springs Rhododendron Garden,** a riot of color each spring, with seven acres of rhododendrons, azaleas, and hybrids. See the Relocation chapter for more details on these neighborhoods.

NORTH & NORTHEAST PORTLAND

Northeast Portland and its neighbor North Portland are home to the same blend of industry, commerce, culture, and houses that characterize the rest of the city. Beautiful older houses line tree-shaded streets in neighborhoods such as **Laurelhurst, Irvington,** and **Alameda.** Attractive shopping areas draw people from around the region. The popular **Lloyd Center** is the largest single shopping destination in the area (see Shopping). By light rail, Lloyd Center is just minutes from downtown. Around Lloyd Center, the **Northeast Broadway Business District** is blossoming, and just to the east, the delightful **Hollywood District** offers a blend of charming houses and retail businesses.

Portland's **Convention Center** lies between the Lloyd District and the river, its 150-foot-high twin spires stamping their distinctive profile on the city's skyline. The center's walls, lamps, and tiles display handsome

detail, and plaques in the lobby carry insightful quotes about Oregon. A Chinese dragon boat is suspended at the base of the center's south spire, while a dramatic bronze pendulum sways below the north spire. Large murals by Lucinda Parker and Bill Hoppe celebrate Oregon's natural bounty, and outside, temple bells from Portland's sister cities Sapporo, Japan, and Ulsan, South Korea, offer friendly greetings to visitors.

The MAX line stops outside the center's north entrance and also serves the adjacent **Rose Quarter,** a 43-acre complex, featuring the **Memorial Coliseum** arena, the **Rose Garden** arena, **One Center Court** entertainment complex, and four parking garages. The Rose Quarter hosts a variety of sports events, including those of the **Portland Trailblazers,** college basketball, and indoor-soccer teams (for more on these, see Recreation and Spectator Sports). The arenas are also booked with rodeos, circuses, concerts, ice shows, and other spectacles, and they are linked to the nearby Convention Center to accommodate the numerous trade shows and conventions that Portland hosts.

Other neighborhoods farther north, such as **Alberta, Mississippi, St. Johns,** and **Kenton,** offer their own charms and have been swept along with the tide of urban redevelopment to find new identities. These areas, rich in history and blessed with many well-maintained parks and green spaces, hold some of the city's best-kept secrets. Read more about these in the Relocation chapter.

i Portland's Washington Park station is the home of the deepest light-rail stop in the nation, at 260 feet below Earth's surface. En route to the elevators that take you to the zoo, stop to look at the core rock samples and read about the geology of the West Hills.

Close-up

How to Talk Like a Native

While Oregonians, especially natives, don't have any revealing regional accent, we do have a vernacular. To aid you in communicating effectively here in Portland, we offer the following list of local phrases and pronunciations.

The Banfield: I-84, which runs east from Portland to eastern Oregon and beyond. A major commute route.

City of Roses: A popular nickname for the city of Portland.

The Coast: The beaches along the Pacific Ocean anywhere between Astoria, Oregon, and the California border.

Couch Street: Pronounced "Kooch."

Fareless Square: The area of downtown, including the transit mall and the Lloyd Center on the east side, where rides on buses and light-rail vehicles are free (hence, fare-less).

Glisan Street: Pronounced "Glee-son."

MAX: More formally the Metropolitan Area Express, this is the light-rail system operated by Tri-Met. The system runs from Hillsboro to Gresham, to the airport, and to North Portland. Do not get caught riding MAX (outside Fareless Square) without a ticket or valid transfer.

OHSU: Oregon Health and Science University.

OMSI: Oregon Museum of Science and Industry. Pronounced "AHM-zi."

Oregon: Correctly pronounced "OR-uh-gun," never "OR-uh-gone."

PDX: The baggage handlers' and airport code for Portland International Airport. Frequently used as shorthand for Portland.

Sauvie Island: To sound like a native, call it "So-vee's" Island.

The Schnitz: The Arlene Schnitzer Concert Hall, named after the grande dame of one of Portland's most prominent families.

The Sunset Highway: US 26, which runs west from Portland to the Oregon coast. Another major commute route and perpetual construction zone.

Willamette: The Willamette River. This river divides Portland into east and west neighborhoods before flowing into the Columbia at Kelley Point. Residents on each side have strongly held opinions about the other's attitudes, political perspectives, lifestyles, and personalities. The correct pronunciation is "wil-LAM-et," not "WILL-a-met."

VANCOUVER

Vancouver was originally a settlement created to supply the vast Hudson's Bay network of fur trappers. Now it is one of Washington's fastest growing communities. This scenic Northwest city, named after British explorer George Vancouver, has 55 parks and playgrounds inside city limits, including the **Burnt Bridge Creek Greenway** and the **Discovery Trail.** The **Vancouver National Historic Reserve** is a partnership that manages of historic sites at **Fort Vancouver, Columbia Park,** and **Pearson Field,** one of the oldest operating airfields in the nation. Vancouver is also known for its celebration on the Fourth of July, when it stages the largest fireworks show west of the Mississippi.

OUTLYING AREAS

You will also find charming towns throughout the greater Portland area, including **Beaverton, Lake Oswego, West Linn, Tigard, Tualatin,** and **Hillsboro** on the west side, and **Troutdale, Fairview, Gresham, Milwaukie,** and **Oregon City** on the east side. These prodigiously growing communities tend to have more new houses and strip malls than Portland proper, but their rural roots are evident if you know where to look. These towns are technically considered suburbs, but they also have their own distinctive economic centers and personalities. These areas and others are profiled in greater detail in the Relocation chapter.

PORTLAND'S BRIDGES

Portland is a city of bridges: More than 10 span the Willamette River, from the St. Johns Bridge at the north end to the Sellwood Bridge at the south. Because Portland is a deepwater port, the five bridges in the heart of downtown are drawbridges, letting large ships pass through. Each bridge has singular characteristics. The Hawthorne Bridge, for example, is the oldest operating vertical-lift bridge in the nation, while the Steel Bridge is a rare example of a bridge with twin decks capable of independent movement. Besides being useful, Portland's bridges are beautiful: They add charm to the cityscape, especially when viewed from the Eastbank Esplanade. For bridge fanatics, the Oregon Department of Transportation (ODOT) maintains a meticulous website that features the engineering and historical details of our bridges: www .oregon.gov/odot/hwy/geoenvironmental/ historic_bridges_Portland1.shtml. And for the rest of us, here are Portland's bridges, from north to south.

- **St. Johns Bridge (1931):** The St. Johns Bridge is a beautiful, distinctive suspension bridge with 400-foot towers and Gothic arches. It links outer Northwest Portland with the North Portland community of St. Johns.
- **Fremont Bridge (1973):** The Fremont Bridge is the newest bridge, but its beautiful arches have shaped the cityscape as profoundly as the older bridges on the Willamette. It's the longest bridge in Oregon and, at 902 feet, is the longest tied-arch bridge in the entire world. It carries traffic from I-405 and US 30 to I-5.
- **Broadway Bridge (1913):** This drawbridge extends Broadway across the river from Northeast Portland to downtown, and it bears the distinction of being the largest rail bridge in the world—that means that its counterweights roll back and forth on bull wheels above the deck. But many Portlanders think of it as simply the "red bridge."

- **Steel Bridge (1912):** Upon completion the Steel Bridge was immediately hailed as an exemplar of imaginative engineering. It is one of the only known dual-lift bridges in the world: The lower deck, accommodating Amtrak and freight trains, lifts independently from the upper deck, which carries light rail, trucks, and cars. The Steel Bridge River Walk allows bikes and pedestrians to cross the churning Willamette River just 30 feet below.
- **Burnside Bridge (1926):** This bridge was designed by Joseph B. Straus, who also designed the Golden Gate Bridge. It is a drawbridge that provides good city views as well as subtle aesthetic details, such as the turrets on the operator's house.
- **Morrison Bridge (1887, 1905, 1958):** When first built in 1887 by the Willamette Iron Bridge Co., the Morrison Bridge was the largest span west of the Mississippi. It was rebuilt in 1905 and again in 1958 as a drawbridge. The Morrison Bridge is between the Hawthorne and Burnside Bridges, and it provides entrances to and exits from I-5. Leaving I-5 southbound at the City Center exit, which takes you to the Morrison Bridge, provides one of the loveliest views of downtown Portland, especially at night when the river, bridge, and city are illuminated.
- **Hawthorne Bridge (1910):** The Hawthorne Bridge is the oldest bridge across the Willamette in Portland. It was finished in 1910 and remodeled in 1998–99; it now includes beautifully wide sidewalks and bike paths, making it a favorite for pedestrians and cyclists. The Hawthorne Bridge, lovely as it is, demands more patience than some bridges in town because it has a low clearance—53 feet at low water. In the spring, when the

water is high, the Hawthorne Bridge raises even for small river traffic such as tourist steamer ships—and, joke residents, kayaks and canoes. Just so you know, on the east side of the river, the Hawthorne Bridge leads to Hawthorne Boulevard, but on the west side, Hawthorne turns into Main and Madison Streets.
- **Marquam Bridge (1966):** A freeway bridge built in the 1960s to accommodate the city's increased traffic, the multilane, double-deck Marquam Bridge provides a panoramic view of the Willamette River, Tom McCall Waterfront Park, and downtown Portland that is unrivaled, but the bridge itself is no beauty. Connecting I-5 to I-84 East on the east side and I-405 North on the west side, with major traffic arteries merging and dividing at both ends of it, it carries large volumes of busy traffic.
- **Ross Island Bridge (1926):** The Ross Island Bridge sits high above the river. The bridge has pretty balustrades and an expansive view, but its aesthetic appeal is diminished by a high volume of speeding traffic. The Ross Island Bridge carries US 26 over the Willamette, connecting to Arthur Street on the west side and to Powell Boulevard on the east. Besides the volume of traffic, its other drawback is that the westside approach, which connects to Barbur Boulevard, SR 43, and Arthur Street, is confusing.
- **Sellwood Bridge (1925):** The Sellwood Bridge allows just two lanes of traffic to flow from SR 43 on the west side to the Portland neighborhood of Sellwood on the east side. It includes sections of the original Burnside Bridge, torn down in 1925.

GETTING HERE, GETTING AROUND

Bordered by mountains, flanked by rivers, surrounded by fertile farmland, the Portland Metro area is well known for its beautiful setting. But don't let those high mountains fool you: Portland accommodates many modes of transportation and allows easy travel once you arrive. The territory is well served by trains, planes, and buses, and its public transportation system is comprehensive.

Portland International Airport, or PDX, is the regional airport for all of Oregon and much of southwestern Washington. From here, in addition to its national and international service, commercial air service provides flights to Eugene, Salem, and Medford. Feeder and regional airlines also serve Pendleton and Klamath Falls in eastern and southern Oregon, in addition to providing flights to Newport and North Bend on the Oregon coast. Flights to the airport in Redmond, Oregon, will take you to the popular resorts and natural attractions of Bend and the rest of central Oregon.

Portland's Amtrak station operates trains to and from Seattle, Los Angeles, and Chicago, as well as nearby towns such as Corvallis and Eugene. Greyhound buses provide ground transportation in all directions, and buses run regularly to and from Seattle, Tacoma, and Olympia; Boise; Denver; Salt Lake City; and major cities in California.

Two interstate highways intersect Portland. I-84 runs east and west through the Columbia Gorge from Portland to Idaho and beyond, and I-5 runs through Portland on its way from Canada to Mexico. Often you'll hear references to the I-5 Corridor, the stretch of I-5 that runs from Portland to Eugene.

From I-5, routes travel west across the Coastal Range to the Pacific Ocean and US 101 and east through several mountain passes, across the Cascade Mountains to central and eastern Oregon. During the winter some of the passes through the Cascades are closed. Those that remain open year-round may be subject to periodic closures due to weather. Traction devices (chains and studded tires) are often required for winter travel through the Cascades (and at times, through the Coastal Range). The Oregon State Police strictly enforce laws requiring motorists to carry traction devices.

NAVIGATING THE AREA

This is the Great American West, so travel distances are greater than in other parts of the country; for instance, Seattle, the closest large city, is three to four hours' drive north. But one of the most prized features of the Portland Metro area is its proximity to so many beautiful areas of recreation, nature, and culture. Year-round skiing at Timberline on Mount Hood is a 90-minute drive from the city center. A loop around Mount Hood to Hood River and then back down the Columbia Gorge is a pleasant way to spend the day, as is a trip to the Johnson Ridge Observatory at Mount St. Helens. The spectacular Oregon coast is less than two hours from Portland, and the heart of Oregon's wine country is no more than 45 minutes from downtown. (See Day Trips for more information on these outings.)

You will find that Portland is not difficult to navigate once you understand its idiosyncrasies. As we described in How to Use This Book, the city is divided into east and west by the Willamette River and north and south by Burnside Street. These serve as your orientation marks, and addresses and street numbers are organized around them. If you're on Southwest 5th Avenue downtown, you'll know that you're 5 blocks west of the Willamette River. Similarly, Burnside Street is the starting point for street addresses, and these rise in number the farther north or south that you travel from Burnside. So if your Southwest 5th Avenue address happens to be 423, you'll know that you're about 4 blocks south of Burnside.

GETTING HERE

By Air

PORTLAND INTERNATIONAL AIRPORT
7000 Northeast Airport Way
(503) 460-4234, (877) 739-4636
www.flypdx.com
Portland International Airport—which we call PDX (its aeronautical code)—is notably clean, light, and pleasant, with many comforts to serve the weary traveler. At times it feels more like an upscale shopping mall than an airport, and indeed, it has won top honors for its shopping and concessions from airport retailers across the nation—as

well as accolades from the travelers who actually use them. *Conde Nast Traveller* has called PDX America's best airport for business travelers more than once—its easy access to downtown and its free wireless service being among the top reasons.

PDX is also safe. As elsewhere in the United States, travelers and their bags are now subjected to vigorous security checks, yet security lines and baggage screening are efficiently managed. There has not been a major civil airline crash at the airport since 1978, when a United Airlines DC-8 ran out of fuel and landed about a mile short of the runway. The airport's crews are experienced in responding to the Oregon winters, and the airport is rarely closed. But bad weather in other parts of the country, especially in Denver, Chicago, Los Angeles, and San Francisco, can cause delays in flights heading for Portland. At certain times of the year, particularly in the fall, early morning fog can wreak havoc with departure times at PDX, and some regional flights are affected by local weather at their intended destinations.

Arriving in Portland

Once you've arrived at PDX, you'll find a cadre of helpers to provide directions; they can point you to your connecting flight gate, the correct baggage carousel, or any other location within the airport complex. Airport service workers offer transportation to and from the passenger gates in electric carts. They can also point out the specially designated "meet and greet" areas: Unticketed persons are forbidden to go past security checkpoints, so if someone is meeting you, you will find them there.

Free wireless Internet access is available throughout most of the main terminal level of the airport. Besides the customary amenities—telephones, express package drop-offs, workstations with computer ports, fax machines, stamp machines, and ATMs— you can shop at some of the area's best stores. In the main terminal's Oregon Market, look for reading material at Powell's Books, sportswear at Norm Thompson's, woolen goods at Pendleton, athletic footwear and apparel at Nike, and souvenirs from our state at Made in Oregon. The restaurants at PDX tend to feature Pacific Northwest products and are nearly all locally owned. Thus the food options are quite decent (and fairly priced), and you'll be able to sample local and regional craft beers, delicious pastries, and other treats throughout the airport. Even better, shopping, food, restrooms, telephones, and other services are available on both sides of the security check, especially along Concourse C. Shops and restaurants are generally open from 6 a.m. to 9 p.m. daily. Coffee and espresso from Starbucks and Portland's Coffee People can be found throughout the airport—including a wee Starbucks bar by the escalators next to the baggage claim area.

Ground Transportation

Transportation from the airport is available by light rail, taxi, and other ride services. You can, of course, also rent cars. Car rental agencies are on the terminal grounds, though several of them have only kiosks there.

Light Rail: The Red Line

Portland's light-rail system, **MAX,** is a convenient way to get downtown from the airport. The Red Line serves downtown and PDX: It takes about 40 minutes and costs $2.35, one-way. Trains are just outside the baggage claim area, and they are well marked with

prominent signs. To take the Red Line into town, purchase your ticket prior to boarding the train at one of the vending machines inside the terminal, near the doors leading to the trains or outside near the track. You'll need to buy an all-zone ticket. The vending machines will accept $1 bills, change, and—for several tickets—credit cards. (You can buy tickets ahead of time online and have them mailed to you, if you are well organized; see http://trimet.org/store/index .htm.) Once you've bought your ticket, be sure to validate it in the machine prior to boarding, and hang onto this ticket for your entire ride—it acts as proof of payment. Cheerful TriMet transit authority employees are usually standing by to help you figure out tickets, destinations, and other problems. Trains to downtown leave about every 15 minutes at peak times and slightly less often at other times. See the TriMet entry later in this chapter for more information on the MAX line.

Other Ground Transportation

For other means of transport, you will find the Ground Transportation Center across the first roadway on the lower level of the airport, just across from the baggage claim area; that is, it is just east of the main terminal, in the direction of the parking garage. Posted signs will tell you whether you are in the right section for your chosen mode of transport; you can also ask the airport service personnel who are always in attendance to direct you. They can also help you get a taxi—only certain companies can serve the airport, so they'll make sure you are in one that's legitimate. Taxis to downtown Portland should cost about $30; the trip downtown takes from 20 to 40 minutes.

ℹ️ The best bargain for transportation from PDX is the light-rail MAX line—just $2.35 for a ride into town.

You will also find a number of other shuttle and towncar services in the Ground Transportation Center. The prices for these will vary depending on the number of passengers, the distance you will travel, and the luxuriousness of the vehicle. Shuttles and towncar services, unlike taxi service, are unregulated, so be sure to clarify the price before you begin your journey. The best way to find a shuttle service is to use the widget on the PDX website: www.port ofportland.com/PDX_Grnd_Trnsprtn.aspx. PDX maintains this comprehensive website and includes links to all shuttle and towncar services, as well as to taxi service, to Portland and beyond, so ground transportation should be pain-free to find and easily arranged online or by phone.

Rental Cars

For car rentals at the airport, go to the parking garage's first floor. The agencies with offices in the garage include **Avis Rent-A-Car** (503) 249-4950, **Budget Rent-A-Car** (503) 249-4556, **Dollar Rent-A-Car** (503) 249-4793, **Hertz Rent-A-Car** (503) 249-8216, and **Enterprise** (503) 252-1500. Some car rental agencies have kiosks just outside the car rental center in the parking garage; these include **Alamo/National** (503) 249-4900 and **Thrifty** (503) 254-6563.

Once you've left the airport, it should take 20 to 30 minutes to reach downtown, and there are clear directions to the freeways from the airport access roads. Airport traffic is funneled onto I-205. To reach downtown,

you will take I-205 South to the I-84 West exit. Follow I-84 to I-5, where you should follow the signs to City Center.

By Train

AMTRAK AT UNION STATION
800 Northwest 6th Ave.
(503) 273-4865 (station information),
(503) 273-4866 (daily arrival and
departure information),
(800) 872-7245 (reservations and
schedule information)
www.amtrakcascades.com

One of Portland's most charming postcard views is Union Station, with its brick clock tower that actually keeps good time. Our town's classic train depot, built in the 1890s, is one of the oldest operating train terminals in the United States. Its appeal is evident in its high ceilings and marble floor, and its historic photographs add to the adventure of traveling by rail. Because Union Station is part of the downtown Portland transit mall and falls within the Fareless Square boundaries, you can take a bus from the train station to downtown Portland for free.

Union Station is an important stop on several major rail routes. The Empire Builder, a passenger train that originates in Chicago, stops here, as does another classic train, the Coast Starlight, which runs daily from Los Angeles and to Seattle. Amtrak's Cascade route features the state-of-the-art, Spanish-built, high-speed Talgo, an ultramodern "tilt" train that runs from Eugene to Vancouver, British Columbia. If you're a train fan, consider a day trip north to Seattle on the Talgo. If you tire of the scenery, you can plug in your laptop and settle in with one of the microbrews served on board.

By Interstate Bus

GREYHOUND LINES
550 Northwest 6th Ave.
(503) 243-2361, (800) 231-2222
www.greyhound.com

Portland's Greyhound Lines bus station is a remarkably clean and modern terminal on the far northern end of the city's transit mall adjacent to Amtrak's Union Station, both of which are a short walk from downtown. The station has plenty of seating, a concession wall, and a small, pleasant cafe. Greyhound is the only transcontinental bus line serving Portland. The Greyhound terminal is included in the public transportation system's Fareless Square, so once you've arrived, it is easy to connect with city buses.

By Car

As the Portland Metro region has grown, so has the amount of traffic and congestion. During rush hours, 7 to 9 a.m. and again from 3:30 to 6 p.m., car and bus traffic pours into downtown from all directions. Those going to high-tech jobs in Washington County have a reverse commute, but their numbers create rush-hour traffic in both directions on freeways, the region's main arterials, downtown streets, and often on secondary streets.

You will want to bear in mind a few things as you travel the city. The downtown area is laid on a grid of one-way streets, so look carefully before making a turn lest you find yourself heading straight into traffic. The major southbound street is **Broadway;** the major northbound street is **4th Avenue; 10th and 11th Avenues** are also important north- and southbound streets. **Naito Parkway** (formerly called Front Avenue) runs along the Willamette River; it permits both north- and southbound traffic. Important eastbound streets are **Market, Alder,** and **Columbia;** westbound arterials include **Clay, Washington,** and **Jefferson.** Burnside allows both east- and westbound traffic, but the places where you are allowed to make a left turn off Burnside are rare in the downtown area.

Two major streets, **6th Avenue** and **5th Avenue,** are the arterials for the bus and light rail system downtown, making up a large component of the transit mall. This is helpful to if you're driving downtown because you must be alert to the traffic markings. Some blocks along these streets are for mass transit only, some blocks allow cars, and some blocks funnel cars right into "turn only" lanes. Car drivers should also pay attention to the signs that warn you not to turn on red lights, because these signs prevent cars from being hit by MAX trains. Furthermore, you must allow buses the right-of-way if you are driving behind them and they are signaling to pull into traffic. A flashing red yield sign on the bus will let you know if you are hogging the road illegally.

You should know a few other important streets and highways in the area. **I-205,** the freeway that takes you to the airport, will also take you south around the eastern edge of the city of Portland to communities such as Oregon City and West Linn before it reconnects with I-5 just south of Lake Oswego. To the north, I-205 takes you across the Columbia River into Washington State, hooking up with I-5 north of Vancouver. **SRs 99E** and **99W** are also critical roads. They are the eastern and western sides of SR 99, the principal thoroughfare of Oregon before I-5 was built, which splits in two just north of Eugene. The directions "W" and "E" designate which side of the Willamette River you are on. South of Portland, SR 99W is also called the West Pacific Highway, but in the city limits it has several names. In order, from south to north, they are Barbur Boulevard, Naito Parkway, and, when it finally crosses the Willamette again, North Interstate Avenue. Similarly, the East Pacific Highway, 99E, is also called McLoughlin Boulevard from Oregon City until just north of the Ross Island Bridge. At that point, SR 99E splits into a northbound arterial called Grand Avenue, and a southbound arterial called Martin Luther King Jr. Boulevard (or MLK). These two rejoin north of Broadway to form Martin Luther King Jr. Boulevard. Both SR 99W and 99E merge into I-5 immediately south of the Columbia River.

Driving east and west over the hills that divide the city from the western suburbs can present some difficulties. The main route, **US 26,** is responsible for some of the worst traffic in the city, just west of downtown, where it is called the Sunset Highway. This is the principal highway between downtown Portland and the west side of the metro region, and it gets backed up in the Sunset Tunnel, which takes cars under the west side of the hills, backed up again as it climbs the Sylvan Pass, and backed up yet again at the interchange with SR 217. To travel east and west, you might try a couple of alternative routes. Burnside will take you over the hill into Beaverton from downtown; when it splits in two, follow Southwest Barnes Road to SR 217. The Beaverton-Hillsdale Highway, or SR 10, can be a good choice; you can also take I-5 south to SR 99W or to SR 217. But all these routes will present the driver with traffic, and they might take you well out of your way.

Another caveat: US 26 turns into a business route when it hits downtown Portland's west side. To follow it east through town, on your way to Mount Hood, for instance, you must be attentive to the signs that direct you toward the Ross Island Bridge, where the highway turns into Powell Boulevard for miles until it passes through the eastern Multnomah County town of Sandy and becomes a proper highway again.

Broadway can also be confusing because it extends from Northeast Portland (where it is called "Northeast Broadway") across the Broadway Bridge to downtown Portland, where it is technically named "Southwest Broadway." But nobody calls it that—downtowners call it just plain "Broadway." While Broadway passes through downtown, it takes the place of 7th Avenue, so you will find it between 6th and 8th Avenues. And after it passes through downtown, it turns into Broadway Drive. Look carefully at the street address of your destination.

Road Safety

Driving on the freeways through the heavy Oregon mist requires particular attention. At higher speeds, hydroplaning on a sheet of water can occur, and stopping distances stretch when roads get wet. Spray from passing cars, buses, and trucks can muddy windshields, blocking a driver's vision before the windshield wipers can clear the water. Sudden entry into unseen pools of standing water, especially in the fall when leaves clog drains, can cause a driver to momentarily lose control. In winter, freezing rain and invisible black ice can make driving difficult for everyone, but especially for those who exceed speed limits.

Please don't drink and drive. Driving under the influence of intoxicating drinks or drugs is a serious offense in Oregon. If your trip calls for a visit to the wine country and a tasting of the vintages, take along a designated driver or limit your imbibing. It is also illegal to have an open container of an alcoholic beverage in your vehicle. Oregon's public safety officers are professionals who take their responsibilities seriously.

Distractions should also be kept to a minimum. As of January 2010, it was illegal to operate a motor vehicle while using a mobile communication device—phone or text—unless you have a hands-free adaptor. Both hands, in other words, must be kept on the wheel.

Bicyclists have an equal legal right to the road, and drivers of motorized vehicles are required to stay out of marked bicycle lanes. Special green pavement markings alert drivers to places where they must be particularly watchful of bicycle right-of-way; areas where bike lanes cross auto turn lanes are notorious for accidents, and the city is trying to make them safer for everyone. Also, you should know that it is legal for motorized wheelchairs to travel in bike lanes. And in downtown Portland you'll also find marked skateboard routes: You'll need to share the road with them too.

i Oregon is one of two states in the country that prohibit self-serve gas stations. Don't try to fill your tank yourself, or you will be descended upon by irate attendants. Unfortunately, our laws do not mandate oil checks or cleaning of windshields; these you may have to do yourself.

Speed limits are usually well posted. For cars, the speed limit is 55 mph on open highways, 65 mph on freeways outside metropolitan areas, 25 mph on residential streets, and 20 mph in business districts and school zones. Photo radar will occasionally enforce these limits, but signs will warn you if the area is patrolled by this system. Driving in Oregon is governed by the basic rule that a driver must always drive at a speed that is reasonable under existing conditions on all roadways at all times. To obey this basic rule, you may have to drive at a slower speed than the legal posted speed limit if conditions warrant it.

Getting to the Airport

To reach the airport, take the Airport Way West exit off I-205, which leads directly to the airport terminal, the car rental lots, and hotels on the airport's property (see our Accommodations chapter for those hotels near the airport). This exit will take you to the economy and other parking lots, to car rental agencies, and to the terminal.

Parking at the airport is not difficult. There are three main areas: the economy lot, the long-term lot, and the parking garage. If you plan to leave your car at the airport while you are gone, use the economy lot, which lies 2 miles east of the airport terminal. Rates are $10 per day, $3 per hour, with the seventh day free. Free PDX shuttles run from the lot to the terminal every seven minutes. (Be sure to remember whether you parked in the red or blue section.) Use the long-term lot for shorter stays exceeding four hours. Rates are $3 per hour and $16 per day maximum, and shuttles are available from this lot. (You can also walk to the airport through the garage tunnels, which are carpeted, well lit, and spacious.) The parking garage rate is also $3 per hour, but it will cost you $24 per day. There is also valet service for $10 per hour or $30 per day. For updated parking information, call (877) 739-4636 before leaving for the airport or check the airport website, which will let you know how full the parking lots are. In case you need it, the parking folks also provide free jump starts and flat-tire service. You can pay for parking with cash, debit cards, and major credit cards.

Once you arrive at the departing flight deck of the terminal, you can give your bags to the sky cap for many airlines or you can take them inside and check them there. All checked baggage is now screened, so allow for extra time if you are checking bags.

Airlines that serve PDX include the following:

- **Air Canada,** (888) 247-2262
- **Alaska Airlines,** (800) 252-7522
- **American Airlines,** (800) 433-7300
- **Continental,** (800) 523-3273
- **Delta Air Lines,** (800) 221-1212
- **Frontier,** (800) 432-1359
- **Hawaiian Air,** (800) 367-5320
- **Horizon Air,** (800) 547-9308
- **Jet Blue Airways,** (800) 538-2583
- **Seaport Airlines,** (888) 573-2767
- **Southwest Airlines,** (800) 435-9792
- **United and United Express,** (800) 864-8331
- **US Airways,** (800) 428-4322

i If you have rented a car that must be returned at the airport, fill the gas tank before you leave for PDX. There are no gas stations on the airport's grounds. Once you are on I-205 or I-84 en route to the airport, you will need to leave the freeway to get gas.

Other Airfields

Besides PDX, the Port of Portland owns and operates three other airfields that are open for general aviation: Portland-Hillsboro, Portland-Mulino, and Portland-Troutdale Airports, all of which can be reached at (503) 944-7000 or through the Port of Portland, (800) 547-8411.

PEARSON FIELD
1115 East Reserve St., Vancouver, WA
(360) 696-1280
www.cityofvancouver.us/pearson
Pearson Field, next to Fort Vancouver Historic Site and within walking distance of downtown Vancouver, has been operating since 1905, making it the longest-running airfield in the United States. Still open for general aviation, it has a 3,300-foot lighted runway and a Fixed Base Operator to help with refueling and other pilot needs. (See the Attractions chapter for more information on Pearson Field.)

GETTING AROUND

Parking

Parking on downtown streets during business hours takes some patience, especially given downtown Portland's grid of one-way streets. Meters generally cost $1.60 per hour and allow parking for periods of time between 15 minutes and 5 hours. Cars are frequently monitored to make sure drivers don't overstay their welcome. Once a parking patrol member has started to write you a citation, it is yours. Parking after 7 p.m. is free in most areas, but in some—for example, near the Rose Quarter and at the Convention Center—metered hours extend to as late as 10 p.m. The meter will indicate the hours of enforcement.

Portland has replaced its old coin-operated parking meters with SmartMeter stations. These central pay station machines work by issuing paper stubs that you adhere to your curbside window. The SmartMeters are convenient; you can pay with coins or with debit or credit cards. SmartMeters work like this: First, park your car and locate the closest pay station. If you're using a debit or credit card, press the button to purchase increments of 15 minutes, or press the "maximum time" button, which buys you the full allotment of time in that meter zone. Your parking purchase must total at least $1.60 if you're using a debit or credit card. When you have indicated all the time you want, press the green button, and the pay station will print a receipt that states how much time you've purchased and when it expires. Be patient—sometimes the meters need to "think" for a minute or two while they are contacting your bank account. Affix the printed receipt to the curbside window, so that the expiration time can be seen clearly from the outside. The great thing about SmartMeters is that you can take the receipt with you and park at a different SmartMeter somewhere else.

Municipal parking garages are an alternative to on-street meters. There are six clearly marked Smart Park garages in downtown Portland, where parking is $1.50 an hour for the first four hours (after that, it's $3 to $5 per hour). On the weekend you can park at Smart Park for $2 to $6 for the whole evening when entering after 6 p.m. Many downtown merchants will validate your Smart Park ticket for two hours of free parking if you spend $25 or more in their stores. Private garages are also an option, of course.

Public Transportation

TRIMET
4012 Southeast 17th Ave.
(503) 238-RIDE (trip information)
http://trimet.org
TriMet is Portland's award-winning mass transit system, comprising the bus, light-rail, and streetcar systems, and it is noted for its efficiency, comprehensiveness, and accommodation. Operating in three

counties (Multnomah, Washington, and Clackamas), TriMet's buses are scheduled on routes that cover almost 600 square miles. The downtown transit mall extends all the way to Union Station for connections to Amtrak and to Greyhound bus service. Downtown Portland's Fareless Square, bordered by the Willamette River, Northwest Irving Street, and I-405, provides free rides within its boundaries and along the transit mall, where riders can transfer to the light-rail service, MAX. MAX reaches from eastern Multnomah County west to Hillsboro in Washington County, with trains scheduled every 15 minutes during the day. MAX has four lines: the Blue Line, which runs east and west between Gresham and Hillsboro via downtown Portland; the Red Line, which runs from the Beaverton Transit Center through downtown to the airport; the Yellow Line, which travels north and south between downtown and the Expo Center, along Interstate Avenue; and the Green Line, which runs from Portland State University east to Clackamas Town Center. In addition, the WES (Westside Express Service) commuter line links Wilsonville, Tigard, Tualatin, and Beaverton with downtown Portland and beyond. It runs each weekday in the morning and afternoon, every 30 minutes. Smaller conventional buses and vans now provide service on less-traveled suburban routes, and there is a wheelchair-accessible special service.

Fares—which apply equally to buses, light-rail trains, and streetcars—are based on a geographic zone system: $2.05 for one or two zones, and $2.35 for all zones. Fares are good for a one-way trip and are discounted for senior citizens and youth. Children 6 and younger ride for free. Bus drivers will not give you change, though dollar bills are accepted on the bus. A day ticket ($4.75) can be used on buses, streetcars, and light rail, traveling to all zones, and you can also get discounted fares if you buy weekly or monthly passes. These passes are widely available throughout the city at many drugstores, grocery stores, and bookstores. The TriMet website has a comprehensive list of outlets.

All TriMet tickets and transfers are good on any TriMet route. Passengers receive a time-sensitive transfer that also serves as a receipt. On the bus and streetcar, unless the rider has a pass or transfer, fares are paid upon boarding, but on MAX, they must be purchased and validated before boarding. MAX tickets are available from machines at every station. After you purchase your ticket but just before you get on the train, insert your ticket in the validator machines at the MAX stops. These machines stamp your ticket with the date and time. MAX tickets, streetcar tickets, and bus transfers can be used interchangeably; they are good for an hour or so past the time they are validated. Hold onto your ticket or transfer! TriMet inspectors can ask for proof of fare payment, and there is a hefty fine if you don't have proof that you are riding legally.

Bus routes vary in frequency and how early and how long each bus travels its route, but during peak times on the most traveled routes, buses run at least every 15 minutes if not more often, as do MAX trains. Schedules for individual bus lines and the light-rail lines are free and commonly available at banks, stores, post offices, bookstores, and dozens of other locations, or accessible on the web at http://trimet.org.

All stops are marked by blue and white signs displaying the route numbers of the buses serving that line. Many are well lit, with covered bus shelters to protect you from

Transit Tracker

Say you're at your office one evening in the middle of winter. Say it's raining in that bone-chilling, soul-killing way that can characterize winter in Portland. Say you have to wait outside to catch your bus. Instead of taking a chance of dying of exposure, why not try Tri-Met's transit tracker? This incredibly useful service uses GPS to tell you when the bus is due to arrive at your stop—real time, not scheduled time. Check out the Transit Tracker website—http://trimet.org/transittracker/about.htm for instructions about accessing this tool via the web, cell phone, and other mobile devices.

the rain and wind, but not all stops are so well equipped. On the transit mall, there are more elaborate shelters with route maps and video screens displaying information and arrival times for the next bus. The system is divided into regions, designated by regional symbols; these symbols mark service to specific areas from the transit mall.

TriMet has an excellent safety record, but don't leave your common sense at home. After 8 p.m. you can ask the driver to let you off the bus any place that he or she can stop safely; many drivers will also stop at night if you wave the bus down between established stops. Be observant when boarding buses: Those marked with an "X" or "I" are express buses that most commonly run during commute hours. After leaving the transit mall, they will stop only at major stops until they reach a local transit center. Most drivers

Close-up

Go by Tram

It's early morning, and quiet. The sun is stretching into the eastern sky, turning the clouds a rosy shade of pink. At the lower terminal of the **Portland Aerial Tram,** next to a large health-care center, a substantial number of people are already in line, ready to board. They are wearing white lab coats; they are wearing bike garb; they are wearing jeans; they are wearing suits. However they are dressed, they are waiting for one thing: for the silver oval tram car to settle into its dock so that they can board and take a three-minute ride to the top of Marquam Hill. There, they will go off to classes, jobs, or appointments at the main campus of Oregon Health and Science University (OHSU), a level-one trauma center and cutting-edge biomedical research hospital, which stands on a hillside above the city of Portland.

The Portland Aerial Tram opened for business in December 2006. At that time it began ferrying passengers from the top of the OHSU Marquam Hill campus to its beautiful outpatient facility, the OHSU Center for Heath and Healing, 3,300 feet (1 kilometer) away. OHSU was built on donated hillside land over many decades. It occupies a large cluster of buildings on the east side of Marquam Hill, part of the network of hills that stand guard over the west side of the Willamette River. As the university expanded over the years—adding clinics, improving its research capacity, attracting patients to its cutting-edge facilities—it ran out of room to grow. Eventually, the reclaimed South Waterfront district was proposed as the best place to expand, but physically connecting the two sites remained a challenge. The geography, as well as the Portland values of livability and proper city scale, made it impossible to simply build a new road from the river to the top of the hill.

Planners concluded that a tram, such as the kind that takes skiers up to the top of alpine terrain, would not only be a viable solution, but could be an interesting one. After all, it made sense: mountain trams transport passengers long distances over challenging terrain in extreme weather conditions. How complicated could it be to create one to transport employees, patients, and students 3,300 feet in less challenging terrain and less challenging weather? As a result, the second commuter tram in the United States—the first is on Roosevelt Island in New York—was built.

---

are very careful to announce that they are driving an express route. If in doubt, ask. Tri-Met's drivers, with rare exception, are courteous and knowledgeable and recognize the long-term value of being helpful to all riders.

C-TRAN

2425 Northeast 65th Ave.,

Vancouver, WA

(360) 695-0123, (503) 283-8054

www.c-tran.com

C-Tran is the bus service for Vancouver and Clark County, Washington. By arrangement with TriMet, C-Tran also offers service across the Columbia River to downtown Portland. To get from Vancouver to Portland, the ticket price is $2.40. C-Tran and TriMet honor one another's tickets, so an All-Zone ticket for TriMet can be used on C-Tran, except for the Portland Express; the fare for this convenient trip is $3.25.

The tram has two stations connected by a cable system that traverses an intermediate tower of 197 feet. The cars ride 175 feet above the ground at the highest point, and the gain in elevation from the lower dock to the higher is about 500 feet. The two cars operate in parallel, propelled by an engine at the lower terminal by the Center for Health and Healing. En route, the cars pass over the congested arterials of I-5, Barbur Boulevard, and Macadam Avenue. But most people aren't looking at the ground. They are looking at the spectacular view, with Mount St. Helens dominating the northern landscape and Mount Hood, directly east, reigning over all, with the carpet of the Willamette River, the skyline, and the hills of Portland stretched out before it. On a good day, you can see all the way to Mt. Rainier, but even rainy, gloomy days provide an interesting view, with the mists rising from the river and the streets glistening below.

To ride the Portland Aerial Tram: Tickets are purchased from a kiosk at the lower terminal at OHSU's Center for Health and Healing. (This outpatient facility also has an excellent cafe and coffee bar, just so you know.) Tickets cost $4, though children ages 6 and under ride for free, as do patients, visitors, and employees of OHSU (including Doernbecher Children's Hospital). The ticket kiosk takes coins and credit or debit cards, but not bills. Tickets are collected only on the way up, but all tickets are round-trip. If you are a patient or visitor, you will need to get a pass from your provider. If you have a monthly or annual TriMet pass or annual streetcar pass, you can ride for free as well, but ordinary TriMet transfer passes are not accepted. The ride takes about three minutes, or a bit longer if it is windy.

The easiest way to get to the tram is to take the streetcar, which stops directly at the Center for Health and Healing on its southbound and northbound routes. It's also easily accessible by bicycle, and there is bike parking available; you can also take your bike on board. If you're driving, your best bet is street parking—metered spots are available on the blocks nearby.

The tram operates weekdays from 5:30 a.m. to 9:30 p.m., on Sat from 9 a.m. to 5 p.m., and on Sun from mid-May through mid-Sept from 1 to 5 p.m. It's closed on legal holidays. The tram departs about every 10 minutes. For the latest info, be sure to check the tram website, **www.portlandtram.org.** The website also provides maps and directions, as well as streetcar maps and schedules so you can plan your trip.

Streetcars

For the first half of the 20th century, Portlanders used streetcars to get around town. Now Portland has brought them back in order to connect the major Westside business districts. Streetcars now travel a route that extends from the South Waterfront district on the Willamette, through Portland State University north to Good Samaritan Hospital (between Northwest Lovejoy and Northwest Northrup at Northwest 23rd), traveling through the Pearl District and along 10th and 11th Avenues. This means you can drive downtown for shopping, then hop on a streetcar to visit Powell's City of Books at 10th and Burnside before your lunch reservation in the Pearl District, all without having to move your car. In 2011, the city planned to extend streetcar service once again to the east side of the river, to the Lloyd district.

Like the bus, streetcars stop every 2 to 3 blocks, and they run from 5:30 a.m. to 11 p.m. Mon through Thurs and until 11:45 p.m. on Fri. Sat hours are from 7:15 a.m. to 11:45 p.m. and Sun from 7:15 a.m. to 10:30 p.m. They arrive every 12 to 15 minutes during peak hours and a bit less frequently at other times. Well-marked, glass-covered streetcar stops, however, are equipped with electronic screens that helpfully note when the next streetcar will arrive.

Fares follow the same schedule as the MAX and the bus, and their tickets and transfers are all interchangeable. Deposit your fare in the farebox when you board. Fareboxes take only $1 and $5 bills and coins—you'll have the least frustration if you pay with exact change. If you've bought tickets elsewhere, simply validate the ticket once on board. (Riding within the Fareless Square is still free.) While the streetcar may be an old-fashioned form of transportation, these are thoroughly modern, with air conditioning, low-floor center sections, and full wheelchair access. They are clean and efficient.

Those with a nostalgic bent can still ride an old-fashioned streetcar. The Vintage Trolley, a trolley operation using replicas of the streetcars that once served the city, runs on Sun from Feb through Dec. For more information check TriMet's useful website at http://trimet.org, which includes an itinerary of historic buildings that the trolley passes as it travels along. The Vintage Trolley charges no fare but welcomes donations.

Taxis

Portland, Oregon, isn't New York City or Washington, D.C., where taxis are a way of urban life. Good luck trying to flag one from the corner: They will rarely, if ever, stop. However, you can telephone for one. If you're walking around downtown, the best cab-finding solution is to head to a hotel and have the doorperson call a cab. If you're at a restaurant, the maitre d' will usually call one for you. If you know your plans for a specific trip or destination, phone ahead and schedule a cab. Fares start at $2.50 and go up $2.30 per mile; you'll also pay an extra $1 per additional passenger. Cab fare from the airport to downtown for two passengers and their luggage should run about $30. Portland cab companies include the following (also see the By Air section for more information on taxi and towncar services):

BROADWAY CAB
1734 Northwest 15th Ave.
(503) 227-1234

GREEN CAB
10118 East Burnside St.
(503) 234-1414

NEW ROSE CITY CAB
1533 Northeast Alberta St.
(503) 282-7707

PORTLAND TAXI
12624 Northeast Halsey St.
(503) 256-5400

RADIO CAB
1613 Northwest Kearney St.
(503) 227-1212

Sharing a Car

Portland is a great city for those who like to walk, bike, or use public transportation. Yet even if you have liberated yourself from car ownership, you may find yourself needing to use a car occasionally. That's where **Zipcar** comes in: It is a cooperative that allows its members access to cars across the city, distributing the cost and hassle of owning a car among all its members. Members are charged for the number of hours they use the cars and the number of miles they drive them, portioning the fees for insurance, gas, repair, and cleaning among everyone. Cars, trucks, minivans, and even cute Mini Coopers and other sports cars are available all day, every day, at specific locations around town. To use a car, you call ahead to make a reservation, pick up the car at the designated spot, and return it to the same location at the time you have arranged. For more information contact Zipcar at (503) 328-3539 or online at www.zipcar.com.

Bicycling & Skateboarding

More and more people are riding their bikes in Portland, and many of these people are commuters. The city estimates that nearly 15,000 bicycles cross the Hawthorne Bridge each day, compared with 200 in 1975—representing almost 20 percent of all vehicles that cross the bridge. Cyclists are allowed on most of Portland's downtown bridges. The city—which has developed a comprehensive **Bicycle Master Plan**—has established nearly 200 miles of bikeways that include both off-street paths and bike lanes along streets. Special blue zones warn motorists that cyclists have the right-of-way in these lanes and that cars must yield to bikes when cars are attempting to turn a corner. Bright green boxes painted on the pavement at intersections tell drivers that bikes have the right of way. Such attention to bicycle riding has earned Portland accolades across the nation, and it is routinely touted as an unusually bike-friendly big city, likely the most bicycle-friendly urban area in the country.

Portland has a vigorous city-sponsored bicycle office: check them out online at www.portlandonline.com/transportation. This office can provide maps and other information about bike routes, bike parking, safety, and commuting. The **City of Portland Bicycle Program** continues to expand and improve the region's network of bike paths, and they have posted signs all over town that tell cyclists how far, and in which direction, their destinations are. Bike storage lockers may be found in many parts of the city, and all TriMet's buses and MAX light-rail trains are equipped with bike racks.

Portland's reputation is in part due to the efforts of the **Bicycle Transportation Alliance (BTA),** founded in 1990. This award-winning advocacy outfit has been tireless in its efforts to establish the infrastructure that allows Portland to be a capital of bike riding—advocating for more bike lanes, encouraging local developers to meet their legal requirements for bike and pedestrian access, providing safe storage lockers for bikes, and developing other initiatives to promote two-wheeled travel. They work with employers to promote bike commuting, which saves firms the steep cost of providing downtown parking. They initiated the campaign to allow bike access to the mass transit system and have been successful at creating bike access to most of the bridges that span the Willamette River—measures that have dramatically increased the number of bike commuters. Their insistence that streets should include people as well as cars has been great for the local economy: The successful redevelopment of the Northeast Broadway area around the Lloyd Center, with its bike lanes, wide sidewalks, and mellower traffic speeds, can be directly linked to the efforts of the BTA. And bicycles are at the heart of many new small businesses that capture Portland's independent spirit: Custom bike builders, athletic-wear designers, helmet innovators, and even transportation consultants are all making good livings thanks to early work by the BTA.

BTA organizes bike parking at festivals and other community events, carries out bicycle safety programs in the schools, and helps sponsor the annual Bridge Pedal (see our Festivals and Annual Events and Recreation chapters). Proceeds from the event not only benefit Providence Hospital but also help sponsor more bike programs. BTA may be reached at (503) 226-0676 or by visiting their informative website, www.bta4bikes .org.

Bicyclists aren't the only ones using human-powered wheels to get to work, school, and beyond. Skateboarders have joined them, having won a victory in 2001, when the city of Portland allowed them access to downtown and added their rights and responsibilities to the bicycle code. Now that skateboarding has become decriminalized, preferred skateboard routes have been designated, which you will find on green signs throughout the 200 blocks of downtown. Those who wish to ride their skateboards through town must follow a few strictly enforced rules: They must wear helmets if they are younger than 16, and they must wear lights at night, among other things. And tempting though it is, they must refrain from skating on the sidewalks. To learn more about biking and skateboarding in the Portland area, see the Recreation chapter.

Walking

Walking in Portland is one of its chief pleasures. Miles of paths line the waterfront, inviting pedestrians to ramble. Not only is the downtown area clean and well maintained, but the little villagelike neighborhoods that make up the city encourage residents to walk to the store, the bank, the library, dinner, even work. The city has found that promoting foot traffic is a smart business move. And moving your legs to get to your business can also be a smart move; on any given morning, you will find pedestrians strolling across downtown bridges, taking advantage of their commute time to exercise their legs, minds, and souls as they prepare for their day. If you're thinking of relocating, you might consider the walking potential of any prospective neighborhoods. You might even find a great job in your own neighborhood and be able to walk to work. See the hiking section in the Recreation chapter and the Portland's Parks chapter for more excellent walks in the area.

HISTORY

But for the toss of a coin, you might be reading the *Insiders' Guide to Boston, Oregon.* Early settlers Asa Lovejoy and William Overton brought their canoe ashore at a clearing in the woods along the Willamette River. Both men agreed that it looked like a promising site for a town. But Overton, a drifter from Tennessee, lacked the 25 cents he needed to file a land claim. So he struck a deal with Lovejoy: They would share the 640-acre site if Lovejoy would put up the money, and the two filed a claim in 1842. But soon, Overton tired of the pioneer's life, and he sold his half of the claim to Francis Pettygrove. By 1845 the settlement in the clearing in the woods had grown enough so that the two owners knew they had to name their site. Pettygrove, a native of Maine, favored the name Portland, while Lovejoy, who came from Boston, wanted to name it after his fair city. The two men agreed to settle the matter by flipping a copper penny. Pettygrove won, and you can still see the "Portland Penny" on permanent display at the Oregon History Center.

EARLY HISTORY

Of course, the story of Portland and the surrounding area begins thousands of years before these 19th-century events, and well before Europeans ever touched Oregon's shores. The first migration to Oregon occurred during the Ice Age, when sea levels fell, exposing a narrow strip of land across the Bering Sea. The game animals that traveled across in search of warmer lands were followed by small bands of nomadic Asian hunters as early as 30,000 years ago. Historians believe that the first Native Americans, including the Klamath, Modock, Bannock, Nez Perce, and Chinook tribes, came to Oregon between 10,000 and 12,000 years ago. The coastal tribes relied heavily on abundant salmon, shellfish, seals, and the occasional stranded whale. The tribes farther inland lived on game and altered the landscape as they burned forests and grasslands to attract

their prey. This last group, the nomadic hunters and gatherers, were the ones to first greet the early European fur traders who reached the Oregon territory even before Lewis and Clark. At first they welcomed these strange visitors, and accepted their gifts, including guns, whiskey, trinkets, and tools.

The first European to see the Oregon coast was probably Juan Rodriguez Cabrillo, a Spanish sea captain who attempted to map the Pacific coast in 1543; however, he did not set foot on land. Sir Francis Drake is said to have had that honor in 1579 when he claimed the area for England in the name of Queen Elizabeth. That claim, however, was hollow, for it would be another 200 years before the next English vessel reached Oregon. Numerous European ships landed on the Oregon coast in the late 16th century and the early 17th century; however, those expeditions revealed little about the inland regions. By 1750 Russian trappers had worked their way down through Alaska and Canada to the Oregon shoreline in search of otter, but they did not establish a colony, choosing instead to build Fort Ross along the northern California coast in 1812. In fact, no less than four nations laid claim to Oregon—Spain, Russia, Britain, and the United States—but not one built a single settlement to signify a legal presence.

In 1788 John Meares sailed right past the mouth of the Columbia River, and in 1792 Captain George Vancouver also missed it, leaving the second largest river in the United States to be discovered by Captain Robert Gray of Boston, who named it after his vessel, the USS *Columbia*.

In the early 1800s Oregon (and the American West in general) was still very much an uncharted place. Easterners heard tall tales about the western mountains and desert swarming with fierce savages, and about abundant resources, but few had been there.

The Native Americans that lived in the area that would become Portland were anything but savages, however. The tribes that lived here—the Kalapuyas, the Clackamas, the Molalla, the Tualatin, the Chinook, the Multnomah, and the Wapato, among others—had sophisticated, multifaceted cultures well supported by the area's abundance. Many of the tribes were quite wealthy. Some of these groups were river tribes, who built large dwellings along the Willamette, Clackamas, Pudding, and other rivers. Other tribes—the Molalla, for instance—lived farther upland, in the foothills of the Cascades. The Molalla were a more nomadic hunting tribe, riding horses east and north toward the Columbia.

While there were occasional conflicts among these different groups, it was largely a peaceful region, with little war. Instead, these tribes had elaborate networks of trade, both within and among all the tribes in the region, as well as with the Eastern trappers who began to show up in the early 19th century. They had a lot to trade too. Though these tribes did not plant crops, many engaged in protoagricultural practices. For example, they burned the grassy fields to harvest grasshoppers, to flush out camas seed, and to ensure the health of the meadows. Division and specialization of labor was common, as were advanced systems for storing the roots, berries, nuts, elk, bear, and salmon that they gathered, hunted, and fished. And much legend and ritual were dedicated to thanksgiving and appreciation for all that the gods had given them in this beautiful place. Hundreds of thousands of people lived here for 10,000 years before Eastern settlers had ever heard of the place, dwelling in villages large and small, speaking a variety of languages, living out their own histories.

The Lewis & Clark Expedition

President Thomas Jefferson planned a secret mission in 1803: to send a small party of men overland to the Pacific—a bold venture that no one before had even attempted. Congress covertly approved the trip, along with its budget of $2,500, because these explorers would be venturing outside US jurisdiction into British territory. Jefferson was looking for an expeditious water route to the Pacific via the Missouri River, its tributaries, and a legendary River of the West said to flow down from the Rockies to the Pacific, in hope that the distance between the east- and west-flowing rivers would be a one-day portage. It would be a simple route west for traders, emigrants, and adventurers. Aware of the opportunity, Jefferson also charged the group with collecting scientific information about the region's interior.

President Jefferson chose his neighbor, longtime friend, and personal secretary, Meriwether Lewis, to lead the contingent across the Louisiana Purchase and to the Pacific coast. Lewis, in turn, wisely selected frontiersman and mapmaker William Clark to be his coleader.

In the spring of 1804, Lewis and Clark, along with 31 men and the intrepid Newfoundland hound, Seaman, left St. Louis and started up the Missouri River heading west. Over the next two years the group—eventually christened the "Corps of Discovery"—would traverse present-day Missouri, Nebraska, the Dakotas, Montana, Wyoming, Washington, and Oregon. The journey took so long that the few insiders who knew about it feared that the members of the expedition had perished. But on December 5, 1805, Lewis and Clark reached the Pacific Ocean and Clark wrote in his diary, "We now discover that we have found the most practicable and navigable passage across the continent of North America." In reality, he couldn't have been further from the truth.

The route discovered by Lewis and Clark was far too difficult for others to follow. Indeed, no pioneer wagon ever did follow their trail. In fact, Lolo Pass, where their expedition crossed the treacherous Bitterroot Mountains in western Montana, is a rough haul even today—two centuries later. But because their detailed maps and notes provided a wealth of scientific data, the West was no longer an uncharted mystery, and their expedition was celebrated as a success. Although they examined only a

small portion of the Northwest Coast and the Columbia River, they gathered much valuable and accurate information about the rest of the Northwest from friendly native peoples. Their reports stirred excitement in the East; their vivid descriptions of a land of bounty created an "Oregon fever" among fur traders who had previously trapped and traded in the Rocky Mountains.

The Fur Trade & Fort Vancouver

The second major westward expedition was not funded by a government but was backed by one of the world's richest men—John Jacob Astor, who whetted his appetite for adventure by reading about Lewis and Clark's great journey. By 1810 Astor saw an opportunity to make a new fortune: a fur-trading enterprise at the mouth of the Columbia River. But one dilemma stood in his way: How could he get his men safely across the uncharted American West? He had a couple of ideas and tried both a land and a sea route.

In 1811 he dispatched an overland party to follow the trail of the early explorers and to establish trading posts. He also sent another party there by sea, in a ship traveling around Cape Horn. The ship arrived safely but was destroyed afterward in a skirmish with Native Americans.

The land expedition also had problems. At a particularly dangerous spot on the Snake River, known as Caldron Linn, one of the canoes capsized, drowning at least one man and losing a large portion of much-needed supplies. Worse, the party soon discovered that the river did not become more placid downstream and that it was too treacherous to navigate. They came to the conclusion that there was no quick and easy route to the Pacific, an assessment that would stymie pioneers for the next hundred years.

Astor's overland party finally did make it to Oregon, but the enterprise was in deep trouble. Their only hope was to send a few men back East to get help from Astor. Robert Stuart led the mission back to St. Louis—an arduous journey that took nearly a year. But Stuart made an incredible discovery along the way. In what is now the state of Wyoming, he found a 20-mile-wide gap in the Rocky Mountains where wagons could pass. Named South Pass, this route would unlock the door to western migration, and more than a half-million emigrants would eventually ride their Conestoga wagons through to the other side. Where Lewis and Clark had valiantly failed, Robert Stuart succeeded through a twist of fate.

Even before Robert Stuart's lucky discovery, adventurous entrepreneurs were at work in the western mountains. These "mountain men" were solitary fur trappers, and most had no home, no money, and no possessions—except what they wore and carried on their backs. They lived completely off the land, on a diet of buffalo, elk, and mountain goat. Many trappers roamed constantly in search of beaver pelts; many married Native American women and earned the respect and fondness of various tribes. Some were hired by the trading companies exploiting the area, while others remained freelancers; still others eventually settled down on land claims.

The companies that hired these men and bought their pelts played a crucial role in the shaping of Portland. John Jacob Astor's Pacific Fur Company did eventually establish a presence in the area, but it was not as great as that of its competitor: the Hudson's Bay Company, run by the British, who wished to control these fertile Northwest lands and secure for themselves the pelts and other riches that the territory promised. The Hudson's Bay Company, established in 1670, was an experienced operation. It had many outposts west of the Rocky Mountains from Alaska to Mexico. But supplying them was expensive and difficult (as Astor too discovered). Thus, the company decided to build a settlement that could sustain itself and perhaps produce enough surplus to furnish other outposts in the West, reducing the need for the costly ships that the company used to bring supplies to its people.

i Some historians believe that the name *Oregon* is derived from the French *ouragan,* meaning "storm" or "hurricane," because early French-Canadian trappers called the Columbia River the "River of Storms."

In 1825 the Hudson's Bay Company sent Dr. John McLoughlin to build a fortified settlement along the Columbia: Fort Vancouver, on the north side of the river. Its location was ideal—it was close enough to the sea that it could receive trading ships and send them back laden with pelts, and it was on a beautiful, richly soiled plain well out of the dangers of annual flooding.

Fort Vancouver became the administrative site and supply depot for the Columbia Department of the Hudson's Bay Company. Its goal was to make it impossible for Astor and the other fur companies to gain a foothold in the area, by establishing a huge network of trappers, traders, and Native Americans to harvest as many furs as possible, even if that meant eradicating an animal population in the area. To accomplish this, the fort became a self-sustaining community, with fields of grain and vegetables, dairies, and orchards. Mills were built for processing lumber and grain. Barrel-makers, bakers, and blacksmiths were hired and brought to the fort. Schools and churches were formed, and a hospital was built and maintained. By the time the first pioneers stumbled out of the mountains in 1842, Western civilization was well established.

McLoughlin was the chief administrator of Fort Vancouver for nearly 20 years, and without him, it is hard to say how the American pioneers would have fared. McLoughlin was a fascinating figure. He had good relations with the native peoples, and his principled administration was admired by many, though—like that of any good administrator—it was not without controversy. He enforced the company policy of protecting its interests while respecting the trade-friendly Native Americans and making no attempt to convert them into Europeans. But the American emigrants were a different story: They posed a direct threat to the comfortable monopoly that the Hudson's Bay Company enjoyed. McLoughlin was dismayed by them, yet he could not keep them out, since the legal claim of the British to the territory had not been established. At the same time, he felt compelled to help the pioneers as they arrived, sick and starving. His solution was to attempt to bring them into the fur trade, and to this end, he helped these emigrants establish themselves in the Willamette Valley, a difficult choice that was often in conflict with his duties to the Hudson's Bay Company.

In 1846 the British and American governments settled the territorial dispute, and Oregon became a territory of the United States. But under this treaty, British and other citizens could retain their rights to the land they had settled. McLoughlin

established Oregon City as a hamlet for retired trappers from the Hudson's Bay Company and continued his work helping the pioneers, whose journey ended when they reached McLoughlin's new hometown. Yet no good deed ever goes unpunished, and McLoughlin's good deeds were no exception. He had wisely governed Fort Vancouver; he was respected by the native nations; he had helped hundreds of pioneers; he was a prudent and farsighted steward. Naturally, then, he developed new political opponents in the territory, who convinced the US Congress to block his claim to land that he had cultivated for more than 30 years. He died in sorrow and in poverty in 1857. Later Oregonians regretted his treatment, restoring some of the property to his heirs in 1862. In 1953, Oregonians sent a statue of John McLoughlin to represent the state in the National Statuary Hall Collection in the United States Capitol in Washington, D.C., officially recognizing his contributions.

AGE OF PIONEERS

Explorers who followed Lewis and Clark, such as John Frémont, were often so upbeat that they made the trip west seem easy and enjoyable, which it definitely was not. They were encouraged in their reports by the US government, who wanted to make sure these resource-rich lands stayed out of the hands of the Russians and the British.

Oregon Trail

Driving this great movement was more than just positive reports. In 1843 the federal government allotted 640 acres of land to every adult homesteader and 160 acres to every child, with hopes of anchoring the United States' claims to the Northwest Territories.

Most of those who came as far west as Oregon made the land trip. However, some came by water and did so even before a land route was established. The sea route never was a popular choice, though. The fare was prohibitive, and most westward-bound pioneers came from central states far from seaports. Also, the sea journey often took up to a full year compared with the wagon journey, which took five to eight months.

Those who did come by land took the route that came to be known as the Oregon Trail (although it actually forks in southern Idaho, with a lower extension ending in California). Legend enjoyed by Oregonians to this day has it that those who were greedy for gold headed south at the fork to California and those who wanted a better life headed north to the Oregon Territory. Nearly 2,000 miles long, the main route west stretched from Independence, Missouri, to Oregon City, Oregon. Portions of it followed the Platte River for 540 miles through Nebraska to Fort Laramie in present-day Wyoming. The trail wound along the North Platte and Sweetwater Rivers to South Pass in the Wind River Range of the Rocky Mountains. From there the main trail went south to Fort Bridger, Wyoming, before turning into the Bear River Valley and north to Fort Hall in present-day Idaho. The Oregon Trail followed the Snake River to Salmon Falls and then went north past Fort Boise. The route entered what is now Oregon, passed through the Grande Ronde River Valley, crossed the Blue Mountains, and followed the Umatilla River to the Columbia River. Shorter and more direct routes were developed along some parts of the trail, but they were often more difficult.

The first organized party of emigrants to actually reach the Oregon Territory came with the American pioneer physician Elijah White. Under the leadership of John Bidwell, an Ohio schoolteacher, this group loaded their wagons and left Missouri in 1841 and in 1842 reached Oregon. The terminus of their journey was the future site of Oregon City; later settlers would head for the verdant Willamette Valley. During the 1840s thousands of pioneers settled there, where wheat, fruits, and vegetables thrived. Others settled higher up, for gold prospecting and to harvest Oregon's bountiful supply of Douglas fir trees.

The Oregon Trail directed the flow of westward expansion and permitted the settlement and development of the Pacific Northwest. Before the completion of the first transcontinental railroad in 1870, an estimated 350,000 pioneers followed the Oregon Trail westward, more than all the other routes combined.

In Oregon, the trail's route has remained a principal course of east-west travel to the present day, though it lies buried beneath I-84. The road crosses a diverse range of terrain—the rugged Blue Mountains in northeastern Oregon, the dry plateaus between Pendleton and The Dalles, the awesome Cascade Mountains and Columbia Gorge section, and even the geographic end of the trail in Oregon City, where the Willamette Valley settlements all began.

i Of the estimated 350,000 settlers who migrated west on the Oregon Trail, at least 20,000 died en route. Cholera was the most common cause of death.

PORTLAND'S EARLY DAYS

As the Native American way of life was disappearing, the settlers were busy creating a new one. Gradually the Oregon Territory began to acquire the sheen of civilization. A dozen years after the first wagon trains arrived at the end of the Oregon Trail, the hamlets along the Willamette began sprouting business districts with general stores, blacksmith shops, tanneries, well-furnished hotels, and white-steepled churches. In Portland the crude log cabins of the frontiersmen were gradually giving way to tidy frame houses with glass windows, ornamental woodwork, and papered walls. A pristine tract of forestland in 1844, Portland boasted 821 residents by 1850, making it the region's most populous community. Mail arrived by steamship, which took the route around Cape Horn, and was distributed to the 40 post offices in the area. And thanks to the vision of New England sailor Captain John Couch, who chose Portland over Oregon City as a deepwater harbor for his shipping, the city soon became known as a port deserving its name.

As proper civilization took hold in Portland, the city also attracted a few lawless individuals who've served to provide color for our local history. One such person was Portland's "Sweet Mary," who created a floating brothel. Another was Joseph "Bunco" Kelly, a hotelier known for shanghaiing young men and selling them to ship captains short of crew members. Kelly carted them off when they were drunk. Upon waking, the young men had bigger problems than a hangover. Eventually, however, the wilder side of Portland, with its teeming saloons and shady houses of ill-repute, was tamed by an indignant citizenry. The prospering economy was turning Stumptown into a real city, complete with officials intent upon creating a structure of law and order. Rules of decorum came to Portland in the

1870s, when it became illegal to fire a pistol downtown or drive your carriage faster than 6 miles per hour. The town gained its most notable nickname in 1889 when local artist, writer, and bon vivant C. E. S. Woods called for an annual rose show. The Portland Rose Festival was launched that year in what would soon be known as the "City of Roses." Since the replacement of the downtown wharves in 1929 with a seawall stretching along most of the city's shoreline on the Willamette River, it has become a tradition to welcome a fleet of US and Canadian warships to dock during this festival.

i Oregon's pioneering spirit extends to many areas. Among other firsts, it was the first state to officially register all its voters, the first to directly elect US senators, the first to create an initiative system—and in case none of the above worked out—the first to develop a system for recalling public officials.

Part of the early economy was agriculture. In 1847 Henderson Lewelling brought the first apple, cherry, peach, plum, and pear saplings into the Willamette Valley, beginning a new agricultural venture. In 1849 the California gold rush created a huge demand for these crops and other staples, thus boosting Portland's economy. The first crop of 100 apples was sent to California mining camps, where there was such a scarcity of fresh fruit that scurvy (caused by a vitamin C deficiency) was a leading cause of death. For a time the apples sold for the sum of $5 apiece, the going rate for a week's room and board. Other Oregon goods, ranging from lumber to eggs, remained in constant demand, which in turn fueled a new rush of men and women eager to farm in the Willamette Valley. In 1851 the city of Portland was officially incorporated. (For more details about Portland's early history, see the Relocation chapter, especially the Linnton and Oregon City sections, and the Area Overview chapter.)

In 1853 Washington split from the Oregon Territory, claiming land north of the Columbia River, which continues to form part of the interstate boundary. The next year, Oregon voters rejected statehood because they were split on whether to enter the United States as a slave state or as a free state. Although slavery was voted down, 7,277 to 2,645, only 1,081 men voted to let free Black men settle in Oregon compared with 8,640 who were opposed to their presence. Statehood initiatives were also rejected in 1855 and 1856. However, on Valentine's Day, 1859, Oregon became a state, with Oregon City, the largest city in the territory, becoming the capital and regional center for all the Oregon Territories.

Indian Treaties Ignored

In the 1860s prosperity continued for Portland's residents as the Oregon Steam Navigation Company secured a monopoly on all shipping on the Columbia River. By 1870 Portland boasted the largest population (9,565) in the Pacific Northwest until the Alaska gold rush of 1897 fueled Seattle's rise. In 1883 the transcontinental railroad arrived in Portland with President U. S. Grant on board. This linkage by rail enabled export of lumber, beef, salmon, and other goods to the major eastern cities, triggering the biggest economic and population growth spurt in the state's history.

Sadly, this led to the further subjugation and maltreatment of the state's indigenous peoples. Impatient settlers and loggers repeatedly trampled Indian treaties by taking land reserved for tribal peoples. Private property was a foreign concept to the Native Americans in the area, who believed the forests and fields were community properties for the general welfare of all. The friction intensified as miners stampeded into areas where silver or gold was found. Native Americans, who were neither taxpayers nor voters, protested the violations in vain. Battles and hostilities sporadically broke out throughout the West. In Oregon, Chief Joseph and the Nez Perce were routed from their homes in the Wallowas to eventually surrender in southern Canada. The Modoc tribe was forced off their land and herded across the California border where they held 1,500 troops at bay in the lava beds for six months. These conflicts were repeated around the western states until the last organized tribal resistance died out in the 1890s.

Logging

Logging was a cornerstone of the economy, and the timber industry was king in Oregon, pressuring Congress to repeal the Forest Preservation Act of 1891, opening up millions of acres of public land in Oregon and other northwestern states for huge clearcuts. Theodore Roosevelt responded by setting aside large forest reserves where timber operations were prohibited. These reserves eventually grew into the USDA Forest Service, which later compromised his intent by allowing timber sales, a source of controversy that lingers today.

The Lewis & Clark Centennial Exposition

Lewis and Clark shaped Portland long after

they departed the quiet native trails that lined the Columbia. Portland derives much of its appearance—even today—from the successful, extensive world's fair held here in 1905 to celebrate the 100-year anniversary of their expedition. The Lewis and Clark Exposition drew thousands of visitors to Portland and precipitated an economic boom, accompanied by a wave of building and development, especially in Northwest and Southwest Portland. Hotels and other civic buildings were constructed to capitalize on the wave of visitors. Few of the fair's actual structures remain—most of them were dismantled, and more than a few burned down. The fair's buildings were beautiful but not designed to last. Yet the hotels, department stores, and other pavilions that were built throughout the city remain today, furnishing the architectural bones of the city.

The Lewis and Clark Exposition also changed the appearance of the nation: It was here that plywood was introduced.

i When Portland's Esther Pohl Lovejoy was appointed to the Portland Board of Health in 1905, she became the first woman to lead the health bureau of a major American city. She put herself through medical school by working at the hosiery counter of the Lipman and Wolfe department store.

THE WAR YEARS

Workers & Population Growth

During World War I thousands of unskilled workers swarmed to Portland to work on Swan Island, a bustling center of shipbuilding and repair. But compared with World War II, the war to end all wars caused only a ripple

in Oregon. It was World War II that forever altered the shape of the Portland area.

Henry J. Kaiser's Oregon Shipbuilding Corporation began building freighters of the famous Liberty Ship class when World War II was less than a month old. The first Kaiser shipyard in the Portland area was the St. Johns Yard. At the end of one year, it launched 36 ships. By war's end, the yard had built 141 vessels, including Liberty Ships and their successor, the Victory Ship.

i Lone Fir Cemetery, on Southeast 20th between Morrison and Stark, holds the earthly remains of early Portlanders. These Oregonians—some with important historical names, some with ignominious ones—lie side by side, speaking eloquently of our common fate.

During World War II the demand for wartime workers and the passage of tens of thousands of enlisted men and women through Oregon swelled the state's population from less than 1.1 million in 1940 to more than 1.5 million in 1950. The city of Portland's 1940 population of 305,000 jumped to 374,000 residents in just three years.

Minority Groups

The Rise & Fall of Vanport

Portland's new residents included large numbers of emigrants from the deep South: They arrived by the trainload, lured away from the poverty and oppression to work in the wartime shipyards of Henry Kaiser. Between 1940 and 1945 Portland's African-American population surged from 2,100 to 15,000.

The state was not always hospitable to minorities, and over the course of its history had created laws limiting the freedoms of everyone who wasn't white and Protestant. For example, Oregon's Ku Klux Klan once boasted a membership of 25,000 and even elected a leader, Grand Dragon Walter Pierce, as governor of the state. Pierce sponsored legislation in 1922 that barred all Catholic schools in the state in addition to attempting to deny African-American citizens their right to vote.

But the war efforts and the workers needed to sustain them created a dilemma. Henry Kaiser was busy building the Liberty Ships for the war effort, yet these new workers had nowhere to live. The sudden increase in population strained the city's ability to meet even the most basic needs of these war workers. The city authorities in Portland dragged their feet, not wanting to create housing for this influx of workers—who might then decide to stay. So Kaiser went around the city authorities and applied the same rapid building techniques to housing war workers as he did to making warships, assembling practically overnight the city of Vanport, just outside the city limits of Portland. It was built to sustain the workers, including providing for their families: It had schools, medical clinics, shops, even 24-hour day care, since many of Kaiser's employees were women with children. Nearly 70,000 workers and their families lived in this city. The major drawback was that it was built on a flat floodplain between the Willamette and Columbia Rivers.

Rapidly, Vanport became the state's second-largest city. Three years after the war, about 19,000 people still lived there. On Memorial Day, 1948, the rivers, swollen by rain and melting snow, broke the dikes protecting Vanport and swept the town away, killing 18 people. The city's entire population, then about one-fourth African American, became homeless.

Vanport was never rebuilt and today West Delta Park stands on the site of this former community.

Relocation Camps

African Americans were not the only minority group to suffer maltreatment. The Pearl Harbor bombing created widespread fear of espionage, sabotage, and an invasion aided by Japanese-American citizens. Under Executive Order 9066, issued in February 1942 by the federal government, Japanese-American citizens in certain sensitive areas were forced to relocate.

When the US Army declared Oregon, California, and Washington "strategic areas," they forced more than 110,000 Japanese Americans into 10 relocation centers. More than 4,000 Oregonians of Japanese descent were moved to the Portland Assembly Center, formerly the Portland International Livestock Center. Between May and September of 1942, they lived in former animal stalls and barns, guarded by military police, while permanent relocation camps were built farther inland. Several years later, the Executive Order was rescinded, but the Japanese-American population lost their homes, businesses, and farms.

World War II in Portland

The war was closer to Portland than many people imagined. In June 1942 a submarine of the Imperial Japanese Navy surfaced a few miles off the Oregon coast. Pointing her stern toward a suspected US submarine base, the ship fired on Fort Stevens. In order to conceal the exact location of their coastal defense guns, the frustrated defenders were forbidden to return fire. Fort Stevens thus became the only military installation in the continental United States to come under direct enemy fire during the war. This was the first attack on the US mainland since the War of 1812. But it was not to be the only Japanese attack here. Many ships were torpedoed off the Oregon coast. For years after the war, rusting mines drifted onto shore. Even today, fishing boats still pull up their nets and find a World War II–era bomb, torpedo, or mine.

Also, in September 1943, the Japanese launched a single-engine float plane that dropped phosphorus bombs in the Oregon forest northwest of Brookings and on other parts of the West Coast. These were the only bombs that fell on continental American soil during the war; their primary purpose was to start forest fires that would create fear and divert troops from the war effort. Of the hundreds of balloon bombs launched by the Japanese, 45 landed in Oregon. Fortunately, most of these fire starters fizzled in the Oregon rain. But one landed near Bly, a town of 750 people in southeastern Oregon, killing one adult and five children. These were the only civilian deaths from enemy action in the continental US during the war.

One long-range target for these bombs may have been the US Army base at Camp Pendleton. Here General Jimmy Doolittle trained B-17 bomber crews heading for England and for the famous attack on Tokyo. It was after Doolittle's highly symbolic raid that the bombs were dropped on our West Coast.

POSTWAR PROSPERITY

War's end brought more changes to Portland and Oregon. Returning veterans enrolled in large numbers at colleges, started families, and bought houses. During the postwar years, Portland prospered, like most of the nation. Wood products and fisheries filled the state's coffers in the postwar building boom, and Portland, as the major city in Oregon, benefited greatly. In the late 1960s and early 1970s, Republican governor Tom McCall, a true visionary, guided the state through a challenging phase by making controlled growth and environmental protection the top priorities of state government. One of his many important achievements was to lead a controversial but farsighted legislative effort to keep the coastline open to the public. As the economy was bolstered by the booming agriculture, timber, fishing, and tourism, many Oregonians enjoyed a period of economic growth and security. Then, in keeping with a national trend, residents and businesses began leaving the inner city in favor of the suburbs. Not all urban shops and homes were replaced with new ownership, and certain areas began to slide downhill. Gradually, islands of neglect began to appear in Portland's inner city. In the 1980s many huge projects of the Portland Development Commission focused on areas such as the riverfront and the downtown square area and neglected neighborhoods in Southeast, North, and Northeast Portland. A prime example is Pioneer Courthouse Square, a central plaza used for festivals, concerts, and lunches away from the office.

By the 1990s the timber industry, while still critical to Oregon's economy, was waning as old growth stands of trees were diminished by decades of overcutting and poor resource management. The fishing and salmon industries were, likewise, crippled by years of heavy gill netting and drift netting. Meanwhile, manufacturing was growing, fueled by telecommunications and computer technology industries in the Willamette Valley. From the late 1970s and mid-1980s, Portland's suburbs, particularly the Silicon Forest in Washington County, made huge strides, and manufacturing and high-technology companies began moving to the area, attracted by cheap water, utilities, space, and a high standard of living.

Oregon's position, between the states of Washington and California and connecting to the Pacific Rim nations, puts it in a large economic sphere that continues to generate growth. But the growth is not without controversy. As both Oregon and Portland continue to expand, arguments about how much to grow and where to grow have become more heated and intense. Mixed-use development, housing, apartments, and business continue to spring up along light rail lines and other innovations in transportation, such as the Portland Streetcar. The city's splashy megaprojects of the 1980s are now replaced by smaller, more community-driven developments in such places as Alberta Street in Northeast Portland. While the trend in the 1970s and 1980s was flight from the urban areas to the suburbs, since the 1990s people have returned to the city, starting businesses, fixing up old houses, and developing new properties. The results are increased jobs, housing, and livability for all Portlanders. By focusing on developing the city, rather than allowing unregulated sprawl, Portland is better equipped than most cities to meet the challenges of the 21st century.

"The past is not dead. It isn't even past," observed William Faulkner. He was talking about the American South, but it's also true in Portland, even in ways that we may not notice. We drive down McLoughlin or Pettygrove, we visit the Multnomah or Clackamas County libraries, we rush by an old pioneer cemetery or restored farmhouse from the 19th century, but rarely do we give thought to the people who walked here before us—pioneer, fur trader, or Native American. Yet our lips echo with their names and our feet tread the same earth. Their spirits live on.

ACCOMMODATIONS

Visitors to Portland will find a variety of motel and hotel offerings, from the basic to the sublime. They range in style, in price, and in location, but no matter where you plan to stay, you should be able to find a place to lay your head and suit your needs. Portland's bed-and-breakfast inns offer visitors an alternative to hotel rooms, as well as a chance to explore the individual neighborhoods that make up the city. Staying in a bed-and-breakfast inn allows you the chance to see why people have chosen to live here and how the region's history, climate, geography, diversity, and growth have shaped their lives.

Price Code

The following price code for hotels, motels, and bed-and-breakfasts in this chapter is based on an average room rate for double occupancy during high season. While there is no sales tax in Oregon, there is a room tax of 12.5 percent.

Please note that many hotels and motels change their room rates frequently, so the ranges we have quoted in this chapter are meant simply as a guide to point you in the right direction, not as the final word on the cost of your stay. Most hotels have a range of room prices; this code is meant to reflect a typical weekend rate for a double or queen room for two adults, unless otherwise noted.

$ . . . . **Less than $90**
$$ . . . . **$90 to $140**
$$$ . . . . **$140 to $190**
$$$$ . . . . **More than $190**

ACCOMMODATIONS

The Lion and The Rose,
North & Northeast
Portland, 52

**The Marriott Hotel–City
Center,** Southwest
Portland, 47

The Marriott Hotel,
Southwest Portland, 47

Silver Cloud Inn, Northwest
Portland, 49

$$

Ace Hotel, Southwest
Portland, 41

The Blue Plum, North &
Northeast Portland, 52

**Georgian House Bed
& Breakfast,** North &
Northeast Portland, 52

The Heathman Lodge,
Vancouver, WA, 50

Hotel Modera, Southwest
Portland, 45

Jupiter Hotel, Southeast
Portland, 49

The Mark Spencer Hotel,
Southwest Portland, 46

**McMenamins Kennedy
School,** North & Northeast
Portland, 50

**Terwilliger Vista Bed &
Breakfast,** Southwest
Portland, 51

$

Bluebird Guesthouse,
Southeast Portland, 49

Clinton Street Guesthouse,
Southeast Portland, 51

HOTELS & MOTELS

You will find certain chains well represented throughout the Portland Metro area. For example, Marriott's Courtyard, Fairfield Inns, and Residence Inns, offering consistently clean and comfortable rooms, can be found in Beaverton, Southeast Portland, Hillsboro, Tigard, downtown, the Lloyd Center, North Portland, at the airport, and at other hubs. So can the Homewood Suites and the Garden Inns by the Hilton chain, Holiday Inn Express, Phoenix Inns, Ramada Inns, and many other well-known chains. The area around the Convention Center and Lloyd Center has large Doubletree and Holiday Inns that are well attended and host many meetings and events. We figure you know about these reliable places already, so in this guide we have concentrated on the standouts in the area, including some in these chains where appropriate. We also focus on the hotels in the center of town, but we've included some options for other parts of town as well.

As Portland's star as a destination for tourism rises, new hotels, guesthouses, and vacation rental services have arrived

> ### Vacation Rentals
>
> With its renowned restaurants, proximity to the Willamette Valley wine country, and energetic cultural scene, Portland is becoming a vacation destination—and that means an emerging market for vacation rentals. Some good sources? Try **Historic Hawthorne Rentals** (www.historichawthornerentals.com) for its stylish eastside locations. **Vaction Rentals By Owner** (www.vrbo.com/vacation-rentals/usa/oregon) and the very popular **Craigslist** (www.portland.craigslist.org) are also reliable sources as well, though the former has more Portland-specific rentals.

to meet the demand for rooms. Many of these, but not all, are found downtown. Not surprisingly, it is expensive to park your car downtown, where hotels charge about $30 per day. Some hotels do offer free parking for guests. Some provide valet parking at their own facilities or nearby garages; others offer their guests discounted parking at local garages. Parking outside of the downtown area is less expensive. However, whether you stay downtown or elsewhere in Portland, you may not need a car at all. Downtown is well served by the MAX line from the airport, the train station is a short cab ride to the downtown core, and it may be simpler just to be car-free.

Southwest Portland

✳ACE HOTEL   **$$**
1022 Southwest Stark St.
(503) 228-2277
www.acehotel.com
This Ace Hotel, though an offshoot of its Seattle brother, is very Portland, with an indie aesthetic and an attitude to match. It is indeed named after the card, which can be either high or low, and this theme is evident throughout. The 79 rooms vary widely in standards of luxury. The most expensive room costs about $250, while rooms with shared baths—or even those with bunk beds designed to house touring bands—run about $95. The hotel is furnished with locally designed things as well as salvaged ones, and many of the features from the residential hotel that existed there beginning at the turn of the century have been repurposed. That said, it is a very stylish hotel, and you might not know these things were old or recycled unless we told you. Local artists were hired to create murals throughout the hotel, but it's not just the artwork that is soulful. The lobby is very comfortable and attractive, with couches and free Wi-Fi (throughout the hotel, actually). Even the business center on the mezzanine radiates West-coast hip, providing MacBooks around a large table for you to check your Gmail, as well as a couch for work-induced narcolepsy.

The Ace Hotel is not for everyone. You should be forewarned that it is going for something other than the standard hotel experience, and adjust your expectations accordingly. For example, you will not find free coffee or newspapers, though delicious coffee is available right next door at the excellent Stumptown coffee shop. Soaps are handmade, but not overabundant, and you may be sharing a bathroom or using a glassed-in shower in your room. The hotel can also be noisy, given its location off Burnside and its ancient age. This hotel may not be the ideal choice for a romantic honeymoon or a tense business trip, but it could be ideal for a weekend getaway with friends, especially since its common spaces are so enticing and its location so central.

ℹ Try the Portland Visitors Association website for deals on hotel rooms and help with planning your meeting: www.travelportland.com.

AVALON HOTEL AND SPA   **$$$**
4650 Southwest Macadam Ave.
(503) 802-5800, (888) 556-4802
www.avalonhotelandspa.com
The Avalon Hotel and Spa is a beautiful hotel with a special difference: It is the only hotel in the area dedicated to providing spa services as part of its mission and built—in an environmentally friendly way, no less—with these services in mind. And Portland residents, who don't usually stay in Portland hotels, believe this was a wise move. This hotel delights residents and visitors alike. Its commitment to old-fashioned luxury and service have made it an instant classic.

The Avalon is in an attractive building south of downtown on the Willamette River, in the South Waterfront district. It offers 99 rooms, 18 of them suites. Public spaces and rooms alike are outfitted with sleek but comfortable furnishings and plush rugs. Many rooms have balconies that look out on the Willamette, to Mount Hood, and beyond. Bathrooms, which feature marble, wood, and stone accents, are spacious. The concierge staff is outstanding. Room service is available from 6 a.m. to 11 p.m., and the full-service Rivers restaurant offers breakfast, lunch, and dinner. To keep things pristine, no smoking or pets are allowed.

Spa services are worth the extra cost. The slate-floored spa, which is downstairs, features an excellent array of services—including massages, facials, and pedicures—that promise restoration to tired bodies and souls. Body wraps of various concoctions of mud, antioxidants, and unguents are especially alluring. Don't miss the Raindance room, with its Vichy and Swiss showers.

THE BENSON HOTEL $$$$
309 Southwest Broadway
(503) 228-2000, (888) 523-6766
www.bensonhotel.com

A grand and historic Portland building, the Benson has been the hotel of choice for visiting US presidents and other dignitaries since 1912, when it was built. Its builder, lumber baron Simon Benson, spared no expense, importing rare Circassian walnut paneling, Austrian crystal chandeliers, and Italian marble to adorn this beautiful hotel. This commitment to superior quality remains, and the Benson's simple but exquisite furnishings and service offer a fine balance of warmth and elegance.

The 287 guest rooms and suites are spacious, amply furnished in a traditional style with pleasing modern touches. Amenities include complimentary high-speed wireless, access to the fitness center, and umbrellas in every room. You can also request Tempur-Pedic Sleep System mattresses. The Grand Suite features a baby grand piano, a fireplace, and a Jacuzzi, and penthouse suites offer delightful views of the city around you.

The Benson's London Grill restaurant has been a Portland favorite for generations. Its downtown location is convenient to galleries, theaters, restaurants, and shopping, and the convention center is a short MAX ride away. Even if you don't stay here, drop by the lobby bar for a drink.

i Traveling with Fido? The Governor Hotel, the Benson, and the Heathman, all downtown, are proud to accommodate your dog. The Hotel Vintage Plaza even has an honor bar just for your pooch. For a list of dog-friendly hotels in Oregon, visit Pets Allowed Hotels at www.pets-allowed-hotels.com/us/Oregon/PORTLAND/index.html.

EMBASSY SUITES PORTLAND
DOWNTOWN $$$$
319 Southwest Pine St.
(503) 279-9000
www.embassysuites.com

The Embassy Suites, which occupies the site of the historic Multnomah Hotel, is a beautiful modern luxury hotel that retains the site's old-fashioned charm. This sophisticated hotel offers guests 276 two-room suites done in a traditional and restful decor. The east-facing rooms afford views of Mount Hood, 60 miles distant. Amenities are good—they include 24-hour room service, a heated indoor pool, a sauna and whirlpool, and a well-equipped athletic center. A full breakfast and a nightly hosted manager's reception are included in the room rate. Guest rooms include voice-mail service, microwaves, refrigerators, wet bars, high-speed Internet access, 25-inch color televisions, and Nintendo systems, in addition to the coffeemakers, irons, hair dryers, and other expected conveniences. A day spa in the hotel, Salon Nyla, features Aveda products and offers pedicures, massages, and other wonderful treatments to help get rid of your jet lag. And conference suites with a combination of meeting and sleeping space make this hotel an excellent conference site. (It boasts 22,000 square feet of meeting and banquet space, including a lovely ballroom.)

The building has a colorful history. Not only has it hosted celebrities from Elvis Presley to Charles Lindbergh, it is the only hotel in Oregon to serve as an airport, however briefly. As part of the 1912 Rose Festival, Silas Christopherson flew his Curtiss pusher biplane off the hotel's roof. The *Oregonian* wrote that the flight would never be done again, but they were wrong. In September 1995 Tom Murphy, a pilot from Hood River, Oregon, with permission from more than two dozen government agencies, duplicated the flight during the building's remodeling.

THE GOVERNOR HOTEL $$$
614 Southwest 11th Ave.
(503) 224-3400, (800) 554-3456
www.govhotel.com
The historic Governor Hotel is an inviting luxury hotel rooted in the past but offering every modern convenience. Early-20th-century murals depicting the travels of Lewis and Clark, as well as mahogany woodwork, deep leather chairs, and a fireplace make the lobby a comfortable retreat. The beautiful stained-glass dome in the adjacent restaurant captures the grandeur of the building, which is a National Historic Landmark. A well-executed historic restoration extends throughout the hotel, including the 100 guest rooms.

The Governor's rooms come in a variety of styles, from luxury suites to simpler guest rooms, but each is decorated in pretty, pale colors. Some rooms have fireplaces. All rooms come with the standard luxury hotel amenities such as coffee, room service, newspapers, voice mail, wireless Internet access, phones, irons, hair dryers, and robes. But you'll know you're in Portland by the recycling program and the windows that open to clean Northwest breezes.

You'll find a Starbucks in the lobby, and just outside the door is the Portland Streetcar line. The Governor is ideally situated close to downtown shops, galleries, and restaurants. Jake's Bar and Grill, a younger sibling of the original Jake's, one of Portland's oldest and most popular restaurants, is adjacent.

✳THE HEATHMAN HOTEL $$$$
1001 Southwest Broadway
(503) 241-4100, (800) 551-0011
http://portland.heathmanhotel.com
This popular and elegant downtown hotel is in a superb location next to Portland's Performing Arts Center and within a few blocks of the Portland Art Museum and the Park Blocks. Known for its attention to detail and its outstanding restaurant, the Heathman Hotel is also distinguished for its collection of work by local and regional artists and by such contemporary American artists as Andy Warhol. The 150 rooms offer a complete array of luxury-hotel amenities. Rooms are furnished in beautifully warm tones and offer high-definition televisions. All rooms have hard-wired secure Internet access, with

free wireless access in the lobby areas. The minibars are stocked with snacks from Pacific Northwest companies.

The Heathman Restaurant has long been one of Portland's best; the adjacent Marble Bar is a beautiful place for an evening cocktail. Tea is served every afternoon (reservations strongly suggested) in the Tea Court Lounge. This lounge, with 25-foot ceilings, a handsome fireplace, and a grand staircase to the mezzanine, is an original part of the hotel, and it's a favorite spot to read, relax, or just people-watch. Evenings in the lounge feature light jazz or piano performances by some of the area's best musicians. There is 24-hour room service, and guests can arrange sessions with personal trainers in the fitness suite. The unique mezzanine library—where you can actually check out the books—offers signed editions by authors who have been guests at the hotel, including Tom Wolfe, John Updike, and Alice Walker. Finally, the Heathman has an outstanding multilingual concierge staff who will find you tickets to local shows, make your dinner reservations, hook you up with sightseeing tours, and fulfill other special requests.

THE HILTON–PORTLAND $$$$
921 Southwest 6th Ave.
(503) 226-1611
www.hilton.com
In the center of Portland's vibrant downtown, the Portland Hilton features a well-lit, contemporary facility that boasts 782 guest rooms and 40,000 square feet of meeting space. The updated and airy rooms, some with views of Mount Hood and the Cascade Mountains, are 100 percent nonsmoking, though pets are allowed. The nicely furnished lobby features a two-story atrium, entrances

on both Southwest Broadway and Southwest 6th Avenue, and well-defined spaces with couches, chairs, and tables providing privacy and quiet. There is an attractive display of works by regional artists, and just off the lobby there is a warm, dark-paneled bar and restaurant. The Portland Hilton Athletic Club includes a large indoor pool, a Jacuzzi, sauna and steam rooms, aerobic classes, and exercise equipment as well as the services of fitness trainers and a massage therapist. Serving an international clientele, the Hilton offers foreign currency exchange and a multilingual staff. Here too the concierge staff is remarkably attentive and knowledgeable; they will help you arrange your dinner and entertainment, as well as help you find your way around the city.

✳HOTEL DELUXE PORTLAND $$$$
729 Southwest 15th Ave.
(503) 219-2094, (866) 895-2094
www.hoteldeluxeportland.com
This stylish hotel lies just south of the Pearl District, west of downtown and off the MAX line very near PGE Park, so it is convenient to everything. The hotel's decor pays homage to the era of the classic studio films, with stills from memorable movie moments lining the corridors and coolly elegant rooms. But its amenities are strictly 21st century. Flat-screen HDTVs adorn each room, and each room also comes equipped with high-speed, wireless Internet access and an iPod station (as well as iPod menus, if yours isn't jiving with the ambience). You can have your choice of a variety of styles of pillow, and the Spiritual Menu and "Make It So" button will help you meet all the rest of your needs. Most important, the beds are supercomfy. The Hotel DeLuxe occupies the space of the late, lamented Mallory Hotel.

We were sad to see the Mallory sold, but its offspring is an entirely worthy successor that has gained many accolades for its wonderful atmosphere. Be sure to check out the hotel bar, The Driftwood Room—a fine spot for a pre-dinner cocktail.

HOTEL FIFTY $$$
50 Southwest Morrison St.
(503) 221-0711, (877) 237-6775
www.hotelfifty.com

This urbane and contemporary spot quite near the Willamette is a lovingly upgraded and refurbished hotel that offers excellent value and an outstanding location. Hotel Fifty will provide you with the standard amenities of a modern hotel, including free wireless, snug memory foam beds and cool linens, iPod docks, and large, capacious showers. In addition, all rooms are smoke-free. Parking is $20 per day, but the hotel is very, very close to the MAX line, so in theory you don't need a car. One nice touch is that they will let you print your boarding pass without your incurring the usual business-center fees that hotels like to add. Another amenity, H50, is not some random oxygen species, but is in fact a nice bistro that is perfectly suited for its location.

*THE HOTEL LUCIA $$$
400 Southwest Broadway
(503) 225-1717, (877) 225-1717
www.hotellucia.com

The comfortable, well-designed Lucia is well located at the northern edge of the heart of downtown, close to all the major business, tourist, and shopping districts.

This attractive little hotel features a polished, Pacific Rim aesthetic that is soothing after a tough meeting. The Lucia pays close attention to detail and thoughtfully provides pillowtop mattresses and plush robes, flat screen televisions, iPod docks, and high-speed wireless Internet access (for a daily fee) in its 128 rooms. Other nice touches include therapeutic Tazo teas, Torrefazione coffee, and Aveda bath products. Rooms feature a contemporary decor in soothing greens and earth tones and luxurious white linens. The hotel's restaurant features an outstanding Thai menu that is also available for room service.

The Hotel Lucia also features a permanent collection of the photographs of David Kennerly, the Pulitzer Prize–winning Oregonian and personal photographer to President Gerald Ford. His distillations of national life and international events are on display throughout the public rooms and in the guest rooms as well.

*HOTEL MODERA $$
515 Southwest Clay St.
(503) 484-1084
www.hotelmodera.com

The guests of the Hotel Modera are indeed lucky pilgrims to find themselves at this sleek temple of West Coast cool comfort. The rooms provide down blankets and many other soft things, large desks and free wireless for your intellectual needs, and bath products full of healthful antioxidants. Its gleaming modern decor feels fresh, it has free Wi-Fi and big flat screen TVs, and it's well located, very close to the Portland Farmers' Market (see the Festivals and Annual Events Chapter) and great downtown shopping. It offers a number of room options—multi-room suites as well as singles—and fantastic Internet specials; we recommend checking their website directly for the best deals. Free passes to 24-Hour Fitness down the street are yours for the asking. They offer parking on site, but the hotel is right on the MAX line and within easy walking distance to the streetcar. The restaurant, Nel Centro, is run by David Machado, one of Portland's top chefs, and it provides a beautiful and unusual view of downtown. A favorite part of the Hotel Modera is the large courtyard—an exemplar of urban landscape design, with a living wall and fire pits. What could be better than a summer evening in a high-design courtyard, with a cocktail, a loved one and a fire pit, right in the heart of downtown Portland?

HOTEL MONACO $$$$
506 Southwest Washington St.
(503) 222-0001, (888) 207-2201
www.monaco-portland.com

Rooms at the Hotel Monaco are like French salons, decorated in creamy tones accented by beautiful modern fabrics in complementary orange, periwinkle, and deep browns, with eclectic furniture and opulent linens. There are 229 rooms, a number of them one-bedroom suites, but all rooms come with fine amenities that include state-of-the-art 32-inch plasma televisions, speaker phones and voice mail, Wi-Fi, and plenty of work space, as well as coffeemakers and complimentary Starbucks coffee to assist you through that really tough deadline. Meeting space is also available in the hotel.

This hotel occupies a building listed in the National Registry of Historic Places. Guests are just a block from Pioneer Courthouse Square, and public transportation, food carts, and shopping are all very near. And don't miss the in-room spa services—not only are massages available, but indulgences such as facials and foot treatments are offered as well.

HOTEL VINTAGE PLAZA $$$
422 Southwest Broadway
(503) 228-1212, (800) 263-2305
www.vintageplaza.com

Featuring a wine country theme that extends to the names of most rooms, to the interior color scheme, and to a nightly tasting of Oregon wines at the lobby fireplace, the romantic Hotel Vintage Plaza is an intimate downtown hotel with an atmosphere and style that cushion guests from the fatigue of travel, touring, or business. The Vintage Plaza has everything a guest would want. The rooms are private, warm, comfortable, and tasteful, and they include complimentary high-speed wireless Internet. All aspects of the hotel's service are personal and highly polished. There are "starlight rooms" with conservatory windows that let natural light flow into the room, and some two-story townhouse suites. Pazzo Ristorante occupies the ground floor; its Northern Italian cuisine touched by Northwest influences is popular with locals too. The hotel, on the north end of downtown, is close to major shopping, cultural, and business districts.

THE MARK SPENCER HOTEL $$
409 Southwest 11th Ave.
(503) 224-3293, (800) 548-3934
www.markspencer.com

The Mark Spencer is a particularly good choice for extended stays in Portland, and it has special packages for artists—especially actors, directors, and other performance-art personnel—who are making lengthy visits. The hotel's clientele also includes business travelers and new residents relocating to the area. Perhaps more modest and conservative than some of the newer and trendier downtown hotels, the Mark Spencer's location offers convenience and value in its 101 rooms and suites. Rooms come with fully equipped kitchens, spacious closets, both on-site laundry and valet service, access to an athletic club, cable television, voice mail, the *New York Times,* and free Wi-Fi. Afternoon tea is served daily in the lobby, wine tasting is offered in the evening, and a light breakfast in the morning. In the same block as Portland's renowned Jake's Restaurant, the Mark Spencer is just across Burnside Street from Powell's City of Books and close to both the MAX and streetcar lines. The hotel also has a great value for out-of-town art lovers: special arts packages that include tickets to theater, museum, and other events in addition to accommodations.

i Even if you're not staying in them, Portland's beautiful downtown hotels are good places to visit. The Marble Bar at the Heathman, the lounge at the Benson, and the bar at the Ace Hotel are but a few of the agreeable spots to while away an hour before dinner.

THE MARRIOTT HOTEL–CITY CENTER $$$
520 Southwest Broadway
(503) 226-6300, (800) 228-9290
www.marriott.com

The renowned Marriott service and the plentiful amenities you have come to expect are here presented in a boutique hotel setting. This hotel features nearly 250 rooms and 10 suites on 20 floors; it's got a cocktail lounge and a restaurant on the premises; it's in the heart of downtown but close to the Pearl District, the Chinese Garden, and the river. It's a good hotel for the business traveler: The rooms have high-speed Internet access (fee-based), and the hotel provides a generous

amount of meeting space. The paneled lobby is quite lovely, with a big chandelier and a sweeping staircase just right for making a spectacular entrance.

THE MARRIOTT HOTEL $$$
Downtown Waterfront
1401 Southwest Naito Pkwy.
(503) 226-7600, (800) 228-9290
www.marriott.com

Across Naito Parkway from the Willamette River and the Tom McCall Riverfront Park, the uppermost of the Marriott's 503 rooms perch 14 stories above street level, offering fine views of Mount Hood. A popular choice for business travelers and meeting and convention attendees—who will find organized facilities and very friendly service—the hotel also attracts its share of tourists. The Marriott includes two restaurants, two bars, an indoor pool, and a 24-hour athletic club. This is a full-service hotel in the broadest sense of the word, with some wheelchair-accessible rooms. The Marriott is convenient to Portland's financial district and government buildings and to all downtown attractions, as well as to recreation areas along the Willamette River.

✱THE NINES HOTEL $$$$
525 Southwest Morrison St.
(503) 222-9995
www.thenines.com

When Macy's took over the historic and venerable Meier & Frank department store, they apparently gazed across the street to Pioneer Courthouse Square and thought—this landscape needs a hotel. And so they created one, the kind where town cars glide up to the front and deposit silky guests who are whisked efficiently inside by doormen.

Occupying the upper nine stories of the 1909 building, The Nines is a gorgeous hotel, balancing its historic exterior with a lovely, modern interior that provides the expected amenities of a luxury operation, such as a VIP floor, spacious and comfortable rooms, cozy beds, soft linens, and a multilingual staff. Wireless service is free in the lobby and other public areas. It is part of the Starwood chain, and in spite of its luxury status, it offers great value: there are many Internet specials, and, if you are not in possession of a town car, it is incredibly convenient to stay there, since the MAX line from the airport stops right across the street.

THE RIVERPLACE HOTEL $$$$
1510 Southwest Harbor Way
(503) 228-3233, (800) 227-1333
www.riverplacehotel.com

On the bank of the Willamette River, the RiverPlace Hotel offers rooms and suites facing the river or with a north view of the city's skyline. During the summer the hotel's patio is a good spot from which to view the frequent displays of fireworks, not to mention an unending, colorful stream of runners, in-line skaters, skateboarders, dog-walkers, cyclists, and people out for a stroll. The river hosts a 24-hour parade of tour boats, sailboats, personal watercraft, barges and log-tows, dragon-boats, yachts, kayaks, and the occasional sailboard.

Separated from the core of the downtown by busy Southwest Naito Parkway, guests can walk along the Tom McCall Waterfront Park to reach downtown's stores, galleries, and other attractions. There is also a small group of shops and stores along the esplanade, facing the river. The hotel is near the streetcar line and a short ride away from the Portland Aerial Tram.

The lobby is elegant, filled with large, artistic displays of fresh flowers, and the staff is well trained, polite, and attentive. Rooms are comfortable, with large baths and contemporary decor, featuring the usual amenities of a quality hotel—free Wi-Fi (in public areas), DVD and CD players, cushy robes, and luxurious bath products. Guests are given breakfast and have access to the adjacent RiverPlace Athletic Club, for a small fee. An excellent restaurant is on-site: Three Degrees, which offers regional specialties beautifully prepared.

THE WESTIN PORTLAND $$$$
750 Southwest Alder St.
(503) 294-9000
www.westinportland.com

One of the nicest downtown luxury hotels, the Westin imparts the feeling that its guests are the most important creatures in the world with the lushness of its surroundings and the attentiveness of its service. The rooms are elegant, with iPod docking stations on the night stands, cozy down duvets on the beds, and oversize, walk-in showers in the bathrooms. For events, the hotel has a number of different-size meeting rooms, as well as a ballroom. The Westin is able to make use of its corporate resources to provide desirable services like the Westin Kids Club and Business Office rooms, and the service is also remarkably thoughtful and charming. The Daily Grill restaurant serves attentively prepared American cuisine from 6:30 a.m. to 11 p.m. weekdays and Sat and Sun from 7 a.m. to midnight; 24-hour room service is also available.

Northwest Portland

INN AT NORTHRUP STATION $$$
2025 Northwest Northrup St.
(503) 224-0543, (800) 224-1180
www.northrupstation.com

The Inn at Northrup Station is a welcome addition to Northwest Portland, where there are few hotels. This stylish place features suites that balance a hip aesthetic with contemporary comforts. Its rooms are brightly colored and filled with modern furniture, with dramatic marble and granite in the bathrooms and kitchens. The hotel's large rooms also include the standard amenities, as well as little luxuries such as private decks and balconies, iPod docks, large flat-screen televisions, and wireless Internet. The Inn at Northrup Station is well located between the lively shopping and restaurant districts on Northwest 21st and Northwest 23rd Avenues—and it's right on the streetcar line, offering easy access to the Pearl District and downtown Portland. There is no restaurant on site, but there is free parking. It is good for extended stays.

SILVER CLOUD INN $$$
2426 Northwest Vaughn St.
(503) 242-2400, (800) 205-6939
www.silvercloud.com/portland.php
This Silver Cloud Inn is situated in Northwest Portland, at the edge of an industrial area. Yet not only is it well placed for business travelers, it is also convenient for anyone wanting to explore Northwest Portland. The hotel is tidy, quiet, and within walking distance of good restaurants, an eclectic mix of small shops, a brewpub, and coffeehouses. Close to the intersection of the area's main freeways, the hotel is also near the chic shopping districts on Northwest 23rd and Northwest 21st Avenues.

The hotel offers covered parking, a fitness center and spa, a complimentary breakfast, large flat-screen televisions, and high-speed Internet access in all the rooms. Pets are welcome. The hotel's location allows easy access to the highways following the Columbia River to the Oregon coast and to those leading east to Mount Hood and the Columbia Gorge.

Southeast Portland

BLUEBIRD GUESTHOUSE $
3517 Southeast Division St.
(503) 238-4333, (866) 717-4333
www.bluebirdguesthouse.com
Something beyond a hotel but not quite a bed-and-breakfast inn, the Bluebird Guesthouse brings much-needed and novel accommodations to Southeast Portland. The seven charming guest rooms and the public areas in this repurposed vintage Portland house are decorated with vivid colors and comfortable furniture. The Bluebird offers a light breakfast in the morning, but you may use the spacious kitchen to make any kind of meal you like—and if you don't feel like cooking, the Bluebird is within easy walking distance of a number of Portland's best restaurants, as well as coffeeshops, bars, retail, and other urban eye candy. It's also a 10-minute drive to downtown Portland, as well as convenient to public transportation. Two rooms have private bathrooms; the others share two and a half bathrooms (translation: no waiting). There are an ironing board and laundry facilities on site; towels, soap, shampoo, and so on are provided. Children ages 4 and older are welcome. One thing you should know: There are no televisions. However, there is a computer that guests can use, and there's free Wi-Fi, too, for those who've brought their laptops.

✳**JUPITER HOTEL** $$
800 East Burnside St.
(503) 230-9200, (877) 800-0004
www.jupiterhotel.com

The Jupiter Hotel is at the center of the revival of "Lo-Bu"—Lower Burnside, on the east side of the Willamette River—and it has won accolades for its approach to hospitality since the minute it opened. The Jupiter is a restyled motel built in the 1960s, and the hotel evokes that era's Land-of-Tomorrow, modern sensibility. Its 80 rooms are divided into the "quiet" side and the "party" side, which is important information depending on how you view proximity to the adjacent Doug Fir Lounge (one of Portland's hottest night spots). The hotel offers the important amenities, as well as chalkboard doors for doodling, an outdoor fire pit, and Blu Dot furnishings.

North & Northeast Portland

*MCMENAMINS
KENNEDY SCHOOL $$
5736 Northeast 33rd Ave.
(503) 249-3983, (888) 249-3983
www.mcmenamins.com/
427-kennedy-school-home

The wonderful Kennedy School is one of our favorite recommendations for out-of-town guests. This unusual 35-room inn inhabits a pretty ex-school (now on the Historic Register), reclaiming classrooms and offices to provide comfortable and spacious rooms for guests. These rooms are charmingly decorated with rich colors and cozy, vintage furniture. Rooms include king- and queen-size beds, phones and modems, as well as private baths. Guests have access to free wireless Internet. A soaking pool invites guests to linger, and the restored gym is available for a game of pickup (as long as it's free of banqueters). It's also close to the Alberta neighborhood, with its outstanding restaurants and shopping.

These are all good reasons to love the Kennedy School, but the inn is far more than a guesthouse. This extensive campus is a destination for much of Portland—not only neighbors, but people from all over town frequent the bars, restaurants, and theaters (for both movies and live music), drawn by the convivial ambience and the six-barrel brewery. The Kennedy School is very popular for meetings, reunion dinners, parties, and all manner of gatherings. It is an engine of neighborhood activity, helping to inspire the regeneration of surrounding blocks.

Vancouver

THE HEATHMAN LODGE $$
7801 Northeast Greenwood Dr.
(360) 254-3100, (888) 475-3100
www.heathmanlodge.com

Known for its charming combination of Pacific Northwest lodge decor and modern conveniences, this hotel has a reputation for friendly service and attention. The lobby and other common areas are done in rustic pine, accented by the color and classic designs of Pendleton blankets and pillows; in fact, the 121 oversize guest rooms have Pendleton bedspreads. Most come with desks and fireplaces. All have free wireless Internet access, as well as the usual amenities. This hotel is equipped with an enclosed swimming pool, sauna and whirlpool, and complete fitness center. The 24-hour room service, laundry facilities, free parking, free morning newspaper, and delicious continental breakfast will also add to your comfort. The Heathman's restaurant, Hudson's Bar and Grill, offers excellent cuisine. Across from Vancouver Mall and a host of restaurants and other services, the Heathman Lodge is 15 minutes from the Portland Airport.

i The root word for *hotel* is "hostel" and in Portland we have two: in Northwest Portland at 1818 Northwest Glisan St. (503-241-2783; www.nwportlandhostel.com) and in Southeast Portland at 3031 Southeast Hawthorne Blvd. (503-236-3380; www.portlandhostel.org).

BED-AND-BREAKFAST INNS

Southwest Portland

THE FULTON HOUSE $$$

7006 Southwest Virginia Ave.

(503) 892-5781

www.thefultonhouse.com

The Fulton House offers two well-appointed guest suites in a lovely 19th-century house near Willamette Park along the river, as well as near the Portland Aerial Tram. While the house once served as a floating bordello, it has reformed its character and now provides nothing but the most respectable accommodations. Breakfasts are served buffet style, and treats are offered every afternoon. Both suites have private baths and sitting areas, as well as telephones, cable television, and wireless Internet access. The grounds of the Fulton House are lovely—lush green lawns and water features, beautiful flowers, and a wonderfully spacious porch and patio area. There, you will find a hot tub and an outdoor grill, both of which you may use. The Fulton House also has an extensive wine cellar, from which you may purchase something tasty to go with your grilling.

The Fulton neighborhood is one of Portland's oldest—indeed, it used to be a separate town—and it is filled with pretty houses and cute shops, as well as offering plentiful, free, and safe street parking. Its proximity to the Willamette greenway means that it is well situated for walking and biking along the river, but it is just a few minutes' drive from all the downtown attractions as well.

TERWILLIGER VISTA

BED & BREAKFAST $$

515 Southwest Westwood Dr.

(503) 244-0602, (888) 244-0602

www.terwilligervista.com

Originally built for a prominent Portland family in 1941, the Terwilliger Vista is a large Georgian-style colonial house in the city's west hills. The house is on a half-acre site colored by rose gardens, camellias, and rhododendrons, minutes from downtown Portland but a world away from the usual urban irritants of traffic, noise, and crowds.

All five of Terwilliger's guest rooms are air-conditioned and offer either king- or queen-size beds, private baths, guest refrigerators, cable television, and fireplaces. A two-room suite is also available. Guests can enjoy a full breakfast from 7:30 to 9:30 a.m. in a spacious dining room. Breakfasts are served buffet style and feature healthy and delicious comfort food. A continental breakfast is available in the early morning for those whose schedules keep them from enjoying the full meal. Complimentary sodas, bottled water, port, and sherry are available in the library. The location is convenient to OHSU and the VA hospital, and the beautiful Olmsted-designed Terwilliger Boulevard is nearby, with wide pedestrian paths and city views. Children older than 10 are welcome. Call between 8 a.m. and 9 p.m., PST.

Southeast Portland

✳**CLINTON STREET GUESTHOUSE** $

4220 Southeast Clinton St.

(503) 234-8752

www.clintonstreetguesthouse.com

This four-room bed-and-breakfast in Southeast Portland is in a pretty, thoroughly refurbished Craftsman-style bungalow built in 1913. The house has a lush and productive garden, with much of its produce—including the fresh eggs from the hens in the back—ending up on your breakfast plate. The decor is simple, serene, and vintage, but the extra outlets so you can keep your laptop charged are a thoughtful nod to the present. The Division Street neighborhood offers some stellar restaurants and coffeeshops nearby—it is centrally located and near the busline, but if you are not used to walking much, you might be happier having a car.

North & Northeast Portland

THE BLUE PLUM $$
2026 Northeast 15th Ave.
(503) 288-3848, (877) 288-3844
www.bluepluminn.com
This handsome inn in the Irvington district was built in 1900. It offers four rooms with private baths, some of which can be combined into suites. A major attraction of the Blue Plum is the attentively prepared breakfasts that feature fresh Northwest ingredients. The same attention to delicious detail is found in their afternoon tea. The dining room and living room are spacious and comfortable, with a carved fireplace as a notable feature. The vintage furnishings disguise the modern amenities such as wireless Internet access and convenient public transportation. The Blue Plum is in an excellent location—the beautiful neighborhood is a pleasure for walking, and the inn is very close to the shops and restaurants of Broadway, as well as near the Lloyd Center shopping mall and the Oregon Convention Center. And it's just a short trip downtown.

GEORGIAN HOUSE
BED & BREAKFAST $$
1828 Northeast Siskiyou St.
(503) 281-2250, (888) 282-2250
www.thegeorgianhouse.com
This classic, immaculately maintained Georgian colonial home was built in 1922, and it features a winding staircase, stained-glass windows, and antique furnishings. Guest rooms have either a private or shared bath and are furnished with antiques. The lower-level spacious and very private Captain Irving Room includes a gas-log fireplace; the Victorian Eastlake Room overlooks the deck, gazebo, and English-style gardens, which feature roses and boxwoods and also provide a variety of berries, grapes, and kiwi for breakfast. The Lovejoy Suite, which has the feel of a bridal suite, has a queen-size brass canopy bed and a private bath with clawfoot tub. There is ample parking.

Children 12 and older are welcome in the Captain Irving Room. The inn has discounts for corporate travelers and for those on extended stays. The surrounding residential neighborhood is near public transit, the Rose Quarter, with the Oregon Convention Center, and the Lloyd Center, with its mix of department stores, movie theaters, and restaurants. It's a short drive to downtown, as well.

THE LION AND THE ROSE $$$
1810 Northeast 15th Ave.
(503) 287-9245, (800) 955-1647
www.lionrose.com
This rambling but immaculately restored Victorian in the well-established Northeast Portland Irvington neighborhood could serve as a postcard image of a past era. Convenient to all of Portland and the entire region, this inn is close to the popular shopping and

restaurant district along Northeast Broadway, including the Lloyd district. This inn is listed on the National Register of Historic Places, and its decor and atmosphere create a sense of relaxed elegance. Guests have the option of an early continental breakfast or, a bit later, the real thing. Guests are also served an afternoon dessert tea. The grounds include English-style gardens, a gazebo, fountains, and brick pathways. Smoking is permitted on the veranda.

All rooms have private baths, and the Rose Room features a queen-size bed and a Jacuzzi. Other rooms offer guests the chance to sleep in an antique Edwardian bed, a flat-top canopy bed, or a traditional four-poster bed. Children older than 12 are welcome. Occasionally this inn requires a two-night minimum, especially on weekends and holidays.

A PAINTED LADY INN $$$
1927 Northeast 16th Ave.
(503) 335-0070
www.apaintedladyinn.com
A Painted Lady Inn is a well-wrought little gem in the Irvington area, well situated to take advantage of shopping, restaurants, and entertainment, with easy access to downtown Portland as well. There are three guest rooms, and—a big plus—delicious, seasonal breakfasts served in your room (or the dining room if you wish). The guest rooms are airy and bright, and the common rooms filled with period furniture that complements this pretty house built in 1904. The grounds are lovely and include a back terrace for sunny morning coffee and newspaper-reading—as well as a porch swing.

> **i** The beautiful Irvington district, home to many of Portland's bed-and-breakfast inns and more than 20 officially designated historic sites, was one of the first planned communities in the area. Its success was due partly to strict building codes and partly to the trolley that transported its banker and lawyer residents downtown.

PORTLAND'S WHITE HOUSE $$$$
1914 Northeast 22nd Ave.
(503) 287-7131, (800) 272-7131
www.portlandswhitehouse.com
Completely restored to the grand splendor of 1911, Portland's White House was built of Honduran mahogany by early Portland timber magnate Robert Lyle. It has nine elegant guest rooms, all with private baths and featuring period furnishings and decor. The Garden Room sports a private terrace, and the Canopy Room has, of course, a canopied bed. With a circular drive, massive classic Greek columns, fountains, a carriage house, and Japanese maples, this inn bears some resemblance to its Washington, D.C., namesake. Guests can visit the parlor for sherry or board games. The inn is a local landmark, close to attractions on the city's East Side, and convenient to downtown. This remarkable inn serves a chef's breakfast by candlelight. Children are welcome if you arrange it in advance.

RESTAURANTS

The Pacific Northwest has long been known for its regional abundance. The Kalapuya, Molalla, Clackamas, and other Native Americans who lived in the Willamette Valley ate remarkably well. And it wasn't just the sheer abundance of the game, camas roots, filberts, mushrooms, truffles, berries, and wild greens. It was also the clever way of cooking—for example, smoking salmon over open fires or roasting it on cedar planks. Their legends are notable for their gratitude over their good fortune.

Modern chefs in Portland are equally fortunate. They carry on that same tradition of using regional ingredients and preparing them in clever ways. While most chefs aren't serving camas roots—yet—they have a lot to work with. The Willamette Valley provides some of the most fruitful farmland in the nation, and we also have a mild climate with a decently long growing season. Like the rest of the nation, we are losing family farms. Yet a small but significant countertrend is also noticeable: The area has seen a revival of small, specialty farms in recent years, and local chefs make good use of these farms and the many farmers' markets in the area. The Portland chapter of the Chefs Collaborative, a national organization dedicated to serving Americans sustainably produced food that is local and seasonal, has instituted an innovative program called the Farmer-Chef Connection. This program brings farmers, fisheries, and other small purveyors together with Portland restaurants, a win-win situation for everyone: The chefs get the best and freshest produce imaginable, the farmers get to sell directly to the chef, and we customers get the best food.

OVERVIEW

But the love of the local does not stop at produce. It also extends to the raising of specialty meats such as rabbit, to the crafting of perfect goat cheeses, to the baking of ideal loaves of crusty, chewy bread. And just as earlier inhabitants of the Willamette Valley migrated from Asia, Portland chefs also reflect our nomadic origins in their variety of culinary influences, from Alaska to Zanzibar. For a city of our size, we have an outsize reputation as a food mecca, a reputation that grows daily. As the New York Times recently noted, Portland is enjoying "a golden age of dining and drinking."

Which raises the question of what you should drink with all this bounty. Our region is known especially for its excellent wine and beer, its fine coffee roasters and tea houses. We share the climate of the Burgundy region of France, and many of the varietal grapes that grow well there also grow well here. Hops—the ingredient that gives beer its piquancy—also grow well here. And while coffee and tea don't grow here, chilly, wet winters have given local roasters and tea brewers the necessary impetus to perfect those beverages.

Below are some of our favorite restaurants, both classic and new. This chapter divides restaurants into their geographic locations and by food type. Portland's destination restaurants are found all over the city. Talented chefs are working kitchens all over town, and many neighborhood places are also destinations for loyal followers and adventuresome people looking for something new. Unless noted, all the restaurants listed take the usual credit cards. By Oregon law restaurants have no-smoking policies, and as of January 2009, so do bars and taverns.

Price Code

Most restaurants have offerings at a range of prices. The price code here reflects the general cost of a single entree, excluding drinks, hors d'oeuvres, side dishes, and tips. As with other Portland purchases, there is no sales tax.

$................. Less than $10
$$ .... $10 to $20
$$$ .... $20 to $30
$$$$ .... More than $30

RESTAURANTS

Heathman Restaurant, Southwest Portland, Pacific Northwest Cuisine, $$$$, 61

Higgins Restaurant and Bar, Southwest Portland, Pacific Northwest Cuisine, $$$$, 61

Hiroshi Sushi, Southwest Portland, Asian, $$$, 57

Huber's, Southwest Portland, American, $–$$, 57

Hudson's, Vancouver, WA, Pacific Northwest Cuisine, $$$, 81

J & M Café, Southeast Portland, Cafes & Breakfast, $, 70

Jake's Famous Crawfish, Southwest Portland, Seafood, $$$, 62

Jake's Grill, Southwest Portland, Seafood, $$$, 62

Justa Pasta, Northwest Portland, Italian, $, 62

Karam Lebanese, Southwest Portland, Middle Eastern, $$, 60

Ken's Artisan Pizza, Southeast Portland, Pizza, $$, 77

Kenny & Zuke's, Southwest Portland, Delis & Sandwiches, $$, 59

Lauro Mediterranean Kitchen, Southeast Portland, Mediterranean, $$$, 75

Le Pigeon, Southeast Portland, Pacific Northwest Cuisine, $$$, 76

Lincoln, North & Northeast Portland, Pacific Northwest Cuisine, $$$, 80

Mother's Bistro and Bar, Southwest Portland, American, $$, 57

Murata, Southwest Portland, Asian, $$$$, 58

Navarre, North & Northeast Portland, Small Plates, $$, 80

Noho's Hawaiian Café, Southeast Portland, Hawaiian, $, 73

Nostrana, Southeast Portland, Italian, $$, 74

Nuestra Cocina, Southeast Portland, Mexican, $$, 75

Olympic Provisions, Southeast Portland, Delis & Sandwiches, $$, 71

Original Halibut's, North & Northeast Portland, Seafood, $, 80

Original Pancake House, Southwest Portland, Cafes & Breakfast, $, 58

Paley's Place, Northwest Portland, Pacific Northwest Cuisine, $$$$, 67

Papa Haydn, Northwest Portland, Desserts, $$, 65

Park Kitchen, Northwest Portland, Pacific Northwest Cuisine, $$$, 67

Pearl Bakery, Northwest Portland, Cafes & Breakfast, $, 64

Piazza Italia, Northwest Portland, Italian, $$, 66

Pine State Biscuits, Southeast Portland, Cafes & Breakfast, $, 71

Pix Patisserie, Southeast Portland, Desserts, $–$$, 73

Podnah's, Southeast Portland, Barbecue, $$, 70

Pok Pok and Whiskey Soda Lounge, Southeast Portland, Asian, $$, 69

Por Que No, North & Northeast Portland, Mexican, $, 80

RingSide, Northwest Portland, Steakhouses, $$$$, 69

Roots, Camas, WA, Pacific Northwest Cuisine, $$$, 82

Saburo's, Southeast Portland, Asian, $, 70

Serrato, Northwest Portland, Italian, $$$, 66

Silk Bistro, Northwest Portland, Asian, $$, 63

Southpark, Southwest Portland, Seafood, $$, 63

Tastebud, Southeast Portland, Pizza, $$, 77

3 Doors Down, Southeast Portland, Mediterranean, $$, 75

Three Square Grill, Southwest Portland, Pacific Northwest Cuisine, $$, 62

Toro Bravo, North & Northeast Portland, Spanish, $$, 81

Veritable Quandary, Southwest Portland, American, $$$, 57

Victory, Southeast Portland, Small Plates, $, 78

Vindalho, Southeast Portland, Indian, $$, 73

Wildwood, Northwest Portland, Pacific Northwest Cuisine, $$$$, 68

SOUTHWEST PORTLAND

American

HUBER'S $-$$
411 Southwest 3rd Ave.
(503) 228-5686
www.hubers.com

Self-described as Portland's oldest restaurant, Huber's opened its doors in 1879 as the Bureau Saloon. In 1884 the bartender, Frank Huber, became a partner and the rest is culinary history. One tale tells of the time during the flood of 1894 when chef Jim Louie stood in a rowboat behind the counter serving steamed clams and turkey sandwiches to customers who rowed in from the other side. Still known for its "Roast Young Tom Turkey," Huber's attracts a steady clientele who also enjoy the Philippine mahogany paneling, stained-glass skylights, and a big brass cash register. A flaming Spanish Coffee at Huber's is a rite of passage for all would-be Portlanders. A happy hour (6 to 8 p.m.) features inexpensive appetizers with well drinks at the usual price.

MOTHER'S BISTRO AND BAR $$
212 Southwest Stark St.
(503) 464-1122
www.mothersbistro.com

Chef Lisa Schroeder wants us to eat the kind of homey dishes our mothers and grandmothers made—comfort food such as braised meats, roasts, stews, meat loaves, and other slow-cooked dishes. But these versions are prepared by an expertly trained chef, making them even better than you remember. Many of the recipes are from actual mothers that Schroeder knows. Both the bistro and the (full) bar are comfortable, and the bar, with its cushy velvet upholstery and gilded mirrors, is especially pretty. Schroeder changes her menu to reflect the seasons, but a typical menu might offer a Painted Hills beef burger or an Italian chopped salad, while dinner could bring chicken and dumplings, if you're lucky. Mother's also serves a weekend brunch that might include salmon hash or crunchy French toast dipped in corn flakes. Mother's is consistently excellent, and you should take your own mom there.

VERITABLE QUANDARY $$$
1220 Southwest 1st Ave.
(503) 227-7342
www.veritablequandary.com

The VQ has been a cocktail favorite for years, with its good location at the western edge of the Hawthorne Bridge and its pretty brick patio and its dark, old-fashioned bar. But it has a growing reputation as a destination for American cuisine inspired by Italy—and by the Pacific Northwest. First-rate signature dishes include osso bucco, as well as revolving fish specials (everything from ahi tuna with pineapple and avocado salsa to red snapper with kumquat). Appetizers are excellent—bacon-wrapped dates are a specialty. Also of note here are the remarkable and rare wines offered by the glass. The dining room has some nice views during the day and at night, depending on the table. The service, especially in the bar, is generally excellent. The VQ also offers an outstanding Sunday brunch.

Asian

HIROSHI SUSHI $$$
926 Northwest 10th Ave.
(503) 619-0580

Sushi master Hiroshi Ikegayai uses his connections to find the freshest, most delectable fish available in order to bring you some of the best sushi north of San Francisco. His mastery, however, is not in who he knows but what he does, bringing together deep experience in proper technique with innovation in his approach to flavors. Signature non-sushi dishes include sea scallops—he uses them in many unusual ways; for example, served stuffed with sea urchin and accompanied by a vinegar truffle sauce—as well as monkfish liver served with a miso–vinegar combination. The sushi itself is perfect, whether you are ordering a single–fish dish such as the abalone or a fancy roll. Even the California roll is amazing, with actual crab and the accompanying cucumbers, avocado, and sesame prepared to maximize texture and flavor. You will also find good beer and sake. It's fun to sit at the sushi bar and see what the chefs themselves think Is yummiest. Do this and you won't go wrong. Open for lunch and dinner Tues through Sun.

MURATA $$$$
200 Southwest Market St.
(503) 227-0080

Murata serves excellent sushi in a modest downtown building. But don't let appearances fool you: This is the real thing. The tasting menu, which is very expensive, is worth every penny and is the ideal showcase for Murata's talents. The tangy salads and savory noodle soups are as good as the sushi, but it's the latter that you'll be dreaming about later. Open for lunch and dinner Mon through Sat.

Cafes & Breakfast

BIJOU CAFE $$
132 Southwest 3rd Ave.
(503) 222-3187

The Bijou's excellent breakfasts, lunches, and weekend brunches are a staple of the downtown crowd, and for atmosphere, there are few better places than this urbane and crowded spot. The entrees are attentively made using as many local and organic ingredients as possible. The Bijou makes some of the best French toast, pancakes, and egg dishes in Portland. The oatmeal is served with chopped filberts. The roast beef hash is delicious. And the oyster omelet with bacon and onions is definitely worth the wait you'll endure at the door.

ORIGINAL PANCAKE HOUSE $
8601 Southwest 24th Ave.
(503) 246-9007
www.originalpancakehouse.com

This Portland classic has been serving fabulous pancakes, omelets, and other breakfast fare since 1953. This is the spot that launched the national chain, and it is justly famous for

---

The Food Dude

For the most unvarnished restaurant reviews, news, and gossip, check out Food Dude's blog, An Exploration of Portland Food and Drink at **www.portland foodanddrink.com.** Food Dude started his blog as an antidote to reviews that sounded like advertising, in an effort to create a more reality-based picture of the Portland food and wine scene. He and his team review restaurants anonymously and multiple times, relating their experiences in great detail. As a result, he is irresistible reading for Portland foodies—including Portland chefs, who often lurk here. Sometimes they post too.

its apple pancake—an oven-baked confection with Granny Smith apples and a perfect cinnamon glaze; its puffy, lemony dutch baby; and its house-made corned beef hash. But anything you order here will be good: The restaurant pays detailed attention to the quality of its ingredients, using the best butter, eggs, and breakfast meats it can find. The restaurant has also won—along with Greg Higgins, Philippe Boulot, and other stars—a James Beard award. The Original Pancake House serves breakfast Wed through Sun until 3 p.m.; no reservations. Cash or check only.

Delis & Sandwiches

KENNY & ZUKE'S   **$$**
1038 Southwest Stark St.
(503) 222-3354
www.kennyandzukes.com
This Jewish delicatessen fills a void in Portland. Signature dishes include the Reuben sandwich, as well as its variety of pastrami sandwiches on housemade rye bread. For example, the cheeseburger—while not exactly kosher—is the kind of thing you'll be craving after a long night of dancing and socializing. This beautifully grilled burger is topped with pastrami and melted Swiss. Pastrami sandwiches are also served with egg salad or chopped liver. All of these are delicious. Kenny & Zuke's is also open early and late, a bit of a mitzvah. You can eat their pastrami from 7 a.m. to midnight Tues through Thurs, until 3 a.m. on Fri and Sat, and from 8 a.m. to 10:30 p.m. on Sun.

Eclectic

CLYDE COMMON   **$$**
1014 Southwest Stark St.
(503) 228-3333
www.clydecommon.com

The signature restaurant of the Ace Hotel, Clyde Common is a stylish space that attracts the beautiful people of Portland to its handsome zinc-topped bar and high-ceilinged dining room—a dining room that features communal tables, where you may find yourself sitting next to the beautiful people. Fortunately, the friendly staff makes sure there is also room for you. The scene, however, could be unbearable if the food weren't first-class. Clyde Common is very good with traditional simple dishes such as a salad of radishes, butter, and salt or even roasted vegetables; they are also excellent at spotting synergistic combinations such as foie gras, shallots, and brioche that are more than the sum of their parts. They have an impressive scotch and bourbon list and make wonderful cocktails, overall. The bar on weekend nights is very festive, so if you need a quiet dinner, you might make another choice.

EL GAUCHO   **$$$$**
319 Southwest Broadway
(503) 227-8794
www.waterfrontpier70.com/elgaucho/
_portland/index.htm
While many restaurants in Portland emphasize the local and regional, El Gaucho celebrates the exotic, with its Argentine steak, its ostrich filet with Madeira sauce, and its bananas Foster. The dining room is dusky and serene, with contemporary polished decor but nonetheless an ambience from another era. The service is impeccable—both friendly and understated, with a great deal of tableside attention. And the food is equally good. Starters include a good crab cake, short ribs, and Wicked Shrimp—spicy shrimp with a piquant dipping sauce. The Caesar salad is outstanding. Steaks include the Gaucho (accompanied by lobster

medallions and béarnaise sauce) and a rib steak stuffed with peppers, rosemary, and garlic. There's nothing like a waiter in black tie flambéing bananas Foster at your table to make you feel that civilization has not disappeared altogether.

French

CARAFE $$
200 Southwest Market St.
(503) 248-0004
www.carafebistro.com

A favorite of the downtown crowd for both lunch and dinner, Carafe is the home of one of Portland's favorite chefs, Pascal Sauton. Sauton labored for many years as the corporate chef in restaurants at RiverPlace, but now he has the chance to flex his creative muscles, to the delight of Portland diners. This wonderful bistro is remarkably Parisian, with rows of outdoor chairs facing the street and an elegant but unfussy interior of dusky gold and reddish brown. Its prime location across the street from Keller Auditorium makes it a favorite before shows. But no matter what's playing, the true star will be the superbly prepared food—French classics such as croque monsieur, frisée salad with bacon, baked escargot, duck confit with olives, and bouillabaisse. We especially love the mussels cooked with shallots and cream, but even the lemonade here is impeccably French. The wine selection is full of excellent values, well chosen and in a range of styles and prices—including interesting *vins du table* available in (you guessed it) carafes. Carafe is open for lunch on weekdays and for dinner every day except Sun. It's best to call ahead if a show is playing at the Keller, for the place will be mobbed and you won't get a table without a reservation. Valet parking is available.

Rooms with a View

Feasting your eyes can be almost as satisfying as plain old feasting, and two places to do it are the Chart House and the Portland City Grill.

The **Chart House** (5700 Southwest Terwilliger Blvd., 503-246-6963) is a beautiful spot to enjoy the visual feast of the city as it stretches to meet the foothills and Mount Hood in the eastern distance. The **Portland City Grill** (111 Southwest 5th Ave., 30th floor, 503-450-0030) sits atop the US Bank Tower, where it hands out impressive views that stretch far afield and help you put things in perspective. It's perfect for a romantic drink before dinner.

Middle Eastern

KARAM LEBANESE $$
316 Southwest Stark St.
(503) 223-0830
www.karamrestaurant.com

It's hard to know where to begin a description of this friendly and abundant place: Karam Lebanese not only has some of the most delicious Middle Eastern food in town, but some of the best service as well. The dining room is hospitable, and the menu well priced. You can tell a lot about a restaurant by how it does the simplest things, and in a Lebanese restaurant, you should first look at the pita. Here, it is indescribably warm and fresh, and if yours looks like it is getting cold, the servers whisk it away and replace it with a new basket. Even the drinks are special—both alcoholic and nonalcoholic drinks might be flavored with rose water or tamarind. The hummus is creamy, with just the right proportions of lemon and garlic, the falafel perfectly crisped, and even the tabbouleh is piquant and delicious.

But the main courses are what it's all about. Here, you will find a wonderful variety of dishes: a savory vegetable kabob served with delicate rice and tomato sauce, a chicken schawarma, or a "Meat Mezza," which offers small tastes of many dishes. Karam is especially known for its Goat Bil Tfeen, a stew in which goat is braised in red wine and garlic, and served with bulgur wheat, chickpeas, and potatoes. It is tender and delicious. Desserts are equally good, especially when you order a thick Turkish coffee with them. Favorites include the crispy baklava, as well as the less familiar knafe-B-kaak. This wonderful dish is composed of a mild cheese mixture that is blended with farina, baked, encrusted with pistachios, and served with a fragrant syrup. This dessert might be where ancient peoples got their ideas about the land of milk and honey, and it's yours for the ordering at Karam.

Pacific Northwest Cuisine

CASSIDY'S $$
1331 Southwest Washington St.
(503) 223-0054
www.cassidysrestaurant.com
Cassidy's reputation as a good late-night bar is so firm that we sometimes forget how good the food is. Premium-cut meats, steamed mussels in rich broths, creamy pastas—all these go beautifully with the local wines and microbrews that Cassidy's also features. The bar's dark paneling and old-fashioned wooden refrigerators remind us of Boston or New York, but the food and drinks are definitely Portland.

HEATHMAN RESTAURANT $$$$
1001 Southwest Broadway
(503) 790-7752
www.heathmanrestaurantandbar.com
The Heathman has maintained its stellar reputation as a premier Portland dining room. It uses the finest Northwest ingredients, prepared with rapt attention to detail. The menu varies seasonally, but you can expect standards such as Angus rib-eye steak, roast chicken, and crispy sweetbreads. The Heathman also offers less common dishes—for example, a buttery poached lobster finished at the grill and served with a nuanced sauce. The accompanying dishes—sautéed leeks, creamy whipped potatoes, fresh spring asparagus—are always designed to balance and complement the flavors and textures of the main ingredient. Over the years, the Heathman has featured guest chefs from all over the world to create special events and prix-fixe menus. These chefs have included Angelo "Balin" Silvestro, Michel Brunel, and André Soltner, among others. All this kitchen talent is aided by first-rate service and a simple, handsome decor that includes a collection of fine paintings. Because the Heathman Restaurant is part of the Heathman Hotel, it also serves breakfast and lunch, seven days a week. The breakfasts are exceptional, and if there are power lunches in Portland, you'll find them here.

*HIGGINS RESTAURANT
AND BAR $$$$
1239 Southwest Broadway
(503) 222-9070
www.higgins.ypguides.net
The inventive ways in which chef Greg Higgins uses seasonal, organic food from nearby farms, forests, and streams have won this handsome downtown restaurant the

highest marks from critics—as well as from the customers that fill the restaurant every night. Higgins, who won the James Beard Award in 2002, is discerning and unpretentious in his combinations of textures and flavors, relying on traditional means of cooking adapted to contemporary eating habits. Because the menu is seasonal, it changes all the time; however, diners can always count on at least one vegan dish on the menu in addition to the beef, duck, fish, and other entrees. The bar menu carries some notable staples, among them an incredibly savory hamburger and a luscious pastrami sandwich (Greg Higgins makes the pastrami himself). Higgins has an excellent wine list that emphasizes Northwest wines, and a beer list that features about 150 different brews from the world over. A striking union of textures, colors, and light, the tri-level restaurant looks as good as the food does. The downstairs dining room, with its mahogany paneling and dark carpet, is both romantic and elegant; the middle dining room is vibrant with burnished floors and two-toned walls. And the bar, a local favorite, is at once comfortable and urbane. Higgins is open for lunch Mon through Fri and dinner daily.

THREE SQUARE GRILL $$
6320 Southwest Capitol Hwy.
(503) 244-4467
www.threesquare.com
A beloved neighborhood spot, Three Square Grill is also a destination for Portlanders hankering for some roadhouse cooking Northwest style. Here you might find a beautiful salmon hash, hush puppies with jalapeño jelly, roasted chicken encrusted with herbs, or spicy garlic fries—we say "might" because it depends on what's in season. The chefs make as much as they can on-site, and

that includes the desserts, the hamburger buns, "Bad Monkey" jalapeño sauce, and pickles—in fact, they are also the purveyors of Picklopolis pickles (www.picklopolis.com), the "Pickles of the Future." You can buy them at the restaurant or at the Hillsdale and Portland farmers' markets. Three Square Grill serves dinner every night.

Seafood

DAN AND LOUIS $$
208 Southwest Ankeny St.
(503) 227-5906
www.danandlouis.com
Dan and Louis is an old Portland tradition in a historic downtown building. They served only live oysters from their opening in 1907 until 1919, when they finally got a stove and could make oyster stew. They still serve both these dishes, but they also serve many oystery treats: oysters Rockefeller, barbecued oysters, and fried oysters, to begin with. Dan and Louis is unpretentious and simple; it is the oldest family-owned restaurant in town. Stick with the oyster dishes or fish and chips and you'll be content. Raw oysters are still their specialty.

JAKE'S FAMOUS CRAWFISH $$$
401 Southwest 12th Ave.
(503) 226-1419

JAKE'S GRILL $$$
611 Southwest 10th Ave.
(503) 220-1850
www.mccormickandschmicks.com
Even though Jake's is now owned by McCormick & Schmick's, which technically makes it a chain restaurant (a Portland chain), this restaurant retains its status as a landmark. Founded in 1892 by Jacob (Jake) Lewis Freiman, Jake's Famous Crawfish still has that

turn-of-the-last-century ambience, with its maze of booths snug against brick walls, its antique oil paintings, deep wood paneling, beautiful bar, and crisp white linen. Jake's Grill, the house restaurant for the Governor Hotel, is also a favorite. Portlanders love these places, as much for the tradition of going as for the skillfully cooked steaks and seafood. Jake's Famous Crawfish specializes in high-quality seafood, and it's the custom in many families to take out-of-town guests here for the splendid oysters Rockefeller. Try the Stark Street Sturgeon with basil dijon, Goose Point oysters, or the half-pound king crab legs. Jake's Grill concentrates on comfort food, and favorites here include prime rib, pork chops, and pot roast. The bar at the Grill is also very good.

SOUTHPARK $$
901 Southwest Salmon St.
(503) 326-1300
www.southparkseafood.com
Southpark is evocative of Casablanca—not only in its decor but also in its menu. We like the dining room, where they specialize in using Northwest ingredients—especially seafood—to showcase inventive Mediterranean-inspired dishes such as a bourride made from local seafood or almond-stuffed dates wrapped in delicate slices of Serrano ham. But we like the wine bar even more, with its murals, velvet drapes, and gleaming metallic bar. There, you can get the same menu or choose from the bar menu. The wine list is first class, and so is the service. Southpark is also good for cocktails and people-watching, not so much because it's a scene but because everyone, including the servers, seems to be having such a nice time.

Another nice perk: Southpark will validate your ticket if you park at the garage next door to the restaurant after 5 p.m. Southpark is open for lunch and dinner daily.

NORTHWEST PORTLAND
Asian

BEWON $$$
1203 Northwest 23rd Ave.
(503) 464-9222
www.bewonrestaurant.com
BeWon offers first-rate Korean food in a sleek atmosphere, with attentive and expert service. Korean food is perhaps the least well known of the Asian cuisines, but BeWon is determined to change that. At this elegant little restaurant, you can order the fixed-price menu (about $25), which comes with eight traditional courses, or you can order a la carte. Offerings might include a pumpkin rice porridge, acorn jelly, a stir-fry of oyster and shitake mushrooms, a hand-rolled crepe. Main courses feature dishes such as salt-encrusted mackerel or traditional barbecued pork. But the adventure here is in the side dishes: Dried cod, kimchi, sugared seaweed, and other small tastings are served on tiny plates that can be refilled. The rice wine list at BeWon is also quite good.

SILK BISTRO $$
1012 Northwest Glisan St.
(503) 248-2172
Silk, the showstopper bistro in the Pho Van dynasty, has its roots in a low-key Vietnamese restaurant in outer Southeast Portland that attracted a loyal following of customers seduced by its flavorful and fragrant noodle soups. Silk is the upscale incarnation of the original restaurant, where customers dine in a chic atmosphere permeated with pan-Pacific colors and lines and enjoy ingenious, haute Vietnamese cuisine. Here, you'll find

fewer varieties of pho, but in compensation, you'll find outstanding salads, grilled chicken, and sweet-savory fish entrees. Stellar dishes include Goi Bap Chuoi, a salad composed of banana blossoms, chicken, grapefruit, and mint, and—of course—the pho: either a chicken with coriander or a beef made with round steak and lean brisket. The Chao Tom roll—minced chicken and shrimp wrapped around a small piece of sugar cane—is an intriguing appetizer. But the true stars of the menu are the fresh fish dishes, served steamed, grilled, lightly battered, and any other way the chefs at Silk devise.

Cafes & Breakfast

BESAW'S CAFE $
2301 Northwest Savier St.
(503) 228-2619
www.besaws.com
Besaw's is a neighborhood joint in northern Northwest, and while it serves very good lunches and dinners, we like it especially for breakfast, which is hearty and delicious. They feature all the staples, plus crispy bacon, apple sausages, succulent smoked salmon, and fluffy pancakes. Expect a wait on the weekends. Besaw's has been a restaurant since the Lewis and Clark Exposition in 1905, and its handsome bar dates from that period.

DAILY CAFE $$
902 Northwest 13th Ave.
(503) 242-1916
www.dailycafe.net
The Daily Cafe, a stylish cafe in the Pearl District, serves breakfast, lunch, and dinner—as well as a standout Sunday brunch—and its attention to quality ingredients, seasonal menus, and friendly service has won hearts and minds all over town. The cafe serves breakfast and a bustling lunch, when crowds

gather to sample tarragon chicken sandwiches and chewy panini. Daily specials are also offered, and they range from the soup du jour to special treats such as fried chicken. Dinners feature wonderfully roasted chicken, perfectly broiled rib eye, and other American-style cuisine creatively prepared. Desserts are always good. A word about the brunch: The Daily Cafe serves starters with brunch—for example, delicate little blintzes or rice puddings that just encourage your appetite for French toast, trout, and eggs— so go when you are hungry.

FULLER'S RESTAURANT $
136 Northwest 9th Ave.
(503) 222-5608
Fuller's has been a Pearl District tradition since before it was the Pearl District, and it retains its working-class roots even as the city gentrifies around it. Of course, that's one of its attractions. Fuller's serves egg sandwiches, pancakes, and other traditional breakfast staples all day until 5 p.m on weekdays, 2 p.m. on Sat. It has 28 stools. Don't be surprised to find yourself in conversation with the guy at the next stool; it's part of the routine. Bring cash—they don't take credit cards. Closed Sun.

PEARL BAKERY $
102 Northwest 9th Ave.
(503) 827-0910
www.pearlbakery.com
Pearl Bakery is one of several excellent artisanal bakeries in town, featuring rustic Italian breads, as well as breakfast and dessert pastries. But Pearl Bakery also operates a tiny cafe in its retail operation on Northwest 9th. Here, you will find a wonderful array of panini, focaccia, and deli sandwiches. The sandwich fillings might include roasted

eggplant and tomato pesto or fig and anise. They may offer a gorgonzola, pear, and arugula salad on walnut bread—an inventive variation on a classic fall salad. The breads are outstanding—traditional sourdoughs are favorites but so are country-style loaves such as levain with green or kalamata olives. Breakfast pastries include tempting specialties such as apple coffee cake and pear Danish. Pearl Bakery is a fine way to begin your morning or have an early lunch.

Desserts

PAPA HAYDN $$
701 Northwest 23rd Ave.
(503) 228-7317
www.papahaydn.com
With the onslaught of excellent new patisseries and bakeries in Portland, it is easy to overlook the stalwarts. In Papa Haydn's case, this would be a mistake. It is still a charming place to go for fancy desserts in Portland, with an impressive array of elaborate gateaux, tortes, ice creams, tarts, and cheesecakes. Dishes such as lemon chiffon torte, marjolaine, peanut butter mousse torte, and black velvet cake draw folks with a sweet tooth from all over the city to the comfortable, polished dining room on Northwest 23rd Avenue. But don't overlook the dependably delicious pastas, salads, and grilled chicken and steak. Papa Haydn has another location in Southeast Portland.

French

✳FENOUIL $$$$
900 Northwest 11th Ave.
(503) 525-2225
www.fenouilinthepearl.com
Fenouil is a large, attractive space off the "living room" of the Pearl District, Jamison Square. In fact, Jamison Square feels more like a Parisian "place" every day, so it's fitting that Fenouil should stand guard over it. The cuisine is French too: steak and fries, foie gras terrine, Alsatian salads, onion soup, and so on. The wine list is extensive, and it has a great selection of Spanish and French wines to pair with your nicely prepared rack of lamb. They offer regional dinners that feature the cuisine of various locales in France and other areas of the Mediterranean, accompanied by appropriate wines. These dinners are served at large communal tables, so they allow you to make some new friends as you discuss the virtues of your plate. Fenouil serves lunch Mon through Fri and dinner Mon through Sat.

Italian

FRATELLI $$
1230 Northwest Hoyt St.
(503) 241-8800
www.fratellicucina.com
Fratelli is a pretty restaurant in the Pearl District that features different regional Italian cuisines. It changes its menu frequently, but its high-quality, local, and seasonal ingredients, clever preparations, and poised and gracious servers have won it a devoted clientele. The entrees might include standouts such as salmon with pearl onions and potatoes, linguine with mushrooms and pancetta, or seared free-range chicken wrapped in proscuitto. Antipasti are equally delightful, especially the bruschetta on house-made bread. The candlelit dining room lends a romantic atmosphere to your dinner, and unlike many contemporary restaurants, you can actually carry on a conversation.

GIORGIO'S $$$
1131 Northwest Hoyt St.
(503) 221-1888
www.giorgiospdx.com

Giorgio's is a beautiful and authentic Italian restaurant in the Pearl serving lunch and dinner. Our favorites include the homemade pastas: the browned gnocchi, the delicate ravioli, the robust *pappardelle*. These are all served inventively, perhaps with braised wild boar or juicy spot prawns. Their other dishes—grilled meats, well-prepared seafood and fish, duck breast—are also good. The service is outstanding. During warm weather, you can sit on the patio and enjoy this feasting outdoors and people-watching, if you can look up from your dinner.

JUSTA PASTA $
1336 Northwest 19th Ave.
(503) 243-2249
www.justapasta.com

Justa Pasta is the major pasta supplier to the region's top-tier restaurants, but it is also a great restaurant in its own right, serving dinner and lunch in its small (30-seat) venue—and one of the best bargains in town. Justa Pasta offers several kinds of pasta and sauces at each meal, accompanied by bread from the Pearl Bakery and well-flavored salads. Some of our favorites include the butternut squash–hazelnut ravioli and the mushroom sauce. The pumpkin ravioli, the swiss chard ravioli, and the lasagna are excellent as well. But simpler dishes, such as bucatini in marinara sauce, are also truly satisfying. It is the perfect place for a cozy dinner. It can be difficult to find a seat, but in the summer a small patio creates more room.

PIAZZA ITALIA $$
1129 Northwest Johnson St.
(503) 478-0619
www.piazzaportland.com

This seductive little cafe serves authentic Italian dishes prepared by actual Italians. It is reminiscent of the cafes one finds on the back streets of Rome, with dishes lined up in the case, looking very modest until you bite into them. In this case, you may want to bite into the gnocchi with braised beef or the bucatini with pancetta, or both. Antipasti and salads are perfect as well. Piazza Italia serves lunch and dinner daily.

SERRATO $$$
2112 Northwest Kearney St.
(503) 221-1195
www.serratto.com

Serrato is dedicated to the proposition that eating is meant to be a pleasurable, unhurried event, and the pretty dining room, with its big windows and blond wood, does inspire a bit of lingering over the dessert wine. The Italian-inspired menu is varied, making good use of our region's abundance. Good choices for antipasti might include the tomato and mozzarella salad with olive oil and basil or the potato and spinach tart with arugula and truffle oil. The pastas and risotto are very good; we have had luck with the ravioli in particular, especially when it is stuffed with crab.

Mediterranean

BLUEHOUR $$$$
250 Northwest 13th Ave.
(503) 226-3394
www.bluehouronline.com

Bluehour is routinely noted as the place to see and be seen in Portland, and it does provide a good backdrop for the beautiful people, with its dramatic curtains and low lighting. But don't overlook the food. It is always carefully prepared and well-balanced, and its cheese blights are outstanding. The dishes are inspired by France and Italy, everything from seared foie gras to osso buco. Bluehour is perhaps the slightest bit self-conscious of the role that it plays, and the menu reflects that—the starters are the star of this show. But everything is prepared handsomely, with a touch of adventure. Bluehour serves dinner every night, lunch Mon through Sat, and brunch on the weekends.

Pacific Northwest Cuisine

✳**PALEY'S PLACE**   **$$$$**
1204 Northwest 21st Ave.
(503) 243-2403
www.paleysplace.net
Paley's Place, run by an amiable couple in Northwest Portland, is justifiably one of Portland's favorite restaurants: Between chef Vitaly Paley's imagination and talent and Kimberly Paley's gregarious command of the dining rooms, Paley's Place offers one of the best meals in town. Here, the simplest ingredients are turned into Northwest-nuanced, French-inspired dishes prepared by a masterful chef. The menu is always changing, but you might find garlicky mussels prepared with hand-cut fries; a beautiful cut of Kobe beef; maple-glazed chicken with Granny Smith apples, sour cherries, and smoky bacon; halibut served with lentils, fennel, and fiddlehead ferns; or sautéed sweetbreads with leek potato gratin and pomegranate sauce. The restaurant, residing in a pretty, old house in Northwest Portland, has only 50 seats. Yet its two dining rooms, bar, and patio convey the feeling of a larger restaurant without losing any

intimacy. Paley's is open seven nights a week for dinner only.

✳**PARK KITCHEN**   **$$$**
422 Northwest 8th Ave.
(503) 223-7275
www.parkkitchen.com
On the shady and peaceful North Park blocks—just a few steps from the hurly-burly of Broadway—you will find Park Kitchen, a lovely little restaurant that offers an ever-changing menu of superlative tavern-style cooking. Chef Scott Dolisch is one of Portland's best, and everything here is tempting, beautifully prepared, and chosen with great care. Indeed, Dolisch was featured as one of America's 10 best new chefs by *Food & Wine* magazine in 2004. The menu changes often, but one of the charms of Park Kitchen is how much they make on-site, including hot dogs and potato chips. Breakfasts feature outstanding pastries, as well as comfort-food favorites such as corn bread pudding with bacon and cheddar cheese or house-made English muffins with bananas and peanut butter. Lunches offer an array of soups, salads, pastas, and panini. You might find, for example, tagliatelle with braised lamb and snap peas or mussels steamed with zinfandel. Dinners feature a range of both cold and hot small plates—salt cod fritters with malt vinegar, for instance, or leek and saffron tart—and provide the adventurous diner with many opportunities to experiment. The thoughtful entree choices are kept to a minimum but offer excellent variety nonetheless—grilled pork chops, spring lamb, risotto, and two kinds of fish were the stars of one recent menu. Dessert choices might include creamy butterscotch pudding in oatmeal shortbread, refreshing papaya-lime sorbet with coconut cakes, or an inventive

s'more Napoleon pastry. Their attention to detail extends to the wine list, as well as the fine selection of bourbons and other liquors in the bar. Park Kitchen serves lunch and dinner. It's closed on Sun and open only for dinner on Sat.

WILDWOOD $$$$
1221 Northwest 21st Ave.
(503) 248-9663
www.wildwoodrestaurant.com

Wildwood is a destination spot in Northwest Portland and it has developed a loyal following who come for the fine Northwest cuisine, expertly prepared. The decor is unfussy and contemporary, and many power lunches and dinners happen here, either in the dining room booths or in the busy bar. The seasonal menu offers the very best from our region.

South American

*ANDINA $$$
1314 Northwest Glisan St.
(503) 228-9535
www.andinarestaurant.com

This stylishly renovated warehouse in the Pearl District is a star in the Portland restaurant scene. Comprising a tapas bar, an aperitif bar, a wine shop, and the capacious dining room, Andina showcases the cuisine of Peru to great effect. It is a beautiful restaurant, both in the space itself and in the presentation of the food. One staple is the cooking of fish in lime juice, or cebiche, which is regarded by some as the national dish of Peru. Marinating fish in lime juice breaks down its proteins, just like cooking with heat, but it leaves the texture firm and fresh and it infuses the fish with wonderful citrusness. It is prepared here with onions, cilantro, spicy peppers, and salt, then served with corn and yams. Andina has a number of fish cebiches, but they also serve several vegetarian variations on this dish as well. The meat selections are also outstanding, from simple Peruvian rack of lamb with purple potatoes (the ancestor of all potatoes) to more complex dishes involving stir-fried beef and yucca. Andina also features delicious side dishes—for example, yucca leaves stuffed with cheese and peppers—and salads. The wine list is well-edited; the service at Andina is professional and the servers' knowledge is excellent, which is helpful if you are unfamiliar with Peruvian cuisine. Andina serves lunch Mon through Sat and dinner every evening.

Portland Spirits

In addition to its microbreweries and purveyors of hand-roasted coffee, and artisanal wine, Portland is also home to a number of micro-distilleries. These include **Clear Creek** (eau de vie and brandy), **Rogue Spirits** (gin and rum), **New Deal Distillery** (vodka); and **House Spirits** (vodka, aquavit, and gin).

But how can you tell whether these homegrown brews are better than, say, bathtub gin? To that end, the **Wine & Spirit Archive** offers classes in spirit appreciation, where you can train your palate to be more discerning: www.wineandspiritarchive.com/ classes/certification/spirits.html. They offer the only such certification in the country.

Steakhouses

RINGSIDE $$$$
2165 West Burnside St.
(503) 223-1513
www.ringsidesteakhouse.com/home
.html

Since 1944, over three generations of owners, not much has changed at the RingSide. The prime and choice aged beef, fresh seafood, and excellent wine and service have helped RingSide garner more than 40 regional and national awards. If you're a rib connoisseur, try the 10-ounce RingSide Prime Rib served with au jus and creamed horseradish sauce. Also, don't leave without ordering the huge, luscious onion rings. The desserts, such as the chocolate raspberry torte (made locally by JaCiva), an exquisite Swiss-chocolate layer cake with raspberry filling, are a terrific way to finish off your feast. RingSide is open weekdays for lunch and daily for dinner.

SOUTHEAST PORTLAND

Asian

BIWA $$
215 Southeast 9th Ave.
(503) 239-8830
http://biwarestaurant.com

For a city on the Pacific Rim, and considering the number of Japanese language and cultural programs we have, Portland has surprisingly few authentic Japanese restaurants. Fortunately, Biwa has closed this gap. This restaurant is in the "small plates" style, emphasizing variety in taste and high-quality ingredients. Standout dishes include the vegetable salad, which features cabbage rolls, carrots, and daikon radish in a silky sesame dressing; a savory fried chicken; pork belly; *onigiri*, little stuffed rice and nori sandwiches; and offerings of two different noodle styles.—in particular, the pork ramen is stellar. Biwa is right next door to Simpatica, and chef Gabe Rosen is a close ally of theirs—which is reflected in all the meat dishes, but especially in the gorgeous beef tartare, marinated in sesame oil and garlic. Its dining room offers both booths and counter seats next to the open kitchen. Biwa also has a fine cocktail list, as well as an excellent selection of sake. Biwa is open Mon through Sat.

**❋POK POK AND WHISKEY SODA
  LOUNGE** $$
3226 Southeast Division St.
(503) 232-1387
www.pokpokpdx.com

Inhabiting a teeny hut and a vintage house on Southeast Division, Pok Pok's modest exterior belies its perfect and authentic Thai cooking. Pok Pok serves the cuisine of the northern part of Thailand, in particular the Chiang Mai valley. What does this mean for you? A mouthwatering balance of crispy and soft; of sweet, salty, and spicy; of yin and yang. Everything here is delicious, but the major draw is the roasted guinea hens, cooked on a special rotisserie that was imported just for this purpose. They have a gorgeous crispy golden skin, and the meat is juicy, infused with lemongrass, garlic, and smoke. Another wonderful dish is the Khao Man Som Tam, a dish of coconut rice, caramelized shredded pork, and fried shallots, but pretty much anything you get will be good. Getting seated can be challenging, so many patrons head across the street and down half a block to the Whiskey Soda Lounge, which serves excellent cocktails along with the spicy Pok Pok wings and other bar treats, to wait for their table. (Indeed, some people head straight to the Whiskey Soda Lounge and just stay there.) Visit Pok Pok Mon through Sun. Lunch is served from 11:30 a.m. to 3:30 p.m.; dinner from 4:30 p.m. on. The Whiskey Soda Lounge is open every night starting at 5 p.m.

SABURO'S $
1667 Southeast Bybee St.
(503) 236-4237
www.saburos.com
Serving good sushi in Portland, Saburo's popularity is evident by the crowds who gather outside in the evening, awaiting beautiful slices of velvety, firm fish and magnificent, fresh rolls. The sake list is also good, as are the tempura, noodles, and other traditional dishes. We order these because we can't help it, and they are good, but the true attraction is the sushi. The lighting is bright and the tables are tiny and crowded. There are always long lines, so we have been known to write our names on the list and then sneak up the street for a cocktail.

Barbecue

PODNAH'S $$
1469 Northeast Prescott St.
(503) 281-3700
www.podnahspit.com
Podnah's serves excellent barbecue and its standard accompaniments in an unpretentious setting. It's one of the few places in town to get an iceberg wedge salad, but it's a salad that goes well with the sliced brisket, lamb spare ribs, and pulled pork. These and other smoky delights are made with local meats and served with refreshing slaws, beans, and other sides. Wine and beer are available, as are an impressive array of sodas. It's open for lunch and dinner Tues through Sun.

Cafes & Breakfast

DETOUR CAFE $
3035 Southeast Division St.
(503) 234-7499
http://detourcafe.com
We love this little neighborhood breakfast and lunch cafe, open daily from 8 a.m. to 4 p.m. We love the modern DIY decor and the outstanding service. And we especially love the sandwiches—all of them. A flavorful BLT served on focaccia, for example—the focaccia is wonderfully chewy and fresh (made on-site), and the thick and crisp bacon is complemented by creamy avocado. The Detour Cafe also makes excellent traditional breakfasts and serves great coffee. It's crowded on the weekends, when it serves a bustling brunch to bleary-eyed nightclubbers, so you might try a weekday lunch when it's slightly mellower.

J & M CAFE $
537 Southeast Ash St.
(503) 230-0463
On a quiet side street a few steps up from bustling Martin Luther King Jr. Boulevard is the J & M Cafe, one of the best places for breakfast and lunch in Portland. Wonderful food, an appealing low-key atmosphere, and reasonable prices make this restaurant an outstanding value. They handle the traditional breakfast dishes beautifully. First, the coffee is self-serve, which is a fine thing if you have to wait for your table. When it's time to order, you can't go wrong. The waffles are excellent—crispy on the outside, tender and flaky inside. The eggs are fluffy and savory, the scrambles imaginative—for example, a house-made chorizo with roasted red pepper, cheddar cheese, and sour cream. Their signature dish, the J & M plate, is their own variation on eggs Benedict: here, two basted eggs

on an English muffin, topped with cheese in place of the hollandaise and thick, crispy bacon. The service here is first-rate. Cash only.

PINE STATE BISCUITS $
3640 Southeast Belmont St.
(503) 236-3346
www.pinestatebiscuits.com

Pine State Biscuits began as a stall in the Portland Farmers' Market, but after their lines snaked around the block and they kept running out of food, they opened this spot on Belmont. Here they serve fantastic breakfasts and lunch made with ingredients from their farmers' market friends. Specialties include amazingly delicious grits, as well as good sandwiches and hash browns. Biscuits are good too, but really, the star is the grits. If you never liked them before, you will now. Pine State Biscuits is open from 7 a.m. to 2 p.m. daily. A second location in Northeast Portland at 2204 Northeast Alberta, is equally popular.

Delis & Sandwiches

*BUNK SANDWICHES $
621 Southeast Morrison St.
(503) 477-9515
www.bunksandwiches.com

This sandwich shop in Southeast Portland is routinely compared to East Coast delis, but we think it's distinctively Portland: you can get an incredible meal for less than $10 made with superb local ingredients alongside a variety of your Portland neighbors from the suited to the tattooed. But our friends from the East Coast who routinely do business in Portland make a point of eating here. They are looking for savory sausage and cheese breakfast sandwiches on flaky biscuits, stellar tuna melts, the pork belly Cuban sandwich, an outstanding meatball parmigiano hero, and multiple other creative

fillings. There are options for vegans and vegetarians as well that are just as delicious. In 2009 Bunk was visited by Guy Fieri and was featured on his show, *Diners, Drive-ins and Dives*. Open Mon through Sat, 8 a.m. to 3 p.m. It gets busy at lunchtime.

EUGENIO'S $
3584 Southeast Division
(503) 233-3656
www.eugenios.net

Eugenio's is a tiny, tiny Italian-style deli that serves some of the best espresso in town, as well as absolutely delicious sausage sandwiches (using the best Italian sausage anywhere, from local purveyor Fred Carlo) and thin-crust pizza. The sandwiches and salads are fresh, with novel combinations of high-quality ingredients—for example, the Draper Valley chicken that's used for the chicken salad. It also offers microbrews on tap and has a small but intelligently selected wine list. There are just a few seats, and sometimes half the space is taken up by musicians singing the praises of Eugenio, but if you are patient you will be justly rewarded with a fine, simple lunch or dinner.

OLYMPIC PROVISIONS $$
107 Southeast Washington St.
(503) 954-3663
www.olympicprovisions.com

This delightful salumeria—amazingly, given all the house-cured meats here, Portland's first—has both a retail side and a restaurant side. On the retail side, you can take home savory Italian, French, and Spanish-style salamis and other cured meats, as well as fresh sausages and pates. On the restaurant side, you may want to tarry over beautiful charcuterie, wine, and cheese, as well as sumptuous meat dishes or daily fish specials.

Close-up

Dining at the Cusp: Oregon's Culinary Schools

With all the attention to food in Portland, it is only natural that the city has several culinary schools. And it turns out that these schools are excellent places to have lunch or dinner—the students are cooking food, and someone must eat it. Why not you?

Two of Portland's cooking schools, **Oregon Culinary Institute** and **Cordon Bleu**, both have good restaurants for the adventuresome diner. The immediate appeal is the price: for less than the price of an entree in many restaurants, you can have an entire dinner. Yet it's not just the price that lies at the heart of these appealing institutions: it's also the sense that you're witnessing something significant.

For example, Oregon Culinary Institute has a handsome dining room and a busy kitchen and appears to simply be a stylish restaurant. But dig a little deeper and you'll find a dedication to focused, hands-on, real-world training of future chefs. The Portland area is ideal for training, given the farm-to-table paradise that is the Northwest. And, as OCI president Eric Stromquist observes, the entire city is like a laboratory for chefs, a unique environment that allows them to experiment and learn from one another. Oregon Culinary Institute also emphasizes the values and ethics behind using local and seasonal ingredients. This emphasis is not just a fashion, but also an important component of the discipline—plus, these ingredients tend to be the best products.

At OCI, the student cooks are under the trained eye of a master instructor; they work the dining room as well, wearing their chef uniforms as they practice balancing trays. They are also trained in restaurant management, labor costs, and other critical aspects of learning how to run a sustainable business. For many students who want to own restaurants some day, this training is as important as knowing how to debone a chicken and concoct the perfect consommé. And customers enjoy—along with truly praiseworthy meals—getting to know the students and following their careers as they become rising stars in the culinary firmament.

Tips for eating at culinary institutes:

Most cooking schools have restaurants so that their students can get some real-world experience not only on the line but also in the dining room. The atmosphere is fun and casual. But they are schools, so it's important to manage your expectations. If you eat there, you need to be prepared for service that's a little uncertain and occasional inconsistency from the kitchen. That said, for diners, these school-based restaurants offer superb value—well-priced meals, quality ingredients, and the possibility of surprise.

Oregon Culinary Institute serves a three-course prix-fixe lunch for $9 (seating at noon) and a four-course prix-fixe dinner for $18 (seating at 7 p.m.); beverages not included; and all gratuities benefit the Student Scholarship Fund. To make a reservation, call (503) 961-6200 from 9 a.m. to 6 p.m., Mon through Fri (office hours). You'll find Oregon Culinary Institute at 1701 Southwest Jefferson St.

Le Cordon Bleu's restaurant is called Bleu; it offers a three- or five-course prix-fixe lunch and dinner, and it's available Tues through Fri when classes are in session. Lunch is served from 11 a.m. to 1 p.m. for lunch and from 6 p.m. to 8 p.m. for dinner. Call for reservations (503-294-9770; 600 Southwest 10th Ave., in the Galleria Building).

The wine list is expansive, and there is also a well-edited hard alcohol selection.

Desserts

PIX PATISSERIE $-$$
3402 Southeast Division St.
(503) 232-4407
www.pixpatisserie.com
Pix specializes in pastry—cakes, tarts, tortes, petit-fours—and in chocolates. Here you will find a spectacular Carmen Miranda tart, with glossy fruit in artful balance. You'll find the award-winning Amelie, a chocolate mousse confection that embraces a well of orange vanilla crème brûlée. And you'll find traditional patisserie favorites, such as the Opera, a thin almond cake layered with chocolate ganache and coffee buttercream. Pix supplies many local shops and restaurants, as well as offering a charming retail shop that also serves as a petite cafe. Pix also has a large and sophisticated space at 3901 North Williams St. (503-282-6539), where classes and other events are located.

Hawaiian

NOHO'S HAWAIIAN CAFE $
2525 Southeast Clinton St.
(503) 233-5301
www.nohos.com/clinton.html
Noho's is a popular neighborhood cafe that offers tasty Hawaiian fare. The yakisoba noodles—served with veggies and a tangy sauce—are a favorite, but the menu offers a selection of exotic meals ranging from Korean short ribs to seafood entrees and yummy marinated chicken dishes. Everything is served with white rice and macaroni or green salad on the side and—for those who like to swap and share different foods—family-style meals are always available. Noho's is open Sun through

Thurs from 10:30 a.m. until 9 p.m., and on Fri and Sat they stay open until 11 p.m. The cafe also offers catering services.

Indian

VINDALHO $$
2038 Southeast Clinton St.
(503) 467-4550
www.vindalho.com
Serving exquisite food in the Indian tradition, Vindalho is unlike any other restaurant between Vancouver, British Columbia, and perhaps San Francisco. What Nuestra Cocina is to Mexican food, Vindalho is to Indian food: It displays a proper respect for the flavors and textures while at the same time taking advantage of the amazing basic ingredients the Pacific Northwest has to offer. Vindalho offers many traditional foods—aromatic naan bread, for instance, or lamb kofta (savory meatballs in a Pakistani curry sauce). You will also find beautiful and flavorful salads. For dinner, you may want to sample the curry, the pork, or any of the various preparations of chicken—including tandoori. The lamb is outstanding—grilled perfectly in the tandoori oven, it is succulent and juicy and nevertheless carries that beautiful smoky scent that is the hallmark of meat grilled outdoors. Whatever else you order, be sure to order the condiments—the sides of relishes and pickles that will bring your dishes together into a meal. Vindalho is open Tues through Sun, 5 to 9 p.m; serving dinner until 10 p.m. on Fri and Sat evenings.

Italian

✳GENOA AND ACCANTO $$-$$$$
2832 Southeast Belmont St.
(503) 238-1464
www.genoarestaurant.com
www.accantopdx.com

Genoa was a longtime prix-fixe restaurant that was a perennial favorite, serving high-end Italian fare, and when it closed, it left a hole in the hearts of patrons across the city. Now it is back: it has been gloriously remodeled, and it is headed by Dave Anderson, who served as the chef de cuisine at both Lauro and Vindalho. Here, he brings his perfectionist tendencies to Italian food, reviving the prix-fixe, five-course menu and focusing on different regional cuisines—Roman one night, Neapolitan another, for example. This is the place to go when you want to celebrate something—or when you simply want a It is a fine place for dressing up and enjoying a delectable food and wine. Accanto is the enoteca side; it's bright and casual, but no less delicious. Many people stop here for a cocktail before dining at Genoa next door. Either would be a fine choice for dinner. Accanto is open for lunch and dinner daily and for brunch on Sat and Sun, in keeping with its role as an attractive and upscale but neighborhood-focused café. Genoa is open for dinner Tues through Sun.

GINO'S RESTAURANT AND BAR $$$
8051 Southeast 13th Ave.
(503) 233-4613
www.ginossellwood.com
Gino's is an unpretentious trattoria that serves excellent Italian dishes. Other chefs come here when they go out to dinner. Down-to-earth classics include the wonderful clams steamed in white wine, chili, and butter; chicken Marsala; Grandma Jean's pasta (which comes with two pork ribs); and a tangy Caesar salad. In addition to the reliable favorites, you will find seasonal specials—rich stews of lamb, sautées of shrimp with red chilis, vegetable ragouts with polenta, for example. Seafoods are always fresh; the Painted Hills beef steaks are specially cut just for Gino's. Gino's serves dinner nightly.

NOSTRANA $$
1401 Southeast Morrison St.
(503) 234-2427
Nostrana has behind it one of Portland's favorite chefs, Cathy Whims. The Neapolitan-style pizza is outstanding, as are the antipasti and bruschetta. Pasta dishes feature house-made noodles and sauces inspired by Marcella Hazen. The grilled and rotisseried meats are perfectly done, sharing touches of Tuscany while being, at the same time, all Oregon. On the wine list you'll see a good selection of wines from Italy, though it also has some nice Oregon pinot noirs. Desserts are outstanding, and one in particular is deserving of mention: wood-oven-baked apple crisp with almond cream. This crisp is baked in the pizza oven—which means at about 700 degrees—and while it takes 20 minutes to prepare, its caramelized and creamy goodness is worth waiting for. Nostrana lives in an old grocery store. They have used the space well, placing tables far apart, but warming the restaurant by using cork floors, the pizza oven, and attractive lighting, elements that create an urbanized rustic feel to the place. Nostrana is open for lunch Mon through Fri from 11:30 a.m. to 2 p.m., and for dinner every night.

Mediterranean

CASTAGNA $$$$
1752 Southeast Hawthorne Blvd.
(503) 231-7373
www.castagnarestaurant.com
Castagna is a sophisticated and spare restaurant on the western end of Hawthorne, with a minimalist ambience that allows the food

to take center stage. The presentation here is outstanding, and even simple dishes such as a butter lettuce salad, sea scallops, or french fries are beautifully arranged on large white plates. Castagna could not get away with this emphasis on appearance, however, if it did not back it up with some of the best food in the city. The seasonal menu—on which you might find grilled sea scallops with oyster mushrooms, little agnolotti pasta stuffed with duck confit, sautéed halibut with mussels and potatoes, or grilled rack of lamb—is Mediterranean influenced, with local ingredients providing the foundation. Everything from the white bean soup to the last crumb of bittersweet chocolate tartlet is impressive to both the eye and the palate. There is no place like Castagna in all of Portland. A less formal, and less expensive, cafe right next door, Café Castagna (1758 Southeast Hawthorne Blvd.; 503-231-9959), provides an excellent meal. Here, the ambience is low key, with its stone floor and wooden tables. You'll be happy in either place.

LAURO MEDITERRANEAN
KITCHEN $$$
3377 Southeast Division St.
(503) 239-7000
www.laurokitchen.com
It took almost no time for Lauro to gain a regional reputation when the neighborhood restaurant opened in 2004. Chef Dave Machado, the creative spirit behind Southpark for a number of years, brings his pan-Mediterranean sensibility to this stylish, friendly spot in Southeast Portland. He looks for the right combination of flavor and texture to update classics of bistro cooking, as well as regional specialties. Standout dishes include wonderfully sweet and savory stuffed plums, a fragrant chicken tagine, short ribs, and an amazing custard cooked with port. Wood-fired pizzas and outstanding burgers allow parents to bring children and eat in peace. Lauro also has an excellent selection of reasonably priced wines by the bottle and glass. Lauro's atmosphere is industrial chic—handsome combinations of wood, concrete, and glass—which pays homage to the building's former life as a warehouse yet sacrifices nothing in comfort. Lauro serves dinner seven nights a week from 5 to 10 p.m. and lunches on weekdays.

3 DOORS DOWN $$
1429 Southeast 37th St.
(503) 236-6886
www.3doorsdowncafe.com
3 Doors Down serves high-quality American-Mediterranean fare and pays attention to all the fine details that add to the enjoyment of a meal. The cozy and comfortable setting is a great place to enjoy the restaurant's wide range of house-made pastas. The risottos and Caesar salads are exceptional, as are the pastas and the entire range of appetizers. A signature, must-try dish is the bucatini pasta with meatballs, which is perfectly balanced and savory. The penne with vodka sauce is also a favorite. The bar is a lovely spot for a predinner aperitif. Closed Mon.

Mexican

NUESTRA COCINA $$
2135 Southeast Division St.
(503) 232-2135
www.nuestra-cocina.com
This remarkable restaurant in Southeast Portland serves Mexican food at its finest—not greasy rice and beans, but complex and savory dishes from Mexico's central regions. The service here is both expert and friendly, and the dining room is handsome, with

mosaic tiles and accents of wood. But as pleasant as the service and dining room are, the food is what, rightly, should draw you. For one thing, the tortillas are *heche a mano*—made by hand using a tortilla press. The result is fragrant goodness that gets even better when you add a few drops of chipotle sauce. Salads and other appetizers are fresh and delicious. They offer a great Caesar salad (yes, it is a Mexican dish), ceviche, and savory little tacos made from shredded pork that are not just crowd pleasers but genuine haute cuisine. Entrees include succulent pork and lamb dishes, as well as truly excellent seafood dishes such as prawns cooked with garlic and spicy chiles, served with a perfectly complementary dish of black beans and plantains. Yum. For dessert, the cinnamon ice cream has no equal in town. One warning: The bar area is very, very small, so there are few options for waiting unless it's a summer night and you can chat outside on the sidewalk. But it is worth waiting for a table here. If you do get a seat at the bar, you should try one of the excellent margaritas; they are delicious. Nuestra Cocina is closed Sun and Mon. However, they will serve you dinner Tues through Sat, from 5 to 10 p.m.

Pacific Northwest Cuisine

✳LE PIGEON   **$$$**
738 East Burnside St.
(503) 546-8796
www.lepigeon.com
Le Pigeon inhabits a small space on busy East Burnside Street, a space that is dominated by the open kitchen, a counter around the kitchen for diners, and a number of farmhouse tables. Le Pigeon does not take reservations, and they seat comparatively few people. It's decorated salvage style, with old chandeliers and repurposed chairs. In spite of these humble trappings, Le Pigeon is probably the most innovative restaurant in Portland today. Chef Gabriel Rucker trained in Napa, then established himself here to take advantage of the local ingredients and the atmosphere of possibility.

While he does use the typical local, seasonal approach, he does not fetishize it, and even more important, he uses these elements in completely novel ways. Menus change a lot, but there are some standout regulars—for example, the peanut butter and jelly sandwich with foie gras, served as an appetizer. Duck confit, crispy sweetbreads, and tongue make regular appearances, as do interesting sides such as pickled strawberries or gazpacho with melon. Desserts frequently incorporate foie gras or bacon to accent the silky sweetness of ice cream or the airiness of a profiterole.

But it would be a mistake to think that the push-the-envelope combinations, which have garnered remarkable local and national press, are what drive this restaurant. For when you get down to it, it is the perfectionist technique of Rucker that makes this place sing. Even simple dishes such as roast chicken display an authoritative touch, with crispy golden skin and perfect combinations of texture and flavor in the accompanying sides. When a chef can make the simple things as interesting as the star dishes, you know he is a master. Le Pigeon is open for dinner nightly.

Pizza

APIZZA SCHOLLS   **$$**
4741 Southeast Hawthorne Blvd.
(503) 233-1286
www.apizzascholls.com
Serving authentic New York–style pizza, Apizza Scholls is always busy. Luckily, since

they don't take reservations, the pizza is worth the wait. Carefully crafted using a very hot oven, slow-rising dough, and local ingredients, these pizzas are so good that even New Yorkers like them. Open for dinner Tues through Sat.

*KEN'S ARTISAN PIZZA　　$$
304 Southeast 28th Ave.
(503) 517-9951
www.kensartisan.com

Ken's Artisan Pizza was born because owner Ken Forkish kept having to stay late at his bakery in Northwest Portland on Monday nights, when he first served pizza, because the lines were so long. Now he stays late in Southeast Portland, and the lines are even longer. Forkish uses a 700-degree oven, a perfect pizza technique, and keeps the menu simple, a combination that leads to incredibly satisfying dinners. The menu includes several salads, among them an excellent Caesar, as well as a seasonally changing prosciutto dish. Some kind of roasted vegetable dish is always available; this is dressed with something light and refreshing that plays up the flavors of the vegetables. Pizzas are also seasonal—in the fall you might find a squash pizza, while spring may bring roasted asparagus—but you can count on a Margherita, with tomato sauce, mozzarella, and basil or even arugula. Other regular toppings involve house cured pancetta, anchovies, and Italian sausage. But it is the pizza dough that is the main event: perfectly crusty and chewy and balanced. The wood-burning pizza oven is also used to roast vegetables and cook dessert, which includes amazing cobblers, crisps, crostada, and other baked fruit desserts. Ice cream and other confections are also available. The interior is small but feels spacious because of the high ceilings and spare aesthetic. A

well-edited selection of beer and wine is offered. Service is consistently professional, so even if you have to wait, the staff will see to it that your wait is pleasant. Ken's serves crusty pizza for dinner Tues through Sat.

TASTEBUD　　$$
3220 Southeast Milwaukie Ave.
(503) 234-0330
www.tastebudfarm.com

Tastebud is the bricks-and-mortar version of a popular mobile wood-fired pizza oven that is frequently seen at farmers' markets, most notably the Porltand Farmers' Market on Saturdays on the campus of Portland State University. For those who have stood in the rain to get the delicious chewy pizza with inventive toppings, the chance to sit down with a slice and maybe a good beer is irresistible. Mark Doxtader—who has a genius for bread dough—has been committed to using local, seasonal, and organic ingredients before it was fashionable, so your toppings might include delicata squash, mozzarella, and arugula; pumpkin and leek; or sausage, apple, and onions. They also make amazing Montreal-style bagels. Tastebud is open for dinner Wed through Sun.

Small Plates

*BAR AVIGNON　　$
2138 Southeast Division St.
(503) 517-0808
http://baravignon.com

Proprietors Randy Goodman and Nancy Hunt will tell you that Bar Avignon is just a bar, but don't believe them. This sleek and organic spot along Southeast Division offers a beautifully edited wine collection and wonderful spirits that frame an outstanding selection of small plates. These include silky cured meats, creamy cheeses served with honey and Marcona almonds, just-harvested salads, the ripest fruit, the crustiest bread from Little T American Baker up the street—in short, everything you need to make a complete meal for the entire family, provided they are all over 21 (though children are in fact welcome). It's a lovely spot for a relaxed weeknight dinner. The service is attentive and the atmosphere is enlivening, full of attractive and convivial people who are all evidently enjoying themselves. You should join them.

✳BEAKER AND FLASK $$
720 Southeast Sandy Blvd.
(503) 235-8180
www.beakerandflask.com

Beaker and Flask first attracted patrons because of its molecularly sophisticated cocktails, but its reputation as an important restaurant was cemented when people ordered the food. It's difficult to achieve good cocktail-food pairings, simply because the cocktails tend to overwhelm the flavors of what you are eating, but the chef at Beaker and Flask has overcome this challenge with vigor. For example, the silky deviled eggs are prepared with smoked trout, a combination of textures and flavors that works beautifully with the fruity heat of bourbon-based cocktail. Dishes such as mussels with chorizo, fried razor clams, or even hot wings are prepared with good balance and attention to detail. The space is nice too, with an unusual view of downtown, and the bartending is legendary among Portland diners. Open Mon through Sat for happy hour and dinner.

VICTORY $
3652 Southeast Division St.
(503) 236-8755

This charming spot in Southeast Portland is a favorite with the neighborhood and fans all over town, drawn by the handsome decor—green walls, tin ceilings, and unusual, handmade light fixtures—and by the sweet, sweet servers. In some respects, Victory is the ideal neighborhood restaurant—not because it is perfect, but because it indicates the benchmark quality that Portland restaurants regularly achieve. Here, they specialize in small plates, with a variety of excellent house-cured meats and a savory spaetzle in a delightful cheese sauce as signature dishes. But they also serve fine salads, mussels, a good cheese plate, and other cafe food. Victory has a well-edited wine list and a number of special cocktails that entice even people who don't live 4 blocks away. In fact, the owners of other Southeast Portland restaurants appear at their bar with a regularity that is telling. Victory is open for dinner nightly.

Soul Food

DELTA CAFE $$
4607 Southeast Woodstock Blvd.
(503) 771-3101

Southern food at its most gloriously soulful is the specialty at Delta Cafe. This inexpensive neighborhood place attracts its share of students from nearby Reed College, but it has a loyal following from all over, due to the generous portions of succulent ribs, hush puppies in brown gravy (aka "Pups in a Pond"), and fried chicken with all the trimmings. Funky music, odd furniture, and local art complete the atmosphere. Delta Cafe won't cost you much, but they accept only cash and checks. Open 5 to 10 p.m. daily; the bar is open until 1 a.m. on weekdays, 2 a.m. on weekends.

NORTH & NORTHEAST PORTLAND

Eclectic

✳BEAST $$$$
5425 Northeast 30th Ave.
(503) 841-6968
www.beastpdx.com

Beast is the brainchild of Naomi Pommeroy, and it features not only communal dining but almost communal cooking—cooks and diners all share the same pretty space, all in one large convivial group spread over two tables. Menus are set in advance; they consist of five or six courses (though some of the courses are amuse-bouche size), beginning with soup and ending with dessert, and wine pairings. The star of these menus is meat in many varieties—for example, delicious braised dishes in the winter and perhaps a gorgeous lamb chop in the summer. Always, you will find delicate charcuterie. Beast has two seatings, on Wed through Sat nights, 6 p.m. or 8:45 p.m. They also serve brunch on Sun at 10 a.m. or noon. If you are the kind of person who likes to swap butter lettuce for foie gras, you will be happier in another restaurant. You may want to check the website before you make your reservations. Because of the communal nature of the experience and the size of the kitchen, what they serve is what they serve and they discourage substitutions.

Italian

✳CIAO VITO $$$
2293 Northeast Alberta St.
(503) 282-5522
www.ciaovito.net

Chef Vito DiLullo opened this attractive restaurant to serve his own neighborhood, on Alberta Street, but it has also become a destination dining spot since it opened in mid-2004. Ciao Vito serves honest food beautifully prepared at good value, and in this way, it feels more like Italy or France than Oregon. The focus of the menu is traditional Italian fare using Northwest ingredients, but there are always surprises. Even the simplest dishes—the antipasto, for example—are about 20 times better than anything you're likely to get west of Sicily. The calamari, served with aioli, is crispy, chewy, and delicious. The cured meats are a superb balance of fragrance, smokiness, and salt; the pickled vegetables taste fresh and tangy and are perfectly textured. The spaghetti carbonara is both creamy and earthy, complemented by the house-made pancetta. The chocolate *pots de creme* are worth savoring, no matter how full you are. The wine list is thoughtful, featuring Northwest and Italian wines at exceptionally reasonable prices. The service at Ciao Vito is professional and friendly. The word *handsome* has two meanings—good-looking and generous—and this affordable restaurant embodies both. Ciao Vito serves dinner Mon through Sun from 5 to 10 p.m., except on Fri and Sat, when dinner is served until 11 p.m.

Mexican

AUTÉNTICA $$$
5506 Northeast 30th Ave.
(503) 287-7555
www.autenticaportland.com

Serving food in the style of the Acapulco region of Mexico, Auténtica may defy your expectations. There is a full bar, from which margaritas and other fine drinks flow. Meals begin with three kinds of salsa, and you will want to also order the outstanding guacamole. Seafood cocktails are a house specialty, and they range from a refreshing octopus salad to tangy ceviche. The soups are hearty,

Close-up

The Food Carts of Portland

Anyone visiting Portland will notice, before long, people waiting expectantly in lines in front of bright little trailers that are selling food. Food carts have, of course, a long history—the red popcorn wagon, the lowly taco truck, the roving espresso cart. What's new is the quality of the cuisine: in a town that's wild about food, Portland's food carts offer exquisite food for a single-digit price. All over the city, outdoor food carts are revolutionizing how food is prepared, sold, and eaten.

They are popular with office workers needing some fresh air at lunchtime and with night owls needing food to soak up the cocktails after a hard night of dancing; with teenagers needing a destination and with families out for a weekend stroll. But food carts are not fast food—rather, they serve simple and delicious fare, and the speed it is delivered into your waiting hands may vary. You can get luscious meals for less than $10.

Portland's food carts can be found throughout the city in clusters known locally as "pods"—these are private lots that provide a home to a number of carts. You can also find them at farmers' markets or sharing lots with other businesses. Some are roving—you can keep up with them on Twitter and Facebook. There are more than twenty food cart pods, as well as individual carts, in Portland, so it's good to have a source for up-to-date information. The online guide **Food Carts Portland** (www.foodcartsportland .com) provides peerless coverage of all things foodcart-related. Listed below are a few of the major pods, followed by some of our very favorite carts.

- **Southwest Fifth Avenue between Southwest Oak and Southwest Stark Streets.** While it has no formal name, this is the mother pod, the one that gave birth to all the rest. Also known as "the lunch carts."

- **Southwest Alder Street between Southwest 9th and 11th Avenues.** This is one of the older pods; it has a very international feel, including arguably the best espresso in Portland, at Spella. (We said "arguably".)

- **Cartopia: Southeast 12th Avenue and Southeast Hawthorne Boulevard.** One of the original pods, Cartopia is notable for staying open very late for hungry clubbers on their way home. But you can come early for dinner too. It has lots of long communal, covered tables.

- **Mississippi Marketplace: North Mississippi Avenue, just south of Skidmore Street.** This pod has comfy seating and many (but not solely) vegan carts—it was an early planned, as opposed to spontaneous, cart community.

---

the flatiron steak is grilled perfectly, and the tostada is beautifully seasoned. The tamales are close to perfect. Because this restaurant is attempting to achieve authenticity, some things might surprise you, such as the saltine crackers served with the seafood cocktails. Just go with it. Dinner served Tues through Sun.

✳POR QUE NO $
3524 North Mississippi St.
(503) 467-4149
This is the kind of Mexican restaurant that makes you hungry just by thinking about it. It offers impeccably fresh, well-flavored dishes— the guacamole has nice chunks of avocado;

- **Portland State University: Southwest 4th Avenue and Southwest Hall.** Convenient to downtown, there are many carts in this pod devoted to delights such as pastrami, simple burgers, meatballs, and other things to make carnivores happy.

As promised, here are a few of our best-loved carts—only space prevents us from listing more:

- **Nourishment.** Nothing eases the rough shake of morning better than Nourishment's yummy breakfast burritos at the Hollywood Farmers' Market. Ramona White, the chef, is a fanatic for fresh and local ingredients. You can find her on Sat from 8 a.m. to 1 p.m., on Northeast Hancock Street between 44th and 45th Avenues.

- **Potato Champion.** A pioneer cart in Southeast Portland, Potato Champion is known for its Belgian-style fries, and in particular for its fresh take on the Quebecois dish poutine, as well as its stellar peanut butter and jelly fries: fries with peanut satay and raspberry chipotle sauce. At Cartopia, Southeast 12th Avenue and Hawthorne.

- **Koi Fusion.** Koi Fusion (Find them on Twitter: @KOIfusionpdx) is a mobile cart whose chef, Bo Kwon, has more than 4,000 followers on Twitter—that's how he tells his customers where he'll be. And people will suddenly appear to feast on his deservedly popular Korean-Mexican barbecue and snacks.

- **Sugar Cube.** This dessert-only cart in the Mississippi Marketplace pod (North Mississippi Avenue, south of Skidmore) makes heartbreakingly delicious sweets, including a salty-sweet chocolate-caramel cupcake with a potato chip garnish—trust us, it works—and handmade ice cream sandwiches.

- **Nong's Khao Man Gai.** We like this cart because they keep it simple by reducing the number of choices you have to make to one: this delightful and succulent Thai chicken dish with rice, prepared in a sauce of garlic, ginger, and soy. Find them downtown at Southwest Alder at Southwest 10th Avenue.

- **La Jarochita.** How we love a good taco truck! This Mexican cart is in the mother pod on Southwest 5th Avenue at Stark Street, and its mouthwatering tamales, tacos, and burritos are favorites with the throngs of downtown workers who swarm the place at lunchtime. We like the hurache, which is like a tostada, only made with masa, like a tamale, but you really can't go wrong with their menu.

the carne asada is nice and smoky, and the fish tacos are brightly complemented by bits of mango. Tortillas are handmade and delicious. Also see the location at 4635 Southeast Hawthorne Blvd. There are long, long lines at both places, but the lines move quickly.

Pacific Northwest Cuisine

✳**LINCOLN** $$$
3808 North Williams Ave.
(503) 288-6200
www.lincolnpdx.com

Lincoln is notable for their harmonious pairing of cutting-edge and classic food, of tradition and innovation, and of high style and down home. For example, their beloved house-made pastas are just a little different—serving braised pork belly with malloreddus rather than penne, or lamb ragu with sorcetti rather than gnocchi. This happy balance has led to success: chef Jenn Louis is a James Beard Award nominee. The space is beautiful, the service is excellent, and their happy hour is fine. Truly fine: who wouldn't want a frosty cocktail or a beer along with some baked eggs with cream, olives, and herbed breadcrumbs, or some savory fritters, or a savory little patty melt, on the way home from work?

Seafood

ORIGINAL HALIBUT'S $
2525 Northeast Alberta St.
(503) 803-9600
A small restaurant in a great neighborhood, Original Halibut's serves wonderfully fresh fish and chips that are perfectly textured: crispy outside and tender inside. The chef varies the fish depending on the season and offers several battered delicacies each day. The clam chowder is also excellent.

Small Plates

NAVARRE $$
10 Northeast 28th Ave.
(503) 232-3555
http://navarreportland.blogspot.com/
index.html
Navarre has been at the vanguard of a trend in Portland restaurants—small plates of wonderful food so you can have many different courses in one meal. The courses at this Spanish-inspired restaurant might include deliciously and simply prepared roasted

meats, tangy braised greens, a beet terrine, pickled carrots, or house-cured meats, in addition to cheeses and desserts. Navarre also, like so, so many Portland restaurants, is market-based, meaning that they serve what is in season, even going so far as to have their own personal farmer. You can tell this by the preserves that adorn the shelves and serve as focal points for the decor. Navarre serves dinner every night.

Southern

ACADIA $$$
1303 Northeast Fremont St.
(503) 249-5001
www.creolapdx.com
Located in a cute neighborhood, this handsome New Orleans–style bistro is packed with adventuresome diners who come in search of delicious Creole dishes, expertly prepared. Here you will find soft-shell crab, catfish taco, and jambalaya among the appetizers, as well as a delightful array of entrees such as Pork Chop Galatoire—a chop rubbed with ancho chili and honey, grilled, and served with crawfish, corn bread stuffing, and caramelized onion. During certain hours, they offer a nice fixed-price, three-course menu that features salad, a choice among three entrees, and either bread pudding or Cajun Velvet Pie for dessert. Acadia also has a full bar. They serve dinner Mon through Sat and a special jazz brunch on Sun.

BERNIE'S SOUTHERN BISTRO $$
2904 Northeast Alberta St.
(503) 282-9864
www.berniesbistro.com
This fine bistro serves Southern dinners with nods to the Northwest in its use of some seasonal and local ingredients—though not

only those ingredients, of course. But Bernie's cornmeal-crusted oysters are a nice twist on a local favorite, as are the green tomatoes (the Northwest gardener's yearly problem), here fried and served with smoked tomato coulis, hearty gumbo, fresh corn bread, and green-onion grits cakes. The catfish is plump, and the chicken-fried steak is savory. The appetizers are also notable, especially the hush puppies. Bernie's serves dinner Tues through Sat.

i Oregon and Washington are among the vanguard of artisanal cheesemakers, and the Pacific Northwest Cheese Project is dedicated to making sure we know how blessed they are. Find them at http://pnwcheese .typepad.com.

Spanish

TORO BRAVO $$
120 Northeast Russell St.
(503) 281-4464
www.torobravopdx.com
Toro Bravo carries the Spanish flag for Portland restaurants, as hospitable and friendly as the country, relaxed and sociable, but with outstanding food. It truly is a tapas "bar," and the best approach to take there is to order just a few dishes, hang onto the menu, and then order some more. Toro Bravo reflects the cuisine of many Spanish regions as interpreted by chef John Gorham, which means that it also reflects Oregon. The kebabs, the paellas, the tortillas: Each of these is prepared as a homage to the mother country but with decided Northwest accents. Local favorites Include the coppa steak, prepared with spinach and golden raisins; bacon-wrapped dates; scallops; duck rillettes; and grilled chanterelle mushrooms. Plus there are enough dishes to please everyone from vegans to omnivores.

You can order refreshing sangria, a number of house cocktails, and excellent wines. Toro Bravo is open for dinner nightly.

VANCOUVER
Pacific Northwest Cuisine

HUDSON'S $$$
Heathman Lodge
7801 Northeast Greenwood Dr.
(360) 816-6100
www.hudsonsbarandgrill.com
The chefs who serve the dining room in this comfortable hotel display its original take on the local and seasonal, with expertly prepared fish, fowl, and meat that is savory and succulent. The signature seafood cakes and flatbread are both amazingly delicious, and the wine list, featuring mostly West Coast wines, just right. Hudson's serves breakfast, lunch, and dinner every day.

OUTLYING AREAS
Pacific Northwest Cuisine

ROOTS $$$
19215 Southeast 34th St.,
Camas, WA
(360) 260-3001
www.rootsrestaurantandbar.com
Roots is a delicious spot for all the folks who are too tired to crawl back over the bridge for dinner, as well as those who never left. Why should Portland have all the fun? The menu is a beautiful concoction of whatever is fresh and seasonal—for example, Dungeness crab and line-caught salmon or wonderfully roasted chicken breast. The wine list is thoughtful, and the service friendly. For those of you in Portland, Roots is worth a trip across the river. Roots is open for lunch and dinner daily.

BREWPUBS

Some anthropologists claim that beer, rather than bread, enticed human tribes to abandon the ways of the nomad and settle down to develop agriculture. It was a powerful inspiration. By 3000 BC, the Sumerians were so devoted to the craft of brewing that it had a patron goddess: Ninkasi. If Ninkasi were looking for new recruits for her cult, she would have to look no further than Portland, where new disciples are born every day. Portland may have more microbreweries and brewpubs than any city in the nation—32 at last count—reflecting a climate hospitable to hops and a fanatic devotion to the homegrown. Our climate is excellent for growing hops (we grow at least 14 varieties) and barley, and beer brewing is a long tradition. Combine these resources with the do-it-yourself ethos left over from Oregon's hippie days, and you have a revolution in the making. All over the area, commercial brewers and backyard enthusiasts are creating microbrews, cask-conditioned ales, and other delights.

Some well known names in brewing legend here include Mike and Brian McMenamin, two brothers who have become not just brewers but real estate developers, hoteliers, and visionaries. They have more than 30 enterprises—including pubs, restaurants, hotels, inns, and theaters—throughout the city and beyond, stretching far south into the Willamette Valley and north to Washington. While their shadow has grown long, nonetheless, their pubs are wonderfully Oregon experiences. Many of them have splendid gardens and appealing interiors, and they all have good beer, from old standards such as Crystal, Ruby, Hammerhead, and Terminator Stout, to seasonal and other special beers.

Other important beer names are Fred Eckhardt, the beer writer whose most frequent label is "legendary," because his book The Essentials of Beer Style is regarded as the gospel by homebrewers and international beer judges; the Widmer Brothers, who made hefewiezen a household word (at least around here); and Henry Weinhard, the progenitor of beer production in the area. But many of the best beers in the area don't have well-known names or even their own pubs. Hair of the Dog—who named one of their special ales "Fred" after Fred Eckhardt—is one to keep your eye out for at taps throughout town.

OVERVIEW

Pubs and brewpubs have fast become a way of life for Oregonians, and many of them are very family-friendly, offering simple food and sometimes even craft-brewed root beer. As long as a pub is also a restaurant, most of them will allow children until 10 p.m. in designated areas. It is very common to see families in these pubs, so if you want to bring the little ones, don't be shy.

SOUTHWEST PORTLAND

✳BAILEY'S TAPROOM
213 Southwest Broadway
(503) 295-1004
www.baileystaproom.com
The handsome, minimalist decor of this pub is the perfect complement to the maximalist beer list: about twenty taps and a long list of bottled beers, all showcasing top-line craft brews, some of them rare indeed, and mostly from Oregon. Bailey's offers excellent samplers, and hosts many events where you can meet and mingle with brewers—notably their festive, if somewhat chaotic, anniversary event at the end of July, featuring potent barrel-aged microbrews from Oregon's finest. (They borrow some techniques from the Oregon Brewers Fest and utilize a snifter-and-token system; tokens are made out of beer caps.) While they don't brew their own beer—or make their own food; it's imported from a great Mexican restaurant across the street—Bailey's is a fine introduction to Oregon beer.

✳FULL SAIL BREWING
307 Southwest Montgomery St.
(503) 222-5343
www.fullsailbrewing.com/full-sail-river-place.cfm
Full Sail is a craft brewery that was established in Hood River, and this is its Portland outpost. They were one of the first microbreweries to figure out how to bottle their beer without losing any of its hoppy perfection, and this genius started a revolution in the hand-crafted beer world. A small operation that serves as the research and development arm, the brewery is next door to McCormick and Schmick's Harborside Restaurant and Pilsner Room, where you can watch the team at work through a glass wall. The delicious brews perfected here are put into production at the main brewery up the Gorge (see the Day Trips chapter). Full Sail is known for its ales and lagers, but it offers a range of delicious brews—including tiny-batch beers developed and tested in the brewery and available only at the two tasting rooms (here and in Hood River).

RACCOON LODGE
7424 Southwest Beaverton-Hillsdale Hwy.
(503) 296-0110
www.raclodge.com
On the western outskirts of town, you'll find the Raccoon Lodge, a large pub and brewery designed as a mountain lodge, with high ceilings, ample dining space with wooden booths and Pendleton blanket cushions, wood trusses and wainscoting, and a monster stone fireplace surmounted by an elk's head and horns. This is the home of Cascade Brewing, a fine local outfit. In addition to its excellent beer, you'll find a great pub fare, including a variety of hand-cut french fries and dipping sauces, including Yukon gold, shoestring, tater tots, sweet potatoes, and ale-batter steak fries, all of which arrive in a big bucket with dipping sauce.

TUGBOAT BREWING CO.
711 Southwest Ankeny St.
(503) 226-2508
www.d2m.com/Tugwebsite
This charming little family-owned spot on a downtown side street is in the old tradition of cottage-style, handcrafted brewing—the kind of beer everyone used to drink and that you can only get on-site. The brewery is upstairs; downstairs is the book-lined pub, where you can curl up with a pint and spend a pleasant evening. Tugboat likes to make

powerful British-style beers, and their offerings include a fantastic Extra Special Bitter, a hoppy India Pale Ale, a medium-bodied Hop Red, and a really special cask-conditioned stout. You may also wish to try their interesting Czech bitter brewed with imported Saaz hops. This is a wonderful pub, and there's nothing else like it in the city. The owner also repairs watches—the brewery is housed in a historic watch- and clock-repair shop—in case yours has stopped.

NORTHWEST PORTLAND

*BRIDGEPORT BREWPUB
1313 Northwest Marshall St.
(503) 241-3612
www.bridgeportbrew.com

Bridgeport began in 1984 as the first microbrewery in town, producing 600 barrels per year. Now this groundbreaking, award-winning brewery produces more than 100,000 barrels each year. This picturesque brick-and-ivy brewpub is reminiscent of old German beer halls, especially the spacious upstairs, which is overflowing on the weekends. House standards such as Coho Pacific and Blue Heron are available, as well as cask-conditioned ales, which are naturally carbonated, unfiltered, and stored in kegs called firkins. Every Tues, brewers tap a firkin right on the bar for a fresh full-bodied taste direct from a gravity-fed spigot. Bridgeport offers a variety of British-style ales, including India Pale Ale, Extra Special Bitter, Black Strap Stout, and Porter conditioned in a bottle, keg, or firkin cask. The flagship ale is Blue Heron Amber Ale, brewed in honor of Portland's official city bird. Bridgeport also serves up a fine pizza, with dough made fresh daily from unfermented beer wort.

*DESCHUTES BREWERY & PUBLIC HOUSE
210 Northwest 11th Ave.
(503) 296-4906
www.deschutesbrewery.com

The Deschutes Brewery, originating in Bend, Oregon, is known for its outstanding brews such as Mirror Pond Pale Ale, Obsidian Stout, Black Butte Porter, and the newest, Armory XPA (a pale ale). In this site, Armory XPA is brewed in gorgeous copper vats made in Germany and calibrated with precision. In Portland style, the menu takes the normal pub fare up a notch, with local and organic meats and produce in the delicious burgers, pizzas, and fish and chips. Most of the food is made on site, including the cured meats, pickles, and tartar sauce. The pub is a beautiful space showcasing the virtues of salvage. The space itself was once an auto garage; the bar was carved from a single block of wood rescued from a demolished building; even the urinals, which were found abandoned in a warehouse in New York, are recycled. The interior is both spacious and cozy, with high ceilings, warm colors, and impressive carvings by J. Chester Armstrong, an Oregon artist, in the dining room. The good-natured servers will pour beer and serve you lunch or dinner from 11 a.m to midnight every day.

MACTARNAHAN'S TAPROOM
2730 Northwest 31st Ave.
(503) 228-5269
www.portlandbrew.com

This huge brewery in the Guild's Lake Industrial District at the edge of Northwest Portland shows off its 140-barrel copper brewing vessels by making them a part of its brewpub's interior design. The kettles are from the Sixenbrau Brewery, dating back to the 16th century in Bavaria. Added to this Teutonic

touch are fancy steins and a menu of seafood, schnitzel, sausage, and other grilled
meats cooked on an applewood rotisserie
and grill. A covered patio is open for dining during the winter. As for the brew, the
line includes its gold-medal winning Amber
Ale—the first amber ale in Oregon—as well
as a well-edited collection of porters, Belgian-style ales, and seasonal brews.

MCMENAMINS TAVERN & POOL
1716 Northwest 23rd Ave.
(503) 227-0929
www.mcmenamins.com
This original tavern in the chain is the only
one named after the McMenamin brothers, whose empire now stretches beyond
Oregon. It's a modest little spot a bit north
of the cultural hubbub on 21st and 23rd
Avenues. For a sense of history and a quiet
brew, check it out. Try the Crystal Ale, an
amber ale, or for a lighter taste, the Cascade
Head Ale. Don't be surprised, however, at the
leisurely service.

NEW OLD LOMPOC
1616 Northwest 23rd Ave.
(503) 225-1855
www.newoldlompoc.com
The place that started the Lompoc brewing
empire, this pub is named after a bar in a
movie with W. C. Fields and Mae West, *The
Bank Dick*. Here you will find powerful beers
brewed with great attention to balance.
There are many seasonal brews, but the year-
round varieties are also excellent. We recommend the rich Sockeye Cream Stout and
the Proletariat Red, both strong beers that
warrant total attention. But if you must be
distracted by food, the menu has satisfying
pub fare. Try them all on a sunny Saturday
afternoon on the deck.

ROGUE ALES PUBLIC HOUSE
1339 Northwest Flanders St.
(503) 222-5910
www.rogue.com
This is Rogue's Portland outpost (they are
based on the coast, in Newport), and it
has taken advantage of its good Pearl District location to offer conference rooms and
catering, as well as a Lego table (for those
really tough meetings). This pub also offers
the hard stuff, as well as its excellent beer.
The beers served here include Rogue Red,
Brutal Bitter, Buckwheat Ale, Porter, Stout,
Rogue Smoke, and Maierbock; some of these
are in pressurized kegs. They also usually
offer a cask-conditioned beer.

SOUTHEAST PORTLAND

THE BAGDAD THEATER AND PUB
3702 Southeast Hawthorne Blvd.
(503) 236-9234
www.mcmenamins.com
This is a Southeast Portland landmark and a
great place to uncoil. You can watch a first-
rate movie for a couple of bucks or sit out
on the picnic tables and survey the scene on
bustling Hawthorne Boulevard. One of the
McMenamins' five movie-house brewpubs,
the Bagdad is a Hawthorne-area favorite.
The movies are usually second-run features,
and the lighting and sound quality are very
good. The Bagdad carries the McMenamins
brews that you'd expect: the fruity Ruby Ale;
Hammerhead, a malty, hoppy, English-style
ale; the dark and stout Terminator; a light
and refreshing wheat ale; and a rich, smooth,
porter. Food choices in the pub next to the
theater include nearly a dozen pizza options
and everything from hot Thai noodles to
black bean burritos.

THE BARLEY MILL
1629 Southeast Hawthorne Blvd.
(503) 231-1492
www.mcmenamins.com
This, the granddaddy of all the McMenamins brewpubs, opened in 1983, but the Barley Mill's roots reach back to 1934 when it operated as The Scuttlebutt the year after Prohibition was repealed. It's impossible to miss the cranky old barley mill stationed near the front door. Big picture windows shed light on this groovy place with loads of Grateful Dead paraphernalia and posters. You can choose between the large wooden picnic tables (inside and outside) or the cozy bar and smaller corner booths. There is the usual selection of ales. We like the Nebraska Bitter, the Hammerhead, and the India Pale Ale. Ask the bartender about the daily special, and if you feel adventurous, try the Brewery Taster, a sampler of six different microbrews. The Barley Mill also offers a basic selection of Edgefield Wines, including chardonnay, pinot gris, Riesling, and a few others. As with most McMenamins pubs, the service can be slow, but if you want to see where it all began, bear it with your historical perspective.

BRIDGEPORT ALE HOUSE
3632 Southeast Hawthorne Blvd.
(503) 233-6540
www.bridgeportbrew.com
Bridgeport Breweries is Oregon's oldest microbrewery, and this eastside outpost is one of our favorite spots. The quality of beverages and food is consistently high, and the stylish interior—with its neutral tones and mellow woods—is friendly and welcoming. This pub offers two cask-conditioned ales as well as six regular microbrews. Their most popular brew is the award-winning India

Pale Ale, but we also love Bridgeport's flagship brew, Blue Heron Amber Ale. They also offer some very tasty seasonals, including the Summer Wheat Ale. Although there is no "happy hour" per se, on Mon the India Pale Ale is served in 20-ounce imperial pints for cheap. The Ale House serves lunch seven days a week, and signature dishes include a wood-roasted oyster sandwich, a grilled eggplant sandwich, and the fire-grilled, seasoned ground-chuck Hawthorne Burger. The hand-tossed, 10-inch pizza pies are baked to perfection and complemented with unusual toppings such as grilled zucchini, smoked chicken, and cilantro. The Bridgeport Ale House is as popular with neighborhood families as it is with everyone else; you can feel like a grown-up again, sipping your beer in this attractive pub, even if junior is busy coloring in the high chair next to you.

i You may find the urge to brew your own, if you stay in Portland long enough. For brewing supplies and expert advice, go to *F. H. Steinbart,* 234 Southeast 12th Ave. (503-232-8793; www.fhsteinbart.com), or *Let's Brew,* 9021 8235 Southeast Stark St. (503-256-0205; www.letsbrew.net), and they will help you get set up.

HEDGE HOUSE
3412 Southeast Division St.
(503) 235-2215
www.newoldlompoc.com/hedgehouse_home.html
It's worth a trip across town to spend a summer evening at Hedge House, the latest offering from the expert brewers at Old Lompoc. The pub is in a cute yellow house on Division Street with cozy indoor spaces and a pretty patio. This pleasant atmosphere

is underscored by great sandwiches, salads, and similar pub food—and of course, great beer. Our favorite brew is C-note, a wonderfully hoppy India pale ale, but when the weather is hot, few things are tastier than a cold Fool's Golden Ale. Cheap pints can be found on Tues and weekends.

*HOPWORKS URBAN BREWERY
2944 Southeast Powell Blvd.
(503) 232-4677
www.hopworksbeer.com
This busy pub brews organic, handcrafted beer and serves it in four beautiful spaces: an outdoor beer garden, an indoor family space that includes a play area, a mezzanine, and a bike-up bar. It's not just the beer that's organic. Every inch is devoted to sustainable restaurant practice, from the permeable pavers lining the beer garden to the rain barrels and composting system. But frankly, what you will notice is the excellence of the beer, which wins medals—including the 2008 World Beer Cup gold medal for its IPA and the silver for its bohemian-style lager. You can get sustainable New York–style pizza to go with it.

THE HORSE BRASS PUB
4534 Southeast Belmont St.
(503) 232-2202
www.horsebrass.com
No visit to Portland is complete without a stop at the Horse Brass for a pint of bitter and a game of darts. This gem of a place is a pub in the finest and truest sense of the word, offering plenty of atmosphere and 46 draughts of the finest microbrewed and imported beers, including Rogue YSB, the house beer for the Horse Brass Pub. Since 1976—more than a decade before most Portlanders had even heard of microbrews—the Horse Brass

Pub has been a haven for crafted ales and authentic, home-style British fare. It is a noisy, gregarious place where folks have a smashing good time at the full bar or at one of the large round tables that bring friends and strangers together. The Horse Brass has been notorious for its smoky—very smoky—atmosphere, but in January 2009, an indoor smoking ban at all Oregon bars, clubs, and restaurants went into effect. While a crisis for some Horse Brass fans, this change is welcomed by others. Your frothy pint should taste just as refreshing, and you'll be able to see the dartboard more clearly.

LUCKY LABRADOR BREWING COMPANY
915 Southeast Hawthorne Blvd.
(503) 236-3555
www.luckylab.com
The Lucky Labrador lies on the fringes of Southeast Portland's Industrial District, a sprawling, refurbished warehouse featuring tasty, handcrafted microbrews. There is ample outside seating as well, with views of the surrounding industrial-area street scenes, while indoor scenes include a large mural that is a great takeoff on Andrew Wyeth's famous painting, *Christina's World*. It's a favorite for meetings and groups. The brews are good, especially the robust Black Lab Stout, a slightly malty Konigs Kolsch, and the crispy Top Dog Extra Pale. We also like Hawthorne's Best Bitter, which is an amber-hued, dry-hopped bitter, very characteristic of an English pint. Plenty of good food is available, including deli sandwiches, Bento (Japanese-style rice with vegetables, chicken, or other toppings), and a good selection of vegetarian dishes. There are two other Lucky Lab locations, so you are never far from one: the Lucky Labrador Public

House (7675 Southwest Capitol Hwy.) and the Lucky Labrador Beer Hall (1945 Northwest Quimby).

i Most stores display beer beneath fluorescent lights and can stock only the stuff that flies off the shelves. But at *Belmont Station* (4500 Southeast Stark St., 503-232-8538; http://belmont-station.com), the storage of beer is taken much more seriously. Single bottles are displayed on shelves out front, and the stuff actually for sale is kept in a darkened walk-in that has the demeanor of a bank vault. Stored this way, the beer lasts longer and tastes better.

OAKS BOTTOM PUB
1621 Southeast Bybee Blvd.
(503) 232-1728
www.newoldlompoc.com/oaksbottom
_home.html

From the Lompoc beer empire, this friendly pub aspires to be a "third place"—a place that is not work and not home but elsewhere, and thus one that allows for genuine relaxing and conviviality. To that end, they offer a great kids' menu in addition to their excellent beers, wines, and cocktails, so that everyone can sit down to enjoy themselves. The food is carefully prepared and uses high-quality ingredients, in spite of its humble appearance. Look for the Tatchos: natchos made with tater tots. Trust us, they are great. The pulled pork sandwich is also delicious.

PHILADELPHIA'S STEAKS AND
  HOAGIES
6410 Southeast Milwaukie Ave.
(503) 239-8544
www.phillypdx.com

This is Oregon's most micro of all the micro-breweries, and not only does it serve frosty ales and stouts, but also really good cheesesteak sandwiches. They offer a variety of sandwich styles, all of which are complemented by the handcrafted beers brewed on site, up to 11 of them on tap at a time. A favorite is the ginger hefeweizen, but all of them are pretty yummy. Also available are Tastykake products—it's the only place in town you can have peanut-butter Kandy Kakes with your IPA.

NORTH & NORTHEAST PORTLAND

ALAMEDA BREWING CO.
4765 Northeast Fremont St.
(503) 460-9025
www.alamedabrewhouse.com

Look for the huge copper hop in front of the Alameda brewpub—consider it a beacon for those seeking quality, hand-crafted ales. Alameda's head brewmaster Craig Nicholls is preparing some of the finest microbrews in town, especially the Black Bear Double Stout, which aficionados are calling one of the best nitro-pours anywhere. (Nitrogen causes all those tiny little bubbles that make the "cascading effect" and gives ales that delicious creamy head.) Alameda offers nine unique regular micros along with two or three seasonals and their popular homemade root beer. With well-priced 20-ounce pints, it's a great value. The food is excellent, affordable, and far more ambitious than standard pub grub. Entrees range from whiskey baby-back ribs to artichoke linguini to smoked chicken ravioli. Sandwiches and burgers are standouts too. A children's menu is also available. The atmosphere—galvanized metal, acid-stained floor, and the white maple/stainless-steel hop-yard theme—works splendidly, as the brewery itself is located in the dining area.

CONCORDIA BREWERY
McMenamins Kennedy School
5736 Northeast 33rd Ave.
(503) 249-3983
www.mcmenamins.com
The McMenamins converted this beautiful old brick school into a wonderful neighborhood hub. The Kennedy School is an inn, a theater, a restaurant, and a brewpub—or rather, several pubs, for there are a number on-site. The Courtyard Restaurant occupies the center of the complex; the Detention Bar (which allows smoking) and the Honors Bar are on the periphery. There's also a wine bar—the Cypress Bar.

Beers include the usual McMenamin offerings, plus some guests. Much of the beer is brewed on-site. Food offerings are also standard—sandwiches, fries, salads, and other appetizery things, but with more variety in the entree department. For more information on the Kennedy School, see the Accommodations chapter.

THE LAURELWOOD
5115 Northeast Sandy Blvd.
(503) 282-0622
www.laurelwoodbrewpub.com
A friendly pub in the Hollywood neighborhood, the Laurelwood offers some of the best beer in the city. They were the first in Oregon to brew organic beers, and their attention to detail has paid off: they have won numerous awards and national attention. The Laurelwood crafts a great line of beers including an India Pale Ale, a stout, and a robust porter, along with seasonal beers. The menu is simple, with good beer food: onion rings, tacos, chicken strips, nachos, and savory parmesan-garlic fries. The Laurelwood is spacious and warm; it occupies a classic Portland building that used to house a dinner theater (its 15-barrel brew system is now on center stage). If you miss it during your stay in Portland, you can stop for a pint on your way out of town: you'll find mini-versions on Concourses A and E at the Portland International Airport.

ST. JOHNS PUB
8203 North Ivanhoe St., St. Johns
(503) 283-8520
www.mcmenamins.com
This historic building with its distinctive dome was part of the 1905 Lewis and Clark Exposition held in Northwest Portland. After the festivities commemorating the centennial of that famous journey, the structure was barged across the Multnomah Channel of the Willamette River to St. Johns, a small burg now tied to the mainland by a lovely bridge with cathedral arches. After a long history as a church, fraternal lodge, and a watering hole called Duffy's, the place was purchased by the McMenamin brothers, who turned it into a roadhouse with lots of old-time signs and enough horns on the wall to hang half the hats in the West. It has the usual drinks and menu loaded with the same tasty sandwiches and burgers found in the other historic theaters, schools, and hotels turned into emporiums of suds and grub by these omnipresent entrepreneurs. With the long elegant wood bar, wood-burning stove, and a 7-foot-tall bird of paradise standing sentinel, it is truly like stepping into a time machine. St. Johns, like most of the McMenamin brothers' brainstorms, is full of treasures, including stained-glass windows, a bizarre assortment of hanging lights, Second Empire chairs, and an old-time piano that patrons sometimes play.

i Beer aficionados in Portland still honor their patron goddess Ninkasi with a major festival: the *Oregon Brewers Festival,* held the last weekend of July. The lead-in for that festival takes place the weekend before with the *Portland International Beerfest,* devoted to the part of the brewing world that isn't Oregon. Visit www.oregonbrewfest.com or see the Festivals and Annual Events chapter for more information.

✻WIDMER BROTHERS GASTHAUS
929 North Russell St.
(503) 281-3333
www.widmer.com

The attractive Gasthaus, in an old refurbished 1890s hotel adjacent to the Widmer brewery, serves a complete menu, ranging from beer and appetizers to full dinners. There's plenty of exposed brick and wood lending character to this pub, which seats around 120. Our favorite Widmer Brothers beers include their seasonal beers, but we also thirst for their IPAs—and the special Brothers' Reserve, fleeting runs of unique, small-batch beer that are true labors of love. Widmer Brothers Brewing Company is a top-selling craft brewer in the region and produces seven original European- and Pacific Northwest–style beers. Their flagship ale is America's original Hefeweizen, a cloudy, golden-hued wheat beer that's as easy to

drink as it is to look at. Hefeweizen is bottled and kegged unfiltered and directly from the lagering tank, adding to its robust taste and unique appearance. At the Gasthaus, you'll find a few outside picnic tables, which fill up fast in the summertime. This place is popular with everyone from the Wall Street set to the shipyard workers on nearby Swan Island.

VANCOUVER

SALMON CREEK BREWERY
108 West Evergreen Blvd.
(360) 993-1827
www.salmoncreekbrewpub.com

A delightful addition to downtown Vancouver, the Salmon Creek Brewery is a friendly, upscale establishment that features a handsome bar meticulously hand-crafted from African hardwood and a ceiling of antiqued pressed tin. Salmon Creek offers 18 taps, many of them devoted to house brews, including Red Irish Ale, Golden Ale, Thunderbolt Porter, Nut Brown Ale, India Pale Ale, and the best-selling Scottish Ale. Although Salmon Creek offers almost any kind of sandwich you can think of, including a hefty and exceptionally tasty Reuben, the menu is more fine dining than pub fare, with an emphasis on traditional steaks, seafood, chicken, and pasta dishes. Outdoor patio dining is a pleasant option during summer months.

COFFEEHOUSES

On a chilly Oregon morning, nothing is more enticing than the aroma of freshly brewed coffee. According to the *Daily Beast,* Portland is the second-most caffeinated city in the US, with residents spending an average of $33 per month on americanos, macchiatos, lattes, and other coffee to go. Portlanders have a well-established tradition of hanging out in coffeehouses that predates Starbucks, so you will find all throughout the city many different kinds of coffeehouse aesthetic, from the sleek urbane to the shabby chic. And the word coffeehouse may mean anything from a small espresso bar to a café to a bakery to a combination of tavern and coffeehouse.

Below, we've listed some of the much-loved coffeehouses in the area. We also encourage you to explore for yourself to find your own favorites, because so many good coffeehouses are out there that we could never list them all. We've omitted Starbucks, since you'll find them everywhere, without even trying. You'll also find Peet's Coffee & Tea—Berkeley's riposte to Starbucks—which has made incursions into the Portland market. Peet's has always been excellent, and even if Peet's, like Starbucks, is no longer a small, local business, these Portland shops are welcome variations in the coffee landscape. But our hearts are truly with our homegrown coffee shops, and this is your guide to them.

SOUTHWEST PORTLAND

✳SPELLA
Southwest 9th Avenue & Southwest Alder
520 Southwest 5th Ave.
(503) 752-0428
http://spellacaffe.com
Spella Caffe is renowned in Portland for its authentic Italian-style espresso and coffee. The fragrant microroasts—hand-roasted by owner Andrea Spella—are sold at a coffee cart (9th and Alder) and a café (5th Avenue) by well-trained baristas who know how to draw a proper shot with an old-fashioned espresso machine. Such expertise is not uncommon in Portland, where barista is a respectable profession, but rarely are such beautiful shots pulled by people who are so friendly and unpretentious. They also make superb chai and serve possibly the best affogato (espresso poured over ice cream) in Portland. Spella Caffe is open at 9th and Alder from 9 a.m. to 4 p.m., and open from 7:30 a.m. to 4 p.m. at the 5th Avenue location.

✳STUMPTOWN COFFEE ROASTERS
128 Southwest 3rd Ave.
(503) 295-6144
http://stumptowncoffee.com
Stumptown roasts better coffee than practically anyone at their production scale, but even if they didn't, this great little cafe would be worth a visit. Part coffee shop, part tavern,

part art gallery, and part newsstand, this bright and airy space invites you to spend an entire afternoon. Periodicals are available to read and buy, and the brick walls feature new works by local artists each month. This downtown coffee shop offers a wee bit more than its eastside partners: an imaginative selection of wine and beer. It's also open a wee bit later: 7 a.m. to 9 p.m. Mon through Sat and 8 a.m. to 6 p.m. on Sun.

NORTHWEST PORTLAND

ANNA BANNANAS
1214 Northwest 21st Ave.
(503) 274-2559
A Portland classic, Anna Bannanas lives in a beautiful old Victorian house and serves strong coffee drinks to the bleary-eyed. The atmosphere is funky and unpretentious, and the crowd therefore ranges from sleepy hipsters to purpose-driven professionals. It's a comfy place to settle in and read—they have a lot of good magazines and journals lying about—while you eat one of their wonderful pastries. Check out their milk shakes too.

BACKSPACE
115 Northwest 5th Ave,
(503) 248-2900
www.backspace.bz
Backspace is a great coffeeshop that aspires to be a "third place"—a home away from home, where you can hang out, drink coffee (or beer), play pool, do some work, look at cool art, or maybe hear a show. Its Old Town location, near the MAX line, is convenient and central. But one of the biggest attractions is the networked gaming room, which provides ten terminals where you can settle in with your coffee and play solo or with friends. If you go when there's a band, you'll need to pay the cover.

i In the 1950s and 1960s, Portland's downtown coffeehouses were the incubators for bands such as Paul Revere and the Raiders and the Kingsmen—both of whom had a hit with "Louie, Louie."

✳BARISTA
539 Northwest 13th Ave.
(503) 274-1211
www.baristapdx.com
Barista was founded by award-winning barista Billy Wilson, and at this urbane shop in Northwest Portland, you can sample different roasts much the way you would sample different wines. This means that local microroasts are served alongside Stumptown, with profiles of each kind listed—because not all espressos are alike. While Barista won't tell you how to drink your coffee, the purity of coffee flavor is the focus, so you may want to save your butterscotch latte for another place and just enjoy the rich espresso pulls. They warn you not to call, but we've listed the phone number anyway. They also have a shop at 1725 Northeast Alberta St. Barista is open from 7 a.m. to 6 p.m.

✳COFFEEHOUSE NORTHWEST
1951 West Burnside St.
(503) 248-2133
www.coffeehousenorthwest.com
The star feature of this attractive space on West Burnside is the espresso. It's drawn from perfectly roasted Stumptown beans at the perfect time to grind (several days out of the roaster) and it's drawn *ristretto*-style, which means the first pulse out of the machine. This attention to quality has earned Coffeehouse Northwest loyal customers and many accolades. The location, on trafficky Burnside, is challenging, but the focus on

Close-up

Portland's Microroasters

While many of the coffeeshops listed in this chapter serve Stumptown Coffee, a growing number are starting to purchase, roast, and sell their own coffee beans. This trend in "microroasting" is no surprise in some ways: Starbucks and Peet's Coffee were once microroasters—as was (dare we say it) Stumptown. Microroasting fits in perfectly with Portland's indie, DIY business ethos, as well as its focus on the quotidian, daily pleasures that make life worth living no matter the size of your bank account. Plus it fits with the functional aesthetic that is so much a part of the character of Portland—coffee is a necessity. Why not style it up?

Here are some notable microroasters in Portland. Others are listed elsewhere in the chapter—in particular, Spella and Ristretto have led the recent microroaster renaissance. But look for more to emerge.

Cellar Door Coffee
2001 Southeast 11th Ave.
(503) 234-7155
www.cellardoorcoffee.com
This husband and wife team started, like many DIY roasters, roasting by popcorn popper and progressed to a barbecue before they took it professional.

Coava Roastery
1300 Southeast Grand Ave.
www.coavacoffee.com
One of the top new microroasters, Coava shares its sleek space on Grand Avenue with a firm that features sustainable and Oregon-based bamboo design. They offer coffee flights of their single-origin brews so that you can directly compare different varieties.

Courier Coffee Roasters
923 Southwest Oak
(503) 545-6444
www.couriercoffeeroasters.com
This meticulous and customer-friendly roaster is renowned for their bicycle deliveries throughout Portland from their roastery on Hawthorne. They have a tiny shop downtown serving their excellent coffee. Bean varietals change seasonally.

Heart
2211 East Burnside St.
(503) 206-6602
www.heartroasters.com
This ultra-modern roaster is notable for its single-origin espresso beans—yes, like wine—and its gorgeous shop near the Jupiter Hotel.

Public Domain
603 Southwest Broadway
(503) 243-6374
www.publicdomaincoffee.com
Public Domain is the high-end roastery of the largest coffee roaster in Oregon, Coffee Bean International, which supplies stores such as Target with their house-brand coffee beans. Here, though, you'll find beautifully roasted single-origin varieties and a state-of-the-art Slayer espresso.

Schondecken Roasters
6720 Southeast 16th Ave.
(503) 236-8234
Schondecken roasts and sells their coffee in a cute shop in Westmoreland, where they also sell spices, teas, and herbs. They were here when Stumptown was just a gleam in Duane Sorenson's eye, and they still roast some great coffee.

making perfect coffee has allowed them to overcome this challenge. They make amazing hot chocolate as well, and serve excellent pastries, but truly, this is a coffee geek's paradise.

KEN'S ARTISAN BAKERY
326 Northwest 21st Ave.
(503) 248-2202
www.kensartisan.com

So it's not strictly coffee, but this excellent French-style patisserie and bakery is one of the best places on the Westside to have coffee, or really one of the best places anywhere. Ken Forkish is one of the most important bakers in town, supplying many restaurants, and his pastries are outstanding—perfectly flaky and balanced but never heavy or greasy. Try to go in the morning, when they are freshest. You'll find a line, but the efficient people behind the counter will move you through quickly. The coffee is also very good, and there are many tables so you can read the paper and drink your coffee while you dissect your croissant.

KOBOS COMPANY
2355 Northwest Vaughn St.
(503) 222-2302
www.kobos.com

Kobos was a pioneer of coffee roasting, setting up retail roasting in 1973 and serving espresso beginning in 1981. This major roaster features specialty coffees, wonderful pastries, and a lot more. Teas, herbs and spices, chocolates and Torani syrups, and cooking utensils from around the world are temptingly displayed at their stores. They also sell gourmet kitchen utensils and supplies. And you can buy their delicious coffee

PEARL BAKERY
102 Northwest 9th Ave.
(503) 827-0910
www.pearlbakery.com

Set on a busy street corner, this shop has two full windows lined with counters, stools, and small tables and chairs. The open atmosphere is great for those overcast days when we need every sunbeam we can get. Coffee and espresso or a good selection of fragrant teas are just the things to accompany the exceptional sandwiches, desserts, and breakfast pastries. See the Restaurant chapter for more information.

SOUTHEAST PORTLAND

CAFÉ PALLINO
3003 Southeast Division
(503) 232-0907

Café Pallino is a beautiful Italian-modern cafe that specializes in coffee, pastries, breakfasts, and panini—and gelato. The gelato is housemade and it is as good as anything you will find in Italy. The cafe is also excellent for groups—there are white leather couches and long, long tables, all designed for maximum conversation. But there are also nice smaller tables if you want to hunker down with your laptop and finish writing your blog post for the day. Which you can do, because there's also free Wi-Fi. A good hangout spot.

COMMON GROUNDS
4321 Southeast Hawthorne Blvd.
(503) 236-4835

This coffeehouse, on the eastern side of the Hawthorne shopping district, is both a neighborhood draw and a destination point, one of the best places in the city to read and write with your latte. Graduate students, artists, and writers flock to the place. They stock a good selection of periodicals, from the *New York Review of Books* to *Wired,* and the music is always good. Common Grounds also serves wonderful food to help fire up the neurons. Great cookies, pastries, and other desserts are made right there, and the panini will keep you going.

FLOYD'S COFFEESHOP
1412 Southeast Morrison St.
(503) 230-2167
www.floydscoffeeshop.com
This bright, shiny little coffeeshop in the Buckman neighborhood serves great pastries and strong coffee with lots of friendliness. We like it not only because of the hand-pulled Stumptown shots but also because there are many outlets—one pretty much for every seat—for when your laptop battery is running low. Look for good tunes, comfortable seats for working: you can get a lot of work done here.

THE PIED COW COFFEEHOUSE
3244 Southeast Belmont St.
(503) 230-4866
The Pied Cow is in an old Victorian home that looks like a cheerfully haunted house. Inside it is decorated with brass chandeliers and big comfortable sofas and pillows. It has an inviting porch and an outside dining area that is packed all year long, since it's heated. This coffeehouse has evolved from hippie to hipster, with the addition of a popular hookah bar, which draws avant-garde smokers from all over town. It's also open late. You can bring the children, but you may be spending a lot of time explaining things.

RIMSKY KORSAKOFFEE HOUSE
707 Southeast 12th Ave.
(503) 232-2640

One of the most unique stops in the city, Rimsky Korsakoffee House offers a wide range of specialty coffees, desserts, and live classical music. Open evenings only: 7 p.m. to midnight during the week and 7 p.m. to 1 a.m. on Fri and Sat.

SOUTHEAST GRIND
1223 Southeast Powell Blvd.
(503) 473-8703
www.southeastgrind.com
The Southeast Grind is one of the very, very few coffee shops in Portland that is open 24 hours, seven days each week. This shop is important to know is not only because it is open 24 hours in a row, but it also makes free Wi-Fi available so you can put your caffeinated rush to good use on the Internet. The atmosphere is pine-lodge rustic, and they have a fireplace. They offer doughnuts, sandwiches, and other treats in addition to their coffee.

STUMPTOWN COFFEE ROASTERS
4525 Southeast Division St.
(503) 230-7702
www.stumptowncoffee.com
This first-rate roaster, with numerous shops of its own as well as a wholesale and distribution outfit, offers an outstanding product to coffee shops all over town—and now has outposts in New York and Amsterdam. We can't really call them small roasters anymore, but we still like hanging out in their cool shops. Stumptown rates high on the hangout scale. All their shops exude a sort of post-millennial, photographer-Wolfgang-Tillmans aesthetic. The service is friendly and competent. The Division shop closes about 6 p.m. most nights (unless there's an event), and the Belmont shop (3356 Southeast Belmont St., 503-232-8889) stays open later,

until 9 p.m. Both open early—6 a.m. Also see Southwest Portland. And two doors down from the Belmont shop, you can find the Stumptown Annex, where you can do a coffee tasting and compare these fairly traded, often organic varietals and roasts.

Voodoo Doughnuts

Coffee and doughnuts are a natural pair. For the best doughnuts in Portland, try **Voodoo Doughnuts,** which has made doughnuts into an actual art form. Besides the usual cakes and crullers, you'll find innovations such as the San Dimas, a doughnut with three kinds of chocolate on top—and the Arnold Palmer, one frosted with lemon and tea powder. These punk-rock alternatives to cupcakes can be found at 22 Southwest Third Ave. (503-241-4704) 24 hours every day. They are also licensed to perform legal marriages.

TINY'S
1412 Southeast 12th Ave.
(503) 236-2454
www.tinyscoffee.com
Tiny's is a cool coffeehouse at the intersection of Southeast 12th Avenue and Hawthorne Boulevard. It serves excellent coffee and VooDoo doughnuts to dunk in it, and it's the kind of old-school place where you can hang out for an hour or two. Tiny's serves delicious sandwiches and provides Internet access as well. They are open early and late—6 a.m. to 10 p.m. every day and night.

NORTH & NORTHEAST PORTLAND

ALBINA PRESS
4637 North Albina Ave.
(503) 282-5214
Albina Press is not only justly famous for their delicious coffee, but also for their barista expertise: they hire only the best, the kind that place highly in National Barista championships. The attention to the coffee combined with the capacious feeling of the space makes this an irresistible cafe for writing, reading, or just chatting for an hour or two or six.

ANNA BANNANAS
8716 North Lombard
(503) 286-2030
The North Portland outpost of this great coffeeshop offers a smoke-free environment, a lovely garden, and a play area for the children. There's also a meeting room, if you want to hold your crafting circle there. And of course, like the Northwest shop, you'll be served yummy pastries, muffins, sandwiches, and so on—not to mention coffee.

BEULAHLAND
118 Northeast 28th Ave.
(503) 235-2794
http://beulahlandpdx.com
Beulahland is an ideal hangout spot, and it serves that perfect combination, coffee and beer, so you could stay there all day and well into the night. It's a good place to hang out because of the jukebox (with its great combination of '80s pop and punk), the pool table, and the pinball machine. At night, Beulahland has live music. They also serve simple but good coffeehouse fare (soups, sandwiches), and the beer selection is unboring.

✴FRESH POT
4001 North Mississippi Ave.
(503) 284-8928
www.thefreshpot.com

Portland does not lack small, locally owned coffeehouses, but there's always room for more of a good thing. The Fresh Pot occupies the historic Rexall Drug building in this renewing neighborhood, where it serves beautifully roasted coffee from Stumptown to neighbors and visitors. The Fresh Pot also runs the coffee bar in the Hawthorne Powell's. The Fresh Pot shops offers Wi-Fi to keep you connected and award-winning baristas to keep you caffeinated.

i The Fresh Pot had a starring role as a featured location in 2007's *Feast of Love,* starring Morgan Freeman and Greg Kinnear.

✴RISTRETTO ROASTERS
3520 Northeast 42nd Ave.
(503) 284-6767
www.ristrettoroasters.com

Ristretto serves small-batch-roasted coffee for coffee purists, but even if you are not a purist, you will love this delicious coffee, attentively prepared on an old-fashioned Probat roaster. Good coffee stewards that they are, they will grind whatever kind of coffee bean you would like to try and make perfect, perfect drip coffee out of it. They also serve espresso, of course, and pastries, sandwiches, and other forms of carbohydrate. Free Wi-Fi, too. And you can buy their coffee online.

NIGHTLIFE

There is a kind of seasonal rhythm to nightlife in Portland. In the summer, when it stays light well into the evening, we spend our evenings outdoors—sitting in brewpub gardens, enjoying concerts at the Oregon Zoo or in the park, walking or biking along the Eastbank Esplanade, celebrating the festival du jour at Waterfront Park, or watching the sun slip along the Columbia River and below the horizon. In the winter, we get through the rainy months by amusing ourselves indoors—perhaps we go to dinner and a show. Perhaps we go to Powell's. Perhaps we just go bowling.

Whatever the season, Portland's nightlife is rich and varied. In this chapter, we cover fun for grown-ups: music, bars, dancing. Portland's scene is impossible to pigeonhole—we are not, for example, readily associated with a particular kind of music—but one thing is certain. We love parties. We love First Thursday and Last Thursday (see our Arts chapter); we love our many Waterfront Park festivals; we love those concerts at the zoo. We have a lot to celebrate.

You'll find nighttime things to do all over town, in every neighborhood—though, ironically, the heart of downtown has less street life and more cultural events in the evening. Throughout the area, however, you'll find clusters of people sitting at outside tables, happy and convivial, yet also behaving in a pretty civilized way. Look for beacons of nightlife along Southeast Division, Hawthorne, and Belmont; along North Mississippi and Northeast Broadway; along Northwest 23rd and 21st Avenues; and all throughout the Pearl District.

OVERVIEW

The restaurants, brewpubs, and coffeeshops mentioned in their respective chapters are excellent sources of entertainment, as are the events and happenings listed in the Festivals and the Arts chapters. Good sources of information on who's playing where are the local rags: the *Portland Mercury; Willamette Week;* the *Oregonian's* Arts and Entertainment section, which is published on Friday; and *Portland Monthly's* calendar (see our Media chapter). These papers will also tell you who is reading at Powell's, what's at the Portland Center Stage, and what's going on at Waterfront Park. Below are more ideas for when you are in the mood to go out. Be prepared to pay cover charges for live and house music.

NIGHTCLUBS, DANCING & LIVE MUSIC
Southwest Portland

BERBATI'S PAN
231 Southwest Ankeny St.
(503) 248-4579
www.berbatis.com

Berbati's features a variety of music shows, many new artists as well as old favorites. It's an intimate venue with great sound and therefore a good dance floor. When they are not presenting your beloved eighties punk band, they might be showing an avant garde film or the sporting contest of the day on their huge screen. Berbati's also serves stiff drinks and reasonable Greek food. Pool tables are available too.

CRYSTAL BALLROOM
1332 West Burnside St.
(503) 225-0047
www.danceonair.com
The Crystal Ballroom is a renovated dance hall with a floating floor on ball bearings and rockers. Back when it opened in 1914 as the Cotillion Hall, Portlanders could be arrested for dancing the tango. Since then it's witnessed the likes of Rudolph Valentino, Ike and Tina Turner, Jimi Hendrix, Marvin Gaye, the Family Dog, and the Grateful Dead. The dance hall closed in 1968 and sat empty for 30 years until the McMenamins tackled a major rehabilitation. Now Portlanders are once again enjoying this gracious space with its high-arched windows, curving balcony, rococo paintings, and, above all, that dance floor with a capacity for 1,500. Live bands play throughout the week, and Sunday brings ballroom dance lessons to the public. The dress code ranges from jeans and T-shirt to black cocktail dress or three-piece suit. There are a couple of bars serving microbrews and mixed drinks.

✳DANTE'S
1 Southwest 3rd Ave.
(503) 226-6630
www.danteslive.com

Dante's is one of the hottest scenes in downtown Portland—literally. Not only does it have a fiery oil drum to give the place a purgatorial glow, it also attracts a wildly diverse crowd. Could it be the exotic dancers? The expertly mixed cocktails? No—it's the great shows, from the American-Idol fantasists on Monday's karaoke night to the "Sinferno" cabaret show on Sunday nights. Other nights are equally spectacular, in the sense of providing spectacle, including tattooed dancing girls and other risqué entertainment. Dante's is open Mon through Fri from 11 a.m. to 2 a.m., and on Sat and Sun from 7 p.m. to 2 a.m.

✳FEZ BALLROOM
316 Southwest 11th Ave.
(503) 221-7262
www.fezballroom.com
The Fez Ballroom is a great dance venue that features both house music and live—and it's really about the dancing, as opposed to the other interesting things that could happen in a nightclub. Friday nights feature an eighties-themed party called "Shut Up and Dance," but any night of the week could bring you out on the dance floor.

Northwest Portland

✳EMBERS
110 Northwest Broadway
(503) 222-3082
Embers is a gay dance club that practices tolerance by letting anyone in. With its three stages, it's a great place for dancing, and the music is a fun blend of retro, dance-party, and Top 40. Drag shows are a reliable feature of any night at the Embers. The bar alone is worth a visit.

When you want an old-fashioned cocktail, visit the Marble Bar at the Heathman Hotel to drink in the glamour of an earlier era. Wilf's, at Union Station, serves nightcaps with vintage charm. And the *Space Room* (4800 Southeast Hawthorne) is perfect when you're feeling more George Jetson than Cary Grant.

ROSELAND THEATRE
8 Northwest 6th Ave.
(503) 224-2038
www.roselandpdx.com/roseland-theater

Housed in an old church, the Roseland Theatre is a somewhat chaotic all-ages concert pavilion with a bar and roomy balcony upstairs for those over 21. This is a popular venue that features national acts as well as local music. It fits about 1400 people at a time—standing up; there are only a few seats, and they are in the bar—but sometimes the security makes it seem like there are three times that many. Still, the Roseland has great sound and good stage visibility. Expect to see anyone from Bob Dylan to Bad Religion to Sara Bareilles.

TIGER BAR
317 Northwest Broadway
(503) 222-7297

With minimal signage and a mysterious front door, Tiger Bar has the outward appearance of a private club. Inside it's an after-work, happening scene. For no cover charge you can join the artists, Bohemians, advertising execs, and other Pearl District habitués who come here to chat, sip an exotic cocktail like vodka-fueled Liquid Love or Damianas, and nibble on tiger prawns, pad Thai noodles, and other pan-Asian treats, all against the backdrop of a wall of electronic sound.

VAULT
226 Northwest 12th Ave.
(503) 224-4909
www.vault-martini.com

Signature habanero martinis and other frosty concoctions keep the well-clad patrons of this Pearl District hangout returning. Vault has millions of martinis (okay, 44) to choose from, as well as a long list of other cocktails. The ambience is upscale modern, with the work of local artists festooning the walls, a fireplace, and an 18-foot glass bar. It's also fun for parties—but make sure to arrange them in advance.

Portland has some fantastic deejays, but a couple of our favorites are DJ Anjali and the Incredible Kid, who brought Bollywood to the dance floors of Portland even before *Slum Dog Millionaire*. You can see where they're spinning by checking out their website: www.anjaliandthekid.com.

Southeast Portland

✳ALADDIN THEATER
3017 Southeast Milwaukie Ave.
(503) 234-9694
www.aladdin-theater.com

We love the Aladdin Theater—it presents great national, international, and occasionally local acts in a theater with about 600 seats, with great sound and sightlines. It feels quite intimate, and the performers seem to like it as much as the fans. The lineup is eclectic, and superb. Expect to see outstanding acoustic performers such as Richard Thompson and Norah Jones as well as more rocking artists such as Sleater-Kinney or the Psychedelic Furs. Once infamous for its record-breaking extended showing of the X-rated film *Deep Throat*, the Aladdin

Theater is now famous for blurring the edges between musical genres and booking some huge and widely respected talent. Advance tickets are available daily at the box office out front from 11 a.m. to 6 p.m. and just before the show, as well as through Ticketmaster.

BAR OF THE GODS
4801 Southeast Hawthorne Blvd.
(503) 232-2037
A unique selection of reasonably priced but heavenly tasting microbrews, free pool, and an outdoor patio await you at Bar of the Gods, on the eastern end of Hawthorne Boulevard. Drinks are generous. Booths are cozy. The happy hour is long. On some evenings they show films beneath hanging bunches of plastic grapes.

BLUE MONK
3341 Southeast Belmont St.
(503) 595-0575
www.thebluemonk.com
The Blue Monk started out as a jazz venue but has now expanded into related genres—including swing dancing and belly dancing. Hey, as the Duke said, if it sounds good, it is good. The Blue Monk has a good happy hour, good free pool, and a good cheap cover as well. Upstairs is a fetching contemporary room with an open kitchen, where cooks are busy preparing spaghetti, shrimp scampi, and other mostly Italian dishes. Downstairs, Portland's finest musicians are jamming.

CRUSH
1412 Southeast Morrison St.
(503) 235-8150
http://crushbar.com
This fun club draws Portland's most stylish with its brilliant rooms, great drinks, grooving DJs, and clever events. The lounge features comfortable couches and a wonderful chandelier made of liquor bottles, while the Blue Room is dedicated to a hopping dance floor. Crush is an equal-opportunity employer of go-go dancers, as well, so have fun watching.

⁕DOUG FIR
830 East Burnside St.
(503) 231-9663
www.dougfirlounge.com
The Doug Fir looks like a mountain lodge that has been given a makeover by Danish modernists, and one reason it is popular is that the soft, indirect lighting makes everyone look as if they ought to be carded. The food is really good, and while some might claim that going to the Doug Fir for the food is like reading Playboy for the interviews, they might actually be telling the truth. But the big draw is the club, which is downstairs. This space features some great bands from all over, and it's a great space to see them. It was designed and built specifically to showcase live music, with a fantastic sound system and stage. The Doug Fir is open seven nights. It's right by the Jupiter Hotel (see the Accommodations chapter), which has obvious benefits.

⁕HOLOCENE
1001 Southeast Morrison St.
(503) 239-7639
www.holocene.org
Holocene is dedicated to the avant-garde of the Portland art and music scene, with an uber-modern interior, two large rooms, and a huge bar. Excellent dancing can be had here, as well as similar music experiences—secret shows by famous artists, up-and-coming bands that will be famous shortly, and other attractions keep hipsters crowding the place. The pours are generous.

*PRESS CLUB
2621 Southeast Clinton St.
(503) 233-5656
www.myspace.com/thepressclub
Along with its dinner menu and wine list, the Press Club serves up expertly prepared live and DJ'd music from local greats and beyond. The Press Club is small and intimate but feels wonderfully spacious, a combination that allows the musicians and the audience to bond. For more information see the listing in the Restaurants chapter. A crowd favorite is Swing Papillon, which plays sweet, sweet Gypsy jazz on Wednesday nights. Hear them if you can.

PRODUCE ROW CAFÉ
204 Southeast Oak St.
(503) 232-8355
www.producerowcafe.com
For a long time, the Produce Row Café was a little lonely, serving up beer and playing great tunes in the inner Southeast industrial district. But now it looks like a pioneer, since this area is the leading edge of the culinary scene (see Olympic Provisions and Clarklewis in the Restaurants chapter). Produce Row has been refurbished into a handsome bar and the deck has been refreshed, but it still offers an excellent selection of beer and ales, good pub food, genuine friendly service, and a variety of live music offerings ranging from jazz to bluegrass to folk. The vibe is very low-key and friendly, with lots of great local bands.

SAPPHIRE HOTEL
5008 Southeast Hawthorne Blvd.
(503) 232-6333
www.thesapphirehotel.com
The Sapphire Hotel is a seductive little spot at the very eastern end of Hawthorne Boulevard—good for a date, since there are some plush chairs and sofas, where you can sip well-constructed cocktails and gaze into one another's eyes. There are multiple happy hours at various times of the day, as well as quite good appetizers. They have an especially thoughtful antipasti plate. This place has a romantic soul, but it has a practical side too, and if you have too many cocktails, they'll reach into the common fund and buy you a cab ride home.

North & Northeast Portland

BIDDY MCGRAW'S IRISH PUB
6000 Northeast Glisan St.
(503) 233-1178
www.biddymcgraws.com
This place is an unkitschy, unpretentious Irish bar with a great community feel. Biddy's offers more than creamy Guinness: it also serves up some of the best Irish food in the city, complemented with about 20 imports, microbrews, and hard liquor. Most evenings Biddy's offers live and authentic Irish music.

LAURELTHIRST PUBLIC HOUSE
2958 Northeast Glisan St.
(503) 232-1504
Laurelthirst is a fine Portland neighborhood pub with a talented and creative kitchen, a variety of microbrews, and a good wine selection. It's popular for brunch, and they are deft with vegan food. They also draw some of Portland's most sought-after musicians as well as emerging talent. The pub itself has great atmosphere: Brick walls and plenty of rough-hewn wood lend it character, and the postage stamp–size stage makes the music experience intimate.

✷MISSISSIPPI STUDIOS
3939 North Mississippi Ave.
(503) 753-4473
www.mississippistudios.com
Part recording studio, part concert venue, Mississippi Studios attracts artists from all over to their excellent space. Here, musicians such as Kristin Hersh, Rickie Lee Jones, John Gorka, and Freedy Johnston have all recorded or performed or both. It's a great place to see a show, with a beautiful outdoor garden, bistro, and bar adjacent (called Mississippi Station).

WHITE EAGLE SALOON
836 North Russell St.
(503) 282-6810
www.mcmenamins.com
The White Eagle Saloon—which is now one of the McMenamin brothers' taverns—is indeed a raucous joint when the sun goes down, when people come to dance their blues away. The old brick building is narrow and long, so when you go inside the place, it seems like you're in an elongated basement except for the high ceiling. The crowded feeling can be claustrophobic, but that same closeness makes the enthusiasm more contagious when the bands turn up the heat. Plus, it helps protect you against the ghosts that are thought to roam the well-storied building, which at one point was a stop on the "Shanghai tunnel network."

i The *Shanghai Tunnel,* 211 Southwest Ankeny St., takes its name from Portland's legendary 19th-century practice of "Shanghai-ing" unsuspecting bumpkins through tunnels that ran under the city. A friendly stranger would buy many drinks for a naive fellow, and the next thing the imbiber knew, he was far at sea with a big hangover and a stint as a forced laborer.

POOL

RIALTO POOLROOM, BAR & CAFE
529 Southwest 4th Ave.
(503) 228-7605
http://rialtopoolroom.com
Minnesota Fats may have felt at home in this downtown pool hall with its 15 full-size Brunswick tables, full bar, sumptuous menu, and downstairs off-track betting. In fact, a photo of Jackie Gleason portraying the legendary stickman in *The Hustler* is prominently displayed in the bar. Open every day of the year, the Rialto offers a rack of balls and a long stretch of green by the hour, with daily specials—and not just on the food and drink.

SAM'S HOLLYWOOD BILLIARDS
1845 Northeast 41st Ave.
(503) 282-8266
Sam's has 13 gorgeous 8-foot pool tables and quality pool cues to match. The bar offers a dozen microbrews, and the kitchen prepares a variety of reasonably priced sandwiches and fried foods. We like Sam's because this neighborhood joint is friendly and steady, an excellent atmosphere in which to practice your bank shots.

TOUCHÉ
1425 Northwest Glisan St.
(503) 221-1150
www.touchepdx.com
Touché has a beautiful and competent restaurant downstairs and a fun, smaller pool room upstairs. It's popular, so you will probably wait for a table, but the friendly bartenders will keep you happy as you do.

UPTOWN BILLIARDS CLUB
120 Northwest 23rd Ave.
(503) 226-6909
www.uptownbilliards.com

This is a great pool room with a mellow vibe during the week, and a hopping one on weekends. In addition to its cocktails, Uptown has a great wine selection—plus an excellent happy hour Tues through Sat (which are the days it is open). In addition to the tables, you can play darts and sometimes they will set up the Ping-Pong table for you.

CABARET & COMEDY

COMEDYSPORTZ
1963 Northwest Kearney St.
(503) 236-8888
www.portlandcomedy.com
Comedysportz is an improv club—its schtick is to have comedic teams, a referee, and audience participation to create the evening's entertainment. The audience chooses the "winners." Jokes must be clean, so you can take the kids, and the high audience participation rate makes it fun for groups. They also offer classes and workshops, so you can work on bringing out your inner Zach Galifianakis.

DARCELLE XV
208 Northwest 3rd Ave.
(503) 222-5338
www.darcellexv.com
Darcelle is a classic Portland female impersonator who puts on a fun Las Vegas–style cabaret revue Wed through Sat. On Fri and Sat, Men of Paradise, a Chippendale-style male strip show, takes over at midnight. Unsurprisingly, Darcelle XV is a big favorite with bachelorette parties, but if you want to bring yours, be sure to call ahead to reserve a seat.

HARVEY'S COMEDY CLUB
436 Northwest 6th Ave.
(503) 241-0338
www.harveyscomedyclub.com
This is the longest-running comedy club in Portland. Locals sharpening their act, as well as well-known stand-up comics on national tours, crack up audiences with witty banter. Harvey's has no drink minimums and no purchase required other than tickets to the show.

SHOPPING

No sales tax in Oregon. What else do you need to know? All right, we'll tell you more. Portland is a great town for shopping. Here you will not only find the usual suspects—Gap, Pottery Barn, Banana Republic, and so on—but many interesting, chic, and independent shops. Portland's shopping is organized around its neighborhoods, and some of these neighborhoods have evolved into destination shopping districts; these composites of retail, business, and living spaces have blended in such a way as to create local shops that reflect and sustain the neighborhoods they inhabit. And Portland also has other unusual shopping opportunities. Portland Saturday Market, which takes place every weekend under the Burnside Bridge, proffers some of the most engrossing shopping in town; it's a carnival of commerce from Feb through Dec. For more information see the Festivals and Annual Events chapter or phone (503) 222-6072. Also see that chapter for information on the area's fine farmers' markets.

We begin with an overview of the major shopping districts. Then we break the chapter into many categories, with shops listed alphabetically. (Since many shops have more than one location, we have deviated from organizing them by geography.) Here you'll find sections on Antiques, Books and Periodicals, Clothing, Food, Home Decor, Shoes, and ever so much more.

SHOPPING DISTRICTS

The soul of Portland shopping can be found in its shopping districts. Because the city organizes itself around its neighborhoods, the shopping and business districts play a vital role in creating neighborhood identity and atmosphere. It is possible to find neighborhood shopping so compelling and comprehensive that you won't want to leave your own turf. But that would be a mistake, because the variety of shopping districts gives insight into the character of Portland.

Shopping districts are clustered throughout the city, and we list some of our favorites here—they are all worth prospecting. The retail environment is dynamic and changes a lot, but these districts always have

great shopping. National chains are found in the malls, downtown, and in Northwest Portland; in most of the neighborhoods listed here, you will find primarily independent shops. We encourage you to stroll whatever neighborhood you're in—unless you do a little fieldwork on your own, who knows what fine harvests are in store?

Southwest Portland

Downtown

Department stores, fashionable boutiques, emerging indpendent stores, and Pioneer Place, a pedestrian mall, are the highlights of downtown shopping. Southwest Broadway, Southwest Morrison between 3rd and 10th, and Southwest 10th between Burnside and Yamhill have some excellent shops, including new clothing boutiques established by local designers attracted to the downtown area.

PIONEER PLACE
Southwest Morrison Street, between 5th Avenue and 3rd Avenue
(503) 228-5800
Pioneer Place is a covered mall downtown, with more than 80 different stores. A huge atrium fills the building with light on even the darkest day and is frequently decorated with amazing hanging creations and designs reflecting the seasons. While shoppers are protected from the rain, Pioneer Place reminds them that they are still in Oregon with a series of fountains and tiny waterfalls that evoke the natural landscape. In the atrium, a fountain surrounded by flowers and plants draws children and their parents, who are praying that the little ones won't tumble in as they wish on their pennies. In the food court, a whole series of waterways provides soothing white noise for diners engrossed in conversation. Here, you'll find retail chains such as the Gap and Forever 21, as well as luxury retailers like Louis Vuitton, Coach, and Tiffany.

Multnomah Village
Multnomah really does feel like a village—it is a tight-knit community in addition to its identity as a retail, coffee-shop, and hang-out mecca. Adding to the cohesive feel are the wonderful **Multnomah Arts Center,** 7688 Capitol Hwy., a popular Portland Arts and Recreation facility. You will find wonderful book stores, gift shops, housewares, and an excellent yarn shop, among other things.

Northwest Portland

Northwest 23rd District
This upscale, neighborhood includes a number of shops on 21st, but is known to Portlanders simply as Northwest 23rd. Filled with lovely Victorian homes and countless trees, this neighborhood is one of the prettier balances of the domestic and commercial in Portland, and it's a great walking neighborhood—the pedestrian traffic here is at times so uppity that it stops the automotive traffic. The foot traffic has created a democracy of fashion: The pierced hipsters sipping martinis at the Gypsy coexist comfortably with the bourgeois denizens dining at Wildwood, and that's because there is something for everyone. In addition to locally owned dress shops and high-end housewares, you'll find chains such as the Gap, Urban Outfitters, and Pottery Barn.

i Many downtown merchants will validate your Smart Park parking slips if you spend $25 or more at their shops. It never hurts to ask.

Pearl District
Colonized by starving artists, then domesticated by hipsters, the Pearl District is now becoming the home of the haute bourgeoisie. Evidence of all three classes is readily apparent in the Soho of Portland. Not only are there dozens of art galleries (and a gallery walk the first Thurs night of each month) and an art school (the Pacific Northwest College of Art, 1241 Northwest Johnson), but the housewares, art supplies, furniture, clothing, hardware, and even light fixtures for sale in the area have a distinctly aesthetic quality to them. Powell's is here, as are chains such as Anthropologie, Lululemon, adidas, and Lucy.

Southeast Portland

Hawthorne District

A local favorite, the busy Hawthorne District is Portland's left-coast hip shopping area, where granola meets granita. On the western end of Hawthorne, you'll find some great vintage shops, as well as yarn and fabric stores. On the bustling eastern end, you'll find excellent gift shops, some of the best clothing and shoe boutiques in town, great housewares, and a plethora of music shops. **Powell's** on Hawthorne, 3723 Southeast Hawthorne, and **Powell's Books for Cooks,** 3747 Southeast Hawthorne, are the eastside siblings of the City of Books, and these are smaller and less overwhelming but still feature a fantastic selection and major literary events. Hawthorne is the earthier alternative to the slick Northwest 23rd: You're more likely to get a whiff of patchouli than Chanel No. 5, although the **Perfume House,** 3328 Southeast Hawthorne, can supply either one.

LoBu

On the east side of the Willamette River, Lower Burnside, or "LoBu," has a number of terrific restaurants and shops. This district is transforming before our very eyes, and new shops are opening all the time. Look for good vintage shops—including the remarkable Hippo Hardware (see the listing below)—and design-focused businesses.

Sellwood District

Sellwood, one of Portland's most distinctive and historic neighborhoods, is brimming with charming antiques stores, particularly in the area along Southeast 13th Avenue, which is known as Antique Row. Because the shopping area is so condensed, you can park your car and then get around on foot. Laced in between the dozen blocks of antiques and collectibles stores, you'll find numerous delightful espresso shops and cafes.

Many shopkeepers hang signs on their buildings explaining their original use and date of construction, but our sources say that Sellwood has been known as Portland's antiques source since the 1950s.

North & Northeast Portland

Alberta Street

Northeast Alberta Street is a festive district that has been the focus of much redevelopment over the years.community banks, city government, and neighborhood groups have converged to make this area one of the most vital places in the city. This gentrification is not without controversy, and not every citizen thinks that opening a new Starbucks counts as progress. The source of this renaissance is the distinctive homegrown businesses, ranging from restaurants and art galleries to clothing designers and gift shops, most of which are clustered along Alberta Street between Martin Luther King, Jr. Boulevard and Northeast 33rd Avenue. This is some of the best shopping in town.

Broadway District

Northeast Broadway is a lively east-west stretch of shops, cafes, and offices; its bike-and-foot-friendly design has helped to make it one of the most enjoyable shopping districts in the city. The anchor of all this glittery commerce is the **Lloyd Center,** Oregon's first indoor mall.

North Mississippi

This charming street has some of the best new shops in town, selling everything from gourmet salts to locally designed dresses and beautifully styled vintage shops. There are great restaurants and coffee shops as well, to sustain you during your hunt.

Where Are the Malls?

Sometimes only a big shopping mall will do. The following are the major shopping malls in the area.

Southeast Portland

Clackamas Town Center
12000 Southeast 82nd Ave.
(503) 653-6913

Mall 205
9900 Southeast Washington St.
(503) 255-5805

North & Northeast Portland

Jantzen Beach Shopping Center
I-5 at exit 308, Hayden Island
(503) 247-1327

Lloyd Center
2201 Lloyd Center
(503) 282-2511

Vancouver

Westfield Shoppingtown–Vancouver
8700 Northeast Vancouver Mall Dr. (on Washington SR 500, between I-205 and I-5)
(360) 892-6255

Outlying Areas

Bridgeport Village
7455 Lower Boones Ferry Rd., Tigard
(exit 290, I-5)
(503) 968-8940

Columbia Gorge Factory Stores
450 Northwest 257th Ave., Troutdale
(503) 669-8060

Washington Square and Square Too
SR 217 at Southwest Greenburg Rd., Tigard
(503) 639-8860

Woodburn Company Stores
1001 Arney Rd., Woodburn
(exit 271, I-5)
(888) 664-SHOP

ANTIQUES

Portland is the home of many, many antiques stores. Here is a sampling of them.

CLASSIC HOME & ANTIQUE
1805 Southeast Martin Luther King Jr. Blvd.
(503) 231-8689
www.classicantique.com
Fine antiques from Europe and the United States, in addition to locally designed contemporary furniture and well-made reproductions, make this outpost a destination for citywide shoppers. Lighting and decor items are also good buys here.

✳HOLLYWOOD ANTIQUE SHOWCASE
1969 Northeast 42nd Ave.
(503) 288-1051
http://hollywoodantiquemall.com
This fine collection of dealers has an excellent variety of furniture, art, collectibles, and

tableware. In particular, the variety of furniture is outstanding and of high quality—but much of it is also very affordable. Different dealers have different strengths, but you can usually find beautiful French antiques as well as mid-century modern. The owners are very smart and helpful.

LOUNGE LIZARD
1310 Southeast Hawthorne Blvd.
(503) 232-7575
www.loungelizard.com
Filled with retro furniture and home decor accessories, Lounge Lizard is just the spot for the newly antique. They aim to please— the prices are affordable and the service is friendly. Plus, they have a large selection of great, basic vintage furniture, as well as odd but wonderful other pieces. The lighting selection is excellent. If you never before thought of putting Eames knockoffs in your 1908 Craftsman, you might start thinking about it now.

THE SELLWOOD ANTIQUE MALL
7875 Southeast 13th Ave.
(503) 232-3755
www.sellwoodantiquemall.com
The Sellwood Antique Mall is perfect for either the serious or frivolous collector. It has more than 100 different dealers, so the inventory changes constantly. The mall is one of the largest of its kind in the city, carrying a wide range of items from furniture to dishes to lighting fixtures. It also carries nostalgia items from the 1950s.

✳STARS
7030 Southeast Milwaukie Ave.
(503) 235-5990
http://starsantique.com

Two hundred dealers of antique and collectible furniture, linens, books, clothes, jewelry, dishes, and tchotchkes are here for the perusal of the antiques hunter. Because there are so many different dealers, the Stars empire cannot be comprehensively characterized, but you're more likely to find a country primitive sideboard than a federal one, although you never know. The managers are very good about display—this is one of the most attractive antiques malls around.

BARGAIN & THRIFT STORES

Did we mention there is no sales tax in Oregon? We recycle everything in Portland. For more savings, check out the stores below.

CITY LIQUIDATORS
823 Southeast 3rd Ave.
(503) 238-1367
City Liquidators is a bargain-hunters' delight, packed to the rafters with low-priced stuff. Some of the hardware and tools are priced very low, as are carpets, planters, small pieces of furniture, and kitchen gadgets. The second floor is the furniture warehouse, and some of it is quite decent. We've seen many low prices on couches, armchairs, dining room and bedroom sets, futons, patio furniture, and much more. From pots and pans to entertainment centers and bookcases, City Liquidators offers everything you need to cheaply furnish a home or apartment. They also have a good selection of office furniture, equipment, and supplies. And they also have much that is just odd. The last time we were there, we overheard a man say to his father, "Do you see anything you can't live without?" "Or live with?" was the answer.

COLUMBIA SPORTSWEAR OUTLET STORE
1323 Southeast Tacoma St., Sellwood
(503) 238-0118
It is worth the drive to Sellwood or Lake Oswego (3 Monroe Pkwy., 503-636-6593) to pick up that parka, rain hat, or down vest you've been eyeing at the downtown store for 30 to 50 percent off the price. This nationally distributed sportswear line is Oregon's own; they supply L.L. Bean and other companies in addition to distributing their own gear. Their handsome flagship retail store can be found at 911 Southwest Broadway, downtown.

GOODWILL STORE
1943 Southeast 6th Ave.
(503) 238-6165
Goodwill in Portland is something of a phenomenon, a business model for all the other Goodwills in the nation because it is so successful. It became successful because it is clean and bright, with inventive advertising and a cheerful atmosphere. The selection of men's, women's, and children's clothes is extensive and reasonably priced. You won't waste time weeding out stained shirts and zipperless pants either. The books section is remarkably free of culls and very well organized. The turnover in just one day is fast. Besides clothes and books, there are plenty of domestic items—dishes, fabrics, odds and ends, wall decorations—and a music section with a ton of LPs. Prices are, however, climbing. You will no longer find Coach bags for $4 or vintage pottery for 99 cents. Bargains can be found, but you will have lots of competition, because everyone shops at Goodwill. Goodwill stores are found throughout the city and more are opening every day. Check out the downtown store at 838 Southwest 10th Ave. for the crème de la crème of fashion recycling.

HANNA ANDERSSON OUTLET STORE
7 Monroe Pkwy., Lake Oswego
(503) 697-1953
The long johns, dresses, tights, clogs, and sportswear you and your children have come to know and love are here offered at a reduced price. Hanna Andersson is known for its high-quality, Swedish-style soft clothing in wonderful colors and patterns. (See the following Clothing section and the Kidstuff chapter for more information.)

NORDSTROM RACK
245 Southwest Morrison St.
(503) 299-1815
Every savvy Portlander knows about "the Rack." This is the closest Portland comes to Filene's Basement, and while you probably won't see anyone disrobing in the aisles, there is no lack of competitive shopping. This store is filled with clearance merchandise from Nordstrom stores plus additional items made specifically for the store. You'll find men's and women's clothing and shoes, as well as a changing assortment of accessories, picture frames, and perfumes. Prices can be as much as 70 percent below the full retail price. Additional locatins are at 8930 Southeast Sunnyside Rd., Clackamas (503-654-5415) and in Tanasbourne at 18100 Northwest Evergreen Pkwy. (503-439-0900).

NORM THOMPSON OUTLET STORE
Oregon Mail Order Outlet Store
9 Monroe Pkwy., Lake Oswego
(503) 697-2931
Next to the Columbia Sportswear Outlet Store, these stores are worth the extra effort to find. The Mail Order Outlet Store is a Norm

Thompson spin-off, with an eclectic mix of clothes, accessories, gadgets, household goods, cleaning solutions, cookware, outdoor clothes, and other things from Norm's lesser-known catalogs, Early Winters and Solutions.

PENDLETON WOOLEN MILL OUTLET STORE
2 Pendleton Way, Washougal, WA
(360) 835-1118
www.pendleton-usa.com

This woolen mill, founded in 1912 and the leading producer of the Pendleton line of woolen clothing, is one of the most popular walking tours of the Portland-Vancouver area. The Washougal site offers the largest of the Pendleton Mill outlet stores and features great savings on new apparel, closeouts, and factory seconds. The tours, offered weekdays, afford an opportunity to see the looming of their extraordinary line of woolen blankets, which are collectibles and still sold in trading huts in the southwestern corner of the United States.

BOOKS & PERIODICALS

Portland is a city of readers. We have the largest bookstore in the nation, Powell's City of Books, which is made even larger by the fact that it has a number of branches. However, Powell's can sometimes overshadow the other fine independent bookstores in the area, including interesting book selections at places like the Oregon Historical Society, Portland State University, or the Audubon Society of Portland. We also have the usual national chain bookstores here in town.

*ANNIE BLOOM'S BOOKS
7834 Southwest Capitol Hwy.
(503) 246-0053
www.annieblooms.com

Tucked into the retail center of the Multnomah neighborhood, this store attracts loyal readers from throughout the area who appreciate the selection, the suggestions, and assistance of the well-read staff, as well as the cozy armchairs. The store is also well known beyond Portland proper for its Children's Corner, with books and a play area, and for its collection of titles on Judaism and Judaic culture and art. Annie Bloom's is frequently mentioned as a contender for Portland's favorite bookstore.

*BROADWAY BOOKS
1714 Northeast Broadway
(503) 284-1726
www.broadwaybooks.net

This charming shop in the Lloyd District has a thoughtful collection of diverse literaria. In addition to stocking a good selection of literary works, it sponsors poetry readings and author book-signing events. The owners and their employees are friendly, knowledgeable, and articulate, and the well-chosen selection here reflects their expertise; they have crafted one of the best bookstores in town.

CAMERON'S BOOKS AND MAGAZINES
336 Southwest 3rd Ave.
(503) 228-2391
www.cameronsbooks.com

Before there was Powell's—before there was any other bookstore in Portland—there was Cameron's. Tucked into a downtown storefront, Cameron's features windows filled with well-cared-for copies of *Life, Time, Look, Saturday Evening Post, Colliers,* and other publications from the era of the general-interest magazine. They also have back issues of *Sports Illustrated* and *Playboy* as well as a massive collection of comic books. Cameron's claims to have 100,000 magazines, mass-market paperbacks, and comics in stock and to be the home of the birthday magazine gift.

DAEDALUS BOOKS
2074 Northwest Flanders St.
(503) 274-7742
www.abebooks.com/home/daedalus
Daedalus Books carries many kinds of books, but they specialize in the scholarly ones that are harder to find in other bookstores. For example, their philosophy inventory goes far beyond *Zen and the Art of Motorcycle Maintenance*. They are an exceptional resource for history and literature, as well as classics and linguistics. They carry both new and used books, and there is nothing quite like Daedalus in town.

IN OTHER WORDS
8 Northeast Killingsworth St.
(503) 232-6003
www.inotherwords.org
Once inside this cheerful, cozy outlet for women's books and resources, you'll find a bounty of magazines, videos, cards, gifts, and new and used books. Open seven days a week, the store also sponsors readings and workshops.

LAUGHING HORSE BOOKS
12 Northeast 10th Ave.
(503) 236-2893
This unabashedly progressive and vibrant bookstore advertises itself as a resource for social change. Inside are new and used books devoted to political issues, a bulletin board listing meetings and workshops held by local political action groups, and a gathering space where poets and authors read from their works and actors perform.

LONGFELLOW'S BOOKS AND MUSIC
1401 Southeast Division St.
(503) 239-5222
www.longfellowspdx.com
Longfellow's is a much-accoladed family-run store near the Ladd's Addition neighborhood of Portland—and a desitnation for its many fans, who regularly cite this friendly shop as their favorite. Their specialties include rare books and magazines, but there is a robust general reading section as well. They're open Mon through Sat from 1 p.m. to 5 p.m.—as well as a great online store.

THE LOOKING GLASS BOOKSTORE
7983 Southeast 13th St.
(503) 227-4760
http://lookingglassbook.qwestoffice.net
In the more than 30 years that the Looking Glass Bookstore has been open, it has consistenty offered a well-chosen selection of new books, both paperback and hardcover, and if it doesn't have what you want in stock, the staff can find it and get it to you. The store has an intriguing selection of magazines and journals and an excellent selection of note cards, including those by Oregon and other Northwest artists. For most of its history, The Looking Glass was downtown. The move to Sellwood has allowed it to refocus on four main areas: American and World history, political science, local poets, and contemporary literature. It also has an excellent children's selection—and since the bookstore resides in a cute red caboose with lots of cozy corners for reading, the kids will be occupied while you are browsing.

MURDER BY THE BOOK
3210 Southeast Hawthorne Blvd.
(503) 232-9995
www.mbtb.com

As the name implies, this bookstore is devoted to mysteries—hard-boiled, tea-cozy, police procedural—name your poison and you'll find it here. There are close-outs on sale at the door, shelves of used books, and the newest releases in both hardbound and paperback. Patrons of this unique shop get a newsletter announcing new releases and readings by mystery authors.

✳POWELL'S CITY OF BOOKS
1005 West Burnside St.
(503) 228-4651
www.powells.com

Powell's is getting pretty close to an empire. (And yes, there is a Powell: Michael Powell is the mind and the will behind Powell's growth, positioning, and well-known civic involvement.) With more than a million books in a store covering several levels in a building filling an entire city block, Powell's is the largest bookstore in the country. It even has its own (small) parking garage. Powell's has become an attraction in its own right and really does deserve a visit . . . or two . . . or three. This is a maze of a store, so pick up a map as you enter. Sections are color-coded, and there are plenty of signs to direct you. The staff is helpful, courteous, and knowl-edgeable in case you have to ask directions.

You'll find both used and new books and a separate rare book room. There are books in other languages besides English, and not surprisingly, a small selection of reading glasses. Powell's also has an excellent chil-dren's section as well as a selection of cards, blank journals, and other papery things. The café, with its coffee, tea, and snacks, would be a good place to look through potential purchases if one weren't always getting dis-tracted by the interesting people wandering in and out of the room. The frequent literary readings are a big draw. Powell's is open every day of the year and is usually busy, if not downright crowded; there are other sites at the airport and in Beaverton, 8725 Southwest Cascade, in addition to the other branches listed below. If you're looking for science- and technology-related items, visit the nearby Powell's Technical Bookstore, 33 Northwest Park. Powell's Books for Cooks and Gardeners, 3747 Southeast Hawthorne Blvd., is devoted to cooking and gardening books, and they have a comprehensive selection of these, as well as tools, toys, and crafted artifacts. It's a great spot to track down a birthday or holiday gift for those who like to cook or garden, or practically anybody else. Powell's Bookstore on Hawthorne, 3723 Southeast Hawthorne Blvd., is a general-interest bookstore; it is smaller and perhaps, based on its scale, more user-friendly. This branch also sponsors weekly readings by writers, poets, and performance artists.

Powell's online service is incredibly well organized and useful. Don't tell them, but a lot of people look up the books that interest them before they get to the store. It helps make the experience less overwhelming.

✳READING FRENZY
921 Southwest Oak St.
(503) 274-1449
www.readingfrenzy.com

Reading Frenzy, which specializes in publica-tions by independent presses, sells things that you can't find anywhere else in Portland, and sometimes, anywhere else in the world. In addition to a fine selection of smart maga-zines, this shop carries locally and nation-ally published 'zines, literary quarterlies, and attractively published essays by academics such as Noam Chomksy. Reading Frenzy also serves as a meeting and distribution place for all kinds of alternative causes.

TITLE WAVE
216 Northeast Knott St.
(503) 988-5021

The bookstore for discards from the Multnomah County Library is so good that we don't even really want to tell you about it. Prices for paperbacks start at about $1 and go up from there. For hardbacks—which include both contemporary and older fiction, poetry, mysteries, cookbooks, and anything else you might want—look for prices to begin at $2. You will also find a great selection of books on tape and CD, music CDs, and LPs. Back copies of many magazines are also available, and the videos and DVDs are also worth perusing.

WALLACE BOOKS
7241 Southeast Milwaukie Blvd.
(503) 235-7350

Just a couple of blocks south of the Moreland business district antiques malls and small shops, Wallace Books is an old house with bookshelves in every room. It's fun to browse upstairs and down to find the words you want to snuggle with later as the day winds down. The store has the newest releases as well as lots of new and used genre paperbacks.

Chain bookstores in Portland include:

BARNES & NOBLE
1317 Lloyd Center
(503) 249-0800

BORDERS BOOKS & MUSIC
708 Southwest 3rd Ave.
(503) 220-5911

CLOTHING

✳DUCHESS
2505 Southeast 11th Ave.
(503) 281-6648
www.duchessclothier.com

Duchess has evolved from a fun shop with Western-inspired clothes, reproductions of 20th-century classic silk slips, and petticoats to a purveyor of handsome custom men's suits in a range of historically inspired styles. The suits are also available in a range of prices. But these made-to-measure suits are all beautifully made, affordable, and will be well worth the effort.

✳ELIZABETH STREET
635 Northwest 23rd Ave.
(503) 243-2456

A stalwart of the Northwest 23rd shopping scene, Elizabeth Street features a beautifully edited collection of new and stylish women's clothing and accessories, both fancy and casual.

ELLINGTON LEATHER GOODS
1533 Northwest 24th Ave.
(503) 223-7457
www.ellingtonleather.com

Ellington makes Italian-inspired handbags, wallets, luggage, and other leather items, as well as a sophisticated line of microfiber bags. Their backpack purses are modern classics. Ellington also has a good web store.

✳THE ENGLISH DEPT.
1124 Southwest Alder Ave.
(503) 224-0724
www.theenglishdept.com

Co-owner Elizabeth Dye sells her own work here, as well as that of others. And what is this work? Why, beautiful and feminine clothes inspired by Jay Gatsby's yellow shirts and other literary fashions. Pretty dresses, jewelry, skirts, and tops.

FYBERWORKS
4300 Southeast Hawthorne Blvd.
(503) 232-7659
www.fyberworks.com
Street clothes, beautiful accessories, and workout wear are the specialties here. We go for gorgeous hand-knit scarves, for silk shawls, for natural-fiber jackets, dresses, and tunics, and for the wonderful variety of locally made designs. Fyberworks often carries cute vintage and Portland-made home design objects in its friendly shop.

HANNA ANDERSSON
327 Northwest 10th Ave.
(503) 321-5275
www.hannaandersson.com
Portland is headquarters for this nationally successful catalog shop featuring Swedish-style, high-quality clothing for kids and their moms. Designs are often, but not exclusively, made with cotton jersey. The underwear and pajamas are especially cozy and comfortable; and the clothes wear very well, through at least two children, and so are a good value. The store is clean, light, and wholesome. This civic-minded company passes along gently used Hannas to needy children—isn't that a good reason to shop here?

✳LANGLITZ LEATHERS
2443 Southeast Division St.
(503) 235-0959
www.langlitz.com
Since 1947, Langlitz Leathers has forged a worldwide reputation for crafting the highest-quality leather garments. Their shop is small—less than 3,000 square feet—and crowded. This family-owned business

welcomes visitors and will be happy to show you every aspect of how they create custom leathers. Langlitz creates only about six garments per day. Half are custom built, and the others are built to stock pattern sizes for walk-in customers. Because their prices are relatively low for custom work (between $500 and $1,000 per garment), their services are in constant demand. They have different products, but the Columbia was the first jacket that store founder Ross Langlitz designed—in the mid-1940s—and it remains the flagship of the jacket line, reflecting the traditional look of motorcycling.

✳MARIO'S
833 Southwest Broadway
(503) 227-3477
http://marios.com
Mario's is the best source in town for urbane designer clothing, shoes, and accessories from Armani to Prada. Some readers may be familiar with the clean, spare luxury of the Mario's in Seattle, but this one is the original; it was one of the first residents of The Galleria and therefore may be regarded as a chief contributor to the beautification of downtown— and its residents. The store now inhabits a beautiful space in the Fox Tower.

MINK
3418 Southeast Hawthorne Blvd.
(503) 232-3500
http://shopmink.com
Gorgeous dresses that will help you unleash your inner Daisy Miller: That is what Mink will provide you with—as well as great tees by Velvet and jeans by Joe's Jeans, and all the accessories to go with them. Mink also carries well-selected pieces from local designers. English majors and accountants alike will find something beautiful here.

MOXIE
2400 East Burnside St.
(503) 296-6943
www.moxiepdx.com

Moxie has eco-conscious, stylish, and chic clothing for women and men. Local and West Coast designers are prominent but not exclusive here; you can get Toms Shoes in addition to gorgeous handmade earrings or a cocktail dress.

*ODESSA
410 Southwest 13th Ave.
(503) 223-1998
http://odessaportland.wordpress.com

Odessa sells fashionable clothes with a downtown feel; they have a good eye for singular pieces with distinctive lines. Most lines are from New York, London, and Los Angeles, and they include Isabel Marant, MM6, and Comme des Garcons. Odessa has beautiful evening clothes but also carries beguiling everyday clothes for the fashionista, such as Petite Bateau T-shirts, as well as beautiful home design fabrics from Kerry Cassill. You'll also find some shoes and handbags.

PIN ME APPAREL
3705 Northeast Mississippi St.
(503) 281-1572
www.pin-me-apparel.com/about.html

Because everyone should have access to high fashion, Pin Me proffers lovely and affordable designer clothes in a wide range of sizes: 0 to 16, to be precise. They also have a generous stock of accessories and handbags. They are especially fond of local, Northwest, and Canadian designers, although international names such as Orla Kiely are favorites as well.

PORTLAND PENDLETON SHOP
900 Southwest 5th Ave.
(503) 242-0037

On the east side of the Standard Insurance Building, this store offers the most complete collection of Pendleton clothing for men and women in all of Oregon. Pendleton has always offered classic styles for men and women and excellent value, and they are enjoying a revival. They've updated their clothing lines with a more contemporary look while retaining their well-known fabrics and colors. In addition to clothing, the store carries an excellent selection of blankets and pillows with dramatic designs and colors based on Western and Native American art and symbols.

*RED LIGHT
3590 Southeast Hawthorne Blvd.
(503) 963-8888
www.redlightclothingexchange.com

Some of the best vintage clothing in Portland is found in this large, trendy shop, in addition to resale modern clothes from BCBG, Betsy Johnson, Urban Outfitters, and Bébé. The vintage selection is comprehensive and reasonably priced, with everything from slips to coats. Men and women alike will find wonderful old leather jackets, evening wear, sweaters, and, well, everything you could imagine.

SAVVY PLUS
3204 Southeast Hawthorne Blvd.
(503) 231-7116
www.savvyplus.com

Savvy Plus specializes in high-quality resale and new women's clothes size 12 and up. Most of the apparel is created using natural fibers and made in the good old USA. They also carry some unusual jewelry that is

Close-up

Local Design

Portland has a history of supplying the nation with stylish, well-made clothing, and you've probably heard of Hanna Andersson, Jantzen, Columbia Sportswear, and Nike. You may have even seen local star Michelle DeCourcy's beautiful dresses featured on Oprah. But Portland's increasing urbanity is reflected in the growing number of successful local designers who have set up shop in the past few years, designers who are also receiving national attention. The following shops carry locally made and designed clothing by Portland's rising design stars.

Lena Medoyeff
710 Northwest 23rd Ave.
(503) 227-0011
Well-cut clothes in stunning fabrics—this is the hallmark of Lynn Solmonson, the designer behind the name Lena Medoyeff. These dresses, skirts, pants, and jackets for day or evening are truly alluring, and they'll make you so as well. You'll see a lot of embroidery, some of it by local artisans. Depending, of course, on the season, you may also see duponi silk, velvet, or lightweight wool, but whatever you see, it will be a simple design that allows the beauty of the fabric to stand out. These clothes are rather dressy, but for Portland, a Lena Medoyeff skirt with a T-shirt and flip-flops fit in just right.

Seaplane
2226 Northwest Lovejoy
(503) 234-2409
www.seaplanedesign.com
Seaplane carries clothes that are a modern hybrid of Bond girl, Grace Jones, and Debbie Harry, with a little Marie Antoinette thrown in for good measure. Designers and proprietors Holly Stadler and Kathryn Towers feature beautifully sculpted dresses, sweaters, and skirts, and they share the love by showcasing other designers as well. With their amazing fashions and phenomenal events, this seminal design collective has been featured in the national and international press, putting Portland on the map as a fashion incubator.

Tumbleweed
1812 Northeast Alberta St.
(503) 335-3100
www.tumbleweedboutique.com
Tumbleweed is the home base of designer Kara Larson and her Kara-Line brand of clothing. These urban cowgirl clothes are available throughout the city and the country. Her simple skirts and dresses are charming without being the least bit fussy; they are made of pretty prints in cottons and rayons. We also love the fact that you can talk to the woman who made them. They purvey an entire "rustic romantic" look, but the pieces blend well with things you already own and can really individualize a wardrobe. Beautiful vintage cowboy and other boots, pantaloons, sweaters, and other fabric delights (including a fun basket of remnants) round out the selection.

handcrafted by local artisans. A great source for stylish and fabulous clothing in larger sizes. You can also consign your consumer-tested fashion items for other people to take home and love.

UNA
2802 Southest Ankeny St.
(503) 235-2326
A tiny, beautiful shop in LoBu, Una is renowned for its well-edited collection of locally designed, cool clothes from New York and Los Angeles, and vintage offerings. Look for Portland designers such as Jess Beebe and Sarah Weick, as well as small labels from, well, all over. Una features accessories as well—including some home decor items, so you'll feel like you belong in your new outfit.

> **i** *Portland Mercury* columnist Marjorie Skinner dishes on the latest sales, trends, and other news in her weekly column Sold Out. Read it and you will never wonder what to wear again.

CRAFTS

BOLT
2136 Northeast Alberta St.
(503) 287-2658
www.boltfabricboutique.com
Bolt is a beautiful fabric shop in the Alberta neighborhood with the feel of a boutique rather than a warehouse. The shop features luscious fabrics in contemporary designs, as well as the hippest patterns available. They also offer workshops and advice for the beginner, intermediate, and expert sewer.

✳COLLAGE ART MATERIALS AND WORKROOM
1639 Northeast Alberta St.
(503) 249-2190
www.collagepdx.com
These delightful spaces in the Alberta and Reed College (4429 Southeast Woodstock Blvd., 503-777-2189) neighborhoods carry an outstanding and thoughtful selection of craft supplies. They have an excellent selection of papers and bookbinding supplies, as well as great bonding agents, cutters, and other basics. The expert staff really knows their stuff and can make great recommendations for tricky crafting problems. In addition, they provide a great work space and classes. (See the DIY feature in the Arts chapter).

✳KNIT PURL
1101 Southwest Alder
(503) 227-2999
www.knit-purl.com
A beautiful downtown yarn shop, Knit Purl carries gorgeous yarns, aesthetically pleasing needles and other tools, and a wide, wide range of patterns and books. The staff is very wise and will help you read your confusing pattern in the nicest way possible. They also provide fabulous classes and open knitting circles—as well as knitting celebrity events.

YARN GARDEN
1413 Southeast Hawthorne Blvd.
(503) 239-7950
www.yarngarden.net
We should all honor our work by using the best materials available, and if knitting is your work, Yarn Garden is the place for the best tools. Luscious yarns in every weight, color, and texture; needles; patterns—all your knitting needs are served here. The

staff is so knowledgeable and helpful for beginners and experienced knitters alike that you'll find half the afternoon has passed before you know it. They are open on Wed evening until 8 p.m.; that's when they hold knitting circles at which you can solicit and receive advice, trade ideas, or meet other knitters. Yarn Garden also has a good selection of books.

i If you're planning to woo your sweetie with some homemade cocktails, note that Oregon's liquor stores are state-licensed. That means you have to shop at designated liquor stores, rather than the supermarket, for the hard stuff. They stay open until 7 p.m. and they're closed on Sunday. Be forewarned.

FOOD

Along with the usual chain supermarkets such as Albertsons, Safeway, Thriftway, and Fred Meyer, Portland is also home to a variety of Korean, Vietnamese, Japanese, Lebanese, Mexican, Russian, and German stores and delis. The national chains Wild Oats and Whole Foods specialize in organic and natural foods, with stores scattered throughout the city. Trader Joe's, the California-based chain, has numerous stores here: Look for them in Portland, 4715 Southeast 39th Ave.; in the Hollywood District at 4121 Northeast Halsey; in Beaverton, 11753 Southwest Beaverton-Hillsdale Hwy.; and in Lake Oswego, 15391 Southwest Bangy Rd., next to the Ethan Allen Furniture Gallery. Zupan's Markets can be found in four locations: Belmont, Burnside, Macadam, and Raleigh Hills.

BOB'S RED MILL
5000 Southeast International Way, Milwaukie
(503) 654-3215
www.bobsredmill.com
Bob's Red Mill is nationally noted for its excellent whole-grain products. Although Bob's Red Mill is now a giant, it still does things the old-fashioned way. Their huge, 120-year-old millstones still operate 24 hours a day, grinding out every grain under the sun—into flours, cereals, meals, farinas, and cracks. Bob's Red Mill is also a certified organic processor and carries a vast amount of organic whole-grain products. Their goods—which are free of chemicals, additives, and preservatives—are also kosher certified by the Rabbinical Council of America. The original plant is in a gorgeous, landscaped setting complete with a duck pond, with an attractive and well-organized on-site retail store for everything from rice, beans, nuts, seeds, milk powders, pastas, dried fruits, sweeteners, and other related products, in either bulk or small packages.

IN GOOD TASTE
231 Northwest 11th Ave.
(503) 248-2015
www.ingoodtastestore.com
Gayle Jolley, who for years taught cooking classes at Sheridan (see below), opened this industrial-chic cooking arena in the Pearl District in 1999. Not only will you find the best, professional-quality cookware here, but you will also find specialty foods and a great wine selection. A bridal registry is available. But people come here for the cooking classes taught by excellent local chefs. In Good Taste also offers full-service catering and a lunchtime bistro to refresh those hungry Pearl District shoppers.

*NEW SEASONS
Various locations
www.newseasonsmarket.com
New Seasons is Portland's answer to Whole Foods. After the locally owned Nature's was sold and resold to big corporations, some of its former employees apparently missed having stores that were integral parts of neighborhood communities and driven by local interests. Thus, they founded New Seasons, which is designed to help bring back the local and seasonal to organic food. New Seasons is a full-service grocery store that features natural and organic foods, with exceptional produce and takeout in addition to traditional groceries, wine, and health and beauty aids. Moreover, the service is remarkably friendly and knowledgeable, with an overt commitment to providing an excellent experience for the customer. Delivery service is also available. You will find them all over the Metro area; more seem to be opening weekly—they are very, very popular.

*PASTAWORKS
3735 Southeast Hawthorne Blvd.
(503) 232-1010
www.pastaworks.com
Pastaworks makes fabulous fresh pasta and sauces right on-site, from light-as-air fettuccine to superbly flavorful ravioli. But Pastaworks is not only for pasta—it also sells everything you need to go with it, from the best produce to the most exquisite cheeses to the choicest organic meat. You'll find many local and imported specialty items here, including truffled olive oils from Italy and melt-in-your-mouth ginger cookies from Sweden. Wines are also a strong suit of the store; the Hawthorne branch offers tastings, as well as a fine selection of stemware, cookware, and cooking classes—as well as

the best butcher and cheese counter in the city. In addition, there are a few tables outside where you can sit with coffee and rolls while you watch people shopping on Hawthorne. The City Market location (735 Northwest 21st Ave., 503-221-3002) is known for its wonderful fish and seafood collection, as well as its outstanding butchers.

SHERIDAN FRUIT CO.
408 Southeast 3rd Ave.
(503) 236-2113
www.sheridanfruit.com
Sheridan Fruit Co. is another Portland institution, offering many unusual herbs, exotic plants, and vegetables. It's a big, fun, bustling place to visit, and many people come to the Sheridan market from all around the Portland-Vancouver area. Sheridan's is known for its produce, but also carries an excellent selection of pasta, wine, meat, and cheese. Sheridan's also has a vast bulk section—and they make good espresso too. They are open Mon through Sat from 6 a.m. to 8 p.m.

HOME DECOR

*CARGO
380 Northwest 13th Ave.
(503) 209-8349
www.cargoinc.com
Those pictures in *Elle Decor* of lofts decorated with tansu chests and Indian saris have always looked appealing, but where do you get the saris and tansu chests to decorate with? In Portland, you get them at Cargo, which is a kind of upscale Cost Plus with many beautiful imports, mainly from India and Asia. High-quality silk pillows, baskets, wooden tea chests, bamboo blinds, and so on are all here, as well as sake sets and chopsticks. Cargo is also an excellent place for gifts.

In Vino Veritas

Oregon is wine country and is justly famous for its pinots. Some passionate souls devoted to the blood of the Oregon soil have set up shop, making local wines available and bringing good international wines to the attention of Portland citizens. Each of the shops below likes to focus on boutique or hard-to-find wines; the ambience of each, their tasting events, and their prodigious variety of stock make them all worth visiting (perhaps not all on the same day). Many hold classes and other events, as well. The shop owners are as varied and fascinating as the wines they sell, so ask them about their passions.

E & R Wine Shop
6141 Southwest Macadam Ave.
(503) 246-6101
A wonderful wine shop with suburb service and smart owners, E & R has a nose for some of the best high-end wines available in the world. But they specialize in great wines from Italy. E & R also offers classes and tastings.

Great Wine Buys
1515 Northeast Broadway
(503) 287-2897
This friendly shop has friendly proprietors and a vast selection of wines from around the world.

Liner & Elsen
2222 Northwest Quimby St.
(503) 241-WINE
Liner & Elsen is regularly touted by the local and national press, and rightly so, for they offer outstanding service, selection, and stemware.

Mt. Tabor Fine Wines
4316 Southeast Hawthorne Blvd.
(503) 235-4444
This shop was named as one of the best wine shops in America four years running by *Food & Wine* magazine.

Portland Wine Merchants
Southeast 35th Ave. and Hawthorne Blvd.
(503) 234-4399
This shop is a favorite for Oregon wines and offers an excellent representation from the world over as well.

Vino
Southeast 28th Ave. and Southeast Ash St.
(503) 235-8545
Vino is a charming spot that features value-priced wines that would be difficult to find without the hard work of the owner, Bruce Bauer.

Three grocery stores also deserve mention for their superb wines: the **Pastaworks** at 3735 Southeast Hawthorne Blvd.; the **Fred Meyer** at Hawthorne Boulevard and Southeast 39th Avenue; and any **Zupan**'s (www .zupans.com).

HIPPO HARDWARE AND TRADING COMPANY
1040 East Burnside St.
(503) 231-1444
www.hippohardware.com

Hippo Hardware, a well-known Portland establishment for many years, carries a wonderfully eclectic assortment of plumbing fixtures, doors, lighting fixtures, and salvaged items for older homes. This place is far more entertaining than the average nuts-and-bolts hardware store and is full of functional curios and odd stuff that can be very useful if you know what to do with it (if you're like us and have no idea what it's supposed to do, just ask and someone will be glad to help you). It takes a long time to search through all the offerings, so plan accordingly. They will also custom build lighting fixtures. Don't forget to bring your old fixtures in here for a swap. It is a trading company, after all.

KITCHEN KABOODLE
404 Northwest 23rd Ave.
(503) 241-4040
www.kitchenkaboodle.com

Their motto is "We make your house a home," and they've been doing just that since 1975. Kitchen Kaboodle sells functional, unique house accoutrements, providing not only every possible gadget you might use someday, but the storage unit to put it in. This Portland institution and local chain has stores all over town; and whether you need an electric egg cooker, a potato ricer, an enameled French casserole, or a maple sideboard, you can find it here. The staff is very knowledgeable and friendly—make use of them. That's what they're paid for. A second central location is at 1520 Northeast Broadway (503-288-1500).

THE REBUILDING CENTER
3625 North Mississippi Ave.
(503) 331-1877
http://rebuildingcenter.org

A nonprofit salvage outlet, the Rebuilding Center sells reclaimed hardware, windows, doors, plumbing fixtures, moldings, and lumber. This is the retail outlet of a firm that disassembles houses and other buildings; what is not immediately reused in other projects is sold here. For the recycling-conscious do-it-yourselfer, this place is heaven.

✳REJUVENATION
1100 Southeast Grand Ave.
(503) 238-1900
www.rejuvenation.com

Another Portland landmark, Rejuvenation is well known nationally for its period lighting fixtures, but it also carries new and salvaged plumbing, doors, windows, moldings, and lumber. You'll also find handsome furniture and garden ornaments. This is a terrific resource center for home improvements; Rejuvenation has built a thriving business around helping people restore classic, turn-of-the-20th-century houses. A knowledgeable staff provides useful information and referral lists of competent home rehabilitation specialists. There's a tiny nook for children to play in while their parents browse; the Daily Cafe, inside the store, is a good place for eating lunch while you figure out what to do with the salvaged staircase you've just bought. Rejuvenation also sells their seconds, which can be a fine source for well-priced lighting fixtures and other things.

RELISH
433 Northwest 10th Ave.
(503) 227-3779
www.relishstyle.com

This sleek boutique stocks accessories and home and lifestyle objects with a modern aesthetic, many by local designers. The jewelry selection is outstanding—unusual in its materials and inspired in its lines.

SWEETWATER FARM
1400 Northwest Everett St.
(503) 227-4947
http://sweetwaterfarmfurniture.com
This shop deals in colorful, funky furniture—everything from armoires to entertainment centers—and singular treasures made by artisans from all over the country. David Marsh and Shoestring Creations are the two featured artists, but there are many more. In addition to the furniture, you'll find a striking array of jewelry, lighting, pillows, toys, and other surprises. Sweetwater Farm might be just the place to find the necessary touch of whimsy to go with the Eileen Gray daybed in your modern row house.

THE WHOLE 9 YARDS
1820 East Burnside St.
(503) 223-2880
www.w9yards.com
Specializing in interior fabrics and trim, The Whole 9 Yards has developed a national reputation for its gorgeous fabrics, inventive combinations, and original style. Their chenilles, jacquards, and velvets are renowned, but they carry everything from duponi silk to cotton. They'll help you put together your drapes and upholstery, as well as providing you with general expertise, curtain rods and trim, and their own line of freshly designed, competitively priced furniture. The shop also offers brilliant classes in fashioning slipcovers, curtains, and pillows.

MUSIC

ARTICHOKE MUSIC
3130 Southeast Hawthorne Blvd.
(503) 232-8845
www.artichokemusic.com
Don't settle for banging a gong; stop by this friendly music shop and strum an Autoharp or thump an Irish bodhran with a double drumstick. Here you will find guitars, banjos, mandolins, dulcimers, harps, accordions, and a fascinating assortment of unusual folk instruments. They also buy and sell all kinds of musical instruments and are extremely knowledgeable about the local music scene. Not only do they carry a wide selection of high-quality musical instruments, but they also feature live performances, music lessons, and cool events—among them open-mike sessions so you can show off your best bluegrass licks and a singing circle where you can sing your heart out and practice those harmonies.

✳JACKPOT RECORDS
209 Southwest 9th Ave.
(503) 222-0990
www.jackpotrecords.com
In an iPod era, fabulous Jackpot Records is better than ever, with an outstanding catalog of new and used CDs and vinyl, as well as an online store and MySpace page. This great shop not only has excellent finds in indie music—as well as electronica, jazz, hip-hop, metal, blues, and more—but it also has amazing in-store events featuring bands such as the Decemberists, Sleater-Kinney, and Franz Ferdinand. A second location is at 3574 Southeast Hawthorne (503-239-7561).

✳MUSIC MILLENNIUM
3158 East Burnside St.
(503) 231-8926
www.musicmillennium.com

Music Millennium, a Portland institution since 1969, carries the latest releases from national, international, and local acts in every variety of music, from blues to spoken word and everything in between. The knowledgeable and friendly staff can help you find whatever you're looking for, as well as tell you about exciting in-store performances on the schedule. They also offer the widest selection of classical CDs in the entire city.

2ND AVENUE RECORDS
400 Southwest 2nd Ave.
(503) 222-3783
A voluminous outlet for all musical genres, 2nd Avenue has the biggest selection of hip-hop in town. You can also track down obscure performers on independent labels. Indie, metal, reggae, postpunk, and more are yours for the buying.

SHOES

HALO SHOES
1425 Northeast Broadway
(503) 331-0366
Halo features high-end shoes for fashionistas and their brothers. This cultured boutique specializes in beautiful and chic shoes from Corso Como, Fiorentini & Baker, CYDWOC, Costume National, and hard-to-find lines from around the world. Halo also carries sleek bags and other good accessories. Many of these beautiful shoes are handmade. An outstanding shoe shop, from service to selection.

✳IMELDA'S AND LOUIE'S SHOES
3426 Southeast Hawthorne Blvd.
(503) 233-7476
www.imeldasandlouies.com
Alluring shoes at reasonable prices—that's why stylish Portlanders seek out Imelda's and Louie's. Kenneth Cole, Frye, Franco Sarto, Born, and Secs are some of the lines that Imelda's and Louie's carries; but also look for special handmade shoes from New York, groovy handbags, and really pretty jewelry. Everybody buys shoes here, because the collection is perfectly edited for Portland. A second location is at 935 Northwest Everett St. (503-595-4970).

JOHNNY SOLE
815 Southwest Alder St.
(503) 225-1241
www.johnnysoleshoes.com
Johnny Sole can satisfy almost any shoe craving, from Seventh-Avenue high-fashion diva to Portland-style alternative-culture goth. Favorite lines include Diba, Giraudon, and Kenneth Cole. It's got a stand-out selection of cool yet weather-and-walking-appropriate boots. This light, spacious boutique in the heart of downtown features men's and women's lines.

NIKE TOWN
930 Southwest 6th Ave.
(503) 221-6453
If shopping were a secular religion, Portland's Nike Town, the progenitor of all other Nike Towns in the entire world, would be the Vatican. Nike Town is made of equal parts museum, gallery, temple, and store. Yes, you can buy shoes and other things here, but the real purpose of a visit is to honor the "swoosh" with generous offerings of currency and plastic. From the hip Nike-clad greeters to the spotlighted and enshrined sneakers, this is a cultural icon.

ATTRACTIONS

Visitors come from all over to see what makes the Portland area different from other parts of the country and world. This chapter emphasizes the local and regional attractions—natural, historical, and contemporary—that define and characterize our area. Getting to these attractions is usually simple. Most are concentrated within the city center. Downtown Portland, which is encompassed in our Southwest Portland section, is agreeable for walking, and even if the weather is not entirely cooperative, the distances are relatively short. Fareless Square, a downtown zone along the bus mall (in which bus fare is free), invites visitors to join local residents on buses, MAX trains, and streetcars to get around downtown more easily. Visitors to attractions in outlying areas, such as Fort Vancouver, will depend more on cars. You can still take public transportation, but it requires more planning and commitment.

The entire Portland Metro area is an attraction, full of interesting things to watch, do, hear, and taste. During the spring and summer, expect the occasional parade, especially during the Rose Festival and on the Fourth of July, as well as street festivals, bike races, weekend runs, and even the occasional protest outside some government building. For more information about special happenings, see our Festivals and Annual Events chapter, and for other attractions, such as galleries and museums, see The Arts chapter. Additionally, if you're traveling with kids, you may want to check out the children's museums and amusement parks in the Kidstuff chapter. We have made every effort to report the most current and accurate hours and addresses. However, given the rate of change in the area, visitors are advised to call their destination beforehand to make sure the information is accurate.

Price Code

Prices reflect the cost of one adult admission. Most attractions have discounts for children, students, and seniors, so bring your ID.

$ . . . . Less than $8
$$ . . . . $8 to $16
$$$ . . . . More than $16

SOUTHWEST PORTLAND

BERRY BOTANIC GARDEN $
11505 Southwest Summerville Ave.
(503) 636-4112
www.berrybot.org
Rae Selling Berry was by all accounts a legendary botanist, and her legacy lives on at the Berry Botanic Garden, the site of

her estate. This garden shouldn't be missed, especially during the spring and summer. The 6.5-acre estate features a collection of endangered plant species, the largest public rock garden on the West Coast, and major collections of lilies, native Northwest plants, and rhododendrons in settings that vary from a damp woodland to streamside plantings. The Berry Botanic Garden was the first seed bank in the nation to dedicate itself to the preservation of the flora of an entire region (the Pacific Northwest), and part of its mission is to sustain the botanical heritage of the area through an extensive research program. Classes and events are offered regularly. The garden is open by appointment every day from 9 a.m. to 4 p.m. Because the garden is in a residential area, you'll need to call to make an appointment, but it's not difficult to get one. Also call for directions to the garden. A recorded message will give them to you—be sure to have your pencil ready because they're delivered rapidly. Alternatively, you can look up directions on the useful website, which also has information about current classes and events.

HOYT ARBORETUM   FREE
4000 Southwest Fairview Blvd.
(503) 865-8733 (visitor center)
www.hoytarboretum.org
Hoyt Arboretum, which is part of Washington Park, not only provides more than 900 species of trees and shrubs to observe, but it also provides 183 acres and 10 miles of trails with striking views of the city, Mount Hood and Mount St. Helens, the Coast Range, and the rolling hills to the west, north, and east. Oaks, maples, cherry trees, Douglas fir, redwoods, blue spruce, Himalayan spruce, and bristlecone pine are but a few of the species that keep the arboretum fragrant in

the spring, fresh and cool in the summer, and flushed with color during the fall. For those of us who weren't paying attention during Outdoor School, most species are labeled, and for those who want to learn more, tours are offered during the weekends from Apr through Aug. The trails do twist up and down the hills, so comfortable and sturdy footwear is suggested. A 1-mile section of the Bristlecone Trail is paved for wheelchair access and offers a good introduction to Washington Park. The grounds are open from 6 a.m. to 10 p.m. The lovely visitor center is open from 9 a.m. until 4 p.m. and until 3 p.m. on Sat. It's closed on Sun and major holidays. Admission is free, though for $3 you can take a guided tour.

INTERNATIONAL ROSE
  TEST GARDEN   **FREE**
400 Southwest Kingston in Washington Park
(503) 823-3636
For some residents and visitors, this park is what Portland is about. High above the city, offering an eastern view of the skyline, the Willamette River and its bridges, the snowcapped peaks of the Cascade Mountains (Mount Hood, Mount St. Helens, Mount Adams, and even Mount Rainier on some days), the Rose Test Garden is an almost obligatory stop for visitors. These appealing gardens beckon you to linger awhile, offering many summer concerts, plays, and other outdoor events in addition to lovely views. This site has been a public rose garden since 1917—it's the oldest public rose test garden in the nation. The five-acre gardens offer visitors the sight and scent of 8,000 plants representing some 500 varieties of roses, from those producing fragile miniatures to some with blossoms nearly 8 inches broad. The roses begin to bloom in May and usually

reach their peak sometime in June, depending on the weather. But there will be flowers on the bushes until October, long after all but the most faithful rose fancier have gone home. There are no admission fees or formal operating hours, but there is a $500 fine for picking a flower. See the Portland's Parks chapter for information on other public rose gardens in Portland.

IRA KELLER
MEMORIAL FOUNTAIN   FREE
Southwest 3rd Avenue and Southwest Clay Street
Named after Ira C. Keller, a self-made millionaire with a well-developed social conscience, this water sculpture with misty falls and rectilinear pools is across from the Keller Auditorium in downtown Portland. In spring and summer, downtown workers eat lunch, nap, talk with friends, read, and sun themselves to the soothing sounds of water cascading down the structure's various levels. Children splash in the cooling waters and delight in the fountain's different waterfalls, pools, concrete and metal islands and terraces, and the design's overall human scale.

Ada Louise Huxtable, the New York Times's respected architecture critic, described the fountain as "perhaps the greatest open space since the Renaissance"—no faint praise for a work of public art, especially in a city with many public spaces. There is no admission charge.

*JAPANESE GARDENS $$
611 Southwest Kingston Ave.
(503) 223-1321
(503) 223-9233 (for tours)
www.japanesegarden.com
A Japanese ambassador to the United States once commented that this site in Washington Park is the most beautiful and authentic Japanese garden outside of Japan. Established in 1963, the Japanese Gardens was designed by Professor Takuma Tono, a distinguished landscape and garden designer, and his achievement is remarkable, compressing five different garden spaces— the Flat Garden, the Strolling Pond Garden, a Tea Garden with a *chashitsu* (a ceremonial tea house), the Natural Garden, and the Zen-inspired Sand and Stone Garden—into little more than five acres. The trees and plants, water, and rocks here change with the season, offering visitors different perspectives of color, texture, shape, shadow, and sound throughout the year.

Managed by the nonprofit Japanese Garden Society of Oregon, the gardens are open daily, except on Thanksgiving, Christmas Day, and New Year's Day. Hours vary according to the season, but visitors can be assured of admission between 10 a.m. and 4 p.m. except on Mon, when the garden opens at noon. In summer the last visitors are admitted at 6:30 p.m., with the gates closing at 7 p.m. Guided tours are available, as well as special annual events, including a moon viewing in Sept, a bonsai exhibition in Oct, and an excellent art and gift exhibit and sale

i The Equitable Life building, designed by renowned Portland architect Pietro Belluschi and completed in 1948, was one of the first modern glass towers, and it was a major trendsetter. It was the first building to be clad in aluminum, the first to use double-glazed windows—and the first to be completely air-conditioned. You can find it at the intersection of Southwest Stark and Southwest Washington Streets.

in Dec. A fine gift shop lists a wide range of books on Japanese art, culture, and gardens among its offerings. The Japanese Gardens, save for a few areas, is wheelchair accessible.

MULTNOMAH COUNTY LIBRARY FREE

Central Branch
801 Southwest 10th Ave.
(503) 988-5123
www.multcolib.org

Each day of the week, thousands of citizens stream through the handsome doors of the Central Branch of the Multnomah County Library. While the library's holdings are extensive, it is no mere warehouse for books: It's a major component in the cultural life of the city. The Central Branch is an exemplary balance of intimate and public space, of cool marble and warm wood, of airy reading rooms and snug alcoves, of formal exhibits and cafe conversation. Its popularity attests to the success of this balance.

The library has dozens of programs, workshops, groups, and events that draw in visitors from all over the area. These range from lectures and roundtable discussions with regional writers to Saturday afternoon concerts to brownbag forums on stress relief to printmaking workshops. Its flourishing programs prompted Portland writer Sallie Tisdale to wonder whether the Central Branch wasn't getting too noisy. Fortunately, the Sterling Room for Writers, available by application only, can provide writers with some peace and quiet.

The Multnomah County Library is the oldest public library building west of the Mississippi. Some, but only some, of the highlights include the Beverly Cleary Children's Library (see the Kidstuff chapter), with both cozy reading nooks and high-tech media capabilities. This enchanting room recruits thousands of small new book lovers each year, sustaining their devotion as they get older with good research facilities for school reports and with splendid books, videos, and CDs to entertain them. The Henry Failing Art and Music Library contains one of the most significant sheet music collections in the nation, along with robust collections in the history of painting, photography, and handicrafts. The Meyer Memorial Trust libraries for science and business and for government documents are among the most-used collections in the library. The Grants Information Center provides the necessary data for those who would like to find financial resources for their worthy projects. The John Wilson Room houses rare books and paper-type artifacts, such as the *Nuremburg Chronicle* (dating from 1493). John Wilson was an Irishman who arrived in Oregon in 1849, and his library was the foundation for this collection devoted to, among other things, Pacific Northwest history, Native American books, children's literature, and the history of the book.

The library is open every day: Mon through Sat, from 10 a.m. to 6 p.m., except on Tues and Wed, when it's open until 8 p.m.; Sun, the library is open from noon until 5 p.m. Portland citizens don't like to be far from coffee, so Starbucks operates a small store, and the coffee scenting the air on the main floor adds a piquant Portland touch.

✳OREGON HISTORICAL SOCIETY MUSEUM $$

1200 Southwest Park Ave.
(503) 222-1741
www.ohs.org

The Oregon Historical Society Museum is a fine place to begin a visit to Portland; it covers the history of Oregon from the earliest Indian civilizations through the saga of the Oregon Trail right up to the issues surrounding Portland's light rail. Before you even enter the building, the two eight-story-high trompe l'oeil murals by Richard Haas present dramatic views and symbols of Oregon's past. The West Mural, at Southwest Park Avenue and Madison Street, captures in larger-than-life scale the key members of the Lewis and Clark Expedition including Sacagawea, and her child, Baptiste; Clark's slave, York; and Seaman, the dog. The other mural, visible from Broadway and Jefferson Streets, symbolically depicts early Oregon characters, among them Native Americans, trappers, and settlers.

The Oregon Historical Society Museum, completely renovated in 2003, is neither dusty nor staid. Part museum, part research facility, it's a leading and influential force in the city and state, sponsoring seminars, workshops, festivals, and celebrations, in addition to its extensive library and its own publications. The center holds a fine collection of historical photos, documents, and artifacts. An afternoon spent here will illuminate Pacific Northwest history in surprising and engaging ways.

The museum store offers a well-chosen selection of books on Oregon and Northwest history, attractions, and personalities, many of which are written by Oregonians and other regional authors, and some of which are published by the OHS's respected press. The shop also has maps, trinkets, and jewelry, as well as an excellent selection of postcards, note cards, and prints, many produced by local artists and photographers. The Oregon Historical Society Museum is open Tues through Sat from 10 a.m. to 5 p.m. On Sun, the museum is open from noon to 5 p.m. The research library is open Thurs through Sat from 1 to 5 p.m. There is no cost for children younger than five.

OREGON MARITIME CENTER AND MUSEUM $
At the foot of Southwest Pine Street between the Morrison and Burnside Bridges
(503) 224-7724
www.oregonmaritimemuseum.org
This small museum, housed in a charming old stern-wheeler tug, is filled with artifacts, models, historic paintings, and a collection of navigational instruments recounting Oregon's seagoing history. One room details the regional shipbuilding industry during World War II, and many of the exhibits feature military craft launched in Oregon's waters. The museum includes a small gift shop with a selection of nautical items and books. The museum's hours are 11 a.m. to 4 p.m., Wed through Sat, and Sun from 12:30 p.m. to 4 p.m.

*THE OREGON ZOO $$
4001 Southwest Canyon Rd.
(503) 226-1561
www.oregonzoo.org
The Oregon Zoo is the newest name for a zoo originally established in 1887 with the gift to the city of an animal collection from a wealthy and idiosyncratic Portland pharmacist, Richard Knight. The Oregon Zoo has evolved from a hodgepodge of animals kept at the back of a pharmacy into a world-class research facility, offering a constantly changing mix of exhibits and other amusements. It's an internationally recognized and respected center for breeding Asian elephants, and it features an imaginative re-creation of the African rain forest. It also

is highly committed to educating visitors about the animals of the Pacific Northwest.

The Oregon Zoo continues to make a serious effort to improve the animal habitats. As if in response to a homier atmosphere, the zoo's animal population is remarkably fertile, and the nursery is one of the most popular exhibits with adults, children, and the Portland media.

This well-liked attraction, second only to Multnomah Falls in the number of visitors it receives each year, offers a variety of other diversions that do not focus on animals. The Zoo Railway is a narrow-gauge railroad running two trains, including a replica of the 1960s streamlined Aerostar, along a route through part of the zoo, into Washington Park and the Rose Gardens. The zoo railroad has the only surviving railway post office in the country and you can amuse your friends back home by sending them mail with its unusual postmark. During Halloween and the Christmas season, the Oregon Zoo hosts many special events in which the train plays a role, such as a festival of lights, which is best seen from the train (see the Festivals and Annual Events chapter).

As you might predict, the zoo has a terrific gift shop and several restaurants and refreshment stands, including the AfriCafe, a restaurant that suggests huts found in a traditional African village.

During the summer the zoo hosts a series of concerts on a stage surrounded by terraced lawns. Many of these concerts are free with zoo admission; others cost more. The mild evenings, popular artists, and availability of catered food, regional wines and beer, and coffee combine to make these concerts into events that express the very essence of Portland. Many people bring a picnic (you can bring anything edible except alcohol into the zoo) and sprawl on blankets in the late afternoon sunshine before the music begins. Spontaneous outbursts of dancing will occur in front of the stage. It's a fine thing to see people of all ages and ways of life come together at these events; everyone loves to sit on the big lawns listening to great music under the lovely skies at twilight with friends and families.

The Oregon Zoo is open every day except Christmas Day. Gates are open from 8 a.m. until 6 p.m. from May 15 through Sept 15 and 9 a.m. to 4 p.m. from Sept 16 through Apr 14. There is a $2 fee for parking. The zoo stays open for an hour after the gates close, unless you're attending a special event or concert, when you can stay longer. Admission is $4 for everyone (except children 2 and under, who are always admitted free of charge) on the second Tues of each month. The zoo also features special rides and exhibitions that may incur a separate small fee, and the Zoo Railway has a separate charge of $3 to $5, depending on the loop and your membership status. By car, the zoo is best reached by a well-marked exit from westbound US 26 as it leaves downtown Portland. There is a light-rail station at the zoo, and ART the Cultural Bus also stops at the zoo. On summer weekends and during many concerts, parking can be particularly scarce, so light rail may be the least frustrating way to get here—plus you get $1 off your admission (See the Portland's Parks chapter for more information on the zoo.)

PIONEER COURTHOUSE   **FREE**
555 Southwest Yamhill St.
Pioneer Courthouse, the second-oldest federal building west of the Mississippi, was Portland's first restoration project back in the 1970s. Built in the late 1860s of beautiful

Bellingham sandstone, the Italianate building survived ill-considered plans that would have had it demolished for a mundane office building in the 1930s, for a parking lot in the 1940s, and for a new federal office building in the 1960s. Most of the city's residents don't know it, but you can climb to the cupola of Pioneer Courthouse for a rarely seen view of the city. This is a free trip back to 1877. Hanging between the cupola's eight windows is a series of restored photos of the city in that year by a local photographer, A. H. Wulzen. Many of the photos were taken from the cupola and offer the viewer a most unusual "before and after" scene. To reach the cupola, enter the courthouse (not the Post Office on Southwest 6th Avenue) from Southwest Yamhill Street. There is a stairway to the cupola, though you may have to pass through a metal detector, the times being what they are. Admission is free.

PIONEER COURTHOUSE
SQUARE FREE
**Between Broadway and Southwest
6th Avenue at Southwest Yamhill and
Southwest Morrison Streets
www.pioneercourthousesquare.org**
Pioneer Courthouse Square has been many things during its long life. The site was home to the city's first public schoolhouse; then home to the Portland Hotel, a massive and impressive building that was torn down, to much local dismay, to make way for a parking lot. Now, however, this wonderful piece of real estate is known as "Portland's living room" for its warm blend of red brick, park benches, flowers, sculpture, and coffee. Look at the bricks in the square's open spaces, and you'll see the inscribed names of more than 64,000 Portland residents, companies, and other Oregonians who paid $25 each

to buy the bricks: The citizens of Portland rallied to install this project against some local ill will. (You can still buy a brick, but in these inflationary times, the price has gone up to $100.)

By the early 1970s, downtown Portland was choking on its own traffic, and stores and other businesses were fleeing to the suburbs where parking was easier and the surroundings less threatening, if more bland. Instead of prolonged municipal hand-wringing, Portland ripped up a freeway, tore up almost the entire downtown, and invited pedestrians back into the city's core with a transit mall and free bus rides, wider sidewalks, trees, flower-filled planters, public art, and a squad of uniformed workers paid to keep the streets and sidewalks clean, give directions to visitors, and prevent crime by simply being visible and pleasant. The result has been one of the most honored urban renaissance projects in the nation, and Pioneer Courthouse Square is its epicenter. Food vendors, a flower stand, a Starbucks, and public restrooms add to the charm, and the city's light-rail system runs on two sides of the square, making it accessible to everyone. The Portland Oregon Visitor Association and TriMet both have major offices here, along with maintaining rooms for meetings and other occurrences, and a new facility, Ticket Central, allows people to buy tickets for events around town.

One thing about the decor of Portland's living room: It can surprise you. The square attracts diverse crowds that tolerate and even amuse each other and who, with very rare exception, get along quite well, illustrating the city's acceptance of individuality. Expect to see street musicians, jugglers, pierced and tattooed teenagers, and street people with their studded leather jackets, army surplus camouflage, and assortments of pet dogs, snakes, kittens, and birds—in addition, of course, to tourists, students, and city office workers strolling about. The Weather Machine, a piece of whimsical but functional sculpture, informs passersby of the weather: A blue heron means mist and drizzle, a golden sun goddess predicts clear skies, and a copper dragon warns of approaching storms, heavy rain, and winds. The square is open to all at no charge.

Pioneer Square hosts an unending series of special events (see the Festivals and Annual Events chapter), including contests, cultural festivals, a giant civic Christmas tree, a yuletide tuba concert, a sand castle contest, officially sanctioned skateboarding competitions, and anything else residents can get approved.

POLICE HISTORICAL MUSEUM
JUSTICE CENTER   **FREE**
1111 Southwest 2nd Ave.
(503) 823-0019
www.portlandpolicemuseum.com
You may not want to know the motives of some of the other people visiting here with you, but don't miss this small museum, which highlights the fascinating history of crime and punishment.

The museum displays a retired police motorcycle, a working traffic signal, a collection of badges, uniforms, weapons, handcuffs, and other tools of the trade representing both sides of the cops-and-robbers paradigm. There is also a great collection of historical photos. Current and retired Portland police officers make up the volunteer staff, so mind your manners. Entry to the museum is free, though donations are welcome. The museum is open Tues through Fri, from 10 a.m. to 3 p.m.; you should call ahead.

There's also a gift shop. If you're over 18 you'll need some photo ID since it is, actually, in the building that houses the city jail.

✳**PORTLAND ART MUSEUM**   **$$**
1219 Southwest Park Ave.
(503) 226-2811
www.portlandartmuseum.org
The Portland Art Museum, the oldest museum in the Pacific Northwest, has become an attraction with new dimensions, an attraction that extends beyond the allure of the Pietro Belluschi–designed building and the art within it. The museum has gained much attention for its major exhibitions and even more major fund-raising capabilities. The results have been impressive: After an extensive expansion, the museum now has the space for new galleries, educational facilities, a multimedia room, an appealing public sculpture garden, and a cafe. This new wealth of space has allowed the museum to better feature its important collections in Northwest and Native American art and in European painting, as well as creating space for recent acquisitions. (In 2000 the museum procured the collection of the distinguished New York art critic Clement Greenberg.) But the museum has also become a lively force in the cultural life of the city, enlisting young patrons in its philanthropic drives, arranging family programs, sponsoring lectures and evening events, and generally making a big splash. Hours are Tues, Wed, and Sat, 10 a.m. to 5 p.m.; Sun from noon to 5 p.m.; Thurs and Fri the museum is open until 8 p.m. Reduced ticket prices are available for children and seniors, and the fourth Fri each month, admission is free between 5 p.m. and 8 p.m. For more information see The Arts chapter.

PORTLAND BUILDING   FREE
1120 Southwest 5th Ave.

Completed in 1984, this wonderful, controversial, 15-story building still evokes potent reactions from local, regional, and national architects, designers, critics, local politicians making some point about public spending and public art, and almost everyone who views it. Designed by Michael Graves as the first public building in a postmodern style in the United States, the colorful Portland Building houses an administrative wing of Portland city government, next door to Portland City Hall, so between 8 a.m. and 5 p.m. you can walk around the lobby and other public areas where local artists' works are on display.

Portlandia was installed in 1985 after being barged up the Willamette River and trucked through downtown. This large, hammered-copper statue, which is second in size only to the more traditional *Statue of Liberty,* represents a modern mythological incarnation or descendant of Lady Commerce, the classic female figure on the city of Portland's official seal. With strong, 9-foot-long thighs and a plunging bronze decolletage, *Portlandia* has been called heroic, revealing, X-rated, and even "statuesque." While some still dissatisfied citizens want her relocated to a more (or less) visible location, the statue was designed for this location. She will remain where she is. There is no admission charge.

PORTLAND CITY HALL   FREE
1221 Southwest 4th Ave.

Portland City Hall, built in 1895, underwent extensive renovation during the late 1990s. This ambitious project not only restored this Italianate building's original floor plan

and reestablished its original look and feel but also preserved one of the most historically important buildings in the city. While the building retains much of its traditional appearance on the outside, its infrastructure is modern and energy-efficient. The building has also been made more accessible to the public, and a number of very Portland touches have been added, including a coffee bar, a secured bicycle parking shelter, and a rose garden that replaced a small, inefficient parking lot. The renovation has also restored natural light, air, and color to the interior of the building by uncovering the original skylights, by refurbishing the beautiful woodwork and floor tiles, and by ripping out walls that had enclosed the stairwells, exposing the decorative copper plating that had once adorned them. This renovated space is a beautiful backdrop for Portland's growing public art collection, some of which can be found on display here. There is no charge to visit City Hall or its art and architecture.

i Portland has a comparatively large requirement for public art (2 percent of publically funded projects). You can download a walking map detailing the works on display from the Regional Arts & Culture Council (www.racc.org/public-art/overview-opportunities).

TOM MCCALL
WATERFRONT PARK   FREE
Bordering Naito Parkway and the Willamette River from Broadway Bridge South to River Place

If Pioneer Courthouse Square is Portland's living room, then the Tom McCall Waterfront Park is the city's front yard. The park starts at the Broadway Bridge, stretches south for about 2 miles and then converts into a portion of the Greenway, a path continuing south to Willamette Park, a total distance of 3.25 miles. Once an ugly freeway cut off the downtown from the Willamette River. Led by Governor Tom McCall, planners came up with the Downtown Plan of 1972, which included the removal of the freeway and the creation of open space that would again reunite the city and river. This space would eventually be named Tom McCall Waterfront Park to honor the governor's contribution to restoring the space to the public. Portlanders have adopted the park with such fervor that it is in danger of being loved to death by an unending series of events, including the Rose Festival Fun Center, the Blue Brewers' Festival, Cinco de Mayo, Blues Festival, Fourth of July fireworks, and the Race for the Cure (see the Portland's Parks chapter for more on this park and the Festivals and Annual Events chapter for more on these special outings). The city has installed hardier sod, improved drainage, and made other changes to help the park bear the wear and tear of all these festivities.

Center stage for Waterfront Park is the Salmon Street Springs Fountain at the foot of Southwest Salmon Street. In hot weather, this fountain, with its spurting jets of water, attracts crowds of adults and children who play and splash in the streams of water and the shallow pool. The dock for the *Portland Spirit,* an excursion boat offering cruises on the Willamette, is also nearby.

The Waterfront Story Garden, a light-hearted cobblestone and granite monument to storytellers, is one of a small number of memorials. Another is the Japanese American Historical Plaza, sometimes referred to as the Garden of Stones. This solemn memorial is best walked from south to north. Along the memorial's formal plaza are stones, some broken, some cut, some shattered, to represent the disrupted lives of 110,000 Japanese Americans interned in camps throughout the western United States during World War II. The stones are carved with inscriptions in English (quotations from Oregonians of Japanese ancestry who were interned) and in Japanese (often written in Japan's unique poetry, haiku). Farther north, near the Steel Bridge, is the Friendship Circle. This sculpture emits the sounds of a Japanese flute and drum and honors the Sister City relationship between Portland and Sapporo, Japan.

Across from the Oregon Maritime Museum is the battleship USS *Oregon* monument. The *Oregon,* known as "McKinley's Bull-dog" because of its role in the Spanish-American War, was a turn-of-the-20th-century battleship launched in 1893. Between the two world wars, the *Oregon* was tied up along the sea wall at the foot of Southwest Jefferson Street as a memorial and museum, but in 1942, as a patriotic gesture, the ship was returned to the US Navy. One of the ship's masts was removed before she was reclaimed by the navy, and it is that battleship-gray mast from which the American and Oregon flags fly along the river.

The final monument along Waterfront Park is, unfortunately, little noted. In a tribute to the staff of the Canadian Embassy in Tehran, Iran, who helped a number of American diplomats and their families escape during the yearlong Iran Hostage Crisis, a small group of Portlanders commissioned a plaque honoring their bravery. The monument is often overlooked and at times is not well maintained, but it is a heartfelt tribute to the quiet bravery of the Canadian diplomatic corps and the Canadian nation.

VIETNAM VETERANS
MEMORIAL   FREE
World Forestry Center
4033 Southwest Canyon Rd.

Oregon's tribute to its Vietnam veterans sits on 11 acres of land in the southwest corner of Hoyt Arboretum, above the World Forestry Center. The Vietnam Veterans Memorial honors the 57,000 Oregonians who served in Southeast Asia, listing by name and date of death the state's nearly 800 known dead and still missing. The memorial puts those deaths in a historical context by including references to state, national, and international events occurring at the same time. The site is reverent, graceful, and solemn, and often the only sounds are those of quiet footsteps, the wind, and the hum of distant traffic. As at the national memorial in Washington, D.C., visitors often find personal remembrances—military insignia, campaign ribbons and medals, faded pictures, flowers, toys, candles, photos of sons and daughters, grandsons and granddaughters—left near a name. Each Memorial Day, an honor guard of ROTC cadets from the University of Portland stands a silent 24-hour guard at the memorial. The ceremony and vigil ends with all the names of the dead being read aloud, to show they are not forgotten, and with the haunting sounds of taps echoing through the trees and hills. The monument is open for viewing during daylight hours. No admission is charged.

*WASHINGTON PARK   FREE
Southwest Park Place at Southwest
Vista Avenue
(503) 823-7529

Washington Park is set on 546 acres on the city's West Hills, where it overlooks downtown Portland and east beyond into the mountains. It is the home of the Oregon Zoo, the World Forestry Center, the Japanese Garden, the Children's Museum, and the Rose Gardens. All these attractions are within walking distance of one another, if you're a sturdy walker. The Zoo, Forestry Center, and Children's Museum are right off the MAX stop, and the Japanese and Rose Gardens are about a mile away along the roads or trails of Washington Park. You can also take the zoo train, which has a station at the Rose Gardens, or the TriMet #63 buses that traverse the park and back to town. (You can also take ART the Cultural Bus. ART is a propane-powered bus painted by Henk Pander, one of Portland's best-known artists.)

The simplest way to the park is a clearly marked exit from westbound US 26 as it leaves downtown Portland and climbs over the West Hills toward Beaverton (follow the exit signs that say OREGON ZOO and WORLD FORESTRY CENTER). This highway is easily accessible (and well marked) from I-5 via I-405. Visitors coming from Portland's Eastside can use either the Fremont Bridge or the Marquam Bridge. If you're downtown already, the two easiest ways to enter Washington Park Place are via Southwest Vista Avenue above PGE Park or close to the intersection of Burnside Street and Northwest 23rd Avenue, at the Uptown Shopping Center. This entrance is the most convenient from Northwest Portland.

This is one of Portland's most popular parks. On summer weekends, especially during the Rose Festival, and during any special event or concert in the park, traffic can be vicious and parking all but impossible. Seriously consider light rail, bus, or even a cab or town car as an alternative to driving. See the listing in the Portland's Parks chapter for more information.

ATTRACTIONS

WORLD FORESTRY CENTER MUSEUM $
4033 Southwest Canyon Rd.
(503) 228-1367
www.worldforestry.org

Before Oregon's Silicon Forest, there were real forests where giant trees were felled by handsaws and axes, hauled or floated to mills, and then cut and finished to build the nation's houses and factories. Built by a consortium of timber and related industries, the World Forestry Center Museum offers information and hands-on exhibits emphasizing the forests of the Pacific Northwest and beyond. There are exhibits of petrified wood and a sculpture of a tiger carved from a 1,000-year-old tree for the 1988 Olympics. An intriguing 70-foot talking Douglas fir tree is designed to interest children as it explains to them how it grows. There are also adventure rides—a white-water "rafting" trip and a 45-foot lift up into the tree canopy (these carry small extra charges beyond the price of admission).

The Forestry Center also hosts a range of special activities, including an annual show featuring Oregon woodworkers and carvers and an exhibit of wooden toys. A gallery features rotating exhibits of photography and other art. The Forest Store, the center's gift shop, offers wooden gifts and other items in keeping with the forest theme. The World Forestry Center Museum is open daily from 10 a.m. to 5 p.m. On Wed, admission is discounted to $2 per person. Parking will set you back $2 per car.

NORTHWEST PORTLAND

OREGON JEWISH MUSEUM $
1953 Northwest Kearney St.
(503) 226-3600
www.ojm.org

The Oregon Jewish Museum is the only institution in the Pacific Northwest devoted to Jewish history and culture; it features an archival library with papers and oral histories about the history of Jews in Oregon, permanent exhibits, and changing exhibits of Jewish history both in Oregon and throughout the world. Call for more information or to make an appointment to visit the museum. The museum is open Tues through Thurs from 10:30 a.m. to 4 p.m., on Fri from 10:30 a.m. to 3 p.m., and on Sun from 1 to 4 p.m.

PITTOCK MANSION $
3229 Northwest Pittock Dr.
(503) 823-3623
www.pittockmansion.org

Henry Pittock, founder of the *Uregonian*, the city's daily newspaper and the largest paper in the state, built himself a château 1,000 feet above the city. The mansion stayed in the family for 50 years, until 1964, when it was sold to the city of Portland. This 22-room, 16,000-square-foot, antiques- and art-filled house is now open to the public. Guided tours of the house are offered each afternoon, and visitors can wander through the gardens of roses, azaleas, and rhododendrons. In spring, flowering cherry trees add their color to the grounds. The view is spectacular. The adjoining Pittock Acres offer hiking and walking trails and are part of the Audubon Society's Wildlife Preserve.

The mansion's gatehouse, which once was the gardener's cottage, is now the Gate Lodge, and it is part of the museum complex. The Pittock Mansion is open for public viewing seven days a week from 11 a.m. to 4 p.m., except in July and Aug, when it opens at 10 a.m. The mansion is closed on major holidays, for a few days in late Nov when holiday decorations are being put up, and during Jan for annual maintenance. The Pittock Mansion is often rented by businesses, private groups, and families for dinners, receptions, meetings, and weddings, but these events are limited to evening hours.

PORTLAND AUDUBON
SOCIETY SANCTUARY   FREE
5151 Northwest Cornell Rd.
(503) 292-6855
www.audubonportland.org
The Portland Audubon Society, a nonprofit group with a long and established concern about Oregon's ecology and wildlife, has worked closely with government agencies to further protect Oregon's natural beauty. A leading example is the Audubon Sanctuary, a 160-acre tract surrounded by Forest Park, a 5,000-acre municipal park, and linked to that park's Wildwood and Macleary Trails. The society also provides a Wildlife Care Center, where injured owls, hawks, herons, cranes, and other birds and waterfowl are cared for until they can be returned to the wild.

Audubon House includes one of the best selections of books on natural history and wildlife. There is also an interpretive center, a nature store, and a viewing window overlooking the feeding platforms for resident songbirds. Hours for the sanctuary and gift shop are 10 a.m. to 6 p.m. Mon through Sat and 10 a.m. to 5 p.m. on Sun. There is no admission charge to visit the sanctuary, and trails are open daily dawn to dusk. Pets should remain in the car.

✳PORTLAND CLASSICAL CHINESE
GARDEN $$
Northwest 3rd Avenue and Everett Street
(503) 228-8131
www.portlandchinesegarden.org

The exquisite Portland Classical Chinese Garden, more formally known as the "Garden of Awakening Orchids," is a double-walled oasis built in a traditional Chinese style with extensive help from Portland's Chinese sister city Suzhou. It inhabits a city block at the north end of Chinatown and serves as a retreat from the chaos of urban life. But it's more than a retreat. The garden integrates the elements of water, stone, light, shadow, color, texture, and fragrance to form an enclosed small world that mysteriously feels as though it unfurls the entire universe within its walls.

Mysteries are at the soul of this place, but its physical existence is due to attentive design and careful building. Clever planning makes good use of views and space; you would never know from the outside that the garden holds a lake of 8,000 square feet, and from the inside, it's hard to remember that the sidewalk is 12 feet away. You enter through a series of courtyards designed to help you make the transition from the outer world of hurry and work and wander along paths, over bridges, beside water, and through rooms with enticing names like "Celestial House of Permeating Fragrance" or "Reflections in Clear Ripples." Similarly, pavilions are named after the meditations they are meant to inspire—"Flowers Bathing in Spring Rain" or "Painted Boat in Misty Rain." The Tower of Cosmic Reflections is a tea house run by Portland's Tao of Tea (traditional Chinese tea and snacks).

Within each discrete space is a carefully arranged display of stones, trees, shrubs, flowers, or other components. Classical Chinese gardens, unlike the gardens of the emperor, were built by gentlemen scholars for their own use, so their scale is small, focusing on the well-wrought detail. No pebble is insignificant. Latticed windows give sunshine a template to decorate the elaborate mosaic floors. Banana plants live underneath the rain gutters to allow a beautiful sound to permeate the garden when it rains and the water splashes onto them. Rocks left in Suzhou streams 60 years ago by grandparents to be naturally sculpted by the water have been harvested by grandchildren and placed with delicate care. All five senses are honored in the feel of the stones, the fragrant blossoms, the sound of water, the taste of tea in the tea house, and the sight of, well, everything.

The deliberate re-creation of nature's spontaneous workings—the Chinese garden is meant to inspire you to think about this paradox and others like it. For the scholars who possessed them—scholars who today would be bureaucrats or businessmen—gardens were places of freedom from the pressure and constraints of official life, where their owners could meditate upon the paradoxes of the freedom found in duty or the nature found in culture. One reason the Chinese Garden is powerful is that such paradoxes are not foreign to us moderns. We buy cars and houses in order to be free but then must slave away to pay for the houses and cars.

It is easy to enjoy the garden on your own, but if you want to learn more about its history, traditions, and symbolism, we strongly recommend taking one of the tours. The garden is open daily, from 10 a.m. to 5 p.m., Nov through Feb, and from 9 a.m. to 6 p.m., Apr through Sept. Public tours are offered at noon and 1 p.m., and private tours can be arranged. The garden is wheelchair accessible.

SOUTHEAST PORTLAND

CRYSTAL SPRINGS RHODODENDRON GARDEN $
Southeast 28th Avenue
(One block north of Woodstock Boulevard)
(503) 823-3640

Long periods of gray days create a great appreciation for color in many Oregonians. You can see this in the well-tended public and private gardens that celebrate the coming of spring and summer with tulips, lilacs, daffodils, azaleas, magnolias, roses, and rhododendrons. Beginning in April Oregonians flock to the seven-acre Crystal Springs Rhododendron Garden to savor the brilliant colors of the garden's 2,500 rhododendrons, azaleas, and other plants. While spring is prime time here, the gardens are a delight at any time of the year. In the fall, the Japanese maples and sourwood trees burst into flame, a defiant gesture against the coming monotones of winter. A spring-fed lake attracts a permanent colony of ducks and other waterfowl, not to mention the area's population of birders. Even when the seasons' colors have peaked, the garden attracts visitors looking for solitude and a temporary respite from urban life.

From the first of Feb through Labor Day, on Tues and Wed admission fees are waived. Adult admission is $3 the rest of the time. Children are always free. The park is open from dawn to dusk. (For further information see the Portland's Parks chapter.)

KIDD'S TOY MUSEUM FREE
1300 Southeast Grand Ave.
(at Main Street)
(503) 233-7807
http://kiddstoymuseum.com

This unique and vast collection of toys was inspired by Frank Kidd's automotive business, beginning with toy cars and other transportation vehicles such as toy trains and planes. Eventually, however, Kidd's joy in toy collecting extended to other areas, including a stellar collection of mechanical banks. To preserve the collection, the owner created a museum that is open to the public free of charge. The Kidd's Toy Museum is open Mon through Thurs from noon until 6 p.m., and on Fri from 1 p.m. until 6 p.m. Weekend visits can be arranged by appointment.

LEACH BOTANICAL GARDEN   FREE
6704 Southeast 122nd Ave.
(503) 823-9503
www.leachgarden.org
Beginning in the 1930s, Lila and John Leach, two amateur botanists, started their five-acre garden along Southeast Portland's Johnson Creek. Credited with discovering 11 new species of Northwest plants, the Leaches eventually grew their garden to include some 14 acres. More than 1,500 species of native ferns, wildflowers, shrubs, and irises contentedly grow in the garden. Rock gardens, bog gardens, and an experimental recycling and composting center have recently been added. The garden is open Sun from 1 until 4 p.m. and Tues through Sat from 9 a.m. until 4 p.m. Admission is free. (Also see the entry in the Portland's Parks chapter.)

OAKS AMUSEMENT PARK $$
Southeast Spokane Street at the
east end of the Sellwood Bridge on the
Willamette River
(503) 233-5777
www.oakspark.com
Oaks Park is a throwback to the days when streetcar companies built amusement parks to stimulate ridership. Originally opened in 1905, Oaks Park has survived the demise of the streetcars (and may yet witness their rebirth), the introduction of television and video games, and several floods to amuse and entertain yet another generation of Portlanders. This isn't Disneyland and it isn't high-tech. Nevertheless, the old-fashioned rides such as the Screaming Eagle and the Tilt-a-Whirl, as well as gentler teacups and merry-go-rounds, are still irresistable.

Besides the games of skill and chance, Oaks Park offers a sedately scary tunnel of love, a giant slide, and a small roller coaster. New rides are in the works, as well as the remodeling of some of the creaky buildings. Picnic tables and fireplaces are available for family use, and there are no rules prohibiting bringing in your own food. The usual amusement park menu of cotton candy and deep-fried "food-on-a-stick" refreshments are also offered. The park's roller-skating rink clearly harkens back to a different era of entertainment, but it is still very popular. It is one of the oldest continuously operating roller rinks in the country and the only one with a live Wurlitzer organ. (Skate rentals are available.) The park is open throughout the year, but its high season is clearly during the summer. It also sponsors Fourth of July fireworks, weather permitting. For more information, refer to the Kidstuff chapter. Gate admission is free except for major events such as Oktoberfest (see the Festivals and Annual Events chapter), but rides, games, and roller-skating carry fees.

✳OREGON MUSEUM OF SCIENCE AND
**   INDUSTRY (OMSI) $$**
1945 Southeast Water Ave.
(503) 797-4000
www.omsi.edu

ATTRACTIONS

One of the most popular attractions in Oregon and one of the five largest science museums in the nation, the Oregon Museum of Science and Industry is really a series of very different exhibits and elements. OMSI is a hands-on museum where visitors, especially children, are encouraged to touch things, try experiments, and question why things happen.

Adults and children alike will enjoy the presentations in the large-screen OMNIMAX theater and the variety of programs in the Murdock Sky Theater, a domed theater for programs on astronomy. The core of the museum is a series of specialized exhibit halls, each with different emphases. The Earth Science Hall shakes things up with its realistic Earthquake Room. Other exhibits present information about natural phenomena and allow visitors to discover the complex interrelationships of the earth's elements. The Life Science Hall focuses on human growth in the fullest sense of the term and includes a house and an office illustrating designs for accessible living and assisting technology. At the Information Science Hall, visitors can beam a personal message into the vastness of space and receive information on the knowledge and skills that created technology as we know it and that constantly expand it. In addition to its permanent exhibits, OMSI offers an exciting array of temporary exhibits, such as [title] Body Worlds 3 [end title], a fascinating exhibit in which plastinated human and mammalian bodies were displayed to show their inner workings, or [title] Lost Egypt: Ancient Secrets, Modern Science [end title], which featured the science behind human and animal mummies and other interesting aspects of Egyptian culture seen through the lenses of modern technologies.

While there is a separate admission charge for *USS Blueback*, the US Navy's last diesel-powered submarine, visitors should not miss a tour of this vessel. The *Blueback* tour lasts 40 minutes, and visitors should carefully read the "Tips for *USS Blueback* Visitors" brochure before buying a ticket. This is a real submarine, with confined spaces, no windows, and no onboard restrooms; access is by ladders instead of stairs. Children must be at least four years old and 36 inches tall to tour the submarine.

OMSI is closed Mon except when a public school holiday falls on a Mon. During the school year it is open Tues through Sun 9:30 a.m. until 5:30 p.m. Summer hours are Mon through Sun 9:30 a.m. to 7 p.m. OMSI also offers a variety of camps, classes, field trips, and special programs for students, adults, and families. The facility has an ATM, a cafe, and vending machines. Not surprisingly, there is a large, well-stocked gift shop with a wide range of science-oriented objects, toys, T-shirts, games, and books. Parking is $2.

VANCOUVER

Vancouver's diverse attractions range from the restoration of original Fort Vancouver and Officers Row to the Ridgefield Wildlife Refuge. While Vancouver shares the Columbia River with Portland, the city is historic and vibrant in its own right. The area code for all attractions in Vancouver and Southwest Washington is 360, and it's always a long-distance call from Portland.

CLARK COUNTY
   HISTORICAL MUSEUM $
1511 Main St.
(360) 993-5679
www.cchmuseum.org

A good starting place for a visit to Vancouver, the museum displays a range of historical artifacts relating to the founding and growth of the area. Additional displays and exhibits document the original Native American residents of the region. There is also an exhibit detailing how the expansion of the railroads across the country and along the Pacific Coast changed the area's economy, population, and contact with the rest of the nation. The museum is open all year (except on major holidays) Tues through Sat from 11 a.m. until 4 p.m.

ESTHER SHORT PARK   **FREE**
6th Street and Columbia Drive
(360) 619-1111
This five-acre site is the state's oldest public square and includes the Victorian Rose Gardens and the 1867 Slocum House, an Italianate structure that is one of the few remaining buildings from Vancouver's earliest residential neighborhoods. Moved from its original site during an urban renewal project, the Slocum House now serves as a theater. With downtown Vancouver experiencing a period of renaissance and revitalization, this park, with its gardens and Victorian-era benches, fountains, and lights, serves as an anchor to the city's past.

✳FORT VANCOUVER NATIONAL
 HISTORIC SITE   **$**
1501 East Evergreen Blvd.
(360) 696-7655, ext. 10
www.nps.gov/fova
Fort Vancouver was originally built by the British not only as a fur-trading center, but also as an attempt to solidify Britain's claim to the entire Northwest Territory. One of 34 such forts the Hudson's Bay Company built, Fort Vancouver became an American outpost

in 1846 when a treaty between the United States and Britain established the 49th parallel as Canada's southern border. Now restored and administered by the National Park Service, Fort Vancouver offers a look at frontier life through a range of restored buildings, exhibits and displays, and re-creations.

Adjacent to Fort Vancouver National Historic Site sits Vancouver Barracks, the first military post in the Oregon Territory. From this base, Americans explored Alaska, fought the Indian Wars, provided security to settlers, and developed an early network of roads, dams, and locks. From May 1849 to the present, Vancouver Barracks has been an active military post. To the north of the Fort Vancouver National Historic Site and just across a vast green is Officers Row, an immaculately restored and rare collection of 21 Victorian-era homes built between 1850 and 1906 by the federal government. The houses were the residences for the military officers and other government officials and their families assigned to Fort Vancouver, Vancouver Barracks, and the army's Department of the Columbia. Homes such as these were once common on American military bases, but this is the only entire Officers Row preserved in the nation. Among the army officers who lived on Officers Row were Generals Phillip Sheridan, Benjamin Bonneville, and Omar Bradley. Guests at Officers Row included three US presidents: Ulysses S. Grant, Rutherford B. Hayes, and Franklin Delano Roosevelt. This site is open from 9 a.m. to 4 p.m. daily during winter and 9 a.m. to 5 p.m. during summer.

THE GEORGE C. MARSHALL
 HOUSE   **FREE**
1301 Officers Row
(360) 693-3103

This Officers Row house, now called the George C. Marshall House, was the home for the commanding officer of Vancouver Barracks. Originally built in 1886 and now completely restored and furnished with antiques from the 1880s, the house is home to the local office of Washington's governor. General Marshall, who was awarded the Nobel Peace Prize in 1953, served as Vancouver Barracks' commanding officer from 1936 to 1938 and lived in the house during that period. In 1937 Marshall opened his home to the three Russian fliers who landed at Pearson Airfield after their transpolar flight. The building was later renamed to honor his service to the nation as the US Army's Chief of Staff during World War II and later as Secretary of Defense and Secretary of State. The George C. Marshall House is open seven days a week, except for major holidays, from 9 a.m. to 5 p.m. There is no charge.

HENRY J. KAISER
  SHIPYARD MEMORIAL   FREE
At boat launch In Marine Park, Southeast Marine Park Way and Columbia Way
During World War II, the Henry J. Kaiser Shipyards in Vancouver and Portland turned out 140 Liberty ships, T-2 Tankers, and escort carriers ("baby flat-tops") for the war effort. The city of Vanport, north of Portland, was built to house the 38,000 workers who migrated to the region from throughout the country to build the ships. The workforce included a large number of African Americans who were recruited in the South and brought to Oregon and Washington by the trainload. The descendants of these workers who stayed after the war formed the core of the area's African-American population, which added to the region's cultural diversity.

The shipyards closed shortly after the end of the war and Vanport was destroyed in a postwar flood. Now, only faint traces of the shipyard's wooden ways remain along the river. The three-story Henry J. Kaiser Shipyard Memorial and Interpretive Center recognizes and honors the contributions of these workers not only to the Allied victory in World War II, but also for their continuing contributions to the region's culture and economy. Admission is free. (For more on Vanport and shipbuilding during the war years, see the History chapter.)

PEARSON AIR MUSEUM AT
  PEARSON AIRFIELD $
1115 East 5th St.
(360) 694-7026
www.fortvan.org/pages/
pearson-air-museum
At the east end of the Fort Vancouver National Historic Site, this aviation museum captures the achievements and excitement of the Golden Age of Aviation in the 1920s and '30s. As part of Vancouver Barracks, Pearson Airfield was established in 1905 as a dirigible base. The early, unwieldy lighter-than-air ships displaced the officers' polo ponies, as the airfield is built on a former polo field.

Having welcomed its first airplane in 1911, Pearson Airfield is the oldest operating airport in the nation. The museum's recently expanded facilities include an airplane hangar dating from the 1920s as well as a new theater, computerized flight simulators, and a working aircraft restoration center. While there are some contemporary aircraft on display, the heart of the museum's aircraft collection and related exhibits reflect earlier eras, concentrating on civilian aviation developments during the two decades before World War II.

Pearson Airfield played an important role in the development of airmail service as a center of early commercial aviation and as an early army aviation base. Tex Rankin and Charles Lindbergh flew from this field, and in 1937 the Russian aircraft making the first nonstop transpolar flight landed here. The Soviet Transpolar Monument, displayed outside the museum, commemorates the accomplishments of the three Soviet aviators who made that historic flight. After unexpectedly landing at Vancouver (they were trying to reach California), the aircrew was greeted by General George C. Marshall, then the officer commanding Vancouver Barracks.

The museum also has a well-stocked gift shop and hosts a variety of lectures and presentations on aviation history and several aviation-themed special events throughout the year, including flights of vintage aircraft. The museum is open daily from 9 a.m. until 5 p.m. in the spring and summer and until 4 p.m. in the fall and winter. There is a small admission fee beyond the entry fee into Fort Vancouver.

OUTLYING AREAS

BONNEVILLE DAM   **FREE**
Off I-84 (exit 40)
Cascade Locks
(541) 374-8820
www.nwp.usace.army.mil/locations/ booneville
A half-hour of scenic driving through the Columbia River Gorge will take you to the Bonneville Dam, which has an attractive visitor center with interactive exhibits, short films, and displays that illustrate the history and culture of local and regional Native American tribes. You can watch steelhead and Chinook salmon climbing the fish ladders and boats passing through the locks. There are no restaurants here, but this is a popular picnic stop for schoolchildren on field trips or families exploring nearby trails, so there are lots of picnic tables, some of them covered. Admission is free. Hours are 9 a.m. to 5 p.m. for the visitor center; other areas may be open later.

HULDA KLAGER LILAC GARDENS   **$**
115 South Pekin Rd., Woodland, WA
(360) 225-8996
www.lilacgardens.com
Well worth the drive, the Hulda Klager Lilac Gardens are easy to find. Just take I-5 north of Vancouver, look for exit 21, and follow the signs. It's a lovely garden, especially during the annual Lilac Festival held during April and May each year, when dozens of varieties of lilacs are in full bloom. The lilacs truly flourish and flower on these well-kept and fertile grounds. The house is listed on the National Register of Historic Places and features a large collection of antique dolls and period furniture and artifacts. There is also a small gift shop. The Lilac Gardens are open year-round, but are most popular, and most crowded, when the blossoms are in flower in late spring or early summer. Gardeners from throughout Washington and Oregon come to buy cuttings and seedlings to plant in their own gardens. The Mager House is open for tours during the Lilac Festival (see the Annual Events chapter). Hours are 10 a.m. to 4 p.m. daily.

OREGON MILITARY MUSEUM AT CAMP WITHYCOMBE   **FREE**
SR 212, Clackamas
(503) 557-5359
www.swiftview.com/~ormilmuseum
The Oregon Military Museum is housed in a Quonset Hut on an Oregon Army National

Guard facility. To get here, take I-205 to SR 212, which heads toward Estacada. After ⅛ mile, turn left on Southeast 102nd and follow to the main-gate entrance of the camp. Its displays and exhibits emphasize the history and accomplishments of the Oregon Army, Oregon Air National Guard, and Oregon veterans. With limited space and resources, the museum's collection includes uniforms, artifacts, models, paintings, a small but impressive library and archives, and, perhaps most important, a knowledgeable and helpful staff. The museum also has a significant collection of restored and functional wheeled and tracked military vehicles and artillery pieces. When visiting, ask to see what was called on national television the "Oh, My God Room." This is actually a very large vault containing the museum's significant collection of handheld weapons. Admission is free although donations are welcomed. The Oregon Military Museum is open on Sat and Sun from 9 a.m. to 5 p.m. or by appointment. The staff is very cooperative in arranging private tours. Freedom isn't free, but visiting this museum is—there is no charge.

✳VISTA HOUSE AT
CROWN POINT   FREE
40700 East Columbia River Historic Hwy.
www.vistahouse.com

Officially Crown Point State Park, Vista House was conceived as a monument to Oregon pioneers and to the completion of the Columbia River SR from Portland to Hood River in 1916 (see the Day Trips chapter's section on the Mount Hood–Columbia Gorge Loop). Two years later, the building was completed. The view from Vista House, which is 733 feet above the Columbia River, is one of the state's most popular, dramatic, and beautiful sights. It can be reached by taking the Historic Columbia River Highway (SR 30) off I-84 at Corbett (exit 22), 15 miles east of Portland.

Designated a Natural Landmark of national significance, Vista House is also listed on the National Register of Historic Places. Visitors will not only be impressed by the sweeping views of the Columbia River, the Cascades, and the Columbia Gorge, but also by the endurance of the cyclists who pedal their way up the winding hills to Vista House. Sunsets and sunrises are spectacular. If you plan on photographing the evening or morning colors, bring a tripod, because the winds can cause a handheld camera to vibrate. In fact, you should be prepared for windy times in general. There is a small gift shop inside the building, but the real attraction is the view. Standing on the edge of the viewing area, often facing into the east wind, the sheer magnitude of the meeting of the mountains and river is dramatic. Admission is free. The Vista House is open spring through fall from 9 a.m. to 6 p.m. daily, and on winter weekends from 10 a.m. to 4 p.m., weather permitting; you will find a gift shop and espresso bar as well.

KIDSTUFF

"**I**f a place has a reputation as being great for children," one of our friends once observed, "it's probably no good for adults." Fortunately, he wasn't referring to his native city. Portland is a great place both for children and for the adults who live with them. Many of the area's major attractions—Washington Park, the Chinese Garden, the Oregon History Center—interest persons both small and large, and many of the attractions designed just for children hold a kind of giddy appeal for their guardians. Here, then, are some of our favorite places to go with children in the Portland Metro area and a little beyond.

Price Code

The following price codes reflect the price of a single admission ticket. Designations marked "Free" mean there is no entrance fee, however there may be additional costs for some activities.

$.................Less than $7
$$ ....$7 to $15
$$$ .... More than $15

ATTRACTIONS & MUSEUMS

Portland

ALPENROSE DAIRY   **FREE**
6149 Southwest Shattuck Rd.
(503) 244-1133,
(503) 246-0330 (Velodrome),
(503) 246-2826 (Quarter-Midget Racing)
www.alpenrose.com
We love Alpenrose Dairy, a rich blend of past and present. The dairy has been in operation since 1891 and still produces cream, milk, ice cream, cottage cheese, and sour cream (though the cows have moved west and south to other Willamette Valley farms). As the city encroached on the pastureland in the 1950s, the dairy's far-sighted owners, the Cadonau family, began to incorporate entertainment into their business. Now the dairy includes a wide range of family activities. Dairyville, a little frontier town, faithfully reproduces the pioneer atmosphere through its displays of shops and other buildings. An opera house that seats 600 is the home of a 4,000-pipe organ that used to reside in the old Portland Civic Auditorium.

Alpenrose also features the Alpenrose Stadium, dating from 1956, which still hosts Little League games, including the Little League World Series. And there are several racing arenas: a quarter-midget track, a BMX track, and a beautiful Olympic-style velodrome. All these arenas are humming with activity. The quarter-midget races feature miniature race cars powered by gas or alcohol and driven by kids. The velodrome, one of only 20 in the United States, holds fast races on bikes with no brakes as well as gentler pre-event races for kids.

Alpenrose also hosts a large Easter egg hunt that delights hundreds of children every year, and other events occur throughout the year. The quarter-midget races, bike races, and Little League events are free, with varying schedules. (Little League spectators are encouraged to buy from the concessions, the proceeds of which support the teams, but you may bring in food. No concessions are available for the bike races.) For information on the bike races at the velodrome, check the Oregon Bicycle Racing Association's web page: www.obra.org/track.

JEFF MORRIS FIRE MUSEUM   FREE
Belmont Firehouse
900 Southeast 35th Ave.
(503) 823-3615
www.jeffmorrisfoundation.org
This museum occupies a historic firehouse, and here you will find a collection of antique fire equipment that helps children learn about the history of fire fighting. Predecessors of the modern era include an 1863 hand-pumper, an 1870 hand-drawn ladder truck, and an 1870 steam-pumper engine, as well as lots of fire-fighting paraphernalia. There's also a modern fire engine that helps you learn what it's like to fight fires today. Plus, you can slide down the fire pole. This little museum is the legacy of Jeff Morris, a firefighter who established the safety-education program at the Portland Fire Bureau and who died of cancer in the 1970s. Admission is free; donations are welcome. You should call ahead and plan your visit, since hours are sporadic. Check the website, however, for the Saturday open houses held throughout the year.

✳OAKS AMUSEMENT PARK $$
Southeast Spokane Street at the
east end of Sellwood Bridge on the
Willamette River
(503) 236-5777
www.oakspark.com
An appealing and old-fashioned amusement park, Oaks Park dates back to the Lewis and Clark Exposition in 1905 and has entertained generations of Portland families. Oaks Park inhabits 44 acres on the Willamette and features rides, games, and a roller-skating rink. (It's also the home of the Multnomah County Fair.) The park offers more than two dozen rides, including a Ferris wheel, a carousel, a miniature train, and bumper cars for smaller children and the Teacups, the Frog Hopper, and the Screamin' Eagle for their big sisters and brothers. Go-karts and miniature golf are popular draws, as is the roller-skating. Not surprisingly, Oaks Park is an irresistible birthday party venue. Concessions are available, but picnics are welcome. Parts of the park are closed during the winter, but the roller rink stays open all year-round. Admission into the park is free, except during the county fair and on the Fourth of July; rides, activities, and roller-skating will cost you, though. Ride bracelets are the best value. Games, go-karts, and golf are priced separately. The Oaks Park website has good directions and more information about hours and prices; you can also call, of course. (See the Attractions chapter for more information.)

✳OREGON MUSEUM OF SCIENCE AND
**   INDUSTRY (OMSI) $$**
1945 Southeast Water Ave.
(503) 797-4000
www.omsi.edu
OMSI (pronounced Ahm-zee) is nestled on the banks of the Willamette River and is

home to the state's biggest science exhibitions and laser light shows. It is a preferred destination for wiggly preschoolers on rainy afternoons, as well as for older children on field trips. OMSI has the gift of making science and technology interesting without reducing it to mindless entertainment, and children really love this place. The museum has standout permanent and temporary features. For example, OMSI was the site of Body Worlds 3, co-sponsored by Oregon Health and Science University. This remarkable exhibit focused on the full range of anatomy, featuring plastinated human figures that revealed the mysteries of the body, complemented with exhibits and activities from the region's only academic health center. Among the permanent exhibits, you'll find a fascinating display on fetal development as well as a computer station that allows you to see what your face will look like in the coming decades. Wonderful exhibits cover the geology and weather of the region—and should you want to prepare yourself for the Big One, you will find an earthquake simulator. For children younger than seven, the Discovery Space, with its sand, water, slime, magnets, levers, and other intriguing features, will provide hours of entertainment. Richard Scarry's Busytown is a frequent visitor, much to the delight of the preschool set.

Children also love other parts of OMSI: the USS Blueback (a diesel-powered submarine now permanently moored on the banks of the Willamette), the planetarium, and the OMNIMAX theater with its million-dollar projector and five-story screen. Snacks are welcome; concessions are available too. Expect to pay a separate fee for the OMNIMAX theater, laser shows, the submarine, and the planetarium. OMSI also has a great education program and camp. If you think you'll go a lot, you should buy a membership. They kindly remain open on Mon when Portland Public Schools are not in session during the school year. (For more details, see the Attractions chapter.)

#THE OREGON ZOO $$
Washington Park
4001 Southwest Canyon Rd.
(503) 226-1561
www.oregonzoo.org

The Oregon Zoo is a well-visited attraction, but it has a number of features beyond the extensive and naturally compelling animal exhibits that make it a great place for families. First, children love the exhibits, which attempt to faithfully re-create how the animals would live in the wild. Second, there is a lot for children to do: animals to pet, things to climb on, trails for skipping, benches for resting. Many exhibits allow you surprising proximity to the zoo's creatures; there's nothing quite like the feeling of being mistaken by a butterfly for a flower or having to stop in the aviary to let an exotic hen herd her little chicks across the path or being separated by a mere inch or so of glass from a fierce, hungry-looking Amur leopard. Third, the zoo has a great train. Fourth, the zoo is dedicated to saving animals and teaching people about them. For example, the Oregon Zoo has the most successful elephant management program in the country, and more than two dozen baby elephants have been born here since 1962, when Packy was the first elephant born in the United States in 44 years. Packy still lives here and celebrates his birthday every April.

The zoo also has many special events, programs just for home-schooled kids, and well-run, popular day camps during school breaks. During the winter, Zoo Lights—light displays shaped like animals—draw large holiday-season crowds, even on rainy and chilly winter nights. The zoo train is the best way to see them, but lines are long, so dress warmly. During the summer, concerts that feature jazz, folk, world, and many other kinds of music (many of which are free with zoo admission) entice families to spend the late afternoon at the zoo and then sit down with a picnic dinner. They relax on the amphitheater lawn, swaying to the music and honoring the end of the beautiful summer's day. Sometimes the elephants wander out and sway along with the crowd. These concerts are one of the best things about a Portland summer.

The Oregon Zoo is open every day, except Christmas Day, from 9 a.m. until 4 p.m., except from May 15 to Sept 15, when it is open from 8 a.m. until 6 p.m. The zoo stays open for an hour after the gates close, unless you're attending a special event or concert, when you can stay longer. The Zoo Railway has a separate fee. By car, the zoo is best reached by a well-marked exit from westbound US 26 as it leaves downtown Portland. Parking is $2 per car. The zoo is also accessible via TriMet Bus #63 and the Washington Park MAX stop. On summer weekends and during many concerts, parking can be particularly scarce, so light rail may be the least frustrating way to get here. You can buy tickets online, except for on the second Tues of each month, when admission is discounted to $4 per person. (The zoo is very crowded then, as well.) If you think you'll go to the zoo often, a family membership is a must. (See the Attractions chapter for more information on the zoo.)

PORTLAND ART MUSEUM $$
1219 Southwest Park Ave.
(503) 226-2811
www.portlandartmuseum.org

The Portland Art Museum has a number of programs designed to educate—and entertain—children and their families. Museum Family Days are held four times a year. These programs help children explore the artistic process, inspired by the displays in the museum. Families can make their own works of art—their own Giacomettis, Calders, Klimts, and Monets—as well as learn about the originals through discussions, lectures, and performances. Check the website to find out the schedules. Every week, Family Sundays feature special tours, story times, and art-making activities. And the museum also offers art classes for ages three and older (including adults) on weekend evenings, weekends, and during school breaks. A family membership is highly recommended if you plan to go more than once a year. You'll have access to great programs, and you'll save money. Hours are Tues through Sat 10 a.m. to 5 p.m., except on Thurs and Fri, when the museum is open 10 a.m. to 8 p.m.; Sun from noon to 5 p.m. Family programs can fill up fast, so plan ahead. (For more information see the Attractions chapter.)

*PORTLAND CHILDREN'S MUSEUM $
Washington Park across from the
Oregon Zoo
4015 Southwest Canyon Rd.
(503) 223-6500
www.portlandcm.org

The Portland Children's Museum, which dates from 1949, was wonderfully renovated in 2001 and became an instant hit with local children. It's especially popular with preschoolers, who adore the high-quality, innovative, and varied play spaces, which range from a child-size grocery store and restaurant to the ingenious waterworks room, where children turn cranks and wind pulleys to rush water through pipes and pools (plastic aprons are provided). Other spaces are devoted to dressing up, to music, and to art. The clay room allows children to pound, roll, and shape real clay. Next door is a small room that features a variety of papery workshops—everything from painting with watercolor crayons to sewing little books. (Older children especially like the art workshops, which include pottery painting and the "Garage," a studio for making art out of recycled materials.) All these activities are supervised by friendly, knowledgeable staff. The museum also offers amusements just for babies, various organized events, special activities for the holidays, and spaces for birthday parties, as well as facilities for field trips and group tours. The museum is open Tues through Sun from 9 a.m. to 5 p.m.—they stay open until 8 p.m. on Thurs. Parking costs $2. TriMet Bus #63 serves the museum, and the MAX line makes its Washington Park stop just across the parking lot. The museum is also the home of the Opal School, an arts-based charter school (see the Child Care and Education chapter).

✳WORLD FORESTRY CENTER $
4033 Southwest Canyon Rd.
(503) 228-1367
www.worldforestry.org
The World Forestry Center makes a quiet change from the zoo and offers a cool respite from a hot summer day. This museum is dedicated to educating us about the roles that forests have played in culture and in nature. Its permanent collections feature a number of interesting exhibitions, including one on the history of tropical rain forests. These life-size dioramas were developed in collaboration with the Smithsonian, and they tell the story of three different forest families and their struggles in the changing

tropical woods. The 70-foot talking Douglas fir tree that stands at the center of the museum is also a draw—as are two adventure rides, one featuring a white-water rafting experience and the other, the Canopy Lift, a chance to view the forest from a bird's eye by rising 45 feet into the air. (There are small separate charges for the rides.)

The Forestry Center also features the Forest Discovery Lab for children, which offers hands-on activities such as puppet shows, stories, and building forests. The Center hosts a range of special activities, including an annual show featuring Oregon woodworkers and carvers and an exhibit of wooden toys. A gallery features rotating exhibits of photography and other art. The World Forestry Center Museum is open daily from 10 a.m. to 5 p.m. Wednesday, admission is discounted to $2 per person. Parking is $2.

Outlying Areas

✳A. C. GILBERT MUSEUM $
116 Marion St. NE, Salem
(503) 371-3631, (800) 208-9514
www.acgilbert.org
Pretending you are a Maasai herder, a 19th-century explorer, or a modern astronaut are just a few of the compelling activities available at the A. C. Gilbert Museum in Salem—a truly worthy excursion from Portland. This museum complex, made up of three Victorian houses on the Willamette, is filled with interactive exhibitions that are so interesting you might forget they are supposed to be good for you. It's hard to say which you'll like best. Is it the Frozen Shadow room, which captures your shadow on the wall? Is it the bubble room, where you can inhabit a giant bubble? Perhaps it's the Earth's Fury room, which allows you to build buildings and towns and then wipe them out with floods

and earthquakes. You will also find many other diversions, including a room devoted to puzzles, a toy-inventors' workshop, a toddler room, and wonderful temporary exhibitions, educational programs, and special events. A. C. Gilbert, a Salem native, was a toy inventor who gave us, among other things, the Erector Set and American Flyer trains. This museum is a fitting tribute to his contribution to American childhood. Hours are Mon through Sat 10 a.m. to 5 p.m. and Sun from noon to 5 p.m.

BONNEVILLE DAM AND
FISH HATCHERY   FREE
Off I-84 (exit 40)
Cascade Locks
(541) 374-8820
www.nwp.usace.army.mil/op/b/
Children and their parents will love the beautiful half-hour drive from Portland through the Columbia River Gorge to the Bonneville Dam and its next-door neighbor, the Bonneville Fish Hatchery. The dam's attractive and informative visitor center is brimming with interactive exhibits, short films, and displays that illustrate the history and culture of local and regional Native American tribes. Watching the big boats pass through the locks is truly compelling, as are the dam's huge generators inside the powerhouse. Little ones are entranced by the sight of steelhead trout and Chinook, coho, and sockeye salmon stubbornly climbing the fish ladders, though sometimes older siblings grumble about dam breaching and salmon policy. Summer is the best time to go—that's when the fish are most active. At the fish hatchery, watch the trout and sturgeon that you can feed (25 cents per handful). No restaurants are nearby, so you may want to bring food—there are numerous picnic tables (some covered). On the return trip, take a hike along one of the many trails at or near Multnomah Falls, one of the area's premier attractions any time of year. The Army Corps of Engineers, which operates the dam, suggests that you call before your visit. First, many events for children are held, so you might want to plan for them. And second, increased security measures have made the schedule less predictable. You'll want to make sure it's open before you set out. Admission is free.

ENCHANTED FOREST $$$
8462 Enchanted Way SE, Turner
(503) 371-4242
www.enchantedforest.com
We were grateful to finally have children so that we could have an excuse to visit the Enchanted Forest, just south of Salem and a little bit less than an hour's drive south from Portland. This amusement park features imaginative rides, displays, and activities for children of all ages (though some rides have height requirements). One of the nicest things about this place is the balance between thrilling rides and gentler activities. A half-timbered English Village and a replicated Old West town are fun to poke around, while a bobsled-inspired roller coaster and a scary haunted house provide more adrenaline-inducing entertainment. And the Big Timber Log Ride is a fun, splashy way to cool off on a hot summer day. The fountain features a light show coordinated to its cascading jets. Children also love exploring the storybook-theme displays, including the rabbit hole from *Alice in Wonderland,* the cottage of the Seven Dwarfs, and the home of the Old Woman Who Lived in a Shoe. In addition, you'll find bumper boats, a Ferris wheel, and trails to explore.

The price of admission will allow you into most activities, but a number of the most popular features—including the haunted house, the log ride, and the bumper boats—require an additional fee. Ride bracelets are in addition to the cost of admission, but they are probably the best deal. Concessions are available, but picnics are welcome. Children two and younger are admitted at no charge. The park is easily accessed from the freeway. Take I-5 south from Portland to exit 248 (Sunnyside-Turner) to get there. High season is the summer; then, it's open from !0 a.m. to 5 p.m. during the week and until 6 or 7 p.m. on the weekends. During the fall and winter, it's usually only open on the weekends. Check the website's calendar before you head down.

FARMS

It is a habit of many Portland children to mark the seasons by what's going on at area farms. Summer is berry- and peach-picking season, fall means it's time for the pumpkin patch, winter brings Christmas trees, and spring means tulips. Many local farms have made the most of their naturally interesting happenings and have become attractions in their own right. For a complete guide to local farms, seasonal bounty, and agriculture activities for kids, check Oregon Agri-Business's consumer website: **www.oregon fresh.net.** In the meantime, here are some of our favorites.

✳FIR POINT FARMS   **FREE**
14601 Arndt Rd., Aurora
(503) 678-2455
http://firpointfarms.com
About a half an hour's drive from downtown Portland, Fir Point Farms offers flowers, fresh produce, tours (by reservation), a deli, gift shop, and Tillamook ice cream. In the fall, Fir Point Farms is the host to swarms of pumpkin-picking schoolchildren, and weekends in Oct feel more like a farm exhibit in Central Park than a farm in Oregon, but between the excellent homemade doughnuts and the hay-wagon rides, it's not easy to resist the charm of Fir Point Farms, even with the crowds. A big, slippery slide that dumps you into a pile of hay is a popular entertainment. Other allurements include a spooky hay maze, pony rides, and the chickens, turkeys, cows, horses, and goats. You can feed most of the animals, and the owners have capitalized on the attraction of this activity for city folks by charging 25 cents for a handful of chow. The greedy goats are the most fun to watch as they storm unwary visitors. In addition to their large, wooded pen, the goats have a tree house for their amusement, where they scamper along platforms 12 feet in the air, peering down at gawking parents and children. You can send food up to the goats by means of buckets on pulleys. That alone is worth the trip. Fir Point Farms is open from 9 a.m. to 6 p.m. every day. Fall weekends have the most activities. There is no charge for admission, but rides and games will cost you a small amount.

i If you watch The Learning Channel's *Little People, Big World,* you might know that the family it features, the Roloffs, have a working farm near Hillsboro. Area residents have been purchasing their Halloween pumpkins from the Roloffs for years, and you can too. Their farm is open daily during pumpkin season, and they offer hayrides in addition to golden squashy wonders. Find directions to the farm and harvest-season hours at http://therolofffamily.com/farm/.

FLOWER FARMER $
2512 North Holly Rd., Canby
(503) 266-3581
www.flowerfarmer.com
www.phoenixandholly.com

When you visit the Flower Farmer, south and east of Portland in Canby, you will find yourself with plenty of company—and not all children. The main draw is the train, and in particular Sparky and Fred. Sparky is a pint-size, 30-horsepower diesel engine that pulls the Phoenix and Holly Railroad's 15-inch narrow-gauge train through flower-beds and fields on a winding half-mile circuit of tracks. The bright red caboose is named Fred. Together they attract daily crowds of preschoolers, schoolchildren, seniors, and anybody else with a love of narrow-gauge trains. The train makes its circular journey through tunnels and past fun displays, making a stop at a petting zoo with chickens, turkeys, and a miniature donkey. Another stop brings you to a pumpkin patch, with a colossal hay pyramid that kids love and parents hate. The final stop is the gift shop, with ice cream and other treats, as well as a good selection of dried flowers, fresh flowers, and seasonal produce. The Flower Farmer is open from daily; the train runs on the weekends, The hours may vary, so be sure call or check the website. Many events are scheduled throughout the year, especially at Halloween and Christmas.

THE PUMPKIN PATCH $
16511 Northwest Gillihan Rd., Sauvie Island
(503) 621-3874
www.thepumpkinpatch.com

The Pumpkin Patch on beautiful Sauvie Island swarms with schoolchildren on field trips in the fall, but it's open as early as June.

Its classic red barn is home to rabbits, pigs, and other animals. The u-pick fields are filled with luscious berries (for example, straw-berries, raspberries, blueberries) as well as apricots, nectarines, tomatoes, flowers, and, of course, pumpkins. During the harvest festival, wagon and pony rides keep the little ones busy. An elaborate, scary, dark, and beloved corn maze (or "corn maize" as they like to call it) attracts older kids and adults, especially on crisp fall nights. (Be forewarned: It is very muddy, even when the weather is dry, and it gets cold.) To get to the Pumpkin Patch, take US 30 west to Sauvie Island and circle left under the bridge. This will place you on Gillihan Road, and you'll find the farm after about 2 miles—watch for the signs.

RASMUSSEN FRUIT AND
FLOWER FARM FREE
3020 Thomsen Rd., Hood River
(541) 386-4622, (800) 548-2243
www.rasmussenfarms.com

Rasmussen Farms—an hour's drive east from Portland in the scenic Hood River area—is a destination throughout the year because of its varied harvests of cherries (July), pears and apples (Sept), and pumpkins (Oct). Rasmus-sen's Halloween celebrations make it one of the most popular pumpkin patches around. At the foot of Mount Hood, the beautiful set-ting of this farm would be enticing with or without the pumpkins. Rasmussen is open from April until just before Thanksgiving, 9 a.m. to 6 p.m. daily. (Rasmussen also has a good online store).

SLEIGHBELLS FREE
23870 Southwest 195th Place, Sherwood
(503) 625-6052, (866) 857-0975
http://sleighbells.biz

Oregon produces more Christmas trees than any other state in the union, and during December, you can't drive 2 miles in the countryside without running into three tree farms. Many families begin their holiday season with a trip to Sleighbells on the weekend after Thanksgiving, where they pick out their tree and sip hot cocoa. Sleighbells is more than a tree farm, however; it's a holiday extravaganza. The gift shop features a variety of collectible ornaments from Christopher Radko, Polanaise, Slavic Treasures, Chase, Snowbabies, and Department 56 among other lines (that is to say, breakable things). Wreaths and garlands are available during the season, and gifts and crafts are available year-round. Of note are the strolling peacocks that lend an exotic air. You can choose between precut trees or hacking one down yourself. Sleighbells also offers a variety of different activities throughout the year. It's open from 10 a.m. to 6 p.m. daily.

PLANES, TRAINS & AUTOMOBILES

CANBY FERRY $
South end of Mountain Road, Wilsonville
North end of Holly Street, Canby
(503) 650-3030
**www.co.clackamas.or.us/transportation/
transit/ferry.htm**
The charming Canby Ferry is an echo of the past, when the Willamette was not festooned with bridges. If you follow Holly Road north from the Flower Farmer (see separate entry in this chapter) to the end, you'll reach the ferry, in operation since 1914 and one of the few remaining river ferries in the area. The friendly operator will take you and your car across the river on a platform ferry that holds nine vehicles and takes about five minutes. The ferry tracks peacefully along a cable in the river.

After you cross, you can take Mountain Road north; it will turn into Stafford Road and take you to I-205. (From the other direction, take I-205 to Stafford Road and proceed south, following Mountain Road.) This little journey is one of the favorite details of our trips to the Flower Farmer and Fir Point Farms. Everyone used to cross the Willamette this way, and it's both a welcome respite from modern hurry and a reminder of what we take for granted. There is a small charge for cars; bikes and pedestrians ride free. The Canby Ferry runs from 6:45 a.m. to 9:15 p.m. daily.

**COLUMBIA GORGE
  STERNWHEELER** $$$
Cascade Locks
(503) 224-3900, (800) 224-3901
www.portlandspirit.com
Sternwheelers were once common along the Columbia and Willamette, though now they are a means to a pleasant afternoon or evening rather than a means of transportation. The Columbia Gorge Sternwheeler, as it chugs down and back through part of the Columbia Gorge National Scenic Area, is a fine way to learn about Lewis and Clark, the Oregon Trail, Bridge of the Gods, and the river routes that were the area's first freeways. Boarding begins at Marine Park in Cascade Locks (take I-84 east from Portland to exit 44, which takes about 45 minutes). The cruise takes about two hours. Summer is the best time to go, for you can sit out on the deck and watch the windsurfers race you. The Columbia Gorge also offers a sunset dinner cruise and a champagne brunch cruise on the weekends, but the scenery is enough of a feast. They also offer special events that coincide with the Fourth of July and other holidays as well as dances and many other fun events. The schedule is limited from Oct through May. It's a good

idea either to purchase tickets ahead of time (on their website) or to call ahead, especially during the summer.

CONCOURS D'ELEGANCE $$–$$$
Pacific University, 2043 College Way, Forest Grove
(503) 357-3006
www.forestgroveconcours.org
This classic and vintage car event, held in July, features 40 different classes of automobiles that have been lovingly restored and preserved. It's also a fund-raiser put on by the Rotary Club of Forest Grove, which passes along the proceeds to local community service and scholarship funds. The beautiful Corvettes, Cadillacs, and Model Ts are so different from today's minivans and SUVs that kids can spend a couple hours wandering through the 300-car exhibition. For kids who like cars, this is a fun event and a nice day trip. See the Festivals and Annual Events chapter for more information.

MALIBU GRAND PRIX $$$
9405 Southwest Cascade Ave., Beaverton
(503) 641-8122
www.maliburaceway.com
The Portland version of the Malibu Grand Prix has lots of entertainment for the pre-license crowd, from whizzing round the track in an F-50 to the latest video games to batting cages. The Grand Prix has two racetracks and three go-kart models, and some of them go quite fast (helmets and harnesses are required). The F-50s require a height of 4 feet 6 inches and an age of at least eight, and if you'll be chauffering your children, they must be at least 3 feet 6 inches. The Malibu Grand Prix is a popular site for birthday parties. Hours are Mon through Thurs, 11 a.m. to 9 p.m.; Fri and Sat, 11 a.m. to 11 p.m.; Sun, 11

a.m. to 8 p.m. You'll get a better deal if you buy laps in bulk.

PEARSON AIR MUSEUM $
1115 East 5th St.
Vancouver, WA
(360) 694-7026
www.fortvan.org/pages/
pearson-air-museum
The Pearson Museum, part of the Vancouver Historic Reserve, is committed to preserving the nation's oldest operating airstrip. Its family activities include interactive exhibits at the Children's Hands-on Activity Center, which teaches kids about the science of flight through various stations. These allow kids to experiment with airflow and air resistance, propeller speed, and other interesting things that you've always wondered about. The museum is open daily from 9 a.m. until 5 p.m. in the spring and summer and until 4 p.m. in the fall and winter. There is a small admission fee beyond the entry fee into Fort Vancouver. (See the Attractions chapter for more information.)

PHOENIX AND HOLLY RAILROAD $
2512 North Holly Rd., Canby
(503) 266-3581
www.flowerfarmer.com
www.phoenixandholly.com
This little 15-inch, narrow-gauge train pulls hordes of schoolchildren through the fields of the Flower Farmer. If your children are fans of trains, they will love this one. (See the entry for the Flower Farmer in this chapter.)

SHADY DELL PACIFIC RAILROAD FREE
Pacific Northwest Live Steamers
31083 South Shady Dell Dr., Molalla
(503) 829-6866
www.pnls.org

Something about the Molalla area inspires train building. Pacific Northwest Live Steamers, which dates from the 1960s, was one of the first hobby trains in the area. This beautiful, four-acre private park is devoted to a small-scale railroad featuring handcrafted steam-, electric-, and gas-powered locomotives that wend their way around a 3,800-foot, 7.5-inch-gauge track. The park is open from May to Oct on Sun and holidays from noon to 5 p.m. Admission is free, but (tax-deductible) donations are welcome.

THE SPRUCE GOOSE   **$$$**
Evergreen Aviation Museum
SR 18, 1 mile east of McMinnville
(503) 434-4180
www.sprucegoose.org
This museum is not only the home of the giant Spruce Goose—the Hughes Air H-4 Hercules, which is actually made out of birch—but it also houses myriad aircraft from US aviation history in its 121,000-square-foot facility, including the Apollo Lunar Module. The museum, which is set in the midst of verdant fields in the middle of wine country, features a replica of the Wright brothers' original 1903 craft as well as fighter jets, commercial planes, and, in the spirit of those aviation pioneers, home-built aircraft from the 1990s. It also features an IMAX theater. The museum is open daily from 9 a.m. to 5 p.m. except Thanksgiving, Christmas, and New Year's, with tours at 11 a.m. and 1:30 p.m. Children five and younger are admitted free of charge, and special discounts are available for students, seniors, and military folk, past and present.

**THE WESTERN ANTIQUE AEROPLANE
  & AUTOMOBILE MUSEUM**   **$$**
Ken Jernstedt Airfield 4S2
1600 Museum Rd., Hood River
(541) 308-1600
www.waaamuseum.org
The Western Antique Aeroplane & Automobile Museum, in beautiful Hood River, features not only beautifully restored old planes and cars, but also planes and cars that actually still work. Here you will find Model T's and Studebakers, as well as a very large collection of operating antique planes—among them a rare Curtiss Jenny. The museum also has an extensive restoration program, and they hold numerous events throughout the year where they take the planes up in an inspiring homage to human endeavor.

SPORTS

Portland is a city full of outdoor enthusiasts, and they seem pretty much born that way, but their inclinations are abetted by facilities all over the city. Words can hardly do justice to the extensive, well-run, and popular programs run by the **Portland Parks and Recreation Department.** They offer the greatest variety of sports and other athletic activities in the city, including dancing, swimming, even snowshoeing. They offer class sessions continually and also sponsor team sports such as soccer and basketball. Call them at (503) 823-PLAY. You can also find out about organized team sports by contacting your child's school.

In general, Portland's parks, sports programs, and trails are filled with children. The city has many parks with excellent playground equipment, and much of that equipment has undergone a renaissance in the past few years. Exceptional playgrounds include Washington Park, where the substantial, bright red, blue, and yellow equipment near the Rose Garden is designed to keep preschoolers and their big brothers and sisters occupied for hours; Laurelhurst Park, which has a series of bridges that are good for playing tag; Gabriel Park, with its bright green grassy hills that look like they're straight out of *Teletubbies;* Sellwood Park and its wonderful tall fir trees; and Mount Tabor Park, which has views of Mount St. Helens in addition to its climbing structure and swings. Many school grounds are adjacent to parks and have good equipment, as well. Places that inspire bursts of running in children include Waterfront Park, Pioneer Courthouse Square, the Eastbank Esplanade, the plaza in front of OMSI, and the big lawn at the Oregon Zoo. The Hoyt Arboretum draws families who love to hike, and Powell Butte, just east of town, offers a network of easy trails so that children can explore the vestiges of the old farm it once was. (More information about the parks and their programs in the area may be found in the Portland's Parks chapter, and more information about sports may be found in the Recreation chapter.)

Bowling

Bowling is a fun, inexpensive, rainy-day activity in the Portland Metro area, and many of the area's bowling alleys offer family specials, foolproof bumper bowling, glow-in-the-dark cosmic bowling, and other enticements. Birthday parties are often held at bowling alleys, and many lanes have good deals on packages. Shoes are available at all the places listed below, which are some of our favorites. Smoking is not allowed in bowling alleys (or most other businesses) in Oregon, so the air is now fresher for the kids. See the Recreation chapter for more bowling alleys in Portland.

Portland

AMF PRO-300 LANES $$
3031 Southeast Powell Blvd.
(503) 234-0237

HOLLYWOOD BOWL $$
4030 Northeast Halsey St.
(503) 288-9237

Outlying Areas

SUNSET LANES $$
12770 Southwest Walker Rd., Beaverton
(503) 646-1116

VALLEY LANES $$
9300 Southeast Beaverton-Hillsdale Hwy., Beaverton
(503) 292-3523

Ice-Skating

LLOYD CENTER ICE RINK $$
953 Lloyd Center
(503) 288-6073
www.lloydcenterice.com
This popular ice-skating rink, at the Lloyd Center shopping mall, brings people of all ages to scoot, slip, and skate their way around the ice. Shoppers stand about, sipping coffee, watching beginners lurch past orange cones and pairs of ice dancers whoosh elegantly by. Besides offering ice-skating and hockey lessons, this is a favorite place for birthday parties and all sorts of festive occasions. The Ice Chalet also offers a summer camp for youngsters who are serious about wanting to learn to skate. Ice skates are available to rent.

MOUNTAIN VIEW ICE ARENA $$
14313 Southeast Mill Plain Blvd.,
Vancouver, WA
(360) 896-8700
www.mtviewice.com
Whether you are looking for hockey, lessons, birthday parties, or just a place to wear out the children, the Mountain View Ice Arena is there for you. Public skating times are Mon through Fri, 10 a.m. to noon and 2 to about 5 p.m. and Sat and Sun from 1 to 4 p.m., as well as Fri and Sat nights from 7:30 to 9:30 p.m. Skates are available to rent.

Miniature Golf

Miniature golf is the ideal way to keep those grade-schoolers busy when summer starts to get boring. Miniature golf can be found at the **Family Fun Center** (listed under Games in this chapter) and the **Mount Hood Summer Action Park** (listed under Summer Activities in this chapter). Our favorite is **Tualatin Island Greens** (20400 Southwest Cipole Rd., Tualatin; 503-691-8400 or www.tualatinislandgreens.com). The putting course on this public range consists of 18 famous golf holes reduced to scale, so it will be extra fun for anyone with a serious interest in golf. For the not-so-serious golfers, try **Glowing Greens** (509 Southwest Taylor St.; 503-222-5554), which features glow-in-the-dark pirate miniature golf. They are open on Fri and Sat from noon to midnight and on Sun from noon to 10 p.m. It's a change from the usual birthday party juggernaut.

Rock Climbing

✳PORTLAND ROCK GYM
21 Northeast 12th Ave.
(503) 232-8310
www.portlandrockgym.com

Are your kids climbing the walls? Why not let them do it in a place with a 38-foot rope and bouldering courses? This fun climbing gym also has lots of classes and camps for children—and is a popular spot for birthday parties. The instructors are patient and friendly. The Portland Rock Gym is open Mon, Wed, and Fri from 11 a.m. to 11 p.m.; Tues and Thurs from 7 a.m. to 11 p.m.; Sat from 9 a.m. to 7 p.m.; and Sun from 9 a.m. to 6 p.m. (See the entry in the Recreation chapter.)

Roller-Skating

Roller-skating is available at several rinks throughout the area. You can rent skates or bring your own provided they don't have black brakes. **Oaks Park** (listed under Attractions and Museums in this chapter) is one of the largest and best rinks in the area, and it has a Wurlitzer theater organ besides. The **Mount Scott Community Center** (5530 Southeast 72nd Ave.; 503-823-3183) is the cheapest, a great place for birthday parties. **Skate World** (1220 Northeast Kelly, Gresham, 503-667-6543; and in Hillsboro, at 4395 Southeast Witch Hazel Rd., 503-640-1333) has some good family programs that allow parents in street shoes to help their beskated preschoolers around the rink.

Skateboarding

Portland is a skateboard mecca. It even has designated skateboard paths downtown. Resources for skateboarders include **Cal's Pharmacy Skateboards and Snowboards** (15 Northeast Hancock St.; 503-233-1237), where they will charmingly and attentively help even clueless parents; they also run the Department of Skateboarding, an indoor skate park right next door to the shop. **Cal Skate Skateboards** (210 Northwest 6th;

503-248-0495; www.calsk8.com) also has a fantastic selection. An essential resource is the website www.skateoregon.com, which features a comprehensive guide to all the skate parks in Oregon. And because there are nearly 100, there's probably one near you. For more detailed information about Portland skateboarding, visit http://skateportland.org, where the state of the skate—including topics such as the Master Skateboard Plan (yes, there is one)—is under debate.

BURNSIDE SKATEPARK   FREE
Under the Burnside Bridge on the east side of the Willamette River

This legendary skate park was built by hand by ambitious skateboarders—illegally. But then the city realized that public concrete everywhere would be better served by allowing a place for skateboarders to go, and they sanctioned it. And thus a revolution was born, for the builders of the Burnside Skatepark inspired a national movement. It's still one of the best. There are no fees and few rules here, but if your kids are inexperienced, try to go at off-peak times (early in the day).

CHEHALEM SKATEPARK   FREE
1210 Blaine St., Newberg
(503) 538-7454

This landmark facility is worth a special trip. *Skate Oregon* calls this the best skatepark on Earth, with 29,000 square feet of skatable surface. It was designed and executed with the help of actual skateboarders. There's also a BMX track at the same site, so BMXers are not competing for space. Chehalem Skatepark is free; helmets are required.

Games

ELECTRIC CASTLES WUNDERLAND $
3451 Southeast Belmont St.
(503) 238-1617
www.wunderlandgames.com

Your kids will finally have something to do with the nickels they collect for bottle deposits. Wunderland carries all the hottest video and pinball games, including test games. New games arrive all the time. If you're a pinball wizard, some of the payoffs from video and pinball games can be redeemed for prizes. Wunderland is also a very popular spot for birthday parties. There's a small admission fee; everything else runs on nickels. The Avalon and Milwaukie Wunderland locations also show family-friendly, first-run movies at very good prices. Additional locations are at 10306 Northeast Halsey St. (503-255-7333); 11011 Southeast Main St., Milwaukie (503-653-2222); and 4070 Cedar Hills Blvd., Beaverton (503-626-1665).

FAMILY FUN CENTER AND
BULLWINKLE'S RESTAURANT $$$
29111 Southwest Town Center Loop West
Wilsonville
(503) 685-5000
www.fun-center.com

The Family Fun Center offers a double-story game arcade, batting cages, go-karts, and bumper boats. Miniature golf helps them work on their hand-eye coordination, while a flight simulator provides some high-tech fun. Laser tag is featured as well. The restaurant, Bullwinkle's, specializes in kid-friendly cuisine such as pizza and burgers. A destination birthday spot.

ULTRAZONE $$$

Holly Farm Shopping Center

16074 Southeast McLoughlin Blvd.,

Milwaukie

(503) 652-1122

www.ultrazoneportland.com

The big attraction here: high-tech interactive, laser-tag games. The futuristic atmosphere, with mazes, strobe lights, and special sound effects, adds to the enjoyment. Ultrazone is recommended for kids older than five. Adults like to play too, and corporations will sometimes sponsor team-building events here, so don't be surprised if you spy Joe from accounting.

The Arts

Children have many opportunities to both participate in and watch the performing arts in Portland. In addition to the annual *Nutcracker* performances by the Oregon Ballet Theater and the summer concerts at the Oregon Zoo, you'll find a variety of child-centered theater programs. The puppet theater, **Tears of Joy Theatre,** (503) 248-0557, and the **Oregon Children's Theatre Company,** (503) 228-9571, perform seasonally for children and adults; the **Ladybug Theater,** (503) 232-2346, has ongoing performances for small and big children. Many of these organizations offer wonderful summer camp experiences.

CHILDREN'S LIBRARY AT CENTRAL
  MULTNOMAH COUNTY
  LIBRARY FREE

801 Southwest 10th Ave.

(503) 988-5123

www.multcolib.org

Once you enter the Central Library, take a right turn and discover the Children's Library. As you enter this brightly illuminated treasure trove of books, videos, and artwork for kids, a bronze tree catches your eye. This arboreal fantasy has a hollow trunk for play and storytelling inside. The library has one activity that should keep kids busy during the summer: the summer reading program, which is theme-based and offers prizes. It also offers story times. While you're there, pick up a copy of *InfoLines,* the library's newsletter, which gives information about other library programs and events.

> **i** What better way to spend a summer evening than watching a movie with the family at the drive-in? The 99W Drive-In is happy to oblige every weekend spring through fall. You can find it at SR 99W and Springbrook Road in Newberg (503-538-2738; www .99w.com).

METRO ARTS KIDS CAMP AT
  PORTLAND CENTER FOR
  PERFORMING ARTS

9003 Southeast Stark St.

(503) 408-0604

www.pdxmetroarts.org

Professional educators, visual artists, and performers from the Oregon Symphony, Oregon Ballet Theatre, and various theater companies help students create their own works of art, sing, play instruments, paint, dance, and act in live performances. Some classes charge by the hour, so be sure to call ahead for rates.

NORTHWEST CHILDREN'S THEATER
  AND SCHOOL

1819 Northwest Everett St.

(503) 222-4480 (tickets), (503) 222-2190 (information)

www.nwcts.org

An outstanding operation, Northwest Children's Theater produces frequent and imaginative shows with children in starring roles. Their classes (starting at $150 for 9 weeks) and camps (starting at $135 for 1 week) are first-rate, and they have been responsible for many budding Portland stars. Shows range from interpretations of classic fairy tales such as *Sleeping Beauty* to adaptations of works such as *Alexander and the Terrible, Horrible, No Good, Very Bad Day* to musicals from *Annie* to *Hamlet* to original works, all performed with incredible professionalism.

OREGON CHILDREN'S THEATRE FREE
600 Southwest 10th Ave.
(503) 228-9571
www.octc.org

This professional theater company takes props, makeup, and sets to Portland-area schools to ignite the magic of drama in classroom workshops and assemblies. And then, at Keller Auditorium, this marvelous outfit turns it around by bringing local kids onstage to help present plays and musicals. They adapt great children's classics such as *James and the Giant Peach, A Wrinkle in Time,* and *Lily's Purple Plastic Purse* into accessible and exciting theater. They also have excellent classes. There are tuition costs for the classes, but discounts and scholarships are available.

SUMMER ACTIVITIES

Portland has so many parks and playgrounds and is so close to both the mountains and the ocean that summer is never boring. The chapters on Recreation and Spectator Sports and on Portland's Parks give comprehensive and plentiful accounts of the Parks and Rec activities and programs. The Festivals and Annual Events chapter surveys the best of the seasonal events. There are also lots of summer camps in the area, with focuses in equestrian pursuits, sports (golf, baseball, soccer, basketball, and roller hockey), arts, theater, science, African arts, music, computers, cooking, fashion design, eco-awareness, politics—all in addition, of course, to plain old sleep-away camps with singing around the campfire. (Nostalgic parents don't have to be left out, either: Camp Westwind, on the Oregon coast, organizes a few sessions each summer for parents and children.) OMSI and the Oregon Zoo both offer popular summer camps. The free monthly papers *Metro Parent* and *Portland Family* provide comprehensive lists of camps each year. You can pick them up at any local library, most schools, and many children's stores. The Oregonian also publishes a special section every spring that lists camps in the Portland area. Financial aid for camps is often available; your camp can provide information.

SAND IN THE CITY BEACH PARTY
Pioneer Courthouse Square

Held in early July, this benefit for the Kids on the Block Awareness Program transforms Portland's festive downtown patio into an ocean beach when more than 250 tons of sand are shaped, slapped, and molded into sand castles, dragons, and other wild critters by teams of local businesspeople. In addition to this jovial competition, master sand sculptors give demonstrations, and children can create their own works of art in a kids' sandbox. Food and craft booths are plentiful, too, as well as live music, clowns, and puppet shows. For further information on Sand in the City, see the Festivals and Annual Events chapter. It's free to attend, but donations are welcome. Some activities do have fees, but are usually only a couple dollars. Cash only.

SUMMER ACTION PARK $$–$$$
Mount Hood Ski Bowl on US 26
(503) 272-3206, ext. 1118
www.skibowl.com/summer
Think the only action on the slopes is in the winter? Think again. The clever people at Mount Hood Ski Bowl maintain the Summer Action Park, which offers more than 25 attractions, including a half-mile dual Alpine slide, as well as Indy Karts, miniature golf, bungee jumping, adventure river rides, kiddy jeeps, batting cages, and horse and pony rides. Visit on the way to or from Ski Bowl at Camp Creek, Tollgate Campground, or one of the many gorgeous campsites in lush Mount Hood National Forest just off US 26. Prepare a picnic basket or stop at the Dairy Queen in the nearby village of Rhododendron. Mount Hood is an hour's drive east of Portland on US 26. (For more information see the Day Trips and Recreation chapters.) All-day passes, while running up to $60, include unlimited rides down the Alpine slide; the a la carte menu can add up quickly.

i Part of the challenge with having children is that they get in the way of your yoga practice. Don't let it happen to you: *Yoga Shala* offers child care for some of its classes, so you can put the *chi* back in children. And they offer kids' classes too. See a schedule at www.yogashalapdx.com.

SWIMMING POOLS & WATER PARKS

Portland

THE CITY OF PORTLAND PARKS AND RECREATION DEPARTMENT
(503) 823-7529

The City of Portland offers a host of fun, healthy, year-round activities. In the summer the aquatics programs are exceptionally popular; the swimming lessons are a cherished summertime ritual. The department offers swimming lessons for kids from toddlers on up (adults too!). Young swimmers can get advanced lifeguard certification, take diving lessons, or just come to splash at open swim time. Classes are offered at every pool listed here. Most of the swimming pools are open from early in the morning until late at night, and many offer amusing activities. The pools at the Southwest Community Center, the Eastside Community Center, and at Mount Scott are beautiful facilities with water toys, water slides, current channels, and other enticements. In the summer, the outdoor pools are a big draw, especially the pretty pools at Creston, Grant, and Sellwood Parks. Check out the Portland Parks website at www.portlandonline.com/parks or call the park nearest you for specific information and rates. (See the Portland's Parks chapter for more information and the Recreation chapter for more information about pools.)

Indoor Pools

BUCKMAN SWIMMING POOL $
320 Southeast 16th Ave.
(503) 823-3668

COLUMBIA SWIMMING POOL $
7701 North Chautauqua Blvd.
(503) 823-3669

MATT DISHMAN POOL $
77 Northeast Knott St.
(503) 823-3673

MLC POOL $
2033 Northwest Glisan St.
(503) 823-3671

MOUNT SCOTT SWIMMING POOL $
5530 Southeast 72nd Ave.
(503) 823-3813

SOUTHWEST COMMUNITY CENTER $
6820 Southwest 45th Ave.
(503) 823-2840

Outdoor Pools

CRESTON SWIMMING POOL $
4454 Southeast Powell Blvd.
(503) 823-3672

GRANT SWIMMING POOL $
2300 Northeast 33rd Ave.
(503) 823-3674

MONTAVILLA SWIMMING POOL $
8219 Northeast Glisan St.
(503) 823-4101

PENINSULA PARK SWIMMING POOL $
700 North Rosa Parks Way
(503) 823-3677

PIER SWIMMING POOL $
9341 North St. Johns St.
(503) 823-3678

SELLWOOD SWIMMING POOL $
7951 Southeast 7th Ave.
(503) 823-3679

WILSON POOL $
1151 Southwest Vermont St.
(503) 823-3680

Outlying Areas

✳**NORTH CLACKAMAS**
  AQUATIC PARK $
7300 Southeast Harmony Rd., Milwaukie
(503) 557-7873
www.co.clackamas.or.us/ncprd/aquatic

This Disneyland-ish water world is a wonderfully wet place for the kids to cool off during the long hot days of July and August. With wave pools, wading pools, diving pools, three water slides, and a whirlpool, you can bet the little ones will return home all tuckered out. Adults pay a little more. (See the Recreation chapter for more information.)

i Saturday matinees at the McMenamin pub theaters—the Kennedy School, the Bagdad, and the Mission—are perfect for inexpensive family movies.

SHOPPING FOR TOYS, BOOKS & MORE

PORTLAND SATURDAY MARKET
Southwest Ankeny and Southwest Naito Parkway, just south of the Burnside Bridge
(503) 222-6072
www.portlandsaturdaymarket.com
The Portland Saturday Market, which also runs on Sun, is a characteristic Portland experience that children love. In addition to the vendors of tie-dye, candles, jewelry, pottery, and stained glass, you'll find lively entertainment of every variety (especially music). The food is delicious, and the eye candy is even better. There are special activities just for children, such as performances by Tears of Joy Theatre, children's musicians, and other fun things. Saturday Market takes place from the first weekend in March to Christmas Eve. On Sat the market opens at 10 a.m. and closes at 5 p.m.; Sun hours are 11 a.m. to 4:30 p.m.

Books

BARNES & NOBLE BOOKSTORE
Lloyd Center
1317 Lloyd Ave.
(503) 249-0800
www.barnesandnoble.com
Area Barnes & Noble bookstores not only offer books but also have story times and author events for preschoolers through teens. The Lloyd Center location along with the Beaverton store (18300 Northwest Evergreen Pkwy., 503-645-3046) are two of our favorites, but there are six in the area, all of which typically offer a weekend morning storytime and a Saturday event as well. To see what's on deck, click on the store locator tab on the website listed above. Both the Lloyd Center and Beaverton stores also have toys and games in addition to books. Barnes & Noble stores are spacious and comfortable; most have an in-house Starbucks and free Wi-Fi. Maybe you'll get to browse a little too.

BORDERS BOOKS
708 Southwest 3rd Ave.
(503) 220-5911
www.borders.com/online/store/Home
Borders' book events, signings, crafts, and story readings are typically held on Saturdays throughout the year. We like this downtown spot because of its proximity to the MAX line and its handsome interior, as well as its fantastic selection of music and DVDs, in addition to the books. Their events for children are always festive. There are five Borders stores in the area, all with free Wi-Fi, and they all have cool events for children. To see what's on the calendar, use the store locator tab on the website above; it will take you to the link for the downtown Portland store, or whichever one you prefer, and you can view the store events.

A CHILDREN'S PLACE
4807 Northeast Fremont St.
(503) 284-8294
www.achildrensplacebookstore.com
A Children's Place is a wonderful independent store in the Beaumont neighborhood that offers an impressive selection of books and music for children of all ages. And they have the expertise that comes with focusing on young readers, so they make wise recommendations if you need advice. You can also buy a wide variety of educational toys and puzzles here, as well as games to stimulate those fertile imaginations, a good stock of art supplies, and musical instruments, and they work with teachers and local schools to keep them supplied as well. A Children's Place also hosts many events—including book events for adults—with their Thursday morning storytelling a community favorite.

COSMIC MONKEY COMICS
5335 Northeast Sandy Blvd.
(503) 517-9050
www.cosmicmonkeycomics.com
A fine, large comic store with a wall of Manga and every variety of comic books. Cosmic Monkey is open daily from 7 p.m. They are very kid-friendly and offer summer workshops on how to create your own comics.

EXCALIBUR COMICS
2444 Southeast Hawthorne Blvd.
(503) 231-7351
A premier outlet for comics in the Portland area, Excalibur carries collector's items, books, and alternative comics in addition to their mainstream offerings. Not everything is G-rated, but they do have an impressive selection of children's comics, as well as good service. And you can rent anime flicks and other DVDs from Excalibur.

POWELL'S CITY OF BOOKS

1005 West Burnside St.

(503) 228-4651

www.powells.com

While Powell's City of Books is fully covered in the Shopping chapter, it is worth noting that the children's resources at Powell's are phenomenal. Not only do they carry current favorites, but they have vast holdings of used books, classics, collector's items, and, most important, a knowledgeable staff to help you find the perfect book for your child. Furthermore, they carry excellent educational materials; whether you are a home-schooling parent, a teacher, or simply an interested adult, you will be astonished at the wealth here. Visiting the store is a fine way to spend a day—while Powell's wants parents to watch their little ones and to refrain them from terrorizing the place, they also want to cultivate future readers, so exploring the wares is encouraged. The Hawthorne branch also has a good, though smaller, children's section

Toys

CHILD'S PLAY

2305 Northwest Kearney St.

(503) 224-5586

http://childsplayportland.com

A fine neighborhood shop in the Northwest Portland district, Child's Play features well-made, inventive toys. You'll find a decent selection of seasonal toys and dress-up clothes as well as lines like Playmobil, Lego, and Brio. The wide array of Breyer horses and accoutrements is another big draw. The store also carries books. It's useful to note that the shop has a parking lot (a rarity in the area) and they will wrap your gifts for free.

FINNEGAN'S

922 Yamhill St.

(503) 221-0306

www.finneganstoys.com

At Finnegan's you'll find whole cities of dolls, lots of building blocks, sidewalk chalk, ant farms, flower presses, boomerangs, dump trucks—in short, every kind of toy a child could imagine. Though it is large, it never has that frantic feeling that so many of the big chain toy stores cultivate; even during the holidays when it's really busy, Finnegan's manages to exude serenity. It could be the well-organized and competent staff, or perhaps it's the high-quality toys. They carry a vast selection of Brio, Plan, and Playmobil toys, lovely Ravensburger puzzles, great craft kits, plush toys, books, and more. And you'll find a lot of cool toys for party bags— bubbles, tops, creatures, chalk. The Hello Kitty Photo Sticker Machine, which will turn your image into stickers, is worth a stop even if you don't have any kids. Finnegan's also offers online gift certificates, which is incredibly convenient.

KIDS AT HEART

3435 Southeast Hawthorne Blvd.

(503) 231-2954

www.kidsathearttoys.com

Kids at Heart is a sweet neighborhood store in the Hawthorne shopping district; it keeps area residents supplied with birthday presents, art supplies, Playmobil sets, and Brio trains, but it's worth a trip for nonresidents too. Kids at Heart has a fine collection of dress-up clothes, games, and science-oriented toys—kits turning children into spies and explorers have been recent hits at parties. You won't find Barbie, but you will find Madeline dolls and Groovy Girls in addition to a whole wall of trains and building toys.

Clothes

BLACK WAGON
3964 North Mississippi Ave.
(503) 916-0000, (866) 916-0004
http://blackwagon.com
Black Wagon is a charming store in the Mississippi neighborhood that offers beautiful children's shoes and clothing (from birth to age 12), much of it handmade, organic or recycled fiber, and very chic. In addition to the great clothes, however, they also offer a stylish collection of bedding, decor and furniture, toys, books, and music. Their online store is excellent as well, so you can still shop there after you've gone home.

GRASSHOPPER
1816 Northeast Alberta St.
(503) 335-3131
www.grasshopperstore.com
Grasshopper offers wonderful clothes for children, many of them handmade right there (or down the street at the "mother" store, Tumbleweed). Brands include the store's own Wild Carrots, Kate Quinn Organics, and Picaflor, among many others. There is also a large selection of well-made, lead-free toys. The beautiful space is a pleasure to shop in, and your children will also enjoy themselves, possibly almost as much as you. Grasshopper is open daily from 10 a.m. to 6 p.m. (5 p.m. on Sun and Mon). They have a cool blog too, with things like DIY bubble soap.

HAGGIS MCBAGGIS
6802 Southeast Milwaukie Ave.
(503) 234-0849
www.haggismcbaggis.com
Finally, a store that understands the parental shopper: We are buying things for our children that secretly we want to wear ourselves. So the fancy shoes, wonderful tights, jewels, and very imaginative accessories that also come in adult sizes are a few reasons to shop in this colorful, attractive store. Another reason is the beautiful, clean, and spacious bathroom that stocks disposable diapers for emergencies. And still another: the kids' toys. Yet one more is the big cookie jar. Did we mention the adult sizes?

HANNA ANDERSSON
327 Northwest 10th Ave.
(503) 321-5275
Beautiful, well-made cotton clothes that look good and feel good are the specialty of this amazing Portland store, and it has acquired an international following through its catalog sales since its founding here in 1983. These clothes last a long time—even the tights. The clothes are meant to last for more than one child, so the company has a program to pass on gently used Hannas to needy children. Hanna Andersson is open Mon through Fri 10 a.m. to 6 p.m. and on Sat from 10 a.m. to 5 p.m. (See the Shopping chapter for more details.)

MAMABABY
4029 Southeast Hawthorne Blvd.
(503) 233-8130
www.mamababyshop.com/index.html
Beautiful natural-fiber clothing for children and their mothers (their pregnant and nursing mothers, that is), as well as a fine selection of baby accessories and some toys, draws people from all over town to this cozy shop on Hawthorne. The collection of clothing and accessories for pregnant and nursing women is thoughtful, and the children's clothing is adorable.

MOTHER NATURE'S
2627 Southeast Clinton St.
(503) 230-7077
www.mothernaturesbabystore.com

This is the go-to spot for organic cotton diapers, diaper covers, baby slings, and other organic-fiber baby supplies. They carry lovely skin products for mother and baby, and many BPA- and phthalate-free cups, pacifiers and teethers, including the French classic Sophie the Giraffe, newly discovered as the toy du jour of hip American parents.

NIKE TOWN
930 Southwest 6th Ave.
(503) 221-6454

Nike Town is the high-tech, ultramodern retail outlet for shoes, shirts, caps, and other sports apparel with that famous swoosh logo. The corner store is easy to spot with its life-size metallic silhouette of His Airness, Michael Jordan, on the south wall. Inside are plaques celebrating other noted athletes, interactive displays, multimedia delights, and video theatrics. (See the Shopping chapter for more information.)

POLLIWOG
2900 Southeast Belmont St.
(503) 236-3903
www.polliwogportland.com

Beautiful, beautiful children's clothes for newborns and their siblings up to age six are the specialty of this pretty store in Southeast Portland—though they also sell diaper bags, gifts, wooden toys,. and accessories as well. Shoes from See Kai Run are best-sellers, as well as wonderful baby T-shirts by Glug. Polliwog also carries dresses by Mister Judy, handmade in Portland.

PRESENTS OF MIND
3633 Southeast Hawthorne Blvd.
(503) 230-7740
www.presentsofmind.tv

It is often difficult to find high-quality baby clothing and gifts that are gender-neutral, but Presents of Mind not only has baby and toddler clothing that is in other colors besides pink and blue, it also has baby and toddler clothing that is made by local Portland artisans. Here you'll find soft baby hats made out of recycled cashmere sweaters, cute organic-cotton onesies, and sweet handsmocked dresses, among many other inventive things. See the listing in the Shopping chapter for more information on this wonderful shop.

FESTIVALS &
ANNUAL EVENTS

Almost everything in Oregon, from the sacred to the mundane, seems to have its own festival or event. In this chapter, which is organized chronologically, we cover a wide range of festivals of all types and sizes in Portland and the metro area, surrounding Oregon counties, and in nearby Vancouver and Clark County, Washington. In a culture of mass marketing, mass media, and mass consumption, these celebrations help define and distinguish a particular area, preserving an awareness of local identity and history. Most important, they preserve a sense of place.

Some of the largest events in the area include athletic contests such as the Portland Marathon and the Hood-to-Coast Relay. Other draws feature Waterfront Park: In the summer, Portland's Tom McCall Waterfront Park hosts the Oregon Brewers Festival, the Rose Festival Fun Center, and the Waterfront Blues Festival. The area also has a chance to showcase its farmers' markets during the summer. There you will find specialty and organic food products, flowers and nursery stock, not to mention the area's agricultural bounty (see the Close-up on the Portland Farmers' Market in this chapter). Portland's Old Town hosts the Saturday Market, an open-air craft and food event held each weekend from March until Christmas. Downtown's Pioneer Square is another popular site for performances of all sorts and smaller cultural, art, food, and other festivals. You can find something happening every weekend, somewhere.

Local newspapers and websites are good sources for details about what is going on when you are visiting. The *Oregonian's* Friday A&E section and Homes & Gardens of the Northwest insert all carry detailed listings and calendars of a wide assortment of events in the entire region. *Portland Monthly* magazine maintains an excellent calendar, and the smaller community and weekly papers—notably *Willamette Week* and the *Portland Mercury*—also carry this information. The Portland Oregon Visitors Association (POVA), at (503) 275-9750 or (800) 962-3700, keeps an online events calendar: www.travelportland.com.

Finally, this is Oregon: Outside events are rarely canceled because of weather, though it may occasionally cause changes in schedules and performances. In general, though, the show goes on. Dress accordingly.

JANUARY

REEL MUSIC
Northwest Film Center
1219 Southwest Park Ave.
(503) 221-1156
www.nwfilm.org
The annual celebration of music on film is one of two popular winter events sponsored by the Northwest Film Center. It's held at the Whitsell Auditorium in the Portland Art Museum, and the event features film showings, concerts, and speakers. Admission fees vary, so call ahead.

ROSE CITY CLASSIC ALL BREED DOG SHOW
Portland Expo Center
2060 North Marine Dr.
www.rosecityclassic.org
Portlanders love their dogs, and this event allows owners from throughout Oregon and southwest Washington to show off their pets (or vice versa). Four thousand dogs and their breeders attend this dog extravaganza, complete with agility trials, obedience contests, and breed competitions.

FEBRUARY

CHINESE NEW YEAR
Various locations
Lucky money, fireworks, and feasting—what's not to love about Chinese New Year? This 15-day festival offers parades, parties, and other events to bring in the new year with style. Dancers dressed in traditional lion costumes scare off the evil spirits and bring good luck to Chinatown—an area of town that once housed immigrants from the Kwangtung province of Canton. You can celebrate Chinese New Year at various venues across town, in particular at the Portland

Classical Chinese Garden (503-228-8131; see our Attractions chapter).

PACIFIC NORTHWEST SPORTSMEN'S SHOW
Portland Expo Center
2060 North Marine Dr.
(503) 246-8291
The region's oldest and largest show of its type, this toy show is for those who fish, camp, hunt, and hike. There are hundreds of new products and services along with free seminars, exhibitions, and hands-on demonstrations.

PORTLAND INTERNATIONAL FILM FESTIVAL
Various locations
Northwest Film Center
1219 Southwest Park Ave.
(503) 276-4310
www.nwfilm.org
Whether you like to go to the movies or view films, this festival will provide plenty of entertainment. Expect to see a variety of professional, experimental, traditional, and avant-garde films—as well as lectures, talks and exhibits—during this well-attended event, which sponsored by the Northwest Film Center. Admission fees vary, but in general, the more movies you attend, the lower the cost per viewing, if you buy a pass or block of tickets. Movies (as many as 80) are shown in local theaters over a three-week period. The opening and closing nights feature the Portland premiers of new major movies. Matinee tickets are available.

PORTLAND JAZZ FESTIVAL
Various locations
(503) 228-5299
http://pdxjazz.com

The Portland Jazz Festival celebrates our musical heritage with rare insight and wit. The festival is organized around a new theme each year, and so the featured artists vary. But you will hear luminaries such as pianist Randy Weston, local favorites with international reputations such as Dave Frishberg, as well as up-and-coming stars like tenor sax man Joshua Redman and jazz violinist Regina Carter. The Portland Jazz Festival coincides with Black History Month, and many outreach and education events round out this weeklong celebration.

MARCH

ANTIQUE & COLLECTIBLE SALE
Portland Expo Center
2060 North Marine Dr.
(503) 282-0877
www.palmerwirfs.com
Billed as "America's Largest Antique and Collectible Sale," this extravaganza will have something for everyone. Admission is $7, but there is an additional parking fee. More than 1000 booths fill the Expo Center with intriguing items from the past. They'll appraise your old stuff for $5 per item, too. They repeat this event in July and Oct. Please leave Fido in the RV.

✳PORTLAND SATURDAY MARKET
Southwest Ankeny and Southwest Naito Parkway, south of Burnside Bridge
(503) 222-6072
www.portlandsaturdaymarket.com
Since 1974 Saturday Market (it is open on Sun too) has been another "must see" for visitors. You can enjoy street theater (some intentional, some not), sample from a range of food booths, and buy everything from candles, macramé, pottery, stained glass,

clothing, hemp products, local produce and handmade housewares to furniture and toys, and tools and trinkets. Not as countercultural as they once were, vendors may dress like Deadheads but in reality are small business owners. Everything is made by hand. The market runs until Christmas. During the holiday-shopping madness, it is as packed as any department store or mall. We still have the Cowichan sweaters we bought there in high school, which are now cult items thanks to *The Big Lebowski*, and now you can have one too.

REED ARTS WEEK (RAW)
Reed College
3202 Southeast Woodstock Blvd.
www.reed.edu/raw
This five-day gala of dance, poetry and prose readings, exhibits and musical performances includes the work of Reed students and that of important artists from Portland and beyond. There are performances and master classes, and everything is intellectually and aesthetically stimulating and challenging. And the college's Southeast Portland campus is beautiful, with a small but excellent art gallery, a superb performing arts center, and a great bookstore. Exhibitions are open from noon to 6 p.m.; workshops and events begin in the afternoon and linger well into the evening.

ST. PATRICK'S DAY
Various locations
Portland has turned St. Patrick's Day into a multiday party, with the locus downtown, where **Kells Irish Restaurant and Pub** hosts a street fair, live Celtic and Irish music, and demonstrations of Irish crafts (112 Southwest 2nd Ave.; www.kellsirish.com/portland/festival.html). They also serve beer (Harp and

Guinness flow freely), and you can ward off the damp chill with an Irish coffee or some Irish whiskey.

Other shops, restaurants, pubs, and bars flaunt their Irish heritage or make it up for a day as they join in the celebration. You can get ready for **St. Patrick's Day at Kathleen's of Dublin,** 737 Southwest Salmon, (503) 224-4869, one of the best shops for Irish (and Scottish) merchandise, including clothing, tapes, and CDs; Celtic-inspired jewelry; and teacups and teapots—and Guinness. The **All Ireland Cultural Society,** (503) 286-4812, also sponsors a St. Patrick's Day festival, usually on the actual day (March 17). Check out their website for more information: www.oregonirishclub.org/stpatricksdayfestival.html.

SHAMROCK RUN
Tom McCall Waterfront Park, at Southwest Naito Parkway and Southwest Stark
www.shamrockrunportland.com
One of Portland's most popular running events, the Shamrock Run is a fund-raiser for Doernbecher Children's Hospital Foundation, one of the state's most popular and successful charities. The event includes a Leprechaun Lap, a 1-kilometer run, walk, or jog; the Shamrock Stride, a 4-mile walk; and 5-kilometer, 8-kilometer and 15-kilometer races. The entry fee varies with the runner's age and selected event but includes a T-shirt and the usual goodies.

APRIL

✳AGFEST
State Fairgrounds, Salem
(503) 535-9353, (800) 874-7012
www.oragfest.com
The Agfest is a celebration of the industry that plays a large role in all our lives: agriculture. Here you will find representatives of everyone from angora rabbit breeders to grass seed farmers to orchard growers, who gather here to teach people about their work. The Agfest winds throughout most of the fairgrounds, with many activities and events. Crafts, puppet shows, country dancing, and music are featured, along with farm animals of many varieties. Particular favorites include the horse shows, the llamas, the miniature horses, the sheep shearing, and the petting zoo. You can also take a ride in a wagon pulled by horses or by tractors. Children love to follow the elaborate scavenger hunt in the Ag Country display: Not only do they get to sample Oregon products such as pears, cherries, and shrimp; collect seeds to plant at home; and gather up pencils, candy, and other paraphernalia, but they also learn a remarkable amount. Before you head home, be sure to tour the booths in the main exhibition hall and pick up starter plants for excellent prices, as well as wares from local artisans. This fun event is a favorite with families in the Willamette Valley, and more Portlanders should attend. Admission is $7.50 for adults, while children 12 and under are admitted for no charge. To get to the Agfest, take I-5 to exit 256 (Market Street), and then follow Market west. Turn right (north) onto 17th Street, which takes you directly to the fairgrounds. Be prepared to pay a few bucks for parking.

CRYSTAL SPRINGS EARLY RHODODENDRON SHOW
Crystal Springs Rhododendron Garden
Southeast 28th Avenue and Woodstock
(503) 771-8386
The beautiful Crystal Springs Rhododendron Garden hosts two celebrations of this native

flowering shrub, one on the first Sat in April and the other during Mother's Day weekend in May. The April show features hundreds of early blooms and these signs of spring are the perfect way to remind yourself that the rains will eventually taper off. (See the Portland's Parks chapter for more information about this wonderful public park.)

LILAC FESTIVAL
Hulda Klager Lilac Gardens, Woodland, WA
(360) 225-8996
www.lilacgardens.com
Set on 5.5 acres near the Columbia River, the Hulda Klager Lilac Gardens holds the promise of spring. This is a popular event for color-starved Pacific Northwesterners who spend hours wandering the grounds admiring the hues and smelling the fragrance of both rare and more common varieties of the plant. Bouquets and cuttings are also available for purchase. There is a small gift shop in the farmhouse, and refreshments are available. Donations are welcomed at this National Historic Site.

TRILLIUM FESTIVAL
Tryon Creek State Park
11321 Southwest Terwilliger Blvd., Lake Oswego
(503) 636-4398
www.tryonfriends.org
The Trillium Festival celebrates our native Oregon plant at this quiet 635-acre park, tucked away between Lewis & Clark College and Lake Oswego. The free event features a variety of nature-related and craft activities for children at the visitor/learning center. Visitors can purchase plants, trees, and shrubs to help support the park's educational programs and maintenance. There

---

Blossom Time

The Hood River Valley, east of Portland, is prime orchard country, and during late March and all through April, it is blanketed in pink and white blossoms. A drive to see the peach, apple, pear, and cherry blossoms makes a perfect half-day trip, and whether you take the long route over Mount Hood on US 26 or the shorter way (east along the Columbia Gorge via I-84), your drive will be spectacular. Call the Hood River Chamber of Commerce, and they'll send you a blossom-time brochure: (800) 366-3530.

---

are easy walks along the park's rolling trails and streams and food and music for the body and soul.

WOODBURN TULIP FESTIVAL
Woodburn
(503) 634-2243, (800) 711-2006
www.woodenshoe.com
Emerging from the gray Oregon winter, hundreds of thousands of tulip bulbs burst into color each spring at several nurseries in this small town just south of Portland. Oregonians flock to the varied colored fields, rejoicing at this welcome sign that they survived another winter. Visitors can purchase cut flowers, order bulbs, dine on local foods, and be tempted by the nurseries' bounty and gift shops. The actual dates vary slightly in response to the severity of the winter, but by mid-Apr you can usually count on acres of gorgeous blossoms. During the festival weeks there is a $10 vehicle charge on Sat and Sun; Mon through Fri it's $5.

MAY

CERAMIC SHOWCASE
Oregon Convention Center
777 Northeast Martin Luther King Jr.
Blvd.
(503) 222-0533
www.ceramicshowcase.com
If you want to know what Oregonians do when it can rain from Oct to May, visit this annual event sponsored by the Oregon Potters Association. The show, which is the largest event of its kind in the United States, fills several huge rooms with pottery and ceramics by dozens of potters from throughout Oregon and Washington. Admission is free. There are also cool demonstration rooms, where you can try your hand at ceramic arts, as well as showcase awards that honor all that earthy creativity.

CINCO DE MAYO
Tom McCall Waterfront Park, between
the Morrison and Hawthorne Street
Bridges
www.cincodemayo.org
Portland is a Sister City to several cities throughout the world, including Guadalajara. This is a huge waterfront event celebrating the country's holiday, one of the largest such events in North America. It features Mexican and Latino food, crafts, art, music, and dancing, as well as carnival rides and other festive touches. The entry fee is $6 for those 13 and older, $3 for kids 6 to 12, and $4 for seniors.

CRYSTAL SPRINGS RHODODENDRON MOTHER'S DAY SHOW
Crystal Springs Rhododendron Garden
Southeast 28th Avenue and Woodstock
(503) 771-8386

May brings out the full glory of our indigenous rhododendron, and what better way to honor your mom than by walking with her down the lovely, winding paths of the Crystal Springs Rhododendron Garden? The Garden features thousands of blooming rhododendrons, azaleas, and other plantings all during Mother's Day weekend in May—a spectacular sight. (See the Portland's Parks chapter for more information about Crystal Springs Rhododendron Garden.)

DOGGIE DASH
Tom McCall Waterfront Park
Southwest Naito Parkway and
Southwest Pine
(503) 285-7722, ext. 412
www.oregonhumane.org/doggiedash/
Most races don't allow Fido, but this one encourages dogs of all kinds, since it's a fundraiser for the Oregon Humane Society. Sponsored by a local radio station, the Doggie Dash features two runs: a 1.5 mile event and a 2.5-mile event. Canines and their owners alike participate. The entry fee includes a T-shirt (for the runner) and doggie treats (for the dogs). Costumed runners, both canine and human, are not uncommon. This festive event also features bands, pet trick contests, the ubiquitous vendors, and a dog fashion show.

✳MEMORIAL DAY WEEKEND IN THE WINE COUNTRY
Willamette Valley Wineries Association
(503) 646-2985
www.willamettewines.com
This popular self-guided tour of more than 100 vineyards and wineries includes some tasting rooms that are rarely open to the public. The event features wine and food matches from some of the region's best chefs

and vintners. Advice, maps, lists of participating vineyards and wineries, and other details (telephone numbers, open hours, etc.) are available on the website above. This festive weekend draws thousands into the fertile valley to taste the region's pinot noirs, syrahs, and other notable wines. This is a unique opportunity to try barrel tastings, reserves, and the special vintages that the winemakers like to hold back. The wineries are open for the festival from 11 a.m. to 5 p.m. on Sat and Sun. Many new vintages are ready for purchase and consumption at this point, and you'll have excellent opportunities to get good pricing for these, as well as to take advantage of great discounts on cases and other deals. (For a feel for the region, see the Northern Willamette Valley's Wine Country section in the Day Trips chapter.)

JUNE

CHAMBER MUSIC NORTHWEST SUMMER FESTIVAL
Various locations
(503) 223-3202, (503) 294-6400 (tickets)
www.cmnw.org
Chamber Music Northwest is a highly successful music series that brings together the world's finest musicians to play to sold-out crowds throughout the city. Artistic director David Shifrin, a renowned clarinetist and Avery Fisher Prize recipient, inspires great loyalty in the music community and is able to entice superb artists to reside for the summer in Portland and play together. Ticket prices are reasonable, and series tickets are available, but order in advance for the best seats. Discount prices for rush tickets are available for students and seniors. Most performances are held at Reed College, 3203 Southeast Woodstock; the First Congregational Church, 1126 Southwest Park Ave, or

at the St. Mary's Academy Clark Family Auditorium, 1615 Southwest 5th Ave. The website has good directions and advice about parking. These concerts are truly worth seeing if you can get to one of them—but if not, you can order CDs.

FESTIVAL OF FLOWERS
Pioneer Courthouse Square, between
6th Avenue and Broadway,
Morrison and Yamhill Streets
This event mixes a fair amount of flat, open space and the talent and imagination of artists, volunteers, and 15,000 or so potted annuals. The volunteers turn the flowers into a work of art that honors Portland's beautiful public gardens and other traditions. After a few days, when thousands of onlookers have admired the piece, the flowers are sold to the public at wholesale prices.

LAKE OSWEGO FESTIVAL OF THE ARTS
George Rogers Park, Lake Oswego
368 South State St.
(503) 636-1060
www.lakewood-center.org
This juried show in the pretty Lakewood Center complex in Lake Oswego features not only the creative endeavors of local artists, but also arts and crafts booths, food booths, and activities for children and families. This community event has retained its human scale while drawing a good crowd and some excellent artists.

✳PORTLAND ROSE FESTIVAL
Portland Rose Festival Association
Various venues citywide
(503) 227-2681
www.rosefestival.org
The Rose Festival draws thousands and thousands of visitors every year, and it marks

the beginning of the summer season—no matter what the weather is doing. Besides the selection and crowning of the Rose Queen, there are more than 100 different official Rose Festival events, including three parades, dragon boat races, a carnival on the waterfront, art exhibits, tours of ships from the US and Canadian Navy and Coast Guard, fireworks, concerts, races and a world-class rose show. The Grand Floral Parade is the culminating event: it includes floats, marching bands, drill teams, clowns, the Rose Queen and her court of princesses, and general festive spectacle. Look for the Rose Festival beginning Memorial Day weekend and continuing through mid June, when the Grand Floral Parade snakes it way across the river from Memorial Coliseum through downtown.

PRIDE NORTHWEST
Various locations
(503) 295-9788
www.pridenw.org
Pride Northwest is Portland's annual gay, lesbian, bi, and trans celebration that includes music, events, a fun run, a pet parade, and the great Pride Parade, which is held on Sun. The Pride Parade, a splendid event, draws more than 50,000 people and is Portland's third largest annual parade. There is also a festival of food, crafts, and booths by gay/lesbian-friendly organizations and services.

JULY

A NORTHWEST FOURTH OF JULY
As in other parts of the country, the Fourth of July celebrates not only the national birthday, but the full-fledged arrival of summer. Local celebrations of this holiday reflect a sense of national and local identity, and picnics, block parties, barbecues, concerts,

parades, and fireworks are favorite ways to celebrate. Local weather lore indicates that summer in Oregon begins on July 5. Moist, low clouds can sometimes affect fireworks displays, and chilly temperatures can keep residents bundled up.

There are dozens of neighborhood celebrations and festivals as well as several large displays of fireworks along the Willamette and Columbia Rivers. Oaks Park and Waterfront Park along the Willamette have the two most central displays, and if you position yourself just right along the river, you can see both of them at once. Other venues, such as the Portland International Speedway and PGE Park have also displayed fireworks in the past. All over town, you'll find live outdoor music (especially at the Waterfront Blues Festival, below), barbecues, picnics, block parties, and festivity. Two special regional traditions are listed below, one at Fort Vancouver and one in the little town of St. Paul, south of Portland.

CONCERTS IN THE PARKS
Citywide, various locations
(503) 823-PLAY
Summer in the city: Early evening light softens but still gleams off the river; the current laps gently at the river's banks, a counterpoint to the fading, distant hum of traffic; and music soothes and stimulates the quiet crowd that has gathered at Waterfront Park to hear the Oregon Symphony. Or perhaps the crowd is on its feet and dancing the rhumba at Mount Tabor. Whatever the music and wherever the park, these free concerts are held during July (and often into Aug) throughout the city. You'll find a free concert of one kind or another just about every night of the week. Information about these concerts is available at all Portland Parks and Recreation facilities,

as well as libraries throughout the city. You can also find concert schedules and locations at the Portland Parks website: www.portland online.com/parks.

CONCOURS D'ELEGANCE
Pacific University, 2043 College Way, Forest Grove
(503) 357-3006
www.forestgroveconcours.org
Concours D'Elegance is the largest event of its type in the Pacific Northwest. Organized by the Forest Grove Rotary Club, the event is held on the pastoral campus of Pacific University and features more than 350 classic, vintage, and antique touring and sports cars from virtually every era of automotive history. This is a one-day event, usually held on a Sun in mid-July. Admission for adults is $15, and for children 6 through 16, $7. (Some discounts are available if you buy your tickets ahead of time.) In addition to the display of cars as art and investments, there is a range of musical entertainment and assorted refreshments. Forest Grove is a lovely little town where in typical Oregon fashion, loggers and mill workers share neighborhoods with college students and professors and those who commute to downtown Portland.

DA VINCI DAYS
Oregon State University
Corvallis
(541) 757-6363
www.davincidays.org
This wonderful event, inspired by Leonardo da Vinci, brings together art, science, and technology—with the idea that they should never have been separated in the first place. The festival exhibits show you why. It's a three-day celebration that includes

everything from a regional art show to performances of original dance. There are skateboard and teen band competitions, robotics displays, speakers, a film and video festival, music performances, a children's parade, Ultimate Frisbee, and street theater. A range of demonstrations and hands-on activities related to the yearly theme is also scheduled. You can buy tickets just for the day ($10 if you're 13 or older and $5 if you're between 6 and 12), or for the whole weekend ($15 and $10 respectively).

INTERNATIONAL PINOT NOIR CELEBRATION
Linfield College, 900 Southeast Baker St., McMinnville
(800) 775-4762
www.ipnc.org
The Willamette Valley is renowned for its excellent pinot noir growing conditions, and this celebration features the best wines made from this fine grape. It draws oenophiles and wine experts from throughout the world for three days of tastings, talks and tours, eating, and entertainment. Half of the 60 pinots are from Oregon, and the other half arrive from the world over. The event encourages you to mingle by dividing participants into two groups for activities, which makes for very interesting conversations, especially as the afternoon proceeds. Advance reservations are mandatory—this event sells out fast, even with a ticket price of nearly $900. (Tickets are sold on a first-come-first-served basis, starting in Feb.) The Passport to Pinot Noir is a separate mini-festival held on Sunday afternoon. The $125 admission allows you tastes of more than 60 pinot noirs, food from local chefs, a great lecture, and a Reidel glass to keep. Tickets to this event also sell out quickly.

MOLALLA BUCKEROO
The Buckeroo Grounds
Berkeley Avenue, off SR 211, Molalla
(503) 829-8388
www.molallabuckeroo.com
Since 1913, professional riders, ropers, and other persons skilled in the arts of the Western ranch have been coming to the Molalla Buckeroo (that's Oregon-speak for rodeo). Admission prices vary from about $13 to $15, depending on how old you are and where you sit. Matinee prices are discounted. This event includes dances, barbecues, trail rides, parades, and three days of professional rodeo, all during the Fourth of July holiday.

MOUNT ANGEL ABBEY BACH FESTIVAL
Mount Angel Abbey, One Mt. Angel Dr.,
Mount Angel
(503) 845-3066, (800) 845-82725
www.mountangelabbey.org/
bach-home.htm
This event is an opportunity to hear some of Bach's music superbly performed in the beautiful Benedictine abbey and seminary, set in the lush farmland south of Portland. Each night of the festival opens with a vespers service and then a recital, after which the entire audience gathers outside in groups of four for picnic suppers before heading in for the evening's featured performance. Held on the final Wed, Thurs, and Fri in July, the festival's 500 nightly seats. The abbey has a small, eclectic museum and gift shop, and tours are available by prior arrangement.

✳OREGON BREWERS FESTIVAL
Tom McCall Waterfront Park
(503) 778-5917
www.oregonbrewfest.com

This popular festival draws more than 50,000 people who come to Portland's waterfront to taste our region's excellent local beers and ales as well as those from elsewhere. The festival invites more than 80 brewers from across the continent to show off their craft, many of them from Portland. You can expect to find many styles of beer and ale, ranging from stouts to wheat beers and porters (but only one product from each brewery is allowed). And craft-brewed root beer and cream soda, lemonade, cider, and coffees are also available. A selection of locally prepared specialty foods, most of which may be eaten without utensils, is also available. Local musicians, including some of the area's best performers, offer entertainment. Moderation as well as the use of mass transit, taxis, and designated drivers are all seriously encouraged. While clearly not a family event for those with underage offspring—though children are allowed—the festival encourages enjoyment, beer tasting, and a little bit of education about the brewer's art and product. There is zero tolerance for any type of boisterous, unruly, or other antisocial behavior. All local laws are well enforced by Portland's blue-clad finest, and the event is monitored by the sponsoring association and the Oregon Liquor Control Commission. Admission is free, but visitors must purchase a tasting package that includes a plastic mug and up to 40 tokens. (A basic tasting package is $10, and it includes a mug and 4 tokens.) Additional tokens can be purchased for $1 each; a full glass of beer is four tokens, while a taste is one token. The beer vendors only take tokens—no cash or credit cards. An ATM is available on-site. The festival runs Thurs through Sun of the last full weekend in July.

Completely Fair

With their farm animals, 4-H kids, crafts exhibits, carnival rides, and country music, county fairs provide some of the best summer entertainment around.

In May, the **Multnomah County Fair is at Oaks Park** (call 503-761-7577 for information). In July look for the **Hood River County Fair**, www.hoodriverfair.com, and the **Washington County Fair and Rodeo**, www.faircomplex.com. In August try the **Yamhill County Fair**, www.co.yamhill.or.us/fair; the **Clackamas County Fair** www.clackamas.us/fair; and the **Clark County (Washington) Fair**, across the river, www.clarkcofair.com. For information about all the fairs in Oregon, visit www.oregonfairs.org.

✳**OREGON COUNTRY FAIR**
13 miles west of Eugene on
SR 126, near Veneta
(541) 343-4298
www.oregoncountryfair.org
The Oregon Country Fair is a wondrous alloy of handicrafts, music, magic, performance art, spoken word, Vaudeville, belly dancing, food, arts displays, drum circles, stiltwalkers, alternative ideology promoters, and much more. It's a cultural experience unique to Oregon—indeed, it's a proto-Burning Man, in which Oregon reveals its inner hippie (and its outer hippie commercialism). Order advance tickets through Ticketswest (www.ticketswest.com)—none are sold at the site. Friday, the fair's first day, offers the complete experience with fewer visitors. Some child care is available on-site. Forty thousand people communing in a small town outside Eugene does create some chaos, so be patient. Parking and traffic may give you a lot of headaches. You might instead take one of the buses that Lane County Transit thoughtfully sends out to the fair site. If you do park at the fair, be sure to respect the residents who live near the grounds.

No dogs, video cameras, glass containers, or alcoholic beverages are allowed at this event.

PORTLAND SCOTTISH HIGHLAND
GAMES
Mt. Hood Community College
Northeast 257th Ave., Gresham
(503) 293-8501
www.phga.org
This celebration of all things Scottish features bagpipe bands and soloists, Highland dancers, fiddlers, and those unusual and muscle-straining Scottish athletic competitions. Visitors can enjoy ethnic Scottish foods and beverages and browse a range of imported clothes, jewelry, and other items. Admission is in the $10 to $20 range.

THE ST. PAUL RODEO
St. Paul
(503) 633-2011, (800) 237-5920
www.stpaulrodeo.com
Each July 4th holiday, the rural Willamette Vally town of St. Paul holds one of the best rodeos in the country, with riders competing for prizes in several categories. You'll find food and beverage booths, a carnival with rides and games of chance and skill, Western dancing for grown-ups, lots of music, a traditional small-town Fourth of July parade, and, of course, fireworks. To see the rodeo,

you'll need a ticket; these run from about $12 to $18, depending on the luxuriousness of the seat. And it's best to order them ahead—they are available through Ticketmaster. Parking is free.

SAND IN THE CITY
Pioneer Courthouse Square, between 6th Avenue and Broadway, Morrison and Yamhill Streets
(503) 238-4445
Now you can get even with your parents for all the times they told you "don't bring the whole beach home with you." It's not the whole beach (Oregon has some 300 miles of coastline) but it's enough—270 tons—to allow 18 teams of architects and others to design and build sand castles and other structures in the center of downtown. Amused and intrigued onlookers are allowed to provide unsolicited advice during this three-day fund-raising event for Kids on the Block, an organization that uses puppetry and drama to teach kids about healthy living. The event also includes puppet shows, music, and a children's sandbox. Sand in the City is sponsored by Yoshida, and it's free, with a suggested donation of $3 per person, $10 per family.

STATE GAMES OF OREGON
Venues vary
(503) 520-1319
www.stategamesoforegon.org
The State Games involve more than three dozen "grassroots" sports, ranging from arm wrestling and badminton to footbag (hackey-sack) and pickleball, indoor soccer, and water polo, most with at least two or three categories of competition. More than 16,000 people from throughout Oregon and neighboring states will participate at sites throughout the metro area. The State Games of Oregon are a statewide, multisport, Olympic-style competition (individual and team sports) created by the Oregon Amateur Sports Foundation and supported by proceeds from the Oregon Lottery. With some exceptions, only Oregon residents can compete. Admission for spectators is free. Registration fees vary; call for information.

✳WATERFRONT BLUES FESTIVAL
Tom McCall Waterfront Park
(503) 282-0555
www.waterfrontbluesfest.com
There may be some irony about a four-day blues festival held over the Fourth of July weekend in one of the most livable cities in the nation. The blues are perhaps the American musical genre, rooted in hard times and forged with heartache. If you've been down so long that it looks like up to you, then you may not notice that the festival is held on the green sloping banks of a river with a snowcapped mountain bathed in evening light as a backdrop. Nor would you notice the fireworks that end the Fourth of July concert or the fact that the festival brings some of the nation's, and the Northwest's, finest blues artists to the city. One of Portland's premier events, the Waterfront Blues Festival has been packing them in by land and sea (boaters anchor off the seawall to listen to the music sans admission charge) for more than 15 years. If you don't mind not seeing the performers, spread a blanket on the grass beyond the festival area, close your eyes, and listen with all your heart. Admission is $10 and two cans of food for the Oregon Food Bank—all proceeds go to support the Oregon Food Bank.

AUGUST

ALBERTA STREET FAIR

Between 18th and 30th Avenue along Alberta Street
www.albertastreetfair.com

This blossoming mercantile strip in Northeast Portland celebrates its hipness with a multicultural neighborhood celebration featuring artwork, music, food, children's activities, and a free trolley. If you miss this event, you can enjoy the art galleries, restaurants, and boutiques that are popping up along this busy street by attending Last Thursday Walks every month. (See The Arts chapter for more information on Last Thursday Walks.)

THE BITE OF OREGON

Tom McCall Waterfront Park
www.biteoforegon.com

Portlanders do love their summer festivals—It must have something to do with being able to get outdoors without layers of Gore-Tex and a rain hat. The Bite is another local celebration of food, eating, and conspicuous food consumption, and it draws people from all over to eat their way from one end of Waterfront Park to the other. Restaurants from all over the state ply their wares, top chefs show off for one another in a local *Iron Chef*-style competition, and local breweries and winemakers offer their tempting concoctions. The admission charge of $10 for a weekend pass supports the Oregon Special Olympics. Three stages of music and dancing are also featured.

FESTA ITALIANA

Pioneer Courthouse Square, between 6th Avenue and Broadway, Morrison and Yamhill Streets
www.festa-italiana.org

For a few days in August, Pioneer Courthouse Square turns into a proper Italian piazza. The Festa Italiana is full of strolling musicians, dancing, wine tasting, crafts, games, and the culinary arts of a dozen or so Italian restaurants offering pizza, pastas, and other fare. All this and a wine garden draw an afternoon and early-evening crowd from the suburbs and downtown offices. A bocce ball tournament is a prominent feature, but the biggest draw is the wine-making—including the chance for you to get in on the action by stomping grapes.

FIESTA MEXICANA

Legion Park, Woodburn
http://woodburnfiestamexicana.com

Just down the freeway (south on I-5) from Portland, Woodburn is an agricultural hub with a diverse Hispanic population—and some of the best Mexican food in the Northwest. Less commercial and flashy than Portland's Cinco de Mayo celebration, this event reflects the real lives, food, art, music, and traditions of Hispanic Americans. Admission is free.

*HOOD TO COAST RELAY

Starting at Timberline Lodge, Timberline Access Road off US 26, just off Government Camp
(503) 292-4626
www.hoodtocoast.com

Since 1982, teams have gathered at Government Camp, on Mount Hood, to run a 197-mile relay race all the way to Seaside at the Oregon coast. Twelve people are on each team. The race, which is billed as the largest relay race in the world, attracts more than twelve thousands runners, as well as supporters and spectators, from all over. Walking events are offered in addition to running events, and some of the racewalkers are impossibly fast. This race is very exhilarating and therefore popular; many teams are made up of people who wouldn't ordinarily find themselves in any kind of race whatsoever. Because of its popularity, the organizers have a strict registration policy and expect you to register well in advance. But even if you're not racing, the event is fun to follow, whether you're watching the runners speed through Portland or joining them in celebration at Seaside.

INDIA FESTIVAL
**Pioneer Courthouse Square, between
6th Avenue and Broadway,
Morrison and Yamhill Streets
(503) 645-7902
www.icaportland.org**
The India Festival draws Oregonians whose families originated on the Indian subcontinent, as well as everyone in town who loves Indian food, spices, art, jewelry, arts and crafts, music, and dance. It's a sensory carnival, with colors, music, and aromas blending intriguingly. There's no admission charge for this Pioneer Square event.

MT. HOOD HUCKLEBERRY FESTIVAL & BARLOW TRAIL DAYS
**65000 East US 26, Mt. Hood Village
(503) 622-4798
http://cgs-mthood.tripod.com/huck_
festival.htm**
Events like these are important for the area's suburban and urban populations because they help maintain awareness of the state's agricultural heritage and bounty. While Oregon is currently known for high-tech products, expensive athletic shoes, and tourism, agriculture remains one of the three largest industries. This free event emphasizes the

region's history, for it takes place on part of the Oregon Trail, and the state's natural wealth—in this case, berries. You can buy jams, pies, sauces, tarts, and syrups; enjoy a salmon bake; and take tours of the historic Barlow Trail, which led pioneers around Mount Hood and down into the Willamette Valley. There's also lots of great information about Native American history and that of the Oregon Trail.

OBONFEST
**Oregon Buddhist Temple
3720 Southeast 34th Ave.
(503) 254-9456
www.oregonbuddhisttemple.com**
Set in a residential neighborhood, this is a Japanese-American Buddhist Festival of the Ancestors, which offers another perspective on multicultural life in Portland. The free festival is also an opportunity to learn about the long and not terribly comfortable history of Oregon's Japanese-American community. More cultural than strictly religious, the fest includes Japanese and other Asian foods, crafts, music, and dancing.

STREET OF DREAMS
**Location and specific times vary
(503) 292-1461
www.streetofdreamspdx.com**
To showcase their talents each year, between seven and ten local builders create a custom-designed, -decorated, and -landscaped house in a selected enclave. These are clearly not starter, or even average, homes: Prices begin at more than $2 million. *Extravagance* is the word here. But for $15, you can spend a pleasant afternoon seeing how and where the affluent plan to live. The event, a fund-raiser for local nonprofit organizations, opens with a black-tie tour.

Hors d'oeuvres and liquid refreshments are included. (See the Relocation chapter for additional information.)

TUALATIN CRAWFISH FESTIVAL
Tualatin Commons and Community Park
8535 Southwest Tualatin Rd., Tualatin
(503) 692-0780
www.tualatincrawfishfestival.com

As this once-rural suburb grows into a city, it continues to celebrate a tradition dating from 1957. The event is split between the Commons in downtown Tualatin and the Community Park just a short stroll away. This popular event features parades, a 5K race, remote-control boat racing, a pancake breakfast, and many, many booths. You'll find lots of crawfish dishes, including a crawfish cookoff. Many activities are designed just for the children, and there's plenty of entertainment—music, dancing—for adults as well. There's a small admission fee for entering the events at the Community Park, but not for those on the Commons.

SEPTEMBER

ART IN THE PEARL
Northwest Park Blocks, between West Burnside and Northwest Glisan at Northwest 8th Avenue
(503) 722-9017
www.artinthepearl.com

More than 100 artists gather here each Labor Day weekend for a lively three days of culture and commerce. In addition to artists and high-end crafters selling their wares, musicians and theater groups perform on a central stage. And you can try out artistic pursuits for yourself in the Education Pavilion, which has activities for children and their grown-up friends. And, naturally, you'll find the usual festival food booths.

MT. ANGEL OKTOBERFEST
Throughout downtown Mt. Angel
www.mtangel.org

Despite a long history of German settlers, Mount Angel didn't make Oktoberfest a commercial activity until 1965. Now the event lasts four days, beginning with the traditional Webentanz, or May Pole dance, and it's become the largest folk festival in the state. There are four stages with nearly continuous live music, demonstrations of traditional Bavarian folk dancing, and street dances on Fri and Sat nights. Visitors will also find food booths (German and other) and craft booths. In addition to the traditional Biergarten and Wiengarten, there is now a Microgarten with locally brewed beers. For younger visitors there is a Kindergarten with rides and other entertainment geared for youngsters. Most events are free; entrance into the entertainment stages and beer gardens will cost anywhere from $4 to $12 depending on when you buy it. And yes, it's in September.

✳OREGON STATE FAIR
Oregon State Fairgrounds, Salem
(800) 833-0011
www.oregonstatefair.org

The Oregon State Fair is an American tradition, held the last week before Labor Day (which means it sometimes falls in August). The fair still has strong roots, and support, in the state's rural areas and agricultural and ranching communities and industries, but in a larger sense, the fair celebrates and honors Oregon's past, acknowledges the present, and recognizes the future. The fair offers 4-H and Future Farmers of America displays, animals, and products along with a carnival, horse racing, and booth after booth of food and other products. It is good to know people still bake prize-winning cakes, make pickles and jams, raise hogs, and otherwise occupy themselves productively. The fair draws visitors from throughout the state and region. Tickets at the gate are $11 for adults, $6 for seniors and children ages 6 to 12. Parking is free, but lots fill early. There is also a shuttle from nearby Chemeketa Community College, where you can also park for free.

✳PICA TIME-BASED ART FESTIVAL
Various locations
(503) 242-1419
www.pica.org/tba
The Time-Based Art Festival is a fun, avant-garde 10 days of performance, hosted by PICA (see The Arts chapter) and dedicated to celebrating the aesthetics and art practices of the moment. What does that mean for you? Ten days of lectures, workshops, salons, shows, happenings, exhibitions, films, and parties. Because the festival is dedicated to cultivating the new, the forms these events take resist labels. You might find films by cutting-edge artists and performers. You might find a discussion of what Homeland Security means for artists or hear meditations on how Merce Cunningham has influenced dance. You might find performances by the Headlong Theater, Wally Cardona Quartet, Antony and the Johnsons, Tracey and the Plastics, Lone Twin, Rufus Wainwright or the Wooster Group. You might find events at toney downtown hotels or under gritty urban bridges. You just never know what you might find, so check it out. You can buy tickets to individual events, or you can buy passes ($75 and up) to see lots of events. Art professionals receive special discounts. See www.pica.org/tba for updated event and price information.

SAUERKRAUT FESTIVAL
Downtown Scappoose
Off US 30
(503) 543-2010
www.scappoosecommunity.org
Why a sauerkraut festival? Because Scappoose used to be the home of a Steinfeld's pickle factory. This history is preserved in this annual event in this pretty Columbia River town, about 30 miles west of Portland. You'll find the regular cast of vendor booths and entertainment, a Volkswalk, and, of course, lots of sauerkraut. Admission is free.

OCTOBER

GREEK FESTIVAL
Holy Trinity Greek Orthodox Church
3131 Northeast Glisan St.
(503) 234-0468
www.goholytrinity.org/cGreekFest.html
This is a very popular event drawing visitors from throughout northwest Oregon and southwest Washington who come to enjoy Greek music and dancing, arts and crafts displays, and, of course, gorgeous food. At the gate, you'll trade your dollars for Greek *talents*, which you'll spend on food, icons, and other wonderful things. Visitors are invited to participate in the dancing, and there are tours of the beautiful Holy Trinity Church.

HALLOWEEN PUMPKIN FEST
Fir Point Farms
14601 Arndt Rd., Aurora
(503) 678-2455
www.firpointfarms.com
Fir Point Farms is a real, working farm producing flowers and nursery stock, pumpkins, hay, and a variety of fruits and vegetables. It is also a roadside fruit and vegetable stand where you can buy locally grown produce and flowers. They have an excellent selection

of locally made baked goods (like strawberry-rhubarb pie), dried fruits, mustards, jams and jellies, and fruit butters, and other country merchandise. A couple of times a year, the owners attract good crowds of city dwellers, visitors, and locals for a series of holiday event At Halloween, Fir Point Farms hosts a hay maze and wagon rides. The grounds are filled with carved and decorated pumpkins, and there are pony rides, face painting, and entertainments for children, as well as a giant pumpkin weigh-off.

Rabbits, chickens, and turkeys are on hand for petting and watching, and the farm's goats climb a series of ramps and tree branches to get an aerial perch on the activities. For a quarter you can buy a handful of goat food and winch it up to a platform where the goats are waiting for their reward. No admission is charged, although there are small fees for rides. The farm is a few minutes off I-5 at the Aurora/Canby exit, and there are lots of signs pointing you in the right direction. (See the Kidstuff chapter for more on Fir Point Farms and other pumpkin patches.)

HOWLOWEEN
The Oregon Zoo
4001 Southwest Canyon Rd. in
Washington Park
(503) 226-1561
www.oregonzoo.org
The Oregon Zoo holds many seasonal events, and Howl-a-Ween is one of the favorites. This event lets kids trick-or-treat in a safe environment and learn more about the zoo animals as they go. A scavenger hunt sends them to different places around the zoo, where they answer questions and complete activities. All kids who finish the hunt are given bags of candy and prizes when they leave. Howl-a-Ween is usually held on the weekend closest to Halloween. This event is free with regular zoo admission.

OKTOBERFEST
Oaks Park, at the east end of the
Sellwood Bridge
www.oakspark.com
This Oktoberfest at Oaks Park on the banks of the Willamette River features delicious German sausages and other treats, a sausage-eating contest, oompah bands, polka, and other Germania. For the younger set, a *kinderplatz* (children's place) complete with Radio Disney is a big draw. Visitors will find traditional German foods, beers, and wines supplemented with local favorites, as well. Admission is $5 for adults, $2 for kids, and $3 for those 62 and older. Be alert: Sometimes this event is held in late September.

✳PORTLAND MARATHON
(503) 226-1111
www.portlandmarathon.org
While the 26.2-mile run is the logical centerpiece of this event, this well-organized open marathon, now in its fourth decade, includes a 5-mile run, a 10-kilometer (6.2-mile) walk, a half marathon, a noncompetitive 2-mile kids' run, and a 2-mile Special Olympics run. The ethos of this event is very Portland—inclusive and friendly. But don't try to run if you are not an official entrant. Spectators and supporters can participate in a sports medicine and fitness fair. The Portland Marathon has a reputation as a true people's race, where anyone can enter. It is, however, a qualifier for the Boston Marathon. (For information on other running events, see the Recreation chapter.)

Close-up

Portland's Farmers' Market

From the 1850s to 1941, Portland had a thriving public market. As late as the 1930s, the Yamhill Public Market, in what is now Old Town Portland, was a 5-block spread of booths, stalls, tables, and baskets all loaded with fresh produce, meat, and poultry brought into town daily by farmers and ranchers. The city rented these curbside stalls for 16 cents a day.

Today the tradition continues, with the **Portland Farmers' Market** held in the Park Blocks every Sat, Feb through Dec at Southwest Broadway and Montgomery Street on the campus of Portland State University, and June through Sept on Wed at Southwest Park and Salmon. The Farmers' Market is exceptionally popular, robust, and lively, ever-growing and a national model for how to persuade citizens to buy local.

Founded in 1992, the market has dozens of vendors selling farm-fresh produce, cut flowers and bedding plants, vegetable and herb starts, locally raised organic meat and poultry, smoked and fresh seafood, and artisan breads and cheeses. Much, but not all, of the produce is organically grown. In addition, many vendors offer delicious prepared food featuring local fare.

Open-air markets have been the heartbeat of villages for thousands of years and can still be found around the globe by travelers searching for the real feel of a land and its people. Here in Portland that feel includes the image of mounds of green lettuce heads or a huge tub full of sugar-fried popcorn, the sounds of a fiddle player bowing a jump tune next to a farmer from the Coast Range town of Alsea bagging up a half-pound of goat cheese. You'll find cinnamon twists, croissants, and pastry here, as well as shitake mushrooms and organically grown tomatoes. Gardeners can take home honeysuckle starts and dahlia tubers among many other plants.

As well as the wealth of good food at great prices, the market offers a series of events throughout its season. **Chefs-in-the-Market** cooking demonstrations let you watch some of the best chefs in Portland cooking with farmers' market produce on Sat

---

✳WORDSTOCK
Various locations
(503) 549-7887
www.wordstockfestival.com
Portland is a city of readers, and Wordstock is our annual festival of the book. This gala event brings writers and readers together for three days of workshops, dinners, music, readings by best-selling authors and rising stars, a book fair, a special Children's Festival, and other fabulous events. Past Wordstocks have featured writers such as Ira Glass, Dave Eggers, Gore Vidal, R. L. Stine, Ariel Gore, Ursula LeGuin, Carl Hiaasen, and Donald

Hall. Admission to Wordstock is $7 to $10, depending on your age, but if you're willing to pay significantly more for gala fundraising events, you can mingle with literary stars.

NOVEMBER

CHRISTMAS AT THE PITTOCK
MANSION
3229 Northwest Pittock Dr.
(503) 823-3624
www.pittockmansion.org
Perched above Portland's downtown, the Pittock Mansion (see the Attractions chapter)

at 10 a.m., June through October. Monthly celebrations are an important feature of the market because they underscore the seasonal nature of food, from the height-of-summer **Berry Festival** to the **Summer Loaf Bread festival** held in August, which brings more than 20 area bakeries to the market, along with a wood-burning demonstration oven, featured bread-baking speakers, and amateur and professional baking contests. In September more than 50 peak-season tomato varieties are sliced and placed on paper plates with name tags along a row of tables. It's your tough assignment to taste them and write down your comments. A **Harvest Festival,** held in late Oct, celebrates the season with a pumpkin pie contest, jack-o'-lantern carving, and other fall traditions.

The Portland Farmers' Market—and all the farmers' markets in the area—give Portland citizens the chance to connect with the important people who sustain us, a chance that we don't have very often. It may be the Age of Information, but we still have to eat food that someone grows. And what better way to appreciate your food than to meet the person who grew it?

Portland Farmers' Market
Portland State University
1800 Southwest Broadway at Montgomery
(503) 241-0032
www.portlandfarmersmarket.org
Feb through Dec, Sat 8 a.m. to 2 p.m.
The Portland Farmers' Market is only one of many in the region—there are thriving markets all over the city, notably in the Hillsdale, Hollywood, and Interstate neighborhoods, as well as in Beaverton. For a complete list of all the farmers markets in the city and throughout Portland, check out the excellent **Oregon Farmers Market Association** website, and you will find one nearby: **www.oregonfarmersmarkets.org.**

is the grandest of all Portland's mansions. As such it is appropriately decorated and lighted for Christmas. The usual admission fee applies ($8 for adults, $7 for seniors, and $5 for anyone who is 6-18), but you'll get the added bonus of seasonal music and other delights.

PIONEER COURTHOUSE SQUARE HOLIDAY HAPPENINGS
Pioneer Courthouse Square, between 6th Avenue and Broadway, Morrison and Yamhill Streets
(503) 223-1613
www.pioneercourthousesquare.org

The one Portland tradition visitors must hear (and see) to believe is the annual Tuba Concert. With 100 or more tuba players ranging from symphony members to enthusiastic novices risking badly chilled lips and fingers, the downtown echoes (and echoes) with unique renditions of favorite holiday songs and carols. At times you can almost hear the carolers making a good-faith effort to match the tuba sounds. Don't miss it. The city's Christmas tree is displayed here too, delivered from a local tree farm by a log truck, bringing out the latent Scrooge in many. The tree-lighting ceremony happens right after Thanksgiving, and it is a sight to behold. The city's official menorah is lit nearby when Hanukkah begins.

WINE COUNTRY THANKSGIVING
Willamette Valley Wineries Association
(503) 646-2985
www.willamettewines.com
This popular tour is held the fourth weekend in November, following Thanksgiving Day. Sponsored by the Willamette Valley Wineries Association, the event highlights dozens of wineries and vineyards with new vintages, winery tours, sale prices, and lots of food, crafts, and music. Like the Willamette Valley wine tasting event listed in May, this weekend is a great opportunity to see tasting rooms that are rarely open, get a chance to buy some wine futures, and purchase all your holiday grape beverages.

DECEMBER

FESTIVAL OF TREES
Oregon Convention Center
777 Northeast Martin Luther King Jr. Blvd.
(503) 215-6070
To benefit the Providence Medical Foundation, local designers and celebrities decorate 45 8-foot trees. The trees are auctioned off during opening night, with bids beginning at $500. There are also gingerbread and other displays, holiday entertainment, and demonstrations of arts and crafts. Admission is $5 for adults and $4 for seniors; children 3 to 12 are admitted for $3.

HOLIDAY LIGHTS DISPLAYS
Various locations throughout the city, including:

FESTIVAL OF LIGHTS AT THE GROTTO
Sandy Boulevard and Northeast 85th Avenue
(503) 254-7371
www.thegrotto.org

ZOOLIGHTS FESTIVAL AT THE OREGON ZOO
4001 Northwest Canyon Rd., Washington Park
(503) 226-1561
The darkness of winter nights is charmingly dispelled by these glimmering displays of holiday lights in various neighborhoods and at the Grotto and the zoo. Admission is charged at both the Oregon Zoo and the Grotto. The Grotto hosts the largest choral festival in the Pacific Northwest, with singers from 130 or more school, church, and civic choral groups performing in a 600-seat chapel. The chapel's acoustics are cathedral quality, enhancing the practiced voices of the choirs. The nativity story is told in lighted dioramas, and there is a petting zoo for children. Suitable refreshments—hot chocolate, cider, and the like—are available here. Admission is $8 for adults and $4 for those ages 3 to 12.

The Oregon Zoo hosts a month-long display with thousands of lights on trees and buildings and holiday lights arranged into animal silhouettes that raise and lower their heads or perform other animated gestures. The zoo stays open late, and evenings feature local choirs performing holiday music and adult-size elves bearing treats. The additional charge to ride the Zoo Train is worth it to see the displays from a different perspective. ZooLights can get very crowded, so be prepared for a wait for the Zoo Train and dress warmly!

Various neighborhoods compete with each other for the most lavish displays, though the traditional winner is Peacock Lane. A must-visit street for many years, residents on Peacock Lane have now enlisted computers and fiber optics to enhance their displays. The lights and displays draw visitors like moths to electric flames. Some visitors prefer to drive down the 2 blocks or so, but the traffic backs up fast. Others park nearby, bundle up, and walk up and down the street to admire the displays. Hot chocolate is sold from a little booth to warm those who choose to see the lights on foot.

THE NUTCRACKER
Keller Auditorium
Southwest 3rd Avenue and Clay Street
(503) 222-5538
www.obt.org
Each December, Oregon Ballet Theater features George Balanchine choreography to Tchaikovsky's ballet. This holiday classic sells out every year—though tickets are usually available because they give many performances—and has been a tradition among some Portland families for generations. Reservations are mandatory, but the ticket price range is reasonable.

PARADE OF CHRISTMAS SHIPS
Willamette and Columbia Rivers
www.christmasships.org

Local boat owners decorate their crafts, then form a floating convoy and sail up and down the Columbia and Willamette Rivers each night for several weeks in December. Owners have an informal competition among themselves for the most colorful display and some boats broadcast Christmas carols. All in all, nearly 60 craft participate. If the weather is bad, find a riverside restaurant or bar, order an Irish coffee or a local stout, and enjoy the floating spectacle snug and warm. If the weather is tolerable, try standing on the Hawthorne or Sellwood Bridges over the Willamette south of Portland as the twinkling fleet sails under the bridge upstream and back. Park in East Sellwood and then stroll out onto the bridge. Dress for chilly winds.

SINGING CHRISTMAS TREE
Keller Auditorium
222 Southwest Clay St.
(503) 557-8733
www.singingchristmastree.org
The Singing Christmas Tree is a long-standing, glorious singing event involving 300 singers. There is an actual "tree" involving about half of the singers, and the rest are strategically placed to act out scenes from cherished Christmas tales, both secular and religious. The pageant also features beloved musical performers from Portland and beyond. It's right up there with *The Nutcracker* as a ritual for Portlanders at holiday time.

THE ARTS

Portland has always taken a playful approach to art, starting in the 1970s when our mayor, Bud Clark, was photographed by Michael Ryerson at the bus mall, facing a statue by Norman J. Taylor. The statue is entitled Kvinneakt, or in Norwegian, "nude woman." But Clark was not just looking: He was wearing an overcoat (and not much else else) and flashing the statue. The poster that was subsequently created was called "Expose Yourself to Art," and it was a best-seller that helped set the tone for the arts scene in Portland.

This playful legacy has remained as Portland evolves from a sleepy provincial town to a more sophisticated city. We have the second-oldest museum building on the West Coast, but the spirit of Portland's art is not constrained by history. Thus, the arts are alive here—both the classical disciplines and the experimental counterparts that invigorate and refresh. Because it is comparatively simple and pleasant to live here—one doesn't need a car, for example—the city attracts people who want to make art and who want to start arts-related businesses. These have flourished over the past 10 years and have made important contributions to the economy and overall livability of Portland.

Portland has major strengths in the literary arts, as well as in music, visual arts, and performance. To find the where, what, who, and perhaps why of most of the above, here's a selection of the most intriguing, vital, happening arts outfits in the Portland area. The listing includes performance and cultural centers, arts organizations, dance assemblies, literary venues and groups, a profile of the Portland Art Museum, musical ensembles, arts schools, theatrical troupes, and visual arts opportunities.

CULTURAL CENTERS & ARTS ORGANIZATIONS

COMMUNITY MUSIC CENTER
3350 Southeast Francis St.
(503) 823-3177
www.portlandonline.com/parks
Community Music Center was built in 1912 and served the neighborhood as a fire station until it was abandoned mid-century. Now beautifully renovated, it's a training center for hundreds of music students in the Portland area who present their recitals at the center. Most of those school-age musicians who train at the center are learning to play stringed instruments, including violin, viola, cello, and bass. Many students go on to play with the Metropolitan Youth Symphony and Portland Youth Philharmonic. The center, a member of the National Guild of Community Schools of the Arts, is also a recipient of Chamber Music Program grants from the Amateur Chamber Music Players

Foundation. The Community Music Center also hosts concerts in its acoustically sophisticated performance space.

MULTNOMAH ARTS CENTER
7688 Southwest Capitol Hwy.
(503) 823-2787
www.portlandonline.com/parks
This former middle school on the northern edge of Multnomah Village is now a learning center for artists, musicians, and craftspeople from all over the Portland Metro region. MAC offers a full menu of tai chi, yoga, and art classes for everyone, from toddlers dabbling with mom and dad to preteens learning cartooning, to serious graphic artists using the right side of their brains. There are burgeoning theater, music, and dance departments as well as classroom and hall rentals. It is also home to the Basketry Guild and Portland Handweavers Guild. Visit the website to download a catalogue.

OREGON POTTERS ASSOCIATION
(503) 222-0533
www.oregonpotters.org
The nonprofit Oregon Potters Association presents a large exhibit of works by more than 400 Oregon and southwest Washington clay artists every year at the Oregon Convention Center, 777 Northeast Martin Luther King Jr. Blvd. Admission is free to the exhibit, which features clay art including dinner and functional ware, jewelry, sculpture, outdoor garden sculpture, tile work, fountains, and vessels. Throughout each day artists will demonstrate their individual techniques. Attendees can learn how to make a vessel with a potter's wheel or be entertained with a bit of pioneer history while watching artists throw pots on an old wagon wheel.

Confluence Project

Lewis and Clark's expedition in 1804 heralded many changes for the people who lived in the Pacific Northwest. As the bicentennial of that journey was celebrated, local Native American tribes and civic groups asked artist Maya Lin, who designed the Vietnam Veterans Memorial in Washington, D.C., to help them commemorate this anniversary. The result is the **Confluence Project,** a series of seven installations along the Columbia River, designed and shepherded by Lin with the participation of everyone from schoolchildren to respected community elders— including artists, architects, city planners, and even state departments of transportation. The sites are in varying stages of completion, but they include a stunning land bridge at Fort Vancouver, where the Klikitat meets the Columbia River, an installation at the Sandy River delta, and a large, completed project at Cape Disappointment, where the Columbia meets the Pacific Ocean. For more information, directions, and events concerning this remarkable project, visit the project's website: www.confluenceproject.org.

THE PORTLAND CENTER FOR THE
PERFORMING ARTS
1111 Southwest Broadway
(503) 248-4335 (box office)
www.pcpa.com

Looming as the centerpiece of the city's cultural district, the Portland Center for the Performing Arts hosts more than 900 events, entertaining more than one million ticketholders. The center comprises a number buildings and theaters within buildings, with the main box office at 1111 Southwest Broadway. The Arlene Schnitzer Concert Hall, just to the north, is the grande dame of the performance halls. A building with a grand past, it's currently the home of the Oregon Symphony and host to several traveling theater productions, lectures, and other entertainment. Just south of the Schnitzer is a complex with two theaters: the Newmark Theatre and the Dolores Winningstad Theatre. The Dolores Winningstad Theatre is an Elizabethan or "black-box" theater with 292 seats; the Newmark Theatre is a 916-seat room designed to emulate the Edwardian-style theaters of Europe.

Of note, Keller Auditorium on Southwest 3rd Avenue between Market and Clay Streets, is a spacious theater with a capacity of 3,000 seats—and it's the venue for traveling Broadway shows.

PORTLAND INSTITUTE FOR CONTEMPORARY ART
224 Northwest 13th Ave.
(503) 242-1419
www.pica.org
Dedicated to bringing innovative and relevant contemporary art, music, and theater to Portland, this advocacy group and gallery is also known for its former Dada Ball where even the most staid bureaucrats astonished the crowd with their outrageous costumes. PICA has also staged many other memorable events, such as *Monsters of Grace,* a multimedia opera by Robert Wilson and Philip Glass, and the work of performance artist Karen Finley.

PICA provides residence and other forms of sustenance to artists, as well as education, exhibition, and performance programs. Its Time-Based Art festival (see our Festival and Annual Events chapter) is the culminating event of Portland's summer season. This lively avant-garde gala, modeled on the Edinburgh Festival in Scotland, celebrates every kind of performance art. PICA has become a major cultural force in Portland, attracting the loyalty of artists and patrons alike. There is a resource room with hundreds of exhibition catalogues, periodicals, DVDs, and books on contemporary art, as well as an archive of all past PICA productions. Hours are Mon through Fri, 10 a.m. to 5 p.m. It's open to the public.

DANCE

OREGON BALLET THEATRE
818 Southeast 6th Ave.
(503) 222-5538 (tickets), (503) 227-0977 (administration)
www.obt.org
The Oregon Ballet Theatre presents classics such as *Giselle* and *The Nutcracker* as well as showcasing the work of new choreographers. Artistic director Christopher Stowell, known for his own precise technique as a dancer in the San Francisco City Ballet, brings that same athletic precision to his work with the Oregon Ballet Theatre corps—but goes beyond that to really make use of dance as a means of expression. He is also committed to live music, which makes the experience of watching the Oregon Ballet Theatre even more exciting. Although most of the performances are at the Keller Auditorium and the Newmark Theatre (see the Portland Center for the Performing Arts for more information), Oregon Ballet Theatre also takes to smaller stages such as Lincoln Hall at Portland State University as well as touring

engagements throughout the United States. Oregon Ballet Theatre also has an outstanding classical ballet school.

WHITE BIRD DANCE
5620 Southwest Edgemont Place
(503) 245-1600
www.whitebird.org
White Bird Dance brings exciting dance performances to Portland with most shows staged at the Arlene Schnitzer Concert Hall, but a few performances require more intimate venues. White Bird Dance has sponsored the Paul Taylor Dance Company; Ballet Hispanico, the nation's leading Hispanic-American dance company; and the Diavolo Dance Company, a group that leaps, spins, and flies through the air. White Bird also collaborates with local dancers to create innovative choreography and sponsors education and outreach programs for the Portland Public Schools and other groups.

FILM

CINEMA 21
616 Northwest 21st Ave.
(503) 223-4515
www.cinema21.com
Cinema 21 is the front-runner in the small contingent of art and foreign film houses in town. With its single screen, loose-sprung seats, less-than-impeccable sound, and gently worn lobby, this neighborhood movie house has redefined itself as the place to catch a cult favorite, the big hit at Cannes, a black-and-white B-flick, or a martial arts marathon just in from Taiwan. Tickets are $8, $7 for students, and $5 for children and seniors.

CINEMAGIC
2021 Southeast Hawthorne Blvd.
(503) 231-7919
This little blue box is a classic with a jukebox in the lobby and a steady parade of classic films and contemporary ones—sometimes second-runs, but often not, especially for international and independent films. Plus, the old-fashioned movie theater atmosphere is alluring. Tickets are $4.50 before 6 p.m. and $6.75 after 6 p.m. Cash and checks only.

CLINTON STREET THEATER
2522 Southeast Clinton St.
(503) 238-8899
www.clintonsttheater.com
Once exclusively a film theater, this multipurpose rumpus room offers poetry readings, performance art pieces, concerts, and movies of various genres, including science fiction, foreign, classic, and art films, most of which are decidedly not mainstream. Tickets are $6; matinees are $4; and on Tues, all shows are $4. The *Rocky Horror Picture Show* is a regular feature, showing every Saturday night at midnight—since April 1978, in what is undoubtedly the longest run of the cult favorite. All shows after 7 p.m. are for those 21 and over (except *Rocky Horror*). Cash only.

HOLLYWOOD THEATRE
4122 Northeast Sandy Blvd.
(503) 281-4215
www.hollywoodtheatre.org
Open since 1926 this grand movie parlor is not only a splendid place to see a movie, but it's also a cultural center with classes, events, and workshops. This theater has been restored to its original glory, and it offers one of the few screens in town devoted to art and foreign films, as well as Hollywood classics, old and new.

LAURELHURST THEATER AND PUB
2735 East Burnside St.
(503) 232-5511
www.laurelhursttheater.com

This classic neighborhood movie house offers pizza, wine, and microbrew beer with second-run films, independent films, and classics at $3 per show for adults 21 and older. On weekend afternoons, children accompanied by an adult can see the matinee shows; children's tickets are $1. (All shows after 3 p.m. are for ages 21 and older.) Check it out for its neon swirl out front and along the ceiling.

NORTHWEST FILM CENTER
1219 Southwest Park Ave.
(503) 221-1156
www.nwfilm.org

An adjunct of the Portland Art Museum, the Northwest Film Center is an educational facility with a broad curriculum of filmmaking, screenwriting, and similar classes that can lead to a certificate of film study. The film center also houses a media arts resource center, and happily for the rest of us, it is also a terrific conduit of current and classic art and foreign films. Costs for classes vary depending on length and topic. Call the center for more information on tuition. Every year the center sponsors three major festivals: an international film festival that brings dozens of award-winning movies from all over the globe; the Northwest Film and Video Festival featuring work by regional filmmakers, animators, and cinematographers; and Young People's Film and Video Festival. Films are screened at the museum's Whitsell Auditorium, Southwest Park and Madison; the Guild Theatre, Southwest 9th Avenue; and local Regal Cinemas.

The Portland International Film Festival is the biggest film event in Oregon. It is two weeks of screen madness, with nearly 100 films from 30 countries shown at theaters all over town. The Northwest Film and Video Festival, while not so large, is in some ways more interesting. It not only showcases local talent, but it brings in important independent filmmakers, such as Todd Haynes, Gus Van Sant, and Matt Groening. The institute also sponsors a cool festival devoted to sound and vision: the Reel Music Festival.

LITERARY ARTS

The literary arts are where Portland truly shines. With Powell's—the biggest bookstore in the country—as a foundation, Portland has one of the most well-read citizenries around, and writers like to visit Portland because people actually attend their book signings and are likely to read the books. The three major branches of Powell's (Burnside, Hawthorne, and Beaverton) have author events almost daily. Another lively literary place is the downtown Borders (708 Southwest 3rd St.; 503-220-5911)—this store has signings, discussions, and performances in its bright little cafe. But many of the bookstores in town have author-related events (see the Shopping chapter for these stores), and sometimes these smaller venues provide more personal interaction with the writers. Local colleges—especially PSU, Reed, and Lewis & Clark—also sponsor author events and discussions. The *Oregonian, Willamette Week,* the *Mercury,* and the stores themselves are all good places to check to see who is in town.

Two other important literary events are **Literary Arts Inc.'s Portland Arts and Lectures** series, which features writers with national and international reputations—such as David Sedaris, Ira Glass, Annie Dillard,

Adrienne Rich, and Seamus Heaney—who speak at the Arlene Schnitzer Concert Hall to sell-out crowds; and **Wordstock,** featured in this section.

LITERARY ARTS, INC.
224 Northwest 13th Ave., #306
(503) 227-2583
www.literary-arts.org
In addition to the Portland Arts and Lectures Series, this busy bunch sponsors Oregon Literary Fellowships, Writers in the Schools, and the Poetry in Motion project. Portland was the first city on the West Coast to launch a Poetry in Motion program, and ours also includes poetry from local schoolchildren. Literary Arts also sponsors the Oregon Book Awards at which writers and their friends gather every year to watch as book awards are presented for poetry, fiction, literary non-fiction, drama, and work aimed at young readers.

MOUNTAIN WRITERS CENTER
2804 Southeast 27th Ave., #2
(503) 232-4517
www.mountainwriters.org
Since 1973 Mountain Writers has been sponsoring readings, lectures, and classes for writers. Its invited speakers have included Nobel Prize–winning writers as well as brand-new voices, from all over the world and from the Portland Metro area. Programs include readings at local colleges and universities— as well as regular readings at the Press Club—outreach to high school students, residencies in Portland for visiting writers, and sponsorship of visits by writers to rural areas. But it is most well known for its eight-week workshops and short-term master classes. These are open to emerging writers.

i Portland is the home of the literary journal *Tin House,* which also publishes books and sponsors an excellent writing workshop each summer at Reed College. Faculty have included luminaries such as Charles D'Ambrosio, Anthony Doerr, Denis Johnson, Walter Kirn, and Abigail Thomas. The workshop also gives writers opportunities to meet with editors and agents. Find out more at www.tinhouse.com.

✳POWELL'S CITY OF BOOKS
1005 West Burnside St.
(503) 228-4651
www.powells.com
The preeminent venues for literary readings in the Portland area are arguably the three Powell's bookstores: the Mothership on Burnside, the Eastside store on Hawthorne (3747 Southeast Hawthorne Blvd., 503-235-3802), and the store in Beaverton (8725 Southwest Cascade Ave., 503-643-3131). All three have authors' readings in the evenings throughout the week. Expect everything from writers who are on the top-10 list to those who are just starting their careers or causing a hubbub with offbeat books. Schedules are available at all stores and advertised in local newspapers and magazines. Often, while the novelist, poet, or journalist is signing books after the reading, you can have a chat with these intriguing scribes.

MUSIC

✳CHAMBER MUSIC NORTHWEST
Various locations
(503) 223-3202, (503) 294-6400 (tickets)
Chamber Music Northwest, under the inspired direction of artistic director David Shifrin, promotes the diversity and exquisite beauty of chamber music, old and new. This

Close-up

Wordstock: A Book and Literary Festival

In early October, Portland is at its best—the sun shines a buttery light on the city; the leaves are washed with orange, red, and yellow—and the beautiful fall weather tilts our thoughts toward reading. That's when it's time for **Wordstock.**

Wordstock is a festival devoted to all things book-related. It comprises readings, lectures, teachers' workshops, workshops for kids, music, films, discussions, play readings, dances, dialogues, and anything else that can be connected to the word. For the price of a movie and popcorn, you can spend the entire weekend immersed in a book.

Founded by journalist, teacher, and ex-professional-baseball player Larry Colton, Wordstock started out as a way to raise funds for writing programs in schools. It has grown to involve more than 200 writers, more than 100 exhibitors, and thousands of attendees. *The New York Times,* C-SPAN, and major presses join small presses and local cultural organizations; teachers work side by side in master classes; kids practice narratives; ordinary readers listen and talk and read.

And then there are the writers, who come to talk to their readers and with one another. There are many ways to be a writer in this world, and Wordstock takes advantage of this felicitous variety by inviting all kinds of them. In the past, Wordstock invited stars such as Gore Vidal, Dave Eggers, R. L. Stine, and Joyce Carol Oates. For the first few years, this formula worked well—people lined up to sit in an audience and listen to their heroes. But something felt like it was missing. Then, says executive director Greg Netzer, the festival staff had an epiphany: there was too much focus on national stars. What was missing was community.

Wordstock began as a way to support an organization called Community of Writers, a program devoted to helping teachers learn to teach writing more effectively. When the festival relied on superstars, the sense of community was tenuous. So why not make Wordstock into a genuine and sustainable community by having the festival *be* about the community? They rethought the guest list, and—based on response from

organization, housed at Reed College, brings renowned soloists and ensembles for a year-round program of music, lectures, films, symposia, master classes, and other events. Their season is divided into a summer concert festival and a fall-winter-spring series, and they are often organized thematically. Guest artists have included such stars as Bill T. Jones, the Orion Quartet, and Anne-Marie McDermott. Chamber Music Northwest also collaborates frequently with other groups in town—White Bird Dance, PICA, the Oregon Symphony, for example, as well as making good use of the Reed College faculty. Many events include intelligent lectures and discussion about the music, its history, and its context. Their concerts are usually held at Reed College and elsewhere. Wherever they are, however, you should make the effort to see this outstanding series. See the Festivals and Annual Events chapter for more information.

OREGON REPERTORY SINGERS
909 Southwest Washington St.
(503) 230-0652
www.orsingers.org

the audience—made Northwest writers central, featuring well known writers such as Timothy Egan and Ursula Le Guin who live in the Northwest, but also local heroes such as Oregon poet and noted teacher Kim Stafford and *Willamette Week* publisher Richard Meeker.

Netzer points out that stories, narrative, are made in community; community provides new ways of sharing these stories—sometimes on film, sometimes in performance, sometimes in the simple telling of a tale. Wordstock has augmented this process of community-building by pairing writers and creating interactions; by being open-minded about what counts as literary, so new audiences are hooked. Making local writers central to Wordstock sustains this community-building process beyond the weekend of the festival itself: audiences and writers alike carry these narratives back into the neighborhoods in which they dwell.

Investing in the local community of writers had some beautiful unintended consequences. Ultimately, the original mission—to support the Community of Writers—has been achieved and expanded in innovative ways. Not only were audiences and writers more engaged, but this strategy also allowed them to build alliances with local organizations that were fellow travelers in the literary world—local stores, museums, other businesses, who have welcomed the chance to be a part of this appealing event.

And still, national writers want to come. Originally, Wordstock had to pursue New York publishers. Now, they do not have to be wooed but are wooing Wordstock. They want to come because Portland itself is a draw—Wonderful food! Powells! No sales tax! Great shopping! Readers! But the seductive pull of the (lowercase) community of writers also draws them, once again manifesting the truth that the universal may be found in the particulars of Portland, Oregon.

Wordstock takes place at various locations but primarily at the Oregon Convention Center. Call (503) 549-7887 or check www.wordstockfestival.com for more information.

Also see our Festivals and Annual Events chapter.

The 60-plus voices of the Oregon Repertory Singers present neglected classics as well as contemporary pieces to international acclaim. Directed by versatile conductor Gilbert Seeley, the group often joins the Portland Baroque Orchestra to reinterpret work by Handel, Mozart, and Bach. They also have an extremely well-run youth choir program, with 170 children in 6 choirs.

✳OREGON SYMPHONY
923 Southwest Washington St.
(503) 228-1353
www.oregonsymphony.org
This ensemble of world-class performers and conductors routinely delivers outstanding music. The sensitive and exciting principal conductor of the Oregon Symphony is the European-trained Carlos Kalmar, who also serves at the helm of Chicago's Grant Park Music Festival. He has won the hearts and ears of Oregonians, aided by concertmaster

Jun Iwasaki. In addition to playing classic symphonic music, the Oregon Symphony keeps it fresh with innovative events such as playing a live accompaniment to Alfred Hitchcock's film *Psycho*.

PORTLAND BAROQUE ORCHESTRA
1020 Southwest Taylor Ave.
(503) 222-6000
www.pbo.org

The Portland Baroque Orchestra is devoted to the performance of classical and baroque music on original instruments (or replicas) to provide an authentic experience of the great composers. It is worth attending a concert to hear them play music written between 1600 and the mid-19th century on these instruments. To enhance this time travel, visiting soloists on violin, cello, and harpsichord join the orchestra to render historical versions of Handel, Haydn, and Mozart.

PORTLAND CHAMBER ORCHESTRA
(503) 771-3250
www.portlandchamberorchestra.org

Music for the chamber orchestra, a group that numbers about 35, is intimate but powerful—the size of the group allows greater flexibility compared with ensembles that are bigger or smaller. And Portland Chamber Orchestra takes full advantage of this in their repertoire; for example, their interpretation of Handel's *Messiah* is stunning. Also, they will often accompany stand-out soloists, such as pianist Mei-Ting Sun. This nimble group sometimes pairs with the ballet or other groups to increase the fun.

PORTLAND YOUTH PHILHARMONIC
421 Southwest Hall St.
(503) 223-5939
www.portlandyouthphil.org

Portland Youth Philharmonic has a long history as the country's first youth orchestra. In 1912 Oregon's first children's orchestra was christened as the Sagebrush Symphony. This group turned into the Portland Junior Symphony in 1924 and then in 1930 it settled into its current title. The Youth Philharmonic has two full symphony orchestras, as well as a strong orchestra for younger students.

THEATER

ARTISTS REPERTORY THEATRE
1515 Southwest Morrison St.
(503) 241-1278
www.artistsrep.org

A charming black-box theater is home to this company, known for taut performances of new plays and classics. A good example is *Metamorphoses*, by Mary Zimmerman— a recipient of the MacArthur "genius" fellowship. ART's beautiful space has two separate theaters; both are intimate and actor-focused—the ideal environment for its cutting edge performances that include many West Coast and world premieres.

DO JUMP!
Echo Theater
1515 Southeast 37th Ave.
(503) 231-1232
www.dojump.org

This one-of-a-kind physical theater and dance troupe has been celebrated since its beginning in 1977 for its distinctive choreography, which also features aerial acrobatics and live music. Do Jump! now regularly performs at the downtown Newmark Theater and tours the nation, but its home is still the unpretentious Echo Theater just off Hawthorne Boulevard. That's also the home of its wonderful camps and classes that teach stilt walking, trapeze flying, aerobatics, and other gravity-defying tricks to children and adults. Do Jump! has become a classic Portland experience.

IMAGO THEATRE
17 Southeast 8th Ave.
(503) 231-9581
www.imagotheatre.com

Imago Theater blends physical comedy, acrobatics, and pathos, and somehow brings all of these characteristics together to perform award-winning shows that have traveled as far as Broadway. This boundary-blurring company performs new works as well as adaptations of classics. They are best known for their comedy Portland's most avant-garde theater ensemble, Imago tackles edgy drama and comedy that slice across theatrical history from Japanese Noh to Sartre's *No Exit* to contemporary works by emerging playwrights. When Imago is not touring the globe, Portlanders line up to see their newest, strangely captivating performances.

MIRACLE THEATRE GROUP
425 Southeast 6th Ave.
(503) 236-7253
www.milagro.org

Comprising Miracle Mainstage, Teatro Milagro, and Milagro Bailadores, this Portland-based operation is the largest Hispanic arts and cultural organization in the Pacific Northwest. Since it started in 1985, Miracle Theatre has offered Hispanic theater, arts, and cultural experiences throughout the region, particularly to low- and moderate-income Spanish-speaking audiences and those in rural settings who often don't get to see quality drama. Mainstage presents four English-language plays by Hispanic playwrights and two festivals each season on the Portland stage. Teatro Milagro is the group's

touring theatrical company that journeys to rural communities in Oregon, Idaho, Montana, Washington, and Wyoming, where it invites local amateur actors and youth-at-risk to join the troupers onstage. Milagro Bailadores, a touring dance company, travels to schools throughout the western United States, where it entertains as well as informs audiences about Latin American dance and music.

PORTLAND CENTER STAGE
128 Northwest 11th Ave.
(503) 445-3700
www.pcs.org

Portland Center Stage, our city's only fully professional resident theater company, presents its dramas and comedies in the Gerding Theatre, a beautiful LEED-certified (Leadership in Energy and Environmental Design) building in the Pearl District. Recent productions have included *West Side Story*, the *Fantasticks, Grey Gardens, Sunset Boulevard*, and a wonderful adaptation of Ken Kesey's novel *Sometimes a Great Notion*. PCS also shows compelling Christmas shows such as *The Santaland Diaries* and *A Christmas Carol*. Tickets prices depend on seating and day of the week. In addition, PCS sponsors an intensive playwrights' festival each summer.

PORTLAND OPERA
211 Southeast Carruthers St.
(503) 241-1802
www.portlandopera.org

Since the early '60s, the Portland Opera has been presenting operas that have earned the group a ranking in the top 15 opera companies in the United States. It was also the second company in the United States to use supertitles (English translation projected above the stage). This will come as good news to those who find it difficult to follow the plot through aria after aria, though not all opera fans are pleased. As well as presenting classic operas such as *Aida, Carmina Burana,* and *The Mikado,* Portland Opera became the first opera company in the world to sponsor a subscription series to national touring Broadway musicals. This "Best of Broadway Series" has brought *The Sound of Music, Sunset Boulevard, Les Miserables, Mamma Mia, Wicked,* and many more crowd-pleasers to the Keller Auditorium.

TEARS OF JOY THEATRE
700 Northeast 136th Ave.,
Vancouver, WA
(503) 248-0557, (360) 695-3050
www.tojt.com
A puppeteer ensemble that has grown far beyond the days of Punch and Judy, Tears of Joy Theatre, based in Vancouver, Washington, has been delighting kids and adults for years with its mythologically driven dramas, life-size puppets, and wondrous costumes. As well as touring through the United States, Tears of Joy also performs at the Winningstad Theatre in Portland. Tears of Joy also has a Puppet Camp where children ages 7 to 12 get to join the puppeteers in creating their own puppet plays. Kids build puppets and masks and learn performance skills. These camps, usually during summer, are funded by the city of Vancouver.

> **i** The Regional Arts & Culture Council is an important source for arts education, advocacy, and stewardship in the Portland metro area. And it's also the best place to find out about about Portland's substantial public art program. Visit them on the web at www .racc.org.

VISUAL ARTS

The two major events in the Portland visual arts scene are **First Thursday** and its reverse image, **Last Thursday.** On the first Thurs of each month, galleries, shops, and museums are open into the evening in the Old Town, Pearl, and downtown districts. Even on rainy nights, these are festive and crowded events, with street musicians, performing artists, and exhibitionist art students lending a carnival air to the evening. First Thursdays are usually the evenings that new exhibitions are opened. It is great fun, but parking in the Pearl can be maddening. Like us, you can park in a downtown garage and take the streetcar to the Pearl.

Last Thursdays are a kind of Bohemian retort to First Thursdays. This event is held on Northeast Alberta Street, and it includes the galleries that are sprouting thickly in this area of urban renewal. On Alberta pay special attention to the exhibitions and receptions at Guardino Gallery, Onda, Talisman, and everywhere else along this vibrant little strip, a celebration of the carnivalesque.

THE ART GYM
Marylhurst University
17600 Pacific Hwy.
(503) 699-6243
www.marylhurst.edu/theartgym
Unlike many college art museums and galleries that, for better or worse, only reflect work undertaken by faculty and students, The Art Gym at Marylhurst is a consistently exciting venue for contemporary artists in and out of school, often out on the cutting edge. Once the gymnasium for this private school, the 3,000-square-foot gallery is large enough to hold sizable sculptures and large installations. The Art Gym is open Tues through Sun noon to 4 p.m.

AUGEN GALLERY
817 Southwest 2nd Ave.
(503) 224-8182
www.augengallery.com

A venerable institution in Portland's art world, the two locations of the Augen Gallery (additional location is at 16 Northwest Davis St., 503-546-5056) sustain its reputation for eclectic fine art with a large collection featuring not only local artists but internationally renowned masters such as Stella, Hockney, Motherwell, and Warhol as well. Put this gallery on your itinerary when you begin your sampling of art during your First Thursday stroll.

BLACKFISH GALLERY
420 Northwest 9th Ave.
(503) 224-2634
www.blackfish.com

This influential gallery is an important stop on any tour of visual art in Portland. Here, the artwork of the nation's oldest artists' cooperative is displayed during monthly exhibits. Examples of this widely varied effort include abstracts, weavings, and sculpture. The gallery is open Tues through Sat 11 a.m. to 5 p.m.

BLUE SKY GALLERY
122 Northwest 8th Ave.
(503) 225-0210
www.blueskygallery.org

Blue Sky was established in 1975 as the Center of the Photographic Arts to promote the glories of that medium and cultivate innovative talent. Since then, the gallery has been a fierce advocate of local photographers as well as showcasing international artists. The gallery is open Tues through Sat noon to 5 p.m.

ELIZABETH LEACH GALLERY
417 Northwest 9th Ave.
(503) 224-0521
www.elizabethleach.com

One of Portland's premier art scenes, Elizabeth Leach Gallery, located in the spacious Hazeltine Building in the heart of Old Town, represents both Northwest and national artists in monthly exhibitions. This gallery features cutting-edge work, and attendance on First Thursday is practically required. Hours are Tues through Sat, 10:30 a.m. to 5:30 p.m.

GUARDINO GALLERY
2939 Northeast Alberta St.
(503) 281-9048
www.guardinogallery.com

This gallery in Northeast Alberta Street has its finger on the pulse of emerging talent, with high-quality exhibits of local painters, printmakers, and sculptors. When you stop by the string of galleries, studios, and shops on Alberta that celebrate Last Thursday, be sure to visit Guardino Gallery. Chat with the Guardinos, who are happy to share their thoughts on the artists on display as well as their own ongoing creative work. Or you can stop by any time Tues through Sat from 11 a.m. to 6 p.m., or Sun from 11 a.m. to 4 p.m.

LAURA RUSSO GALLERY
805 Northwest 21st Ave.
(503) 226-2754
www.laurarusso.com

One of Portland's largest and most prestigious galleries, Laura Russo Gallery offers classical and controversial artwork by the Northwest's finest artists as well as young talent in a setting that is itself a work of serene art. The gallery is open Tues through Fri, 11 a.m. to 5:30 p.m. and Sat, 11 a.m. to 5 p.m.

MUSEUM OF CONTEMPORARY CRAFT
724 Northwest Davis St.
(503) 223-2654
www.museumofcontemporarycraft.org
The Museum of Contemporary Craft is dedicated to promoting the beauty of handmade arts in Oregon, sponsoring permanent and traveling collections of exquisite ceramic, glass, metal, and fiber art. Its permanent collections feature regional stars such as Don Sprague and international artists such as Vladimir Tsivin and Gail Nichols, but you will also find much space devoted to emerging artists. The gallery has always been devoted to providing craftspersons with a way to sell their work at a fair price, and the sales gallery here is outstanding, offering expert help for the novice and the seasoned collector. The gallery was founded in 1937, built in part with Works Progress Administration funds, and it is the oldest nonprofit gallery in the country. In 2008 it moved to a handsomely renovated space in the Pearl District, with help from a large grant from investor and philanthropist Paul Allen, and was able to massively expand its offerings. The museum offers family programs on Sun, as well as lectures, discussions, and classes throughout the week. Crafts have long been considered fine art in Portland, and this museum displays the highest form of these ideals.

NEWSPACE CENTER FOR PHOTOGRAPHY
1632 Southeast 10th Ave.
(503) 963-1935
www.newspacephoto.org
This center is devoted to the photographic image, providing resources for students, artists, teachers, and professionals. It has a wonderful gallery space that shows the work of new and established photographers, but it also offers classes, darkroom space (for those who have not converted solely to digital), and help with access to lighting. They also help out artists by reviewing portfolios and teaching workshops on how to market your wares.

i For the latest announcements, reviews, and news about the Portland arts scene, check out PORT at www .portlandart.net. This site, sponsored by the movers and shakers of the Portland art world, features outstanding writing about what's being shown around town and what to think of it.

✳PORTLAND ART MUSEUM
1219 Southwest Park Ave.
(503) 226-2811
www.portlandartmuseum.org
The Portland Art Museum is architecturally and artistically our city's pride and joy even if we quarrel about what exhibits are inside. The second oldest fine arts museum in the Pacific Northwest, it was established in 1892 when business and cultural leaders created the Portland Art Association and ponied up dough to collect a group of 100 plaster casts of Greek and Roman sculpture. It was a start. In 1905 the museum found a physical location at Southwest 5th Avenue and Taylor Street, and in the 1930s it ended up in its current building designed by the noted architect, Pietro Belluschi. In fall 2000 the museum reopened after an extensive renovation in the Hoffman Wing: three floors devoted to Native American art and new exhibit space for European, regional, contemporary, and graphic art. There is also a gift shop, outside sculpture garden, and the Whitsell Auditorium used for ceremonies and films. Now one of the 25 largest

museums in the United States, the Portland Art Museum has a collection of more than 32,000 works of art from American Indian artifacts to Monet's *Waterlilies* to an impressive assembly of Asian art. To display the large collection of Asian paintings, ceramics, prints, and sculptures, three permanent Asian art galleries have been added to the museum's exhibit space. After strolling past a changing gallery that reflects the flavor of the permanent displays, visitors can view art in the Japanese, Chinese, and Korean galleries.

In the fall of 2005, the museum opened its new gallery in the beautifully renovated Mark Building, an old Masonic temple immediately adjacent to the museum. This renovated space provides 141,000 square feet for the new Jubitz Center for Modern and Contemporary Art, as well as two ballrooms, a library, and offices.

The museum frequently stages extravagant touring exhibits featuring art from the ancient to the modern. These have included important collections of artifacts from China and Egypt, as well as the late paintings of Monet and other French masters. The museum also embraces edgy modern art and has an ideal space to show it in the Jubitz Center.

The Portland Art Museum also sponsors numerous events and classes, many of which are family-friendly. The museum is open Tues, Wed, and Sat from 10 a.m. to 5 p.m.; Thurs and Fri from 10 a.m. to 8 p.m.; and Sun from noon to 5 p.m. Admission is free to museum members; nonmember prices are $10 for adults. For information on shows and programs, call (503) 226-2811.

QUINTANA GALLERIES
124 Northwest 9th Ave.
(503) 223-1729
www.quintanagalleries.com
A popular stopping spot in downtown Portland since it opened in 1972, Quintana has a bounty of American Indian and Hispanic art. Walking by its windows is a show in itself with a sumptuous display of Northwest tribal masks and totems as well as pueblo pottery, fetishes, and other crafts from the Southwest. The gallery also has a good collection of photographs by Edward Curtis as well as collector-quality antiques.

RECREATION & SPECTATOR SPORTS

Oregonians have their share of skyscrapers, computer chip plants, and BMW dealerships, but we also have forests, snow-topped mountains, phenomenal river gorges, a 300-mile coastline, one of the most fertile valleys in the world, a lacy network of creeks and rivers, and an extensive system of parks and wilderness areas. Though the great expanse of our state may be crisscrossed with highways, while even our trails may be crowded with exuberant hikers, there is still a wild, true outback here where a soul can find solitude, clean air to breathe, and a vision of unspoiled land, river, or seacoast. The Portland area in particular is home to or close to some of our best outdoor attractions. So Portlanders love to get out and about—to bike, hike, paddle, putt, shoot, set the hook, and slide down our slippery snowy slopes. In this chapter we've listed some of our favorite spots, so you can try out your outdoor or indoor recreational skills in our beautiful Portland setting. We've included a few organizations and commercial operations that can help you on your way.

As for spectator sports, the biggest game in Portland is the National Basketball Association's Trailblazers, but there are lots of other seats to cheer from, including ice hockey with the Winter Hawks and soccer matches with the Portland Timbers, now a Major League Soccer team. PGE Park, a downtown stadium, is the home of the Timbers, while the Blazers play at the Rose Garden. We'll tell you more about these later in the chapter.

RECREATION

NATURE OF THE NORTHWEST INFORMATION CENTER
800 Northeast Oregon St.
(503) 872-2752
www.naturenw.org
Near the Convention Center and Lloyd Center, this information center is open from 10 a.m. to 5 p.m., Mon through Fri. Outdoor recreationists come here to examine books and pamphlets about geology and other natural history features of Oregon. Topographic maps, brochures, and books are also on sale. You can also obtain from them a free publication list from the Oregon Department of Geology—as well as the information-packed website, which has the lowdown on passes, hikes, and other crucial information.

Biking

Bicycling magazine has repeatedly proclaimed Portland the most bike-friendly city in the United States. People ride their bikes to work, to school, for fun, or for sport—no matter how steep the hill or how dreary the weather. TriMet provides help for this popular form of transportation with racks on its buses and light rail. You can store your bike on the front of the bus or train and ride to your neighborhood or out into the country for a recreational spin. There are also many bike repair shops where you can chat with bike mechanics or do the work yourself for a small fee. In short, if you've got skinny or fat tires, a rusty, beloved Schwinn or a shiny new Yeti, this is a great town for biking.

i The most comprehensive source of bike information in town is *BikePortland* (www.bikeportland.org), an online daily bulletin of bike news, policy, and analysis. It also provides an incredibly useful registry of stolen bikes and advice about how to get them back.

Biking Organizations
✴BICYCLE TRANSPORTATION ALLIANCE (BTA)
233 Northwest 5th Ave.
(503) 226-0676
www.bta4bikes.org
With nearly 5,000 members statewide, the mission of the Bicycle Transportation Alliance is to get more people out of cars and on bicycles for the commute to and from work. BTA coordinates its efforts with the Bike Gallery chain and Cycle Oregon to promote cycling as a fun, healthy, and environmentally friendly mode of transport. If you want to work to get more bike lanes and biker-friendly legislation, this is an outfit that will appreciate your help.

PORTLAND WHEELMEN TOURING CLUB
(503) 257-7982 (ride hotline),
(503) 666-5796 (information)
www.pwtc.com
The Portland Wheelmen Touring Club, founded in 1971, promotes cycling via a social organization for cyclists with more than 1,100 members. The primary focus of the club is recreational riding. It sponsors up to two dozen rides on a weekly basis, including rides every day of the year and many evenings. You don't have to be a member to go on a ride, but if you are one, they'll keep your stats for you. The outings are listed in their monthly newsletter, *Riders Digest,* available at most Portland area bicycle shops and in the *Oregonian*'s arts and entertainment section every Fri.

Popular Rides
PORTLAND BRIDGE PEDAL
Bicycle Transportation Alliance
www.bta4bikes.org
Held every August, this urban bike ride brings together a very long string of more than 10,000 participants who bike and hike over bridges crossing the Willamette River. The city closes nine of these spans to auto traffic so that the noncompetitive bikers can claim the bridges as their own. During their 28-mile trek, these pedalers can gaze down at a bustling cityscape, freighters getting loads of wheat at huge grain elevators, and other bikers struggling up the on-ramp. At the end of the ride, a festive get-together celebrates biking with T-shirts, certificates of accomplishment, and vendors selling cold drinks and spicy grub.

Cycle Oregon

Every year, 2,000 cyclists take to the road for seven days, cruising through hundreds of miles of Oregon's most beautiful scenery to raise money for Oregon community development and preservation. **Cycle Oregon** is a fully supported tour—and that means hot showers, excellent meals, massages, folks to carry your gear, and every other detail considered—so you can relax and enjoy the scenery while you pedal. For more information visit the Cycle Oregon website, www.cycleoregon.com.

WORST DAY OF THE YEAR RIDE
www.worstdayride.com

This festive event, sponsored by the Community Cycling Center, celebrates the hideous winter biking weather that Portlanders endure with a 2,000-cyclist ride. You can choose between two loops—an 18-mile urban one or a 40-mile course that takes you out to Hillsboro. Both start at the Lucky Labrador Brew Pub (915 Southeast Hawthorne). Riders show up in costumes but ready for any kind of weather. Proceeds benefit the Community Cycling Center, which uses the funds to give bikes to low-income kids and for other worthy things.

Portland Bike Shops

These shops can help you find a bike, the tools to repair it, all the gear you'll need for soggy commutes, and information about where to ride on the weekend. Some of them will also rent bikes. Others sell custom bikes—a burgeoning industry in Portland. BikePortland (www.BikePortland.org) also has comprehensive information on custom bikes.

i Bike riding can be a great form of exercise for city children. But parents rightly worry about safety: Dogs, cars, and other cyclists can make riding hazardous. The Community Cycling Center is dedicated to teaching children about bicycle safety, riding, and repair. Contact them at 1700 Northeast Alberta St., (503) 287-8786; www .communitycyclingcenter.org.

BECKWITH BICYCLES
4235 Southeast Woodstock Blvd.
(503) 774-3531

BICYCLE REPAIR COLLECTIVE
Southeast 45th Avenue and Belmont Street
(503) 233-0564

BIKE CENTRAL CO-OP
732 Southwest 1st Ave.
(503) 227-4439

BIKE GALLERY
(Six locations; see website)
5329 Northeast Sandy Blvd.
(503) 281-9800
www.bikegallery.com

CITYBIKES WORKER'S COOPERATIVE
734 Southeast Ankeny St.
(503) 239-6951, (503) 239-0553 (for repair shop)

FAT TIRE FARM
2714 Northwest Thurman St.
(503) 222-3276
www.fattirefarm.com

REI
1405 Northwest Johnson St.
(503) 221-1938, (360) 693-0209
www.rei.com

RIVER CITY BICYCLES
706 Southeast Martin Luther King Jr. Blvd.
(503) 233-5973
www.rivercitybicycles.com

VELOCE BICYCLES
3202 Southeast Hawthorne Ave.
(503) 234-8400

Boating

A city at the confluence of two major waterways and surrounded by myriad ponds and lakes, Portland has a lot of boats parked in driveways, moored at docks, and afloat as homesteads. All through summer the Willamette River swarms with nautical traffic, water-skiers zooming the more tranquil waters below Ross Island, and sailboats wending between downtown bridges. And during the winter holidays, volunteer boaters decorate their crafts and line up for the Parade of Christmas Ships as they take a week of chilly nights to entertain Portlanders with their imaginative use of lights shining on dark water.

The Willamette's major launch sites, both operated by Portland Parks and Recreation, (503) 823-7529, are at Willamette Park and Sellwood Riverfront Park. Others are RiverPlace, an elegant moorage close to downtown on the Willamette, (503) 241-8283, and Chinook Landing Marine Park, which has six launch lanes on the Columbia River. The Oregon State Marine Board has an amazingly helpful online guide that details boat ramp information, regulations, route planning, cautions, fishing, and more (www.boatoregon.com). Wherever you launch, be sure to put the children in life jackets: It is required by law. And you'd better put on one yourself too.

Rentals
BLUE LAKE PARK
20500 Northeast Marine Dr., Fairview
(503) 661-6087
From Memorial Day to Labor Day, from 11 a.m. to late afternoon, you can rent a canoe or paddleboat from the Blue Lake dock for less than the price of a matinee. Note: It also costs $5 per car to enter the park.

ISLAND SAILING CENTER
515 Northeast Tomahawk Island Dr.
(800) 303-2470
www.islandsailingclub.com
If you're into sailing, you'll want to check out the Island Sailing Club. Here you can rent a 20-foot Santana for $70 for a half day or $154 for a full day or a 24-foot Wavelength for $254 for a full day on the Columbia. For a more ambitious adventure, the club will rent a charter sailboat for up to a week out of a moorage in DesMoines, Washington, near Seattle. For the uncertain, captains can also be rented.

SPORTCRAFT MARINA

1701 Clackamette Dr., Oregon City
(503) 656-6484
www.sportcraftmarina.com

This is a good rental operation for those who want to boat on the Willamette River. Open year-round Tues through Sat from 9 a.m. to 4 p.m., they rent, with a $50 deposit, solo canoes and kayaks for $20 for two hours and $5 for each additional hour; If you want to rent a craft on Sun or Mon, call for special arrangements.

WILLAMETTE SAILING CLUB

6336 Southwest Beaver Ave.
(503) 246-5345
www.willamettesailingclub.com

If you're going to be here a while, you might consider joining this member-run group dedicated to small sailboats, which moors its craft near Willamette Park. If you're a member you can rent a dinghy here. The club holds meetings and classes and invites members to crew with each other.

Bowling

Bowling never seems to lose its appeal, even with electronic scorekeeping. Below are a couple of favorite lanes.

INTERSTATE LANES

6049 North Interstate Ave.
(503) 285-9881

This bowling alley not only features cosmic bowling—where black lights turn the pins a spooky white, and lasers flash through the air to the beat of cosmic tunes—but it also is completely nonsmoking. They do birthdays and corporate events as well. They serve beer, wine, and pizza. Cosmic bowling happens between 10:30 p.m. and 1:30 a.m. on Fri and Sat night.

International Play

Portland sometimes has the feeling of a provincial European capital. Is it the skyline? The river wall and bridges? Or is it the bocce ball and pétanque players in the city parks? For a little bit of France, join the pétanque players on Saturdays at Portland's own Place de Vosges, Jamison Square (visit **www.laboulerose.com** for a calendar and other information). If you're the bocce type, the Portland Bocce League (**www .portlandbocce.com**) plays tournaments during July and August in the public courts found on the North Park Blocks, Northwest Glisan Street and Park Avenue.

VALLEY LANES

9300 Southwest Beaverton-Hillsdale Hwy., Beaverton
(503) 292-3523
www.valleylanes.com

Home of glow-in-the-dark laser lanes, Valley Lanes also offers bumper bowling for kids. It has 32 lanes open from 9 a.m. to midnight, seven days a week. Valley Lanes also has all-you-can-bowl cosmic bowling—as well as a full-service restaurant and lounge.

Camping

In a region renowned for a vast menu of camping sites, it's hard to pick just a few to recommend, but here are some nearby sites that are at the top of the list. Note that some state parks require a $5 day-use fee; you can also purchase an annual pass for $30. Camping fees depend on the park, the time of year, and the luxuriousness of the facility. For state park information call (503) 986-0707 or (800) 551-6949. If you want to make a reservation (a good idea), call (800) 452-5687. You can register online at www .oregonstateparks.org.

MILO MCIVER STATE PARK
South side of Clackamas River off Springwater Road, 4 miles northwest of Estacada
(503) 986-0707, (800) 452-5687
This spot is an excellent stop for RVs with its 44 electrical hookups and 4 primitive tent sites. Lots of trailheads lead into riverside forests, and plenty of meadows invite roaming about. Open as a park all year, it is available for camping Feb through Nov. To get there take I-205 to SR 212. Make a lazy right turn off SR 212 onto SR 224, which leads to Estacada. From here backtrack down the river on Springwater Road to the park.

✳MOUNT HOOD RECREATIONAL AREA
Mount Hood Information Center
65000 East US 26, Welches
(503) 622-4822, (888) 622-4822,
(877) 444-6777 (campsite reservations)
www.mthood.info
www.reserveamerica.com
You'll find plenty of gorgeous spots in the Mount Hood Wilderness only 60 miles east of Portland. To get there, take I-205 to Southeast Powell Boulevard, which morphs into US 26, the trail up the hill to all the fun.

Backpackers can take one of many trails leading from Timberline Lodge, a National Historic Monument with huge beams and logs for posts and lintels. This justly famous hotel, built in 1937, offers rustic luxury—if such a thing is possible—in its rooms, but campers might be more interested in the wonderful restaurant.

For those who want to stay down in the trees, there are plenty of campsites and picnic areas. With 15 sites on the Salmon River Road, Green Canyon is a charming stop close to a store for stocking up on all that gooey stuff that goes into s'mores.

To get there, take US 26 to Zigzag (70220 US 26; 503-622-3191) then drive 4 miles northeast on the Salmon River Road (2618) to the campground. One of the prettiest campsites in this wilderness area is Tollgate, on the banks of the Zigzag River 1 mile east of the tiny town of Rhododendron. Another good campground, Camp Creek, with 30 sites, lies on Camp Creek Road a short distance beyond the Tollgate turnoff.

One of the largest and most popular campsites in the Mount Hood National Forest is Timothy Lake, acclaimed as one of the 10 best camping spots in the West by *Sunset* magazine. This scenic lake with its postcard view of Mount Hood is easily accessible from Portland. Take US 26 beyond the junction with SR 35 and turn south on Skyline Road and east on FR 57, both of which are marked with signs to Timothy Lake. Once at this huge lake, which is ringed by fir, hemlock, and pine trees, pick a spot at one of its three main campsites, or simply hike or canoe to a more secluded camp. To make a reservation at Oak Fork, Gone Creek, or Hoodview, call (877) 444-6777, the number for ReserveAmerica. For more information on camping in the Mount Hood Recreational Area, call the Zigzag Ranger District at the number above or write to them at 70220 East SR 26, Zigzag, Oregon 97049. A day-use pass will set you back $5; an annual pass is $30.

OXBOW REGIONAL PARK
6 miles east of Gresham on Division

Street

(503) 663-4708

Oxbow Regional Park is a close-in site for tent camping that's open all year and operated by Metro, the regional governing body that runs the zoo, TriMet, and other public services. Six miles east of Gresham on Division Street, this site has 45 tent and RV campsites with no hookups. The cost is $15 per night and a $4 vehicle entry fee. Firewood is $4 per bundle. As in all Metro parks, no dogs are allowed.

Canoeing, Kayaking & Rafting

Paddlers looking for water deep enough for their canoes, kayaks, or rafts can find a launch spot within minutes anywhere in the Portland area. Here, where the Clackamas, Sandy, Willamette, and Columbia Rivers amble together west toward the Pacific Ocean, are stretches of flat calm, cataracts of white fury, and fast water rippling over dappled round boulders. And for those who want to just ease along, there are also a few boat-friendly lakes and ponds. Here's a sampling of aqua-jaunts available close to town.

BLUE LAKE
8 miles east of Portland in the town of Fairview along I-84

Blue Lake Regional Park, at the gateway to the Columbia Gorge, is just 20 minutes east of downtown Portland. Although it gets crowded, it is worth a visit for its accessibility and amenities. Chinook Landing Marine Park, adjacent to Blue Lake Regional Park, is a sizable boating facility with a six-lane launch ramp and picnic area. There are also trails through nearby wetlands for opportunities to view wildlife.

MULTNOMAH CHANNEL

Multnomah Channel is a backdoor watercourse that starts at the southeast tip of Sauvie Island and winds northwest through a lacy wild of sloughs, swamps, and grassy pastures to the little lumbertown of St. Helens and a confluence with the Columbia River. If you want to meander up or down a stretch of the channel, a good spot to launch your canoe or rowboat is the Sauvie Island Boat Ramp at the junction of the Burlington Ferry and Sauvie Island Road, just north of the intersection with Reeder Road. (See the entry on Sauvie Island in the Portland's Parks chapter.) You'll find picnic tables, toilets, and plenty of parking nearby.

ROSS ISLAND

A loop around Ross Island is a great two-to three-hour canoe or kayak trip that will get those kinks out of your arms and back. The put-in spot is Willamette Park in Portland's southwest side. Once in the river cross over to Ross Island, hang a right around its northern tip, and go down the Holgate Channel to the entrance to the lagoon. After you visit this tranquil pond—where you may spy a Swainson's thrush, black-headed grosbeak, or spotted sandpiper—paddle down the channel, around the southern edge of the island, and back downriver to Willamette Park.

SMITH AND BYBEE LAKES
North Portland, 2.5 miles west on Marine Drive off I-5

Smith and Bybee Lakes are the liquid portions of a 2,000-acre wildlife area across the mouth of the Willamette River from Sauvie Island. Here at the confluence of the Columbia and Willamette Rivers is a huge intersection of waterfowl flight paths where federal, state, and regional agencies have established refuges for birds wintering or just passing through. Canoeists and kayakers can paddle quietly among thousands of mallards and Canada geese as well as great blue herons nesting along the shoreline. Osprey are common in the summer, and bald eagles take over their fishing spots in wintertime. Nesting great horned owls have also been sighted. You can reach these lakes by taking I-5 north of Portland to the Marine Drive West exit. Drive west 2.5 miles to the parking lot on the south side of Marine Drive or continue to the Kelley Point Boat Launch farther west on Marine Drive. From the launch it's a short cruise down a slough to the southwest edge of Bybee Lake. Once you arrive at the lakes, if the sun is cooperating, it will be easy to spot lots of Northwest painted turtles basking on logs.

Rentals & Resources
ALDER CREEK KAYAK & CANOE
250 Northeast Tomahawk Island Dr.
(503) 285-0464
1515 Southeast Water St.
(503) 285-1819
www.aldercreek.com
Alder Creek has a great central location, next to OMSI, for renting a kayak or canoe in the downtown area. It's also a good place to rent a canoe or kayak on Tomahawk Island, a close neighbor of Hayden Island, where I-5 crosses the Columbia. This full-service outfit offers a complete line of gear for white-water enthusiasts, as well as low-key paddlers.

PORTLAND RIVER COMPANY
6600 Southwest Macadam Ave., next to Willamette Park
(503) 459-4050
www.portlandrivercompany.com
Portland River Company provides everything

you will need to paddle a single or double sea kayak. It also offers guided tours along the Willamette. First-time kayakers and experienced paddlers alike will enjoy this marine view of Portland. The adventure starts at RiverPlace Marina; crosses over to the historic *USS Blueback,* a submarine docked at Oregon's Museum of Science and Industry; and continues upriver, circling Ross Island, where you may catch sight of great blue herons, osprey, and bald eagles.

i Climbers and other recreators on a budget will appreciate Next Adventure, which carries—in addition to new equipment—a wide variety of used, consigned, closed-out, and traded climbing gear, as well as equipment for lots of other recreational activities. Find them at 426 Southeast Grand Ave., (503) 233-0706 or www.nextadventure .net.

Climbing
A glance to the east or north will suggest that Portlanders have plenty of mountains and cliffs to climb when they get the urge. At roughly 11,235 feet, Mount Hood or Wy'east, as this gorgeous peak is still known, looms above the Cascade ridges. When spring chases the snow up this glacier (the season lasts from May to July), technical climbers grab ice axes and crampons for various ascents suited for novices to masters. It is a relative easy climb until the last 1,500 feet. Due to cagey weather fronts and unstable snow, this last stretch is far more difficult: Rescue units are often plucking unlucky climbers off the steep slope. Other sites that will challenge the crampon crowd are Horsethief Butte, 2 miles east of the Dalles Bridge

on SR 14, and Broughton's Bluff at Lewis and Clark State Park east of Troutdale on I-84. Just 30 minutes from town, Broughton's Bluff offers a number of tough climbs.

MAZAMAS
527 Southeast 43rd Ave.
(503) 227-2345
www.mazamas.org

This 3,000-member mountaineering group is named after Mount Mazama, a huge mountain that blew itself apart to create Crater Lake in southern Oregon. Founded in 1894 when 193 climbers ascended to the summit of Mount Hood, the Mazamas are legendary for all the mountains they've climbed and the resources they provide for their members. To join all you have to do is climb a mountain with a living glacier.

OREGON MOUNTAIN COMMUNITY
2975 Northeast Sandy Blvd.
(503) 227-1038
www.e-omc.com

Oregon Mountain Community—or known fondly as OMC—carries everything for the serious climber and mountaineer, including climbing and backpacking gear, from crampons, axes, and ropes to get you up the mountain to probes, beacons, and shovels in case it falls down on top of you. They also host classes and lectures, run a repair shop, and offer rentals of every kind of ski, snowshoe, and other winter sports gear.

PORTLAND ROCK GYM
21 Northeast 12th Ave.
(503) 232-8310
www.portlandrockgym.com

The Portland Rock Gym was an urban pioneer, seeing possibility in the Lower Burnside neighborhood when no one else did. They can help you do something similar with your climbing skills. When the weather is keeping you off the rocks, or when you want to fine-tune your ascension skills, stop by Portland Rock Gym for some indoor climbing on a 40-foot wall. The Portland Rock Gym has 8,000 square feet of climbing space and offers classes and equipment rentals, as well as yoga classes, camps, and activities for kids after school. The gym is open Mon, Wed, and Fri from 11 a.m. to 11 p.m., Tues and Thurs from 7 a.m. to 11 p.m., on Sat from 9 a.m. to 7 p.m., and on Sun from 9 a.m. to 6 p.m.

STONEWORKS CLIMBING GYM
6775 Southwest 111th Ave., Beaverton
(503) 644-3517
www.belay.com

While Stoneworks has the usual features of a rock gym, and rents gear, holds classes, and sponsors competitions, it is really renowned for its bouldering area, which is more than 2,000 square feet and has drawn national accolades. For a monthly fee you can take advantage of the intriguing overhang bouldering and a large number of different holds. Stoneworks is open Mon through Thurs from 4 to 10 p.m., Fri from 4 to 8 p.m., and on weekends from noon to 8 p.m.

Fishing & Fly-Fishing

Anglers who live in the Portland area can wet their lines all year long. Spring chinook salmon and summer and winter steelhead spawn up the Clackamas and Sandy Rivers, and rainbow trout can be hooked in those streams as well as the Willamette River and in Blue Lake, a popular fishing hole and recreational site. A good spot to land a steelhead is at the confluence of the Clackamas and Willamette Rivers near Milwaukie. The **Oregon Department of Fish and Wildlife**

(ODFW) keeps a minimum of spawning salmon en route to their upstream beds by issuing quotas in Portland-area water. But as long as the season is open, go for it. To find out where they're biting and where it's legal to hook them, call ODFW's 24-hour automated number, (503) 947-6000 or (800) 720-6339, or visit them online at www.dfw.state.or.us/resources/fishing. Fisherfolk can also catch bass and crappies in the Willamette and sturgeon and shad in the Columbia and Willamette as well as in sloughs and bays feeding into those streams. ODFW has a free pamphlet, "Guide to Warmwater Fishing in the Portland Metropolitan Area," which will guide fishers to piers, pilings, and ponds where those lunkers lay about.

Sporting Goods Stores & Marinas
FISHERMAN'S MARINE & OUTDOOR
1120 North Hayden Meadows Dr.
(503) 283-0044
www.fishermans-marine.com
This huge, locally owned store has anything you'd ever want, from bait to spinners to outboard motors, and you might be able to coax the location of a hot fishing hole out of the friendly clerk. They are wise in the ways of the fish that live in Oregon and Washington.

KAUFMANN'S STREAMBORN
11960 Southwest Pacific Hwy.
(503) 639-7004
www.kaufmannsstreamborn.com
Kaufmann's provides fly-fishing equipment, workshops, and worldwide bookings for piscatory outings abroad. This beautiful store has evolved from the days when the Kaufmann brothers tied flies in their parents' garage. Kauffmann's offers classes in spey casting and trips down the Deschutes River, among other things.

Hiking

A visitor to Portland may glance about at all the folks with backpacks, cargo shorts, and bandanas striding about the urban landscape and guess that most of us are heading for a hike. Maybe so—or maybe it's just the fashion here. Either way, an abundance of nearby trails await hikers of all levels, from those wanting a mellow stroll, such as the 2-mile nature path through Marquam Park, to those dedicated enthusiasts who might enjoy the 27-mile Wildwood Trail along the crest of Forest Park. **Portland Hikers** (www.portlandhikers.org) has up-to-date information about trail condtions and a comprehensive searchable database of Oregon (and some Washington) hikes. Here are a few close-in hikes among this wide range of possibilities.

✳COLUMBIA RIVER GORGE NATIONAL SCENIC AREA
902 Wasco Ave., Suite 200,
Hood River
(541) 308-1700
www.fs.fed.us/r6/columbia/forest
Sweltering Portlanders and Vancouverites have a couple of choices for relief from hot summer days. They either head for the coast or the Columbia Gorge. If they choose the latter, they can stretch their legs on lots of shady trails up and down high, heavily forested basalt promontories. If they decide on a hike to the summit, they get an eye-popping view of one of the largest, most scenic river valleys on the planet. This 300,000-acre wilderness encompasses 22 state parks and is crisscrossed with 167 miles of well-maintained to rough trails. From 15-minute walks to 20-mile days, there are hikes for all ages and abilities.

From bluffs above, hundreds of creeks cataract down steep wooded ridges, and waterfalls hide mossy caves. And alongside the creeks are pathways of varying difficulty: Mount Defiance Trail, Wahkeena Loop with Devil's Rest Option, Bridal Veil Falls and Overlook Loop Trail, and Starvation Ridge Trail. To get to all these trails, take I-84 east along the Columbia Gorge to the Corbett exit (number 22). From there you take the Columbia River Scenic Highway, which travels along the top of the southern bluff to Vista Point and then down the cliff to a stretch of magic with all the above hikes and viewpoints easily accessible. Just watch for signs. If you want to plan an excursion to any of these shady glens and sparkling waterfalls, call the number listed here. You can also find out all you need to know by stopping by the Multnomah Falls Information Center in the Multnomah Falls Lodge, a centrally located facility with restrooms, a restaurant, and on-duty rangers. Public spaces in the gorge are overseen by either of the two agencies listed above. There is also more information about the Columbia Gorge in the Day Trips chapter.

DOG MOUNTAIN
Washington SR 14, milepost 53
Columbia River Gorge
Located about 12 miles east of the Bridge of the Gods, Dog Mountain is a popular hike for a reason: spectacular views of the Gorge, the Cascades, and the amazing wildflowers along the way. It's a bit strenuous, with a 700-foot climb in the first half-mile. Then you have the choice to take a steep, direct route to the top of the mountain or a longer but gentler trail. The east trail (the longer trail) has the most impressive views. Both

end up on top of Dog Mountain, a summit of 2,984 feet. You can bring your dog to Dog Mountain, but you both must watch out for poison oak. To get there, take I-205 north to Washington SR 14 and park at the trailhead, milepost 53, on the north side of the highway.

THE MARQUAM PARK TRAIL
Southwest Marquam Street just off
Southwest Sam Jackson Road
(503) 823-5122
A guide with references to stops along the way is available at a nature shelter at the beginning of the hike. The climb leads through leafy bowers until it arrives at Council Crest Park, the highest point within the city limits, at 1,070 feet above sea level.

OAKS BOTTOM WILDLIFE REFUGE
(503) 823-5122
This stretch of wild along the east side of the Willamette is a treat for city dwellers who want to get into the woods in a hurry. To get here from downtown Portland, take the Ross Island Bridge to Powell Boulevard. Turn south on Milwaukie Avenue and just after crossing Holgate Boulevard, look for the parking lot on the west side of the street in the 5000 block. From this trailhead you angle down the hill into the refuge. Another approach is the trail that begins at the north end of Sellwood Park at Southwest 7th Avenue. To get to this starting point, you can take the Sellwood Bridge and bear left after crossing the Willamette. Along with beavers and muskrats, this wetland along the river is home to woodpeckers, warblers, orioles, and great blue and green herons. It can be muddy, so wear appropriate footgear.

OVERLOOK TRAIL
Washington Park
(503) 823-7529
This wheelchair-accessible trail is 0.25 mile of hardened gravel surface connecting the MAX Zoo Station with Hoyt Arboretum. There are also links with the Wildwood Trail (see separate entry in this chapter). The 10-foot-wide path makes frequent switchbacks as it ascends a gentle grade to the top of the hill and the arboretum's outdoor living museum of trees.

You can catch the beginning of the trail across the street from the MAX station at the north end of the World Forestry Center. If you are driving instead of taking MAX, park at the zoo.

TRYON CREEK STATE PARK
11321 Southwest Terwilliger Blvd.
(503) 636-9886
www.oregonstateparks.org
Just south of the Lewis & Clark College campus, Tryon Creek trickles through a deep ravine, the last free-flowing stream in the metro area and one of the few urban streams that still has a steelhead run. Bike paths and wide, paved, woodsy boulevards invite visitors from all over the area to explore the more than 600 acres of woodland. One trail in particular, Trillium Trail, is beautifully and fully wheelchair accessible. At the bottom of the ravine, an interpretive center with nature displays explains the plants, animals, and other features of the park. This site is a happy memory for thousands of kids who've come here on field trips. There is no fee to use this state park.

THE WILDWOOD TRAIL
Near Vietnam Veterans Memorial
in Washington Park
(503) 823-7529
Easily accessible from the MAX Zoo Station, this trail goes over hill and woody dale through Forest Park. At 4,900 acres, this is the largest park within a US metropolis. Free maps of the trail are available at the Hoyt Arboretum Visitor Center at 4000 Southwest Fairview Blvd., which is also on the trail itself.

Ice-Skating

LLOYD CENTER ICE RINK
953 Lloyd Center
(503) 288-6073
www.lloydcenterice.com
While this shopping-mall ice rink offers lessons for young Olympics hopefuls, it is also popular with teens and adults, who swoosh about the ice oblivious to shopping spectators. This rink provides the gamut of lessons, parties, summer camps, broomball, and other icy activities. Admission is $6, with discounts for scouts, mall employees, seniors, and folks in the military. You can rent ice skates for $3. (Also see the listing in the Kidstuff chapter.)

Motorcycling

ROSE CITY MOTORCYCLE CLUB
www.rose-city-mc.org
Tracing its origins back to 1911, Rose City Motorcycle Club is Oregon's oldest AMA Chartered Road Club. Its 250-plus members ride a wide variety of motorcycles, including touring, cruising, and sport bikes. In addition to its internal activities, such as monthly Saturday breakfasts and rides, the club annually hosts the 250-mile Annual Rose City Oregon Tour, which benefits the Oregon Kidney Association. These motorcyclists also join others in a remarkable visit to kids in the Doernbecher Children's Hospital right around Christmas. The sight of

all these leather-clad bikers bearing presents and wearing Santa costumes is definitely memorable.

Roller-Skating

OAKS AMUSEMENT PARK
Southeast Spokane Street north of Sellwood Bridge
(503) 233-5777
www.oakspark.com
Open year-round as part of a surrounding carnival, this large roller-skating rink is vintage Americana, with a huge Wurlitzer pipe organ playing Tues through Thurs nights and Sun. A live DJ is on duty Saturday night. It's a great chance to join everyone as they "skate backwards" to the driving beat of oldies and goldies. Fees are $5.75, $6.75 on Fri and Sat night. (For more information on roller-skating, see the Kidstuff and Attractions chapters.)

Running

Portland—with its miles of trails and mild weather—is a great running town. For one thing, it's in Oregon, where Nike was born. Heroes such as University of Oregon coach Bill Bowerman, along with Phil Knight of Nike, invented the waffle-soled running shoe, and legendary runner Steve Prefontaine brought thrills to the solitary sport. And for another, we have many running events throughout the year. Major races include the Portland Marathon, the Cascade Runoff, the Hood to Coast Run, the Race for the Cure, and the Shamrock Run, but these are just the most well known. A running event seems to happen almost every weekend somewhere within 100 miles of the city. Important resources for Portland runners include several websites: **www.xdogevents**

.com, for extreme running events is one, and Team Oregon, **www.teamoregon.com,** is another really useful website that coordinates running resources in the area, providing links to the Portland Marathon and hosting a calendar of area running events and races. It also sponsors marathon clinics and scheduled practice runs, as well as good running coaches; Team Oregon's coaching programs are very reasonably priced. The Portland Marathon's number is (503) 226-1111; also see the Festivals and Annual Events chapter. Runners should also visit **Running Outfitters,** 2337 Southwest 6th, (503) 248-9820, and **Pacesetter Athletic,** 4306 Southeast Woodstock, (503) 777-3214, for good gear and information about clubs, races, and other events. Popular running trails include Mount Tabor Park and the Wildwood Trail in the Hoyt Arboretum (unpaved) and Terwilliger Boulevard and both sides of the Willamette River (paved).

i You might think you're tough and can run a marathon or schuss down those black diamond runs and barely break a sweat. But until you've tried Studio X's boot camp and power classes, you won't know what tough is. The trainers and classes at Studio X specialize in the science of human movement, and they will revolutionize your approach to moving through space. Find them at 2839 Southeast Stark St., 503-236-7114 or www.studioxfitness.com.

Skiing & Snowboarding

MOUNT HOOD WILDERNESS
Looming above the valley like a white-robed monarch, 11,239-foot Mount Hood is the state's largest peak. During the winter months, the flanks of the mountain draw

thousands to Mount Hood Meadows, Timberline, and other popular resorts for Alpine and Nordic skiing, snowmobiling, and snowshoeing. Also, the area abounds in cross-country ski trails for those who want to get away from it all.

Downhill
COOPER SPUR
SR 35, 23 miles south of Hood River
(503) 352-7803
www.cooperspur.com
Cooper Spur, on the north face of Mount Hood, is a 50-acre resort with 10 ski runs and 2 tubing runs. It's a fine place to learn to ski—most of the runs are beginner or intermediate grade, and the classes are organized around stations so that you can work on the areas you need to improve. Lessons are short so that you can get a lot of practice on the slopes, with instructors available to help you all day long.

MOUNT HOOD MEADOWS
FR 3555, 6 miles north of the junction of SR 35 and US 26
(503) 337-2222, (800) SKI-HOOD
www.skihood.com
This day-ski area is located on the sunny, wind-protected east side of Mount Hood. For 30 years Mount Hood Meadows has enticed skiers and snowboarders to Oregon's most challenging terrain. Currently 10 chair lifts, including 3 high-speed quads, provide access to 82 trails over 2,150 acres. Mount Hood Meadows offers several easy slopes down the mountain and one double black diamond. This is a good place to go if you are a beginner or very advanced.

MOUNT HOOD SKIBOWL
87000 East US 26 at Government Camp
(503) 272-3206, (503) 222-2695
www.skibowl.com
This popular ski bowl is the closest action to Portland, 52 miles east of town. It has a top elevation of 5,056 feet, a vertical drop of 1,500 feet, four double chairs and five surface tows, and 960 acres to play upon. Skiers and snowboarders have 65 day runs and 34 night runs, with the longest run, Skyline Trail, measuring 3 miles. The season generally lasts from mid-Nov to mid-Apr. On the main slope there is the option of going on a separate trail, which includes many jumps, rails, and a half-pipe. Ski Bowl also offers the longest night skiing in America. This resort is an excellent place for first-timers; many great lessons and deals are offered, and the staff are very inviting.

SUMMIT SKI AND SNOW PLAY AREA
US 26 at the east end of Government Camp
(503) 272-0256
www.summitskiarea.com
Summit Ski and Snow Play Area has been open since 1927. It's the second-oldest resort in the United States, with a vertical slope of 306 feet. The slopes at Summit are not steep, so this is a good place to bring beginners. Still, it is also just as great to go there as an intermediate skier. Summit attracts many families, not only for the skiing but also because of the fantastic tubing hills.

✳TIMBERLINE LODGE AND SKI AREA
6 miles north of Government Camp, off FR 50
(503) 622-7979, (503) 222-2211
www.timberlinelodge.com

To get to this resort built in the '30s, turn north from US 26 at the eastern edge of the town of Government Camp and go 6 miles up FR 50. Boasting the longest ski season in North America, Timberline has more than 1,000 acres of snowfields for skiers and snowboarders. Thanks to the Palmer chairlift, skiers have access to 300 acres situated between 7,500 and 8,500 feet in elevation, not to mention some of the most scenic views in Oregon. Because of its terrain, Timberline is a good choice for beginners and intermediate skiers. Overnight lodging is available, but it fills up fast. To book one of the lodge's 59 rooms, call (800) 547-1406. For information regarding snow conditions, call the lodge's snow phone at (503) 222-2211 or (877) 754-6734.

Cross-Country

BERGFREUNDE SKI CLUB
10175 Southwest Barbur Blvd.
(503) 245-8543
www.bergfreunde.org
As the local branch of an international club with more than 2,500 members, the Bergfreunde Ski Club organizes activities that go beyond the winter season. They offer year-round entertainment for active adults, including organized rafting, golf, dance, and theater outings as well as cross-country skiing. Bergfreunde, or "friends of mountains," is a socially lively club for men and women 21 and older. They meet on the first Wed of each month at the Governor Hotel, 614 Southwest 11th Ave.

MOUNT HOOD MEADOWS
FR 3555, 2 miles north of SR 35
(503) 337-2222
This resort offers a full-service Nordic center and 15 kilometers of trails on Mount Hood.

i Snow removal on roads leading to ski areas is costly. To help pay for this service, Sno-Park permits ($20 per year, $7 for three days, or $3 for one day) are required to park legally in winter recreation areas from Nov through Apr. Sno-Park permits can be purchased at ski areas, outdoor stores, or DMV offices. Don't leave home without one!

OREGON DEPARTMENT OF TRANSPORTATION SKI AREAS
(503) 986-4000
www.tripcheck.com/Pages/SPentry.asp
There are 16 Sno-parks in the Mount Hood region operated by the Oregon Department of Transportation. Popular spots are Bennett Pass, Glacier View, Snow Bunny, Frog Lake, and Trillium Lake.

OREGON NORDIC CLUB PORTLAND CHAPTER
(503) 649-9612
http://onc.org
Organized in 1968 by Nordic ski enthusiasts interested in cross-country skiing on public land, the Oregon Nordic Club now has more than 400 members. Activities are usually day and overnight trips, most of which are held on weekends. The Portland chapter of the Oregon Nordic Club also sponsors ski-related special events, including a yearly ski sale, a ski instruction and demonstration day at Teacup Lake, and sanctioned competition. On the first Tuesday of each month, a general membership meeting is held at the Multnomah Art Center, 7688 Southwest Capitol Hwy., with potluck beginning at 6:30 p.m. The website listed above get you information on the week's events.

Swimming

NORTH CLACKAMAS AQUATIC PARK
7300 Southeast Harmony Rd., Milwaukie
(503) 557-7873, (503) 794-8080
www.co.clackamas.or.us/ncprd/aquatic
This popular swimming pool has three water slides and a 4-foot wave pool. The park is open Mon through Fri from 4 to 8 p.m., and Sat and Sun from 11 a.m. to 3 p.m. and 4 to 8 p.m. Admission fees are $4.99 for children ages 3 to 8; $6.99 for those ages 9 to 18 and seniors 62 and older; and $9.99 for all others. Families can get a discount on Sun and Fri. Please don't bring in any outside food or drinks.

TUALATIN HILLS AQUATIC CENTER
Howard M. Terpenning Recreation Complex
15707 Southwest Walker Rd., Beaverton
(503) 645-7454
This aquatics center is located in the Terpenning Recreation Complex, a sprawling 90-acre park in the Tualatin Hills southwest of Portland. A close competitor to the North Clackamas Aquatic Park, it draws folks from all over the region on those muggy days when it's great to take the plunge. Call for drop-in hours. Children who live within the boundaries of the Tualatin Hills Parks and Recreation District pay $1.50 with residency cards; nonresident children pay $3. Adult residents pay $2, while nonresident adults pay $4.

Portland City Pools
Portland Parks and Recreation has six indoor and six outdoor pools at its various parks and centers throughout the metropolitan area. To find the pool nearest your location check www.portlandonline.com/parks. The outdoor pools are open only during the summer. Pool hours vary, but most are open from 6 a.m. to 9 p.m. daily, opening a little later on the weekends. Most of the time, there are lanes devoted to adult lap swim, but these may be taken over during swim team practices or other events. Admission to Portland Parks and Recreation pools varies, but will run about $3 to $4 for adults, about $2 for those 3 to 17, and free for kids 2 and younger. The information line for aquatics is (503) 823-7946.

i If you have special needs or disabilities that have kept you from fully enjoying the great outdoors, try Adventures Without Limits, (503) 359-2568 or www.awloutdoors.com. This outfit sponsors hikes, cross-country ski trips, snowshoeing, indoor rock climbing, and canoe adventures. Fees are charged, but scholarships for day trips and overnighters are available.

Tennis

The Portland Parks and Recreation Department has close to 100 tennis courts in the metro region. Here's a short list of some of the best ones in town.

IRVING PARK
Northeast 7th Avenue and Fremont Street
These courts are well-lit and popular with folks on the inner east side of town.

LAURELHURST PARK
Southeast 39th Avenue and Stark Street
With its tranquil duck pond, huge fir and cedar trees, and sloping lawns, Laurelhurst Park is one of the loveliest and most peaceful spots in town. The two tennis courts here are old relics that are often busy, but it's worth the wait. Plan on playing during the day, for there is no lighting.

MOUNT TABOR PARK WESTSIDE
Entrance near Southeast 62nd Avenue and Main Street

Three courts are tucked against the base of a living volcano and near one of the city's drinking-water reservoirs. They are also along a trail leading up to the top of Mount Tabor and its terrific view of the downtown skyline. Play a few sets under the lights then stroll around the reservoir and up to the summit to catch a spectacular view of the glittering city across the river.

TENNIS CENTER
324 Northeast 12th Ave.
(503) 823-3189
www.pdx10s.com

These four indoor and eight outdoor courts make this one of Portland's most popular facilities. To play you need to make a reservation and pay a fee of $20 per set of 1 hour and 15 minutes for the indoor courts. Open court reservations are available from 6:45 a.m. to 9:10 p.m. Mon through Fri and from 6:45 a.m. to 10 p.m. on weekends. Outdoor courts are available on a first-come, first-served basis. There is plenty of good lighting, lots of easy parking, showers, and restrooms.

Windsurfing & Kiteboarding

On a bright and windy day in the Columbia Gorge, motorists cruising along I-84 on the Oregon side or down-winding Washington SR 14, are entertained by the multicolored confetti of windsurfers' sails sprinkled on the broad Columbia River. Ask any group of windsurfers, and they'll enthusiastically regale you with the wonders of this world-class stretch where the wind blows hard against the sail and boards whip up and down the river.

Hood River is booming with windsurfing shops, manufacturing plants, and windsurfing schools as well as cafes, saloons, motels, and other services aimed at the thousands of visitors with those easily recognizable poles and canvas on top of their rigs. Retail shops in Hood River include **Hood River Windsurfing,** 101 Oak St., (541) 386-5787 or (800) 211-8207; **Big Winds,** 503 Cascade, (541) 386-6086 (these two shops also offer windsurfing schools); and **Windance,** 207 Front St., (541) 386-2131. Check the bulletin boards in these shops for events, classes, and more arcane info appealing to those who scoot around on the water on a surfboat with a sail.

The best spots to launch are the Hook and Event Center at exit 63, off I-84, and the Hatchery and Swell City, a couple of miles west of the Hood River Bridge on the Washington side of Hood River's Sailpark at exit 64.

Yoga

Yoga is very popular in Portland—and has been for years. You will find all varieties of yoga instruction here, from straightforward hatha to more philosophical kundalini. Finding the right yoga studio or teacher is a personal thing, like finding the right therapist, so you may want to try different classes with different teachers until you find one who can challenge you in the right ways. Portland has many yoga studios, but here are several that we have found offer a wide variety of classes and have excellent reputations for outstanding teachers. Expect to pay between $8 and $16 per class. Most studios offer significant discounts if you buy in bulk.

THE BHAKTISHOP
2500 Southeast 26th Ave.
(503) 244-0108
http://thebhaktishop.com

DIANE WILSON YOGA STUDIO
1017 Southwest Morrison St., #508
(503) 227-1726
www.dianewilsonyoga.com

HOLIDAY'S YOGA CENTER
3942 Southeast Hawthorne Blvd.
(503) 224-8611
www.holidaysyogacenter.com

JULIE LAWRENCE YOGA CENTER
1020 Southwest Taylor St.
(503) 227-5524
www.jlyc.com

MOVEMENT CENTER
1025 Northeast 33rd Ave.
(503) 231-0994
www.mcyoga.com

YOGA IN THE PEARL
925 Northwest Davis St.
(503) 525-9642
www.yogainthepearl.com

YOGA SHALA
1812 Northeast Alberta St.
(503) 281-4452
3249 Southeast Division St.
(503) 963-9642
www.yogashalapdx.com

YOGA UNION
2043 Southeast 50th Ave.
(503) 235-9642
www.yogaunioncwc.com

SPECTATOR SPORTS

Auto Racing

This is the American West, so the national love affair with the internal combustion engine, painted and polished sheet metal, and the excessive consumption of imported fossil fuels is in full bloom. Auto racing has everything we love: speed, noise, big and powerful cars, gasoline, beer, fried food, and an absence of cops and dress codes.

PORTLAND INTERNATIONAL RACEWAY
West Delta Park
1940 North Victory Blvd.
(503) 823-7223
www.portlandraceway.com
Portland International Raceway is situated in a big park at the north end of the city, with Mount Hood providing an appropriate background to the drama on the field. The racetrack is to the west of I-5 at exit 306-B. This is where sports cars and motorcycles do their stuff. The raceway also hosts bicycle races, motocross, and other less revved competitions. Admission fees and starting times vary according to the event. The season at PIR is July through Nov, with most races held on weekend nights.

WOODBURN DRAGSTRIP
7730 SR 219 (I-5, exit 271)
(503) 982-4461
www.woodburndragstrip.com
Half an hour's drive south of town, the Woodburn Dragstrip showcases motorcycle, dragster, and funny car events from May through Sept. Classes include pro stock cars, alcohol-run dragsters and funny cars, jet cars, sport compacts, and street-legal drags with mandatory mufflers. Woodburn also sponsors events for junior racers (8 to 17 years). They even have track-side camping spaces available for those folks who don't want to miss a thing. Admission fees and starting times vary according to the event.

Basketball

*THE PORTLAND TRAILBLAZERS
The Rose Garden
1 Center Court
(503) 234-9291, (503) 321-3211 (events)
www.nba.com/blazers

The Portland Trailblazers—who play in the Western Division of the National Basketball Association—are beloved by Portlanders: They get us through the long rainy months of winter and give us plenty of thrills and lots of misery. The team is now owned by Paul Allen, who cofounded Microsoft with Bill Gates. The Blazers are almost always playoff contenders, though they haven't won the NBA title since 1977, when they were led by Bill Walton and coach Jack Ramsey. Still, hope springs eternal, and each new season we think, "This year, for sure!"

The Rose Garden, with seats going from $10 (bring your own oxygen) to more than $150, is one of the best places to be a spectator. It's a great show, with the BlazerDancers swooshing about and many events for the audience. The Rose Garden's 32 public restrooms do have piped-in radio for play-by-play updates, and there are 700 television monitors so you can watch the game while waiting in line for your gardenburger and local brew.

There's a certain cachet about having season tickets or, even better, a corporate luxury box, but these may be hard to get. However, ordinary tickets are usually available even on game day, depending on the opponent. You can often find refreshments-plus-tickets deals and other promotions too. Tickets are available from the Rose Garden box office and from Ticketmaster, (503) 224-4400, which is also partially owned by Paul Allen. The Blazers' season begins in October;

when it ends depends on their skill, luck, opponents, and other playoff-related criteria.

If you go to a game, be prepared to pay a lot for parking. Consider parking and riding: MAX runs to within 100 yards of the Rose Garden and TriMet may eventually figure out, as BART did in San Francisco and Oakland, that they should put on extra trains the nights the Blazers play.

Golf

*SAFEWAY CLASSIC TOURNAMENT GOLF
(503) 626-2711, (503) 287-LPGA (tickets)
http://safewayclassic.com

The Safeway Classic, now held at the Pumpkin Ridge golf course (see the Golf chapter), is tied for second-oldest event on the LPGA (Ladies' Professional Golf Association) tour. Portland has been hosting it since its inception in 1972, and each year the tournament grows in status, with a purse that is now almost $2 million. Even more impressive, the tournament has raised more than $7 million for local charities. It draws more than 50,000 people over the week of the tournament. Weekly tickets are $25; daily tickets are $10; but check for promotional deals, especially if you shop at Safeway.

Hockey

*PORTLAND WINTER HAWKS
Western Hockey League
Portland Memorial Coliseum & Rose Garden, 1 Center Court
(503) 238-6366
www.winterhawks.com

The Hawks, as they are locally known, are another Portland treasure; they've been favorites since they started playing here in

1976. This is a strong, fast-playing team that is a perennial contender for their league's championship. Success on the ice in Portland means a trip to the "big show," the National Hockey League (NHL), for players. The team consistently draws a good crowd, and there are lots of special fan events. While there are no $1-million free-throws from center court, at least once a year the Hawks freeze a good load of silver dollars on the surface of the ice and then let a small number of lucky fans scramble, slide, and slip (sans skates) as they attempt to gather up the coins. The Hawks fly over the ice from late Sept through Feb; games start at 7 p.m., except on Sun, when they start at 5 p.m. Single tickets range from about $15 to $50.

Horseracing

PORTLAND MEADOWS
1001 North Schmeer Rd.
(off I-5 at exit 306-B)
(503) 285-9144
www.portlandmeadows.com
Racehorses have been bred and raced in Portland for nearly a century, though Portland Meadows has only been around since 1946. There are the usual snack bars and restaurants at the track, but you can also sit in the stands with your binoculars, lucky charms, and wallet to watch your favorite race around the oval. Neon light aficionados will appreciate the large-scale animated racehorses adorning the track's entrance, which are visible from I-5. Admission is free and so is parking; some areas of the park may charge a few bucks for prime viewing. The season is from Oct to Apr.

Soccer

✳PORTLAND TIMBERS
PGE Park
1844 Southwest Morrison St.
(503) 553-5400 (information),
(503) 553-5555 (tickets)
www.pgepark.com
The sports landscape in Portland has endured some seismic shaking in the past few years, with many teams falling apart, then re-collecting themselves. But one thing that never changes is Portland's love for soccer—a love that heated up even more when the Portland Timbers announced they would become a Major League Soccer franchise beginning with the 2011 season. John Spencer was announced as the first head coach, Gavin Wilkinson, the general manager. The Portland Timbers began playing in PGE Park in 2001, as a men's A-League team with coach Bobby Howe, to immediate success, making the playoffs their first and second seasons. The Timbers will remain in PGE Park, which will get a complete remodel to house the team.

> **i** Coed kickball for grown-ups is a major deal in Portland, and there are several leagues—complete with interleague rivalries—that organize games and run tournaments: *Underdog Sports* (www.underdogportland.com) and *Northwest Kickball* (www.nwkickball.com) are two of them. It's just like recess. Good times.

Other Spectator Sports

Most of the area's colleges and universities—Portland State University, University of Portland, Lewis & Clark College, and Reed College, among others—have sports programs that may include football, basketball, soccer, and baseball teams.

The University of Portland has consistently produced decent men's and women's basketball teams, as well as championship women's soccer teams. Tiffeny Millbrett, who scored the winning goal in the historic 1996 Olympic gold-medal match against China, was a University of Portland star (and a Portland native).

PSU's Vikings play football at PGE Park, and their men's and women's basketball teams are fun to watch (some years are more fun than others). PSU's women's softball team, which competes in the Pacific Coast Softball Conference, offers free admission. They play at Erv Lind Stadium (Northeast 57th, 2 blocks south of Halsey).

The smaller schools, such as Reed and Lewis & Clark, may not have men's and women's teams that are contenders in all sports, but they play good college ball and attract some excellent track-and-field athletes, rowers, and lacrosse players. And local high school teams are always fun to watch in any sport. There is also a range of amateur teams and leagues playing everything from rugby and soccer to Ultimate Frisbee, lacrosse, and nighttime softball.

PARKS

The Portland Metro area offers an amazing amount and variety of park space, from Forest Park, which, at 4,900 acres, is the largest urban forest in the nation, to Mills End Park, which, at 452 square inches, may be the smallest park in the nation. Portlanders like to weave green spaces, no matter how tiny, into their urban landscape, so that wherever you go in this city, you are never far from a park. Moreover, the parks here serve diverse functions: Many are community gardens, many are educational centers, some are attached to schools and are used for playgrounds, some are golf courses, some are left alone and preserved as wildlife habitats. And some are just old-fashioned parks with benches, swings, and duck ponds.

Whatever their nature, Portland's parks really do offer something for everyone, and they are so much a part of Portland life that we probably take them as a given. Through our parks, countless citizens of all ages have learned to swim, dance, knit, speak Spanish, use computers, paint with oils, identify native plants, and climb mountains.

OVERVIEW

Portland Parks and Recreation manages most parks within the city boundaries; their resources are extensive, and it is easy to get information from them about their many offerings, the breadth and depth of which are astonishing. They put out a useful catalog each season that gives the details of the tennis lessons, swimming lessons, arts and dance classes, and the innumerable other programs; call (503) 823-7529 to request one, or browse online for a downloadable catalog and to register for classes: **www .portlandonline.com/parks.** This website also has a comprehensive and detailed list of all the parks and facilities in the system. The department also runs a compelling Outdoor Recreation Program whose offerings change seasonally but will include things like sea kayaking, sailing trips to the San Juan Islands, classes in fly-fishing, and tours with

historical themes. The **Outdoor Recreation Program** can be reached at (503) 823-5132. For those of you who like your parks raw, the city maintains more than 7,600 acres of space devoted to wildlife, including Smith and Bybee Lakes, Powell Butte, Elk Rock Island, Marquam Nature Park, Oaks Bottom Wildlife Refuge, and Forest Park. In addition, a regional trail system called the 40 Mile Loop, together with the Willamette Greenway Trail, links more than 100 miles of paths throughout the area, forming a network through and around the city. Maps of this system, which was originally inspired by the Olmsted Brothers, are available from Portland Parks and Recreation on the website (**www.port landonline.com/parks**). You can read more about some of these parks and programs in the Attractions, Kidstuff, and Recreation chapters.

The city of Portland is not the only organization that maintains wonderful parks in the area. **Metro,** our regional government, in addition to establishing growth boundaries, keeping up the zoo, and running the mass transit system, is also responsible for a number of parks and grids of open spaces. You can find out more about Metro's parks by visiting them online at **www.oregonmetro.gov.** And the State of Oregon has a fine website that gives a comprehensive look at the parks in the state system: **www.oregon.gov/OPRD/PARKS.** But no matter who is running the parks, we love them. Here, then, are some of our favorites.

CITY PARKS

Southwest Portland

COUNCIL CREST PARK
Southwest Council Crest Drive
(503) 823-7529
High in the Southwest Hills—perhaps higher than anywhere else in the city—rests verdant Council Crest Park. This 42-acre site used to host an amusement park, but the traces of that history have vanished, and now it's a quiet neighborhood park with a large water tower. You'll also find trails, natural areas, restrooms, and picnic tables, and a spot for weddings. But the major draw is the view—from here you can see five major peaks of the Cascade mountains: Mount Hood, Mount St. Helens, Mount Jefferson, Mount Adams, and, on a good day, Mount Rainier. It's an excellent spot to regain perspective.

GABRIEL PARK
Southwest 45th Avenue and Vermont Street
(503) 823-7529, (503) 823-2840
(Southwest Community Center)

A large, multifaceted park, Gabriel Park draws enthusiasts from all over the city. Within the 90 acres of the park, you'll find tennis courts, picnic tables, trails, community gardens, sports fields, and a dog off-leash area. In addition, the splendid Southwest Community Center, which has spotless gyms and pristine swimming pools, gives it that country-club feel. The community center holds the usual breathtaking array of classes and programs; call them for their latest catalog.

✳HOYT ARBORETUM
Washington Park
4000 Southwest Fairview Blvd.
(503) 823-7529, (503) 865-8733
www.hoytarboretum.org
Hoyt Arboretum lies within the boundaries of Washington Park. Its 232 forested acres offer unsurpassed arboreal beauty as well as beautiful views of the city, and it's large enough that you can get into some backwoods areas where you aren't bumping into other hikers every time you round a bend in the trail—though it's popular with trail runners, so be careful when rounding those blind corners. Hoyt Arboretum features a collection of conifers, 10 miles of trails, the vestiges of our rural past, and some striking views of the city and the Cascades. We love to take the Fir Trail all the way to the Pittock Mansion. It only takes about 45 minutes, and the view is stunning. (See the Attractions chapter for more information.)

JAPANESE AMERICAN HISTORICAL PLAZA
Southwest Naito Parkway near the Burnside Bridge
(503) 823-7529
This poignant site along the Willamette River in Waterfront Park just north of the Burnside

Bridge memorializes the Japanese-American citizens who were banished to internment camps during World War II. Cherry trees border the plaza. "Talking stones," sculptures, and other artwork beautifully relate the story of this sad part of our history in the hope that it might not be repeated.

ℹ️ The website for Portland Parks and Recreation allows convenient online registration for classes. Visit www.portlandparks.org.

✴JAPANESE GARDENS
Southwest Kingston Road and
Washington Park Drive
(503) 223-1321, (503) 223-9233 (tours)
www.japanesegarden.com
The Japanese Gardens comprise five different gardens within 5.5 acres and have received, in their nearly 40 years of existence, many accolades for their beauty and fidelity to Japanese traditions. Tours are available. The admission cost is $9.50 for adults and $6.75 for students older than six; college students and seniors pay $7.75. (See the Attractions chapter for a full account.)

PLAZA BLOCKS
(Chapman and Lownsdale Squares)
Southwest 4th Avenue and Main Street
(503) 823-7529
This tiny (1.84 acres) but well-loved park consists of two adjacent city squares and is also known as Lownsdale Park. In 1974 the squares were designated Historic Landmarks; they have been public spaces for about 150 years. Chapman Square, the southern square, was donated to the city by early Portland attorney William Chapman, while Lownsdale Square was contributed by Daniel Lownsdale, who arrived in Portland

in 1845. The squares were originally popular sites for public oratory and other gatherings. And they have a quaint history—at one time, the idea was that women would gather at Chapman Square, while the men would have Lownsdale to themselves. Lownsdale Square is the home of the Soldiers' Monument from 1906, a granite pillar supporting the likeness of an infantryman. This soldier represents Oregon's contribution to the first major force of American troops dispatched overseas, the Second Oregon United States Volunteer Infantry. And two small cannons at the base of the monument are from Fort Sumter; they honor the Northern and Southern soldiers killed during the Civil War. A large bronze elk stands alert right in the middle of Main Street, between the two squares, reminding us of the wildlife that used to graze freely there. It's actually a fountain, built in 1900 at the behest of then-mayor David Thompson. It's hard for modern residents to imagine that the fountain, which has a special drinking trough for horses and dogs, was initially regarded as monstrous by some local residents (notably the Exalted Order of Elks). Later residents objected to its placement in the middle of the road, but it appears that, unlike its natural predecessors, the bronze elk is here to stay.

✴WASHINGTON PARK
Western end of Southwest Park Place
(503) 823-7529
The crown jewel of the city's park system, 145-acre Washington Park is one of the oldest, best-loved, and well-used parks in Portland, offering beautiful scenery; summer concerts; statuary; playgrounds; water reservoirs; fantastic views of Mount Hood, its foothills, and the Willamette Valley; and some of the region's premiere attractions. This is the home

Dog Parks

Your dog needs to run, but you live in the city. Where can Fido get plenty of exercise? Portland has nearly 30 parks with off-leash areas devoted exclusively to dog exercising all day, year-round. Wherever the park, you must clean up after your dog or face fines from the city and the ire of your neighbors. Dogs also should be properly vaccinated, licensed, obedient to voice command, and in other ways model citizens. With so many parks now featuring off-leash areas, there is bound to be one near you. These areas are well-marked, so look for the signs or visit www.portland-online.com/parks and click on the "Recreation" menu for a full list.

distinguished Olmsted brothers, the landscape architects who designed New York's Central Park, to advise them on their own park system. The Olmsteds envisioned a series of parks that would be linked together with greenways all across the city. But they also made some specific suggestions for Washington Park, including the preservation of the natural habitat in addition to formal plantings.

While the major attractions of Washington Park are obvious, some of the minor ones are just as interesting. The first public statue of a woman is here—it's the bronze *Sacagawea*, the intrepid Shoshone who made it possible for Lewis and Clark to navigate the West, which was commissioned for the Lewis and Clark Exposition in 1905. Women all over the nation contributed money to pay for this statue. The park is also home to an arresting Lewis and Clark memorial, consisting of a granite shaft with the seals of the states of Oregon, Washington, Montana, and Idaho at its base; the foundation stone for this memorial was laid in 1903 by Theodore Roosevelt.

Washington Park's attractions also include the World Forestry Center, the Oregon Vietnam Veterans Living Memorial, and the Hoyt Arboretum with its miles of nature trails. And you will find many facilities for recreators of all ages: An archery range, group picnic facilities, stage, covered picnic areas, a soccer field, and tennis courts are all here. And if you have children, don't miss the fanciful play structure just south of the Rose Garden. This bright and inventive gem has slides, bridges, swings, sand, musical toys, ropes, and anything else your children never knew a playground ought to have until now.

of the famed International Rose Test Garden with more than 400 varieties of roses, the Japanese Gardens, the Children's Museum, and the Oregon Zoo (see the Attractions chapter). Besides these world-renowned sites, and the lush trees, shrubs, flowers, and ferns, the park is a treasure trove of history and a tribute to prescient urban planning. Washington Park has been a city property since 1871, when 40 acres were purchased for the development of a park—at a time when most of the city was still wilderness. Early residents thought the city was crazy.

By the turn of the 20th century, however, Portland was glad to have the park, and never more so when they hired the

*WATERFRONT PARK
(Gov. Tom McCall Waterfront Park)
Southwest Naito Parkway from
Southwest Clay Street to Northwest
Glisan Street
(503) 823-7529

This 36-acre city park, which stretches into Northwest Portland, showcases the Willamette River and hums with activity on sunny days. Hugging the west bank of the river, Waterfront Park extends from Southwest Clay Street to the Steel Bridge, 22 blocks in all; it's the site of many Portland events from the Rose Festival to the Brewer's Festival to the Blues Festival (for more information, see the Festivals and Annual Events chapter). It seems as if something is always going on there, but often it's not an organized event, just throngs of joggers, bikers, and those out for leisurely lunchtime strolls along the pleasant waterside pathway. There are basketball courts, fountains, statuary, and opportunities to sightsee, both for people watchers and those more interested in the scenic views of barges and cruise ships passing under the bridges.

You may want to see the Battleship *Oregon* Memorial, erected in 1956 to honor the late-19th-century *USS Oregon*. Also, the benches near the Salmon Street Springs are a great place to hang out on a warm day: You can watch people frolic in a large, beautiful fountain controlled by an underground computer that changes the pattern of the fountain's water jets. If you are an early bird, the morning sunrises as viewed from Waterfront Park are incredibly gorgeous sights, with clear views of majestic Mount Hood and several of the smaller mountains on the east side.

WILLAMETTE PARK
Southwest Macadam Avenue and
Nebraska Street
(503) 823-7529

Nestled along the banks of the Willamette River and just a few miles south of downtown, Willamette Park is undoubtedly one of Portland's busiest and most popular parks. This is a fine place for boating, picnicking, watching the Fourth of July fireworks celebrations, or just hanging around. The parking lot fills up fast, especially in the summertime and on weekends, and some areas of the park itself can get a little crowded. But with more than 30 acres, including a boat ramp, soccer field, tennis court, playground, and hiking and bicycling trails, there's room to spread out. If it's raining and you have an outdoor party or barbecue planned, Willamette Park has covered group picnic facilities.

i If you're interested in exploring more deeply the city wildernesses of Portland, have a look at *Wild in the City: A Guide to Portland's Natural Areas.* This collection of essays is a fine, comprehensive, and detailed guide to the green spaces in our city, published by the Oregon Historical Society and edited by Michael C. Houck and M. J. Cody.

Northwest Portland

COUCH PARK
Northwest 19th Avenue and
Glisan Street
(503) 823-7529

First thing: It's pronounced "kooch." But however you say it, this little neighborhood park, with lovely trees and a playground, is a draw for residents and for the students next door at the Metropolitan Learning Center. And it is a true neighborhood park, even down to its design and execution, which was largely the work of students and neighbors. Its namesake, Captain John Heard Couch, was responsible for the alphabetized street names of this sector of town, which he developed. The park site was originally the estate of one of Captain Couch's daughters and her family.

✳FOREST PARK
West Hills, Northwest Skyline Road, St. Helens
(503) 823-7529
Forest Park is remarkable for many things, one of which is its size. At 4,900 acres, it is thought to be the largest urban forest in America. The city bought the property at the end of the 19th century; they had thought about turning it into a park ever since the Olmsted brothers suggested it would be a good use of the property, and the park, after much debate, was finally established in 1948. Today Forest Park gives Portland residents more than 60 miles of trails for running, walking, and biking. It is a haven for more than 110 species of birds and more than 50 species of mammals, including the human visitors who love to hike and picnic under its lush forest canopy. You'll find Forest Park on the eastern side of the Northwest Hills, once called the Tualatin Mountains, and when you get there, you'll be hiking along some of the same trails—some of which are now paved—that farmers used as shipping routes. Visit the Portland Parks and Recreation website at www.portlandparks.org for a detailed map of Forest Park. Forest Park is also part of the 40 Mile Loop, the regional trail system that winds through the city.

WALLACE PARK
Northwest 25th Avenue and Raleigh Street
(503) 823-7529
Wallace Park is constantly busy with community activities, in part because it is right next to Chapman School and in part because of its namesake, Hugh Wallace. He was the city councilman responsible for this park, and the buzz of activity within it is a fitting tribute. The four-acre park contains basketball and tennis courts, softball and soccer fields, places to picnic and play horseshoes, and a playground. A major feature of this park is the flock of Vaux's Swifts that makes an annual stop on its migration south for the winter. In late August they begin to gather every evening near sunset. As more swifts arrive, they begin to circle a large chimney at Chapman school, which they have adopted as a roost site. All at once, they dive into the chimney, and the sight of 10,000 swifts funneling themselves into their chambers is one to behold. This nightly ritual draws people all through September; they spread out on the lawn with picnic dinners and observe the ritual. The local red-tailed hawks and other raptors have also noticed this, making for high nightly drama. Watching the swifts and the hawks raises many questions—where are the swifts during the day? How do they decide it's time to swirl into the chimney? How do the hawks know it's time to drop by? Luckily, the Audubon Society will often visit the park during the peak of swift-watching season (mid-Sept) to provide answers to these and other burning questions. *NOTE:* Wallace Park does not have a parking lot, and the available parking in this neighborhood is limited. The streetcar stops nearby—we recommend that or bus line 15 or 17.

Southeast Portland

CRESTON PARK
Southeast 44th Avenue and Powell
Boulevard
(503) 823-7529

This green, tree-filled oasis bordering bustling Powell Boulevard is a great place for a summer birthday party or even a quiet, shady lunch. Less than 15 acres, it offers an outdoor swimming pool, lighted tennis court, well-equipped playground, group picnic facilities, and restrooms. While the pool gets very crowded on warm days and is a favorite for summertime swimming lessons, the park grounds are usually quiet and serene on weekdays. Weekends are a different story; many reunions and parties are held here.

CRYSTAL SPRINGS RHODODENDRON GARDEN
Southeast 28th Avenue and
Woodstock Boulevard
(503) 823-7529, (503) 771-8386

Crystal Springs offers the tranquility of a peaceful refuge away from the hurried pace of urban living. In the early spring and summer, its gardens explode in a riot of colors with every size and shade of rhododendron and azalea imaginable. A host of birds and waterfowl also thrives in the sprawling ponds, where children of all ages enjoy feeding the ducks. Crystal Springs also holds annual shows (see the Festivals and Annual Events chapter), at which visitors can see unusual rhododendrons and azaleas not normally found in this area. From Labor Day through Feb, admission is free. From Feb through Labor Day, admission is $3 for those older than 12 if you visit between 10 a.m. and 6 p.m. Thurs through Mon. Duck food is sold separately.

LAURELHURST PARK
Southeast 39th Avenue between
Stark Street and Burnside Street
(503) 823-7529, (503) 823-4101

The Olmsted-inspired Laurelhurst is among the most popular parks in the city for picnics, cookouts, or summer fun. Its 34-plus-acres offer a striking variety of trees, shrubs, and flowers as well as a 3-acre pond with a small island as a centerpiece and many ducks as residents. A paved path circles the pond and the entire outer edge of the park and is well used by early-morning runners and walkers. Laurelhurst is a fine location for larger get-togethers; there's something for everyone to do here, including basketball and tennis courts, a large horseshoe pit, and an excellent play structure. The Laurelhurst Studio is here; it's the Eastside conduit for ballet, tap, and other dance programs in the Parks and Recreation system. The park is gorgeously landscaped; it was once judged as the most beautiful park on the West Coast.

LEACH BOTANICAL GARDEN
6704 Southeast 122nd Ave.
(503) 823-9503
www.leachgarden.org

The Leaches were a couple devoted to plants: John Leach was a pharmacist and his wife Lilla was a botanist. Together they collected more than 2,000 species, some of which they discovered. The Leach Botanical Garden was their estate; its nine acres have been given over to preserving and studying plant life and maintaining a seed bank, as well as preserving the legacy of the couple who made this lovely, botanically diverse sanctuary possible. The grounds include the garden, the manor house, and natural areas. Garden and guided tours are free, and special tours are given by appointment. (For more information see the Attractions chapter.) There's a gift shop and library; classes are offered for adults and children. It's closed on Monday.

MT. SCOTT PARK
Southeast 72nd Avenue and Harold Street
(503) 823-7529, (503) 823-3183
Harvey W. Scott was the editor of the *Oregonian* from 1865 to 1910 and by all accounts was a force to be reckoned with (you can see him in statue form, pointing west, at the top of Mt. Tabor). Mt. Scott Park is named for him. The park encompasses 12 arboreal acres with a playground, softball field, and tennis courts as well as picnic benches. The Mt. Scott Community Center, on the grounds of the park, offers one of the nicest pools you'll find anywhere. Did we say one pool? Make that two—a beautiful lap pool and a fun leisure pool with a great water slide, current channel, and imaginative built-in water toys as well as a separate spa. The facility also has meeting rooms, gyms, classes, an auditorium, and a roller-skating rink. Call for times and fees (which are low—$4.50 for adults).

✳MT. TABOR PARK
Southeast 60th Avenue and Salmon Street
(503) 823-7529
This park affords some of the best views in the city of rugged and stately Mount Hood and Mount St. Helens on the one side and Portland's West Hills on the other. This park is truly a wonderful place for picnics or for walking on wooded trails. Mt. Tabor has a number of reservoirs for Bull Run water, the city's water source; these are contained in whimsical crenellated open reservoirs that

are nonetheless heavily watched. (Don't try to throw anything in!) The 196-acre park also offers basketball courts, a stage for theater or music, lighted tennis courts, group picnic facilities, covered picnic areas, volleyball courts, trails, and public restrooms. The play structure is a big draw for families—they've situated it to take advantage of the sunshine, though the big fir trees still provide plenty of shelter.

Mt. Tabor sits on top of an extinct volcano; this volcano distinguishes Portland as one of two US cities to have an extinct volcano within city limits (the other city is Bend). Many paths, some paved and some not, wind through the park and offer entirely different vistas. Sometimes you feel as though you're in the woods, but right around the bend you may be reminded of an orchard. The hilly terrain makes the park a favorite with runners, dog walkers, mountain bikers, disc golfers, go-karters, and just about anyone who likes a good view and a vigorous climb. Birders may be spotted early in the morning. In fact, the birders are on to something—a sunrise at Mt. Tabor is spectacular and worth the struggle out of bed in the morning.

OAKS BOTTOM WILDLIFE REFUGE
Portland Parks and Recreation
(503) 823-6131
Great blue heron and osprey are the star attractions here, but you can also view 185 other species of birds in this 160-acre refuge. The trail is easy and only 1 mile long, thus it's good for small children. The park is on a floodplain of the Willamette, so the trail can get quite muddy. This park is not wheelchair accessible. (See the Recreation chapter for more information.)

POWELL BUTTE NATURE PARK
Southeast 162nd Avenue and
Powell Boulevard
(503) 823-7259
We love big Powell Butte Nature Park, the site of a long-ago farm—its vestiges there to remind us of our history. Its entrance is unprepossessing, but a walk along the trails is more than rewarding, for soon you will find large meadows that encourage birds of prey as well as raccoons, foxes, and coyotes; shady old orchards; ripe blackberries if you're lucky; and amazing views. It's possible to see a number of peaks from this volcanic mound. Powell Butte attracts mountain bikers, joggers, and a lot of equestrian activity over its 9 miles of trails and 608 acres. There's also a 0.5-mile, wheelchair-friendly trail. You really have to get out and walk or bike around to enjoy this area, which stretches all the way down to Beggar's Tick Wildlife Refuge, a large marshy wetland busy with birds and wildlife.

SELLWOOD PARK
Southeast 7th Avenue and Miller Street
(503) 823-7529
Tall, well-spaced trees distinguish this pretty park, which is a crowd pleaser for its sports fields, excellent playground, and wonderful round swimming pool. The park has both sunny, grassy, open spaces and shady, cool refuges. On the bluff above Oaks Bottom and the Willamette River, you'll get pretty river views as you peer between the trees. Trails link Sellwood Park to Oaks Bottom and Oaks Park. The pool is outdoors, so it's open only during the summer, but it is popular. An abundance of picnic tables encourage large groups—it's a favorite spot for reunions and company parties.

SPRINGWATER CORRIDOR
Southeast Ivon Street to Boring, OR
Springwater Corridor is a 20-mile rails-to-trails route comprising the southeast part of the 40-Mile Loop, basically following Johnson Creek east. It begins at Southeast Ivon Street near the Willamette River in Southeast Portland and ends in the town of Boring, a few miles south of Gresham. The route is a popular trek for walkers, in-line skaters, and those in wheelchairs, on bikes, and astride horses. It's mostly blacktop or chip-sealed surface, with a thin gravel surface on the last 4 miles. The trail takes you through neighborhoods in Portland, eventually spilling you into farmland, wetlands, and nature reserves. There aren't any steep hills or dangerous dips, so even those in need of gentle trails can enjoy this charmingly rural path. One of the trail's delights is a sense of local history that is soon evident as you discover remnants of the old Bellrose rail line and read historical markers that tell how farmers used this very route to take produce west to Sellwood residents and their families and to nearby Oaks Park.

Flanking the route are huge clumps of blackberry vines, lots of sweet peas, long-stemmed blue chicory, Queen Anne's lace, 5-foot-tall mullein, spirea with its fluffy pink cones, dark brown Indian tobacco, and magenta poppies. You will also see a great variety of birds, including hawks, herons, and kingfishers, and you'll see mammals—perhaps even a coyote. Along the way, you'll pass connection points to other trails and spots of interest, such as the Beggars-Tick Wildlife Refuge, a tiny wilderness in the heart of the farm belt. The trail eventually takes you alongside Gresham's city park, with its grassy knolls, nature walks, and recreational facilities before fading to gravel for the last leg of the trail leading southeast to Boring. An excellent map of the trail is available on the Portland Parks website (www.portland-online.com/parks).

WESTMORELAND PARK
Southeast McLoughlin Boulevard and Bybee Street
(503) 823-7529

Expansive, 47-acre Westmoreland Park brings folks from all over town to play baseball—the fields are lighted, and on summer nights they seem to illuminate the whole neighborhood. But Westmoreland also has casting ponds, soccer fields, tennis courts, and a terrific playground to interest people. In addition, the duck ponds lure many kinds of waterfowl, and interesting things happen when the water-birds mingle with the toddlers.

North & Northeast Portland

ARBOR LODGE PARK
North Bryant Street and Delaware Avenue
(503) 823-7529

Portland has many little parks like Arbor Lodge. This small neighborhood park adjoins Chief Joseph School and offers some nice trees, softball and soccer fields, a tennis court and playground, restrooms, a wading pool, and horseshoe pit. On a sunny day this is a wonderful spot to bring a picnic basket and spread a blanket. You can enjoy a magazine while the kids romp on the playground.

CATHEDRAL PARK
North Edison Street and Pittsburgh Avenue
(503) 823-7529

This park—situated on the banks of the Willamette River and one of Portland's most scenic spots—is named after the tall gothic arches that support the St. Johns Bridge, towering above the park and inspiring that sense of awe that you're bound to have in a cathedral. The park, which has a stage, is home to popular summertime concerts; it also includes soccer fields, a boat ramp and docking facilities, and trails. Cathedral Park is often peaceful, belying its lively history—not only is it the site of the very first plat for the village of St. John's, but it is also suspected to have been a favorite fishing site for the Native Americans who lived here before.

COLUMBIA PARK
North Lombard Avenue and Woolsey Street
(503) 823-7529

Healthy competition is a good thing, and when the old city of Albina saw that Portland was developing Washington Park, they were not going to be outdone. They purchased 30 acres on Lombard Street in 1891. Soon after, however, Albina was annexed to Portland. But it took many years before Columbia Park, which was eventually patterned after a park in Berlin, became the handsome, wooded place it is today. In addition to the grounds, the park offers fields for soccer, baseball, and softball, lighted tennis courts, volleyball courts, and a swimming pool.

GRANT PARK
Northeast 33rd Avenue and Ulysses S. Grant Place
(503) 823-7529

President Grant visited Portland three times, but this park, named in his honor, is now more famous for its Beverly Cleary Children's Sculpture Garden, in which Ramona Quimby, Henry Huggins, and his pooch Ribsy, all born of Cleary's lively imagination, are fixed in bronze. (A few blocks away is the actual Klikitat Street, where Ramona "lived," and the neighborhood where author Cleary herself grew up, attending Grant High School in the 1930s.) The sculptures sit atop a fountain, and in the summer, children play there all day long. At Grant Park you'll also find nice sports fields, tennis courts, and a swimming pool.

KELLEY POINT PARK
North Kelley Point Park Road and Marine Drive
(503) 823-7529
This quiet and out-of-the-way 96-acre park is one of our favorite places in the entire Portland Metro area, offering a large sandy beach and views of the Willamette and Columbia Rivers as well as Mount Hood and Mount St. Helens. Picnic tables are scattered all over this park—some are even on the beach—and there is a wide variety of conifers and deciduous trees. The park is named for Oregon advocate Hall J. Kelley, who was a great friend to the state. He wanted to found a city at the convergence of the Willamette and the Columbia, but with 20/20 historical hindsight, it's a good thing he was overruled. Still, the park named in his honor is a wonderful spot, and it provides the anchor for the 40 Mile Loop—a fine legacy, in any case.

PENINSULA PARK AND ROSE GARDENS
North Albina Street and Rosa Parks Way
(503) 823-7529
Portland emerged as a city at a historically astute moment from the perspective of a park lover, and Peninsula Park demonstrates why. Its formal design was characteristic of its early-20th-century era; it is most known for its rose garden, but its striking gazebo

bandstand is also historically important (it's a Portland Historic Landmark and a National Heritage Historical Structure). And its playground, as well as the community center (a city first), made Peninsula Park quite novel when it was finally finished in 1913. (It was also an early example of urban renewal. Previously the site had been home to a roadhouse and a racetrack.) The rose garden is still important, with two acres of roses— almost 9,000 plantings of them. The park, in the Piedmont neighborhood, also includes a softball and soccer field, swimming pool, basketball court, tables for picnics, a fountain, and lawn bowling.

WILSHIRE PARK
Northeast 33rd Avenue and Skidmore Street
Acquired by the city of Portland in 1940, pretty Wilshire Park in the Beaumont-Wilshire neighborhood is popular with softball players and families. Besides the ball field, the 15-acre community park offers some very nice trees, group picnic facilities, a jogging track, a good playground, and ample tables for birthday parties.

Vancouver

FRENCHMAN'S BAR COUNTY PARK
Lower River Road, off Fourth Plain Boulevard, Vancouver, WA
This park offers a lot on its mile-long stretch of sandy beach along the eastern shore of the Columbia River. Activities you can enjoy here include bird-watching, sunbathing, fishing, boating, picnicking, and watching the huge container ships, tankers, and freighters that sail up the waters of the Pacific Northwest's mightiest river. There are plenty of walking trails too, plus eight sand volleyball courts, a grassy amphitheater, and some

playground equipment for the little ones. This spot also affords a terrific view of Mount Hood.

Outlying Areas

BLUE LAKE REGIONAL PARK
Northeast 223rd Avenue between Marine Drive and Sandy Boulevard
(503) 797-1850
www.metro-region.org
Sweltering Portlanders are fond of natural Blue Lake, which is maintained as a regional park by Metro and is just 8 miles east of downtown Portland, making it easily accessible on summer days. The 64-acre lake has 400 feet of swimming beach and—especially fun for the little ones—a special children's "sprayground" (children under 5 are not allowed in the lake, for purposes of hygiene). But there's lots for everyone here—a fishing dock and boat rentals, basketball and volleyball courts, playgrounds, baseball fields, and picnic shelters. A food concession stand will supplement your picnic. The Lake House provides facilities for events such as weddings or retreats. Trails wind their way through the park; these are especially nice for cyclists. The park also hosts numerous programs and events, many of which are geared toward children (see our Kidstuff chapter for more information). You'll need to pay an entrance fee of $5 per car.

ELK ROCK ISLAND
Willamette River, near Southeast 19th Avenue and Sparrow Street, Milwaukie
Elk Rock Island is actually part of the Portland Parks system; it's one of the designated natural areas, given to the city as a preserve for natural beauty that would restore the spirits of the citizens. This big volcanic rock, perhaps the oldest in the Portland area, is an excellent spot for bird-watching and offers some of the most diverse terrain around. Prized spots include herons, hawks, kingfishers, and egrets. This park also includes a hiking trail.

RIDGEFIELD NATIONAL WILDLIFE REFUGE
Northwest 269th Street (Washington SR 501) at I-5, exit 14
(360) 887-4106
www.fws.gov/ridgefieldrefuges/complex/
Situated between Vancouver and Woodland, Washington, this 5,218-acre refuge features pasture, woodlands, and marshland. Much of the wildlife that sustained the area's Native American population and the later European settlers is still found here. The refuge's population includes deer, coyotes, nutria, foxes, rabbits, beavers, and otters—as well as large flocks of migratory birds and waterfowl that travel the Pacific Flyway and either stop and rest in the preserved wetlands or decide to spend the winter there. The refuge's permanent waterfowl and avian population includes herons, cranes, swans, geese, and eagles. There is a well-marked 1.9-mile loop trail that is an easy, if sometimes muddy, walk, even for children. This is a day-use-only area. Though hiking and fishing are allowed, fires and off-road vehicles are not permitted. Binoculars, spotting scopes, and cameras with tripods and long lenses may make viewing and wildlife photography easier. A footbridge over a set of busy railroad tracks is an added attraction, allowing an unusual perspective on the Amtrak trains and the hardworking freight trains running up and down the Pacific Coast. The Ridgefield Refuge Office, 301 North 3rd St., is open weekdays from 7:30 a.m. to 4 p.m., and it has

dozens of informative brochures and a useful map to the refuge. Open from dawn to dusk all year long, the refuge is free to all ages, but leave Fido at home. (Bicycling, horseback riding, and ATVs are also not allowed.) There is a $3 day-use fee.

✳SAUVIE ISLAND
US 30, about 10 miles west of downtown Portland
www.sauvieisland.org

Sauvie Island, a beautiful island of fertile alluvial soil northwest of the city at the confluence of the Willamette and Columbia Rivers, is not, strictly speaking, a park. It is hardworking farm country. But the roads are so pretty, and the u-pick farms, river beaches, parks, and wildlife areas are so enticing, that the entire island seems like a park to many Portland residents who converge there on Saturday morning to pick blueberries or ride their bicycles. This is a mixed blessing. It's good, on the one hand, that we can see the farms that grow our food and that the farms are supported by local dollars. On the other hand, its bucolic nature encourages people to visit, thus increasing traffic and busyness, diminishing the bucolic nature of the place.

In an effort to preserve that nature, some of the island has been set aside in wildlife preserves and parks. The Sauvie Island Wildlife Viewing Area, maintained by the Oregon Fish and Wildlife Department, is an excellent spot for bird-watching. There you will see the ubiquitous ducks and Canada geese, but you may also spy swans, bald eagles, sandhill cranes, herons, and rare species of gull. Winter is an especially good time to look for these birds because many species stop here on the way to warmer places, and some reside here all season, but be aware that some parts of the refuge are closed in

the winter. You'll need a day permit to park at the wildlife area—these are available at most of the small grocery stores that dot the island. The wildlife area is also north of the bridge. For more information about the wildlife area, you may contact Oregon Fish and Wildlife at (503) 621-3488.

More wildlife, as well as human relationships to it, can be seen at Howell Territorial Park, which is part museum and part natural area. This 93-acre park comprises the James F. Bybee House, the Agricultural Museum, old orchards and pastures, and sizable natural areas, including a lake and wetlands. You can see an incredible variety of birds and mammals in the natural areas, while the museums permit a glimpse into the days of the early pioneer settlers, with a fine collection of historical artifacts.

The museums are open during the weekend from the first week of June through Labor Day. The hours are noon to 5 p.m. Guided tours are offered on the half-hour. (You may also reserve the park for special events; the number for that service is 503-797-1850.) To find the park, take US 30 to the Sauvie Island Bridge. Once you've crossed the bridge, follow Sauvie Island Road north for 1 mile, then turn right on Howell Park Road, where you'll immediately see the parking lot on your left.

Sauvie Island Road, by the way, wraps around the whole island. The island is crisscrossed by other roads that wind through farms, orchards, and fields, and following any of them will eventually lead you to something interesting. The u-pick farms that are all over the island are as big an attraction as the parks, and during harvest season—May through Oct—you will find many people picking berries, flowers, peaches, pumpkins, corn, and everything else that grows well here. Farm stands sell produce for those folks who'd rather not get dusty. During October the Pumpkin Patch draws thousands of schoolchildren for hayrides and pumpkin picking; it's a rare Portland child who hasn't chosen a jack-o'-lantern here. You can find this institution by circling under the Sauvie Island Bridge and following the road south. Whichever direction you drive, be respectful of the residents, the cyclists, the chickens, the schoolchildren, and everyone else sharing the road with you. In short, drive carefully!

STATE PARKS NEAR PORTLAND

General information about all state parks is available at (800) 551-6949. To reserve campsites call (800) 452-5687. You can also look up these parks online at www.oregon.gov/OPRD/PARKS.

BALD PEAK STATE PARK
9 miles from Newberg along Bald Peak Road, 5 miles northwest of SR 219 North (Hillsboro-Silverton Highway)
If you're the kind of person who hasn't lost interest in Sunday driving, you might like Bald Peak. A pretty state park near Hillsboro, but high above the Willamette Valley, Bald Peak is still close enough to town to be an alluring spot for a spontaneous picnic on a sunny afternoon (no water, though, so pack your own). Bald Peak offers lovely views of the valley and a number of Cascade peaks in Washington and Oregon, including Mt. Rainier if the visibility is good.

BATTLE GROUND LAKE STATE PARK
**Northeast 249th Street,
Battle Ground, WA
(888) 226-7688 (reservations)
www.parks.wa.gov**

One of the biggest attractions in southwest Washington, Battle Ground Lake State Park tempts recreators from all over the area who are drawn by 280 acres of swimming, fishing, horseback riding, boating, and hiking as well as 50 campsites. The park is 21 miles northeast of Vancouver; it has a splendid lake in the center of an extinct volcano. The park is open from 6:30 a.m. until dusk from Apr to Sept and from 8 a.m. until dusk the remainder of the year. Summer camping is a breeze with the available kitchen shelters and showers—but remember, this park fills up fast. Kitchens with electricity may also be rented for large groups (20 to 150 people); fees depend on the number of people.

CHAMPOEG STATE PARK
**Directly off SR 99 West, 7 miles east of Newberg
(503) 678-1251, ext. 221**
Pronounced "sham-POO-ey," Champoeg State Park is a place where Portlanders flock for the concerts and other events in the pretty amphitheater, but the park has even more to offer. First, there are the trails that cross the 615 acres; these curl through woods, meadows, and wetlands and are wonderful for bicycling or hiking. Then there's the historical interest: The park is on the grounds of the first settlers' government, and two museums and many educational programs and tours help to bring that early history alive. The park is regularly visited by school buses full of children eager to learn what life was like during pioneer days. There is a $5 daily day-use fee, but a $30 annual permit grants access to all day-use areas in state parks across Oregon.

MILO MCIVER STATE PARK
Springwater Road, 4 miles west of
Estacada
(503) 630-7150
Milo McIver State Park is a quiet park less than an hour's drive from downtown—the perfect place to go camping after work. The Clackamas River shoots through here, so you can use the park as home base for kayaking or rafting days. The park also rents horses; its trails and fields are fine country to explore this way. Another attraction is the disc golf course (18 holes). In the summer a variety of recreational and educational programs are offered, in addition to the sweet, simple pleasures of camping: The park has more than 50 sites of various levels of sophistication. Like many other state parks in Oregon, a $5 daily day-use fee is required (unless you want to spring for the annual pass at $30); overnight camping fees depend on the site.

TRYON CREEK STATE PARK
Off I-5 (exit 297)
Terwilliger Boulevard, Southwest
Portland
(503) 636-9886
Lucky schoolchildren have fond memories of this pristine state park that's just a few minutes from downtown, the closest state park to the Portland Metro area. Actually it's within the metro area, which is the reason so many field trips are held here—that, and the fact that so much native wildlife can be found here. One of the few streams in the city that steelhead use for spawning is found here, and the native trillium plant grows abundantly. Tryon Creek State Park has shady trails perfect for biking and walking, and lots of signs tell you about what you're seeing. Much of the park is wheelchair accessible. Day camps are a staple of summer life at Tryon Creek, and guided tours are available as well as a gift shop. These last things are run by the Friends of Tryon Creek State Park; call them at (503) 636-4398. There is no fee to use Tryon Creek.

GOLF

Golf enthusiasts will be happy to discover that their sport has flourished all around the state of Oregon. From courses situated in fertile valleys below the snowcapped Cascades to the high-desert links with fairways framed by lava rock outcroppings, peppery sagebrush, and twisted junipers, this is a golfer's paradise. Many superior golf courses have sprung up in coastal regions, in southern Oregon, and around Bend, the gateway to central Oregon.

Oregon offers an amazing diversity of golf courses, and the Portland Metro area courses are some of the most interesting, challenging, and attractive in the state. With dozens of both public and private courses to choose from, you're sure to find the links to suit you, whether you're a seasoned professional or a neophyte.

Professionals and amateurs alike have found Portland to be a friendly host for tournament play. Portland is home to several major golf tournaments—the LPGA Safeway Classic is a regular events (also see the Recreation and Spectator Sports chapter for more information). The US Amateur Open has been played in Oregon from time to time, most notably at Pumpkin Ridge in 1996, when Tiger Woods won it.

OVERVIEW

It's easy to see why the area has an outstanding reputation for golf. In Portland, and in the numerous courses a few minutes just outside the city, the golf courses are beautifully laid out and meticulously cared for. Small lakes and streams do a good job of defending par, and in the summertime, the greens throughout the region are quite fast. While the terrain is impressive, even for well-traveled golfers, and the facilities are superb, golf in Oregon is an affordable luxury. In Portland, greens fees fall mostly in the $25 to $45 range and sometimes lower. Discounts are available for weekday and off-season play, and afternoon and twilight rates are also common. Factor in relatively low costs for meals (and accommodations, if necessary), and golf here can be a downright thrifty

habit—and a healthy one too. Walking is not only permitted at most of the courses, but here in fitness-oriented Portland, it's also encouraged.

Portland-area courses are open year-round, but May to Sept is prime golfing time. The off-season may be a good time for you to visit a familiar course or to try a new one, because then the courses are quieter and less crowded. In the Portland area alone, about 30 golf courses are open to the public and all rent clubs and carts. The city's four municipal golf courses offer some outstanding golf and lower-than-average greens fees. You can make tee times six days to one hour in advance for the municipal courses—Eastmoreland, Heron Lakes, Red Tail, and Rose City—by reserving them on a

central website, **www.portlandpublicgolf
.com** (or by calling the pro shops directly,
listed below). Also, many area courses offer
discounted greens fees for juniors, seniors,
or both. Senior players can get a need a discount card for the municipal courses—call
Portland Parks and Recreation at (503) 823-
4328 or check www.portlandpublicgolf.com
for more information. Most courses now
have an online reservation system, so be
sure to check their websites. Many of them
also offer online discounts and coupons.
And while reserved tee times are always
recommended, courses are often not as
crowded as they can get in some metropolitan areas, and it is usually possible to find
somewhere you can walk on.

This chapter is devoted to the 18-hole
courses in the area that we like to play the
most, but many more are out there: **Colwood**
(503-254-5515), **Gresham Golf Course**
(503-665-3352), **Meriwether National Golf
Course** in Hillsboro (503-648-4143), **Oregon
City Golf Course** (503-518-2846), **Camas
Meadows Golf Club** (800-750-6511 or 360-
833-2000), and **Three Rivers** (360-423-4653
or 800-286-7765) are fine local courses. And
that's only a few of them. You will also find
lots of 9-hole gems, such as **St. Helens Golf
Course** (503-397-0358) and **McKay Creek**
(503-693-7612). Complete listings of Oregon
golf courses are available at information
kiosks at the POVA information center, the
airport, the zoo, and other tourist gathering
places. *NOTE:* Nonmetal spikes are the only
kind allowed on most Portland golf courses.

Price Code

For one 18-hole round of summer weekend
golf. Cart prices are not included. Rates may
change for senior and junior golfers, during
the week, and winter months.

$. . . . . Less than $25
$$ . . . . $25 to $50
$$$ . . . . $50 to $75
$$$$ . . . . More than $75

PORTLAND

BROADMOOR GOLF COURSE $$
3509 Northeast Columbia Blvd.
(503) 281-1337
www.broadmoor-1931.com
This is one of the friendliest, cheapest, and
most popular golfing locations in Portland
proper. Broadmoor was built in 1931, and
since then it has been a favorite of Portland
golfers, whatever their ability. The 18-hole,
par-72 course unfolds over 220 acres, dodg-
ing water hazards and trees; the billowing
fairways flanked by the Broadmoor Lake and
Slough add aesthetic interest to the techni-
cal challenge of maintaining a low score. In
addition, Broadmoor offers a well-equipped
golf shop and full-service clubhouse. Carts
are optional; tee time reservations are
recommended.

✳EASTMORELAND GOLF COURSE $$
2425 Southeast Bybee Blvd.
(503) 775-2900
www.portlandpublicgolf.com (tee times)
www.eastmorelandgolfcourse.com
Rated one of the top 25 public golf courses
in the United States by *Golf Digest,* Eastmoreland is Portland's oldest and one of its most
beloved greens. Eastmoreland has an endless variety of trees and shrubs on its 6,529
yards and is bordered by Crystal Springs
Lake, the Rhododendron Gardens, and Johnson Creek. The course, which is the site of the
annual city championship, also offers a pro
shop, restaurant, snack bar, reception and
meeting rooms, and a double-deck covered
and lighted driving range. The greens fees

are among the best values of all the local courses. Rates may vary according to the season. Junior and senior rates are available. Carts are optional.

i **Wednesday is Golf Day for the** *Oregonian.* **Check the sports section for the latest news, events, and convenient discount coupons for local golf courses.**

GLENDOVEER GOLF COURSE $$
14015 Northeast Glisan St.
(503) 253-7507
www.golfglendoveer.com
This par-73 course is an excellent place to golf, and it is usually quite busy. Glendoveer, with 36 regulation holes spread out over 280 acres of hills, trees, and water hazards, offers junior and senior rates on the weekdays. This place features a golf shop, driving range, and a great clubhouse with big-screen sports TV and outdoor seating for special events. Regular visitors know this course has a split personality. That's because most of the course swells with hills, except for the front 9 holes of the west course, which are as flat as paper. The east course spans 6,296 yards, while the west course runs 5,922 yards. Glendoveer also offers a pro shop and indoor tennis and racquetball courts; the restaurant and lounge, the Ringside, is a Portland steakhouse favorite and worth a trip even if you're not a golfer.

✴HERON LAKES GOLF COURSE $$
3500 North Victory Blvd.
(503) 289-1818
www.portlandpublicgolf.com (tee times)
www.heronlakesgolf.com
Offering two splendid golf courses designed to try every skill level, Heron Lakes combines a blend of bunkers and water hazards, the latter adding an aesthetic appeal to the technical challenge. The two courses, the Greenback (6,621 yards) and the Great Blue (6,916 yards), which is the flagship of Portland's golf program, were designed by world-renowned golf architect Robert Trent Jones II. Listed by Golf Digest as one of America's top 75 public golf courses, the links-style Heron Lakes has hosted numerous important golf events. In addition to the bunkers and uneven lies, many birds, including bald eagles, Canada geese, and great blue herons, add to its beauty and make life interesting for golfers. Facilities include a pro shop, snack bar, and natural-turf driving range. Holiday fees may be higher. Book your tee time six days in advance—they go fast.

RED TAIL GOLF COURSE $$
8200 Southwest Scholls Ferry Rd.
(503) 646-5166
www.portlandpublicgolf.com (tee times)
www.golfredtail.com
This 7,100-yard championship 18-hole public golf course in Southwest Portland is a redesigned course on the site that was formerly known as Progress Downs. Red Tail has incorporated significant advances in drainage systems—always a problem for Oregon golf—and even during the winter, the ball rolls and springs instead of sinking into muddy grass. In addition to the great greens, the teaching, training, and equipment advice are key features of this course, and the staff is renowned for its teaching ability, with many camps and clinics. They also have state-of-the-art instruction facilities to help you perfect your game. Red Tail is run by Portland Parks and Recreation, so its lush greens and beautiful driving range are available at very reasonable prices.

ROSE CITY GOLF COURSE $$
2200 Northeast 71st Ave.
(503) 253-4744
www.portlandpublicgolf.com (tee times)
www.rosecitygc.com

One of the oldest golf courses in the entire state, Rose City is a challenging course in a beautiful setting. The long par fours and tree-lined, narrow fairways on the 18 regulation holes demand concentration and will test your technical skills. With plenty of hills, sand and water hazards, and trees spread over 6,520 yards, this course plays long and affords excellent scenery. Rose City also has two of the hardest finishing holes in all of Portland public golf. Facilities include a pro shop and a full-service snack bar. Book your tee time up to six days in advance. Lessons can be scheduled with a pro.

WILDWOOD GOLF COURSE $$
21881 Northwest St. Helens Rd.
(503) 621-3402
www.golfnow.com

Beautiful Wildwood on the outskirts of Northwest Portland offers 18 regulation holes on one of the most gorgeous courses in the area. No fewer than three creeks run through the 5,756 yards of hilly greens. You can spend a whole day here, practicing your swing in the driving range, browsing in the pro shop, and celebrating your birdies in the full-bar clubhouse. Lessons are available and tee time reservations should be made a week in advance, but Wildwood can probably squeeze in one or two golfers on short notice. Note that the driving range allows irons only.

OUTLYING AREAS

CHARBONNEAU GOLF CLUB $$
32020 Southwest Charbonneau Dr.,
Wilsonville
(503) 694-1246
www.charbonneaugolf.com

It's no exaggeration to say that this executive course is unique, not only to the area but to the world. Lakes and trees are abundant on the three finely manicured 9-hole courses, which test the skills of beginners and professionals alike. This lush course is a mix of par fours and long and short par threes. The grass driving range is in a bucolic setting with well-tended turf. The practice area is the equal of any PGA Tour site. When you call a week in advance for tee times, you may also want to inquire about the junior and senior rates.

i Make golf a family event by taking the kids to the Children's Golf Course, a pretty par-9 executive course along the Willamette. It features lessons, clinics, and tournaments for young golfers, but grown-ups are welcome too. You'll find it at 19825 River Rd., Gladstone, (503) 722-1530.

LAKE OSWEGO GOLF COURSE $
17525 Southwest Stafford Rd.,
Lake Oswego
(503) 636-8228
www.lakeoswegogolf.org

With an abundance of trees, water, and hills, this splendid 18-hole executive course is both challenging and lovely. Local golfers find the topography the perfect place to practice their short game, and though it's an executive course, Lake Oswego Golf Course has the reputation of being a challenge. The pro shop carries great equipment and the 19th Green Cafe & Grill offers an extensive menu as well. With just 2,693 yards, there are no golf carts here, but lessons are available.

LANGDON FARMS GOLF CLUB $$$
24377 Northeast Airport Rd., Aurora
(503) 678-4653
www.langdonfarms.com

Just off I-5 about 20 minutes south of Portland, Langdon Farms is popular with Portland golfers. This par-71, 18-hole course laid out over 6,935 yards is notable for its unusual contoured terrain. There are few shade trees, so golfers should wear a hat and apply sunscreen when playing on a hot or sunny day. Lessons are available as well as a driving range. Greens fees include cart rental. Rates vary widely—prime-time summer fees are at the high end, but afternoon rates throughout the year offer good value. Several special rates are available at Langdon, among them the one for early birds. Tee times book up quickly—you may need to wait a few weeks. The clubhouse resembles a turn-of-the-20th-century farmhouse, reminding golfers that they're playing in some of the most fertile farmland in the nation.

LEWIS RIVER GOLF COURSE $$
3209 Lewis River Rd.,
Woodland, WA
(800) 341-9426
www.lewisrivergolf.com

Just a half-hour's drive north from Portland, this picturesque public golf course offers gorgeous scenery along the winding Lewis River. The 6,352-yard course is graced with many trees and lakes. Lessons are available. This well-established golf course can handle large groups and tournaments. Besides the driving range and putting green, Lewis River offers a pro shop, restaurant, banquet rooms, and patio dining.

MOUNTAIN VIEW $$
27195 Southeast Kelso Rd., Boring
(503) 663-4869

Exactly one-half of the way between downtown Portland and Mount Hood, this is a dandy place for 18 regulation holes of golf. Mountain View offers plenty of hazards and hills throughout its 5,926 yards and affords a terrific view of Mount Hood. Be sure to ask about hole number 12; with an 18-story drop from the T-box to the green, it is a huge attraction—one of the most unusual holes in the state. Lessons are available. Tee times can be reserved seven days in advance.

i For the most encyclopedic Internet review of golf in Oregon and southwest Washington, visit the truly excellent website www.oregongolf.com. This fine resource gives exhaustive details on each course and links you to the maps to get you there.

✴PUMPKIN RIDGE $$$$
12930 Old Pumpkin Ridge Rd.,
North Plains
(503) 647-4747
www.pumpkinridge.com/golf.cfm

Pumpkin Ridge comprises two first-rate courses, a public course, Ghost Creek, and a private course, Witch Hollow. Ghost Creek stretches over 6,839 beautiful yards, and it is one of the premier golf facilities open to the public on the entire West Coast. Tiger Woods won the US Amateur Open at Pumpkin Ridge in 1996.

Both Witch Hollow and Ghost Creek have bentgrass tees, greens, and fairways. Both are nearly unrivaled in the Pacific Northwest. Amenities include an 18,000-square-foot clubhouse with golf shop, meeting facilities, teaching center, and restaurant. Practice facilities include bunkers, putting and chipping greens, and an expansive driving range. Package deals are available for corporate or tournament outings. Top professional golfers are available for lessons. Fees change with the season, so inquire when you book your tee time. If you plan to golf at Pumpkin Ridge a lot, take advantage of their Ghost Card, which offers a discounted rate for frequent players.

QUAIL VALLEY $$
12565 Northwest Aerts Rd., Banks
(503) 324-4444
www.quailvalleygolf.com
A drive of 30 minutes west on US 26 will take you to the superb Quail Valley Golf Course, which is surprisingly difficult for a course that looks so flat. The difficulty is due to the abundance of water hazards and other environmentally sensitive areas that challenge players in all the right ways. This 6,603-yard course is a favorite for winter play, because it is very well drained.

*RESERVE VINEYARDS
GOLF CLUB $$$$
4805 Southwest 229th Ave., Aloha
(503) 649-8191
www.reservegolf.com
One of the area's newest golf courses, the Reserve Vineyards offers two 18-hole courses in the heart of Willamette Valley wine country. The par-72 courses were designed by John Fought and Bob Cupp, and together these courses offer some of the best golf in the state. The mansionlike, 40,000-square-foot clubhouse includes four dining areas and a deli, a pro shop, a wine-tasting area (there are vineyards on and near the course), locker rooms, a trophy room, and a 2,000-square-foot deck. The club is a popular location for corporate golf tournaments as well as weddings, banquets, and social events, but its claim to national fame is that it has been the home of the Fred Meyer Challenge and the Jeld-Wen Tradition Make tee time reservations up to 14 days in advance.

SKAMANIA LODGE GOLF COURSE $$
1131 Skamania Lodge Way,
Stevenson, WA
(509) 427-2541, (800) 293-0418
www.skamania.com
Don't let this very short par 70 fool you: This course is tough. It is hilly. The rough is brutal. The trees are thick. The extremely tight fairways should encourage you to leave your driver in the trunk. And bunkers lie in wait for you on the green side on several holes. But these challenges—along with the spectacular setting and views—make this one of the most beloved courses in the area. Skamania Lodge Golf Course is about an hour's drive east from Portland through the Columbia Gorge, and it's attached to Skamania Lodge, on the north bank of the Columbia. The impressive views of the Columbia are reason enough to visit. Many Skamania regulars advise you to rent a cart because of the hills. It's also recommended that you call two weeks in advance for tee times, but if you're staying in the lodge, you don't have to call so far in advance. To get there follow I-84 east to the Bridge of the Gods. This toll bridge ($1) will take you across the river, and from there, simply follow the signs.

*STONE CREEK GOLF CLUB $$
14603 Stoneridge Dr., Oregon City
(503) 518-4653
www.stonecreekgolfclub.net
This beautiful par-72 municipal course, designed by Oregon's own Peter Jacobsen,

is situated on 165 diverse acres in Oregon City. The front 9 inhabit a pastoral meadow, and the back 9, wooded wetlands. In fact, water hazards are everywhere—three lakes, four wetlands, and Stone Creek itself. You'll also find views of Mount Hood—and 41 bunkers. This course was designed expressly to challenge and delight players at every level of golf, from the novice to the pro, with rewards for risky shots. The hardest hole is number 5, with its narrow frame of tall fir trees and uphill slope. The 13th hole is also notable; there, your blind tee shot goes over a hill and lands out of view, then you play uphill to a green encircled by majestic firs. Stone Creek provides an all-grass driving range that stretches over 6.5 acres, with six target greens and facilities to practice bunker shots. Club amenities include a pro shop, a full-service deli with three brews on tap, and a clubhouse suitable for parties.

TRI MOUNTAIN $$
1701 Northwest 299th St., Ridgefield, WA
(360) 887-3004, (888) 874-6686
www.trimountaingolf.com

Tri Mountain is close to downtown Portland and even closer to downtown Vancouver; its reputation for sogginess has been improved with drainage systems, and golfers agree that this fun course is well maintained. Sand bunkers are numerous, and 11 lakes that come into play over most of the course's holes keep golfers on their toes. The yardage of this par-72 course is 6,580, and every yard is interesting. Carts are available, as is a full-service clubhouse and an aquatic driving range.

GOLF EVENTS

Oregon has hosted several regular tournaments, the LPGA Safeway Classic and the Fred Meyer Challenge, which PGA notable Peter Jacobsen founded as a fund-raiser for local charities; and the PGA Champions Tour Jeld-Wen Tradition. Of these, only the Safeway Classic remains as a major, regular event. However, roving tournaments of many kinds will alight here, including the US Amateur Open and the U.S.G.A. National Amateur Public Links Championship. Oregon also has its own regiment of local tournaments: The **Oregon Golf Association** is the best source of information on these. They may be reached at (503) 981-GOLF or online at www.orgolf.org.

i The Oregon Golf Association, the local liaison to the USGA, will help you establish your handicap, find out about regional tournaments, and answer your questions about golf courses. Contact them at (503) 981-4653 or www.oga.org.

SAFEWAY CLASSIC TOURNAMENT GOLF
(503) 626-2711, (503) 287-LPGA (tickets)
http://safewayclassic.com

The LPGA Safeway Classic has a purse of almost $2 million; it raises millions for children's charities and is one of the most popular events in Portland golf. Tickets run about $10 per day, $25 for the week, but Safeway shoppers can receive significant discounts—and kids under 17 are free when accompanied by an adult. It's held at some of the Portland area's showcase golf courses; it now makes its home at Pumpkin Ridge (See the Recreation & Spectator Sports chapter for more information on this great golf event.)

DAY TRIPS

A chief pleasure of living in or visiting Portland is its proximity to so many other beautiful places. A two hours' drive west of Portland will take you to the magnificent Oregon coast with its forests, rock formations, and unsullied beaches, while in half an hour, you will be immersed in the rich and fertile Willamette Valley wine country. An easy hour's drive east leads to the awe-inspiring Columbia Gorge and its stunning waterfalls and, by another route, the majestic Mount Hood. If you drive south, in an hour you'll reach the largest and one of the loveliest state parks in Oregon, Silver Falls State Park. So pack your picnic basket, a good map and, of course, your Insiders' Guide, and go discover Oregon firsthand.

SILVER FALLS STATE PARK

SILVER FALLS STATE PARK
SR 214, 26 miles east of Salem
(800) 551-6949 (information),
(800) 452-5687 (reservations)
www.oregonstateparks.org/park_211.php
Silver Falls State Park lies in the foothills below Oregon's Cascade Mountains, east of Salem. Here, one of the most beautiful trails in Oregon, the Trail of 10 Falls, descends to a forest floor covered with ferns, mosses, and wildflowers amid stands of Douglas fir, hemlock, and cedar and the rushing waters of Silver Creek. Silver Falls has one of the highest concentrations of waterfalls in the country, and five of them fall more than 100 feet. This park also has beautiful meadows and excellent facilities, and it's a fine place to spend a day or two. If you aren't in a hurry, the drive to Silver Falls can be part of the fun. Take either SR 99E or I-205 from Portland to Oregon City. Then just follow SR 99E along the Willamette River to Woodburn and then turn onto SR 214, which cuts through the picturesque towns of Mt. Angel and

Silverton on the way to Silver Falls. A faster route is to take I-5 South. Just past Salem, take SR 22 east to SR 214 and head east for 25 miles. From Portland the drive takes about an hour and 15 to 20 minutes.

Once you are at the park, the trails are well marked. (A detailed map of all the trails is available on the park's website, listed above). The well-maintained Canyon Trail, part of the Trail of 10 Falls, winds along the banks of the north and south forks of Silver Creek leading to 11 majestic waterfalls. These range from the grand South Falls (177 feet) to the delicate Drake Falls (27 feet). The trail leads you behind four of these falls to enjoy the cool and misty spray. Canyon Trail is narrow in some places, with steep drop-offs, so it is open to hikers only (no pets). It joins with the Canyon Rim Trail to complete a 7-mile loop.

South Falls, one of the most spectacular sights, is an easy walk from the main parking area and the gorgeous Silver Falls Lodge. The trail descends to the bottom of the canyon and follows the South Fork of Silver Creek

1 mile to Lower South Falls. A quarter mile farther, the trail turns east and follows the North Fork of Silver Creek upstream past at least six more waterfalls.

To hike the entire circuit requires a good three to four hours. For most people who enjoy the canyon at a leisurely pace, the hike is an all-day adventure. But you need not hike the entire trail. Shorter trips may be made by returning via the Ridge Trail or the Winter Falls Trail. You may want to leave a second car at the North Falls parking lot to avoid the 2-mile return hike.

To preserve its pristine nature, there are no shelters, picnic tables, or restrooms along the Silver Creek Canyon Trail, but benches and bridges across the many smaller streams are pleasant spots for a picnic. For safety's sake remember the bicycle trails are also used by hikers and the horse trails are open to bicycles and hikers alike. If you want your day trip to last longer, you will find RV, cabin, and tent camping in the overnight campground.

Some state parks in Oregon charge a nominal day-use fee to cover maintenance costs, and Silver Falls is one of them. You'll need to purchase either a $5 day-use pass or—if you plan to visit a lot of parks—a $30 annual pass that buys access to all state park day-use areas for one year.

i Silver Falls State Park offers 25 miles of trails for horseback riders, bikers, and hikers.

MOUNT ST. HELENS

MOUNT ST. HELENS NATIONAL VOLCANIC MONUMENT
Spirit Lake Highway, Washington, SR 504
www.fs.fed.us/gpnf/mshnvm

Mount St. Helens was once known as "the Mount Fuji of America" because its symmetrical beauty was reminiscent of the famous Japanese volcano. But on May 18, 1980, after nearly two months of smaller earthquakes and steam eruptions, Mount St. Helens began a series of massive, explosive eruptions after an earthquake with a magnitude of 5.1 struck at 8:32 a.m. Within seconds, the volcano's unstable and bulging north flank slid away in the largest landslide in recorded history, triggering a destructive blast of lethal hot gas, steam, and rock debris that swept across the landscape at 684 mph. Temperatures reached as high as 572 degrees Celsius, melting snow and ice on the volcano and forming torrents of water and rock debris that gushed down river valleys leading from the mountain. Within minutes, a massive plume of ash thrust nearly 12½ miles into the sky, where the wind carried about 490 tons of ash across more than 22,000 square miles of the western United States and, in trace amounts, around the world.

The lateral blast, which lasted only the first few minutes of a nine-hour continuous eruption, devastated 250 square miles of forest and recreation area, killed thousands of animals, and left 57 people dead. The eruptions and huge avalanche removed about 4 billion cubic yards of the mountain, including about 170 million cubic yards of glacial snow and ice. The eruption also caused mudflows so severe that they blocked the shipping channel of the Columbia River 70 river miles away.

The volcano periodically spewed steam and ash for several years, eventually settling down enough for the region to rebuild. In 1982 President Ronald Reagan designated 110,000 acres around the volcano as Mount St. Helens National Volcanic Monument.

Trails, campgrounds, and visitor centers were established to accommodate the thousands who visited each year.

Now Mount St. Helens is one of the most popular day-trip destinations in the Pacific Northwest. It is an easy, scenic two-and-a-half-hour drive from Portland. There is a lot to do and see on this trip, so start early in the morning and pack some ice and refreshments in the cooler. Take I-5 to exit 49 (the Toutle/Castle Rock exit), which will lead you onto Washington SR 504 (Spirit Lake Memorial Highway). The first stop, just 5 miles east, is the Mount St. Helens Volcanic Monument Visitor Center (360-274-0962) at Seaquest State Park on the shore of Silver Lake. Don't miss the scaled-down, walk-in replica of the volcano: It really helps kids (and grown-ups, too) understand what's behind all the blasting. A short and easy trail just outside the center leads to a viewpoint overlooking Silver Lake and Mount St. Helens. This facility is operated by Washington State Parks; there is a $3 fee per adult for visiting ($1 for children older than 6), but it is worth it.

Continue driving east past some of the most striking scenery in the Northwest, from the washed-out stretches of the Toutle River to the white carcasses of the fir trees that laid themselves down before the awesome power of the volcanic blast. SR 504 winds around the north fork of the Toutle River, and overlooks along the road offer views of the crater, Castle Lake, Coldwater Lake, and the mountain's northwest lava dome.

Hoffstadt Bluffs Rest Area offers a spectacular view of the landslide that preceded the blast. Elk Rock Viewpoint offers another stunning view into the still sediment-choked Toutle River Valley.

Just 5 miles farther up the road from Coldwater Ridge, SR 504 ends at Johnston Ridge Observatory (milepost 52; 360-274-2140). Only 4 miles from the volcano's crater, this wheelchair-accessible-site affords views of the inside of the crater and its dome. It was named in honor of brave geologist David Johnston, who was keeping watch over the mountain for the US Geological Survey and whose final words warned the world of what was to come. This magnificent center is a fitting tribute. The center also offers an incredibly high-quality movie about the eruption, along with many fascinating, interactive displays and kiosks.

There is much to do on the mountain, so you'll have some decisions to make. Ask for a map of Mount St. Helens at one of the visitor centers or on the website—it will help you understand your options. One great adventure is to circle the entire mountain by following improved forest roads. It is possible to do this from June until the first snowfall—usually in Nov or Dec.

Other monument highlights include Windy Ridge and Spirit Lake, which rose 70 yards as a result of the blast. Consult with visitor center staff about selecting the best route.

You will need a pass to visit the tourist centers at the monument. These can be purchased at any of the visitor centers. Adult multiuse passes are $8; children 15 and under are free. Discounts for seniors are also available. The monument is open year-round, though Johnston Ridge and some of the viewpoints and trails are closed by snow from Oct through May. The visitor centers may be on limited schedules during the winter. If the volcano is active, it may be closed to climbers, though barring a major eruption, the other monument sites tend to remain open.

Pets are welcome at some parts of the monument, but dogs must be leashed where they are permitted. Some areas with especially delicate ecosystems prohibit pets altogether. Take notice of signs.

Excellent picnic and day-use areas are plentiful, but there are few places to purchase food. No overnight accommodations are available on the grounds of the monument, but nearby towns offer lodging, camping, and supplies.

For the most spectacular views of the crater, try to go on a sunny, summer day. But do remember that it is the Northwest, and even sunny days can bring clouds to the mountaintops.

On October 1, 2004, the volcano awoke from its slumber, emitting steam and erupting ash to signal a new phase of geological activity, which is ongoing, rebuilding the dome of the mountain. A volcanic eruption puts daily cares in perspective like nothing else, and despite the potential danger, residents have been enthralled by the reminder that Mount St. Helens has a mind of its own.

i You might hear Oregonians refer to distances in hours instead of miles. Don't be confused—it's just our way of talking. To translate, use an average 50-miles-per-hour figure to account for traffic, stops, and winding roads. So how far from Portland is the Oregon Coast? In distance, about 100 miles. In Oregon-speak, about two hours.

MOUNT HOOD–COLUMBIA GORGE LOOP

When friends visit from out of town and ask what they should do, we send them to the Columbia Gorge. The Gorge showcases our region beautifully, with its dramatic cliffs, tumbling falls, and the mighty Columbia rolling along despite the obstacles we have put in its way. Extending the tour by adding the rich farmland of Hood River and the drive over the archetypical Mount Hood deepens that sense of place, so precious to Oregonians. Here, we recommend an optimal tour of the region, one that you could drive in a day or that you could lengthen with an overnight stay. You can also reverse the drive or easily cut it short. The total length of the journey will be something between 100 and 160 miles, depending on where you stop, where you linger, and where you detour.

These days, cars and trucks race along I-84 at great speed. But before the freeway, drivers had to rely on the road that is now the Columbia Gorge Scenic Highway. This narrow, winding road, with its many moss-covered bridges, was dedicated in 1916 by President Woodrow Wilson. One can only imagine the harrowing journey it must have been when it was the principal route east from Portland. Now it is quieter and less crowded, though on summer days you can still find yourself crawling through the shady forest behind an ambitious RV.

To reach the Gorge along this route, begin by taking I-84 east to Troutdale to exit 17 and follow the signs designating the Scenic Highway. The road takes you through Troutdale, along the swift Sandy River, until you turn up and onto the rural bluffs that overlook the Columbia. Just past the little town of Corbett, you will find the **Portland Women's Forum,** a pretty wayside that provides a spectacular view east of the Columbia Gorge, particularly Crown Point, Rooster Rock, and Beacon Rock, and north into the Washington Cascades.

Just east of the Portland Women's Forum is the road to Larch Mountain, a 29-mile detour (round-trip) that leads to some of the most breathtaking views of the Cascades in the entire area. The road winds through fields and forests until you get to a large parking lot, where an easy, paved trail takes you to a special viewing area that tells you which peaks you are seeing—on a clear day, this can mean a view north all the way to Mount Rainier. Closer in you'll see Mount St. Helens, Mount Adams, Mount Hood, and Mount Jefferson, as well as the verdant, rolling foothills of the Cascades. Larch Mountain also provides picnic areas and other hiking trails, and it's a popular place to watch the Perseid meteor shower in August. (The road may be closed in winter—its final elevation is 4,050 feet.) A note of caution: The Larch Mountain detour is slow going, so it may not be for everyone. And don't bother if the cloud cover is thick. But the payoff is worth it if you have the time and if the weather is cooperative.

Returning to the highway, turn right to continue down the Scenic Highway. After a number of hairpin turns, you will find yourself at **Crown Point Vista House,** a pretty stone building that affords views west and east of the river and the Gorge. Crown Point is especially popular at sunset, when the river washes west into a red and orange sky underlined by the lights of the city and the view east fades into soft purple twilight as the cliffs grow dim. (See the Attractions chapter for more on Crown Point Vista.) East of Crown Point Vista, the highway turns into the forest and provides access to—and views of—the dozens of waterfalls that trickle and gush from the cliffs above on their urgent errand to meet the Columbia below. Many of the biggest falls have waysides, trails, and parks that invite you to explore and linger. Latourell Falls, easily accessible via a paved, 150-yard trail, plummets from a basalt outcropping 250

feet above. Bridal Veil and Wahkeena Falls are next, and then you will arrive at **Multnomah Falls.** Multnomah Falls—at 620 feet, the second-highest waterfall in the United States—is a premier attraction in the state (and indeed warrants a special exit from I-84, in addition to being accessible via the Columbia Gorge Highway). Most visitors are content to view the falls from the viewing area behind the **Multnomah Lodge** (503-695-2376; www.multnomahfallslodge.com), a beautiful historic building that houses a restaurant, gift shop, and information center. For the information center, call the US Forest Service at 503-695-2372. Some visitors venture a bit farther, taking the paved path first to the bridge beneath the falls and then to the top of the falls (1 mile, uphill).

But if you want to hike the entire 3.25-mile loop, you will be rewarded with a verdant walk that takes you along the ridge just west of the falls and past Upper Wahkeenah Falls, before dropping back down to the parking lot. To follow this loop, from the paved overlook spur, you'll continue along the unpaved trail, across the stone bridge, until you reach the junction for the Perdition Trail. Bear right along this trail along the ridge for 1.2 miles. The trail has a number of stone staircases, and just past the steepest and longest set, you will meet the Wahkeenah Trail. Take this, staying to the right and passing Upper Wahkeenah Falls. You'll meet with pavement again about half a mile before Wahkeenah Falls; then stay on the path above the highway for another half mile, until you reach the Multnomah Falls parking lot.

Resuming your trip, the next stop on the Columbia Gorge Highway is **Oneonta Gorge.** Here the reward of the trail, should you choose to take it, is a walk behind the falls. Horsetail Falls is next, before the high-way connects back to I-84 at milepost 35.

Once you are back on the freeway, the next destination is the **Bonneville Dam** (541-374-8820), the oldest Army Corps of Engineers project along the Columbia River. It's fun to watch the salmon struggle up the fish ladder along the dam or to throw chow at the fry in the nearby Bonneville Hatchery. (See the Attractions and Kidstuff chapters for more information on the Bonneville Dam and Fish Hatchery.)

About 2 miles past the Bonneville Dam is the town of Cascades Locks, as well as the Bridge of the Gods, an impressive steel toll bridge that takes you across the Columbia into Washington and to the **Columbia Gorge Interpretive Center** (990 Southwest Rock Creek Dr., Stevenson, WA; 509-427-8211; www.columbiagorge.org). This museum, designed to resemble a saw-mill, offers an absorbing thematic history of the Gorge based on who lived here and what they did. It is a good complement to the **Cascade Locks Museum,** back on the Oregon side (1 Northwest Portage Rd.; open daily May through Sept, noon to 5 p.m.; 541-374-8535). This little museum was formerly the home of a lockman. It dates from 1905 and features many fascinating artifacts and photos from life along the river 100 years ago. In front stands the Oregon Pony, the first steam locomotive on the Pacific coast and the first west of the Missouri. Cascade Locks was built around the site of the navigational pass that allowed boats around a series of Columbia River rapids. Since the building of the dam, of course, these rapids have been submerged, but Cascade Locks is a great stop because of its historic museums, its park, its summer stern-wheeler tours (see the Kidstuff chapter), and its two restaurants:

Charburger (714 Wanapa St.; 541-374-8477), which offers cooked-to-order burgers, home-baked pies and cookies, and striking views of the Columbia; and its neighbor, the **East Wind** (541-374-8380), an old-fashioned drive-in with excellent soft-serve ice cream.

Back on I-84, your next stop will be Hood River. Just west of town, at exit 62, is the his-toric and luxurious **Columbia Gorge Hotel** (4000 West Cliff Dr.; 541-386-5566; www .columbiagorgehotel.com), famous for its dining room views and its lavish five-course farm breakfast. The pretty grounds sit atop a waterfall that plunges 208 feet.

> **i** For maps, trails, and other infor-mation on the Columbia Gorge, call the Columbia Gorge National Scenic Area offices at (541) 308-1700 or visit www.fs.fed.us/r6/columbia/forest.

Hood River is known for two things: windsurfing and orchards. For a span of 70 miles east and west of Hood River, wind-surfers swoop and glide through the chilly Columbia waters, taking advantage of the wind that gusts persistently through the Gorge. Hood River is a pleasant little town, with many charming shops, art galleries, and restaurants. For information about windsurf-ing see the Recreation and Spectator Sports chapter, but also feel free to ask in any of the plentiful surf shops in town. Other stops might include the **Hood River Hotel** (102 Oak Ave.; 541-386-1900 or 800-386-1859; www.hoodriverhotel.com), an appealing 1913 vintage building that houses a good restaurant. Also try the **Full Sail Brewery,** home to some of the finest beer in Oregon (or anywhere). Guided tours are available daily on the hour from noon until 5 p.m. for those older than 13. And all ages are welcome at the pub if they are eating. Pub hours are noon to 8 p.m. daily. The brewery is found at 506 Columbia St. (541-386-2247).

Hood River is a good place to turn around and head back to Portland along I-84. But if you decide to explore further, you will be rewarded.

Follow the main street of Hood River as it angles southeast on SR 35 into the lovely Hood River Valley, home to thousands of acres of orchards and farms. Less than a mile from town, as the highway clings to the hillside, turn up the road marked by the sign designating a panorama point. This will take you to a vista point, with much of this beautiful valley laid before you. Two terrific times to visit the Hood River Valley are during the Hood River Blossom Festival, held in mid-April, and the Hood River Harvest Festival in mid-October. But at any time the trip through this pocket of traditional farmland is a journey beyond life in the city.

After leaving the valley SR 35 starts to curve around the eastern slope of Mount Hood. Soon you begin to catch close-up glimpses of Mount Hood's glacial cap, and if you use your imagination, you can sense the wonder felt by pioneers who opted to take a path around the mountain instead of rafting down the dangerous Columbia. Just before the confluence of SR 35 and US 26, a historical marker announces that you are crossing Barlow Pass, named for Sam Barlow, a trailblazer who found a way down the mountain and set up a toll road. Barlow charged $5 per wagon and 10 cents per head of cattle for those hearty and brave enough to slide and rope their wagons down the muddy slopes and treacherous canyons that are now traversed by US 26. Another historical marker shortly after the Barlow Road marker is a poignant reminder of the cost of this detour.

The **Pioneer Woman's Gravesite** is a short distance from the road; there you can also view intact wagon ruts near the gravesite.

Once on US 26 heading west, there are a number of spots of interest. One is **Trillium Lake,** a picnic site and fishing hole stocked with rainbow trout. To get there take FR 2656 a couple of miles before reaching Government Camp. If it's ski season, you can go to Timberline, Summit Ski area, or Mount Hood Ski Bowl (see the Recreation and Spectator Sports chapter) for some world-class downhill action. Or if you are simply thirsty and hungry, stop at **Mt. Hood Brewing Company** (503-272-3172), at the west end of Government Camp for microbrews and great sandwiches. **Timberline Lodge** (503-272-3311; www.timberlinelodge.com) is worth a visit whether or not you ski and even if no snow is on the ground. This attractive lodge, made of hand-hewn logs and great stones, is a National Historic Landmark built in 1937 as part of the Works Progress Administration (WPA). It stands as a monument to the talents of its builders and to its era. The lodge also features an outstanding restaurant, as well as several cafes and other eating areas. (If you are taking two days, it would make an excellent halfway stop.)

After descending from the ski zone, you'll come to Welches, a mountain town with lodging, shopping, dining, and even golf. **The Resort at the Mountain** (503-622-3101; www.theresort.com) not only offers gracious accommodations but the Three Nines golf course. You might also want to stop here at the Mount Hood Information Center for information on just about everything going on around the mountain.

One last site to see is the **Philip Foster Farm and Homestead** at 29912 Southeast Oregon Hwy. 211 (503-637-6324, www

.philipfosterfarm.com). Follow US 26 west to SR 211 in Sandy, and drive south for 6 miles to the hamlet of Eagle Creek. This national historic site served as many as 10,000 emigrants on the Oregon Trail. Nearing the end of their journey, they ate 50-cent dinners of steak, potatoes, coleslaw, and biscuits at Foster's farm. Foster was an entrepreneurial fellow as well as a restaurateur, and he anticipated and met the needs of weary pioneers. Here they could stock up on fruit, grain, and other supplies and their livestock could partake of the Foster family's hay, before proceeding west and south into the Willamette Valley. Today you'll find a working farm complete with house, barn, garden, orchard, and blacksmith shop. Visitors are invited to help with chores. There is also a picnic spot and a general store. Hours are Fri through Sun 11 a.m. to 4 p.m. June through Aug and just Sat and Sun during Sept.

MARYHILL MUSEUM

The Maryhill Museum, in Goldendale, Washington, across from Biggs, Oregon, is an unusual monument and museum situated where the slopes of the Cascade Mountains fade into the high desert terrain of the eastern Columbia River Gorge. The museum is in a chateau built in 1914 by Sam Hill, the famous developer of the Columbia River Gorge Scenic Highway. (Hill, a Quaker and pacifist as well as an entrepreneur, also built the handsome Peace Arch on the border between Canada and the United States at Blaine, Washington.) Sam Hill named the house for his daughter Mary, building it atop the windy bluffs at a breathtaking spot where you can see the transition in the landscape from the green west to the dry and golden east. The house was never a home, however,

and Hill was persuaded by his friend Loie Fuller, a pioneer of French modern dance, to transform it into a museum. She was also able to help him acquire a good collection of Rodin sculptures to display in it.

Indeed, despite its remote location, the museum boasts an impressive collection of European art as well as Native American artifacts, art, and jewelry. Hill had a number of other influential friends, among them Queen Marie of Romania and Alma Spreckles (of the San Francisco sugar family). Through them, Hill was able to secure many fine paintings and objets d'art. Maryhill is also an official site along the Lewis and Clark Trail, and since 2003 the museum has featured a number of remarkable exhibitions and programs devoted to the bicentennial of their voyage.

Maryhill's grounds are equally lovely. They cover 26 acres, with formal gardens, a sculpture garden, roaming peacocks, and stunning views of the Gorge. The museum (509-773-3733; www.maryhillmuseum.org) is open Mar 15 through Nov 15 from 9 a.m. to 5 p.m. daily. Cost is $7 for adults ($6 for seniors) and $2 for children 6 through 16. The grounds are free. You will find a cafe and gift shop at the museum.

Maryhill also features full-size replica of Stonehenge, 4 miles east of the museum. Hill built it as a monument for the war dead of World War I, and subsequently, the museum has added memorials to Klikitat County soldiers who died in World War II, Korea, and Vietnam. No admission is charged to visit Stonehenge.

To get to Maryhill, take I-84 to the Biggs Junction exit. Take US 97 north to Washington SR 14, traveling west 3 miles to Maryhill, at 35 Maryhill Museum Dr. The drive from Portland should take about two hours.

NORTHERN WILLAMETTE VALLEY'S WINE COUNTRY

In the 1960s Oregon wine pioneer David Lett started planting grapes in the Dundee Hills west of Portland, and everyone thought he was crazy. But he had observed something important. Roughly in the same latitude as Burgundy, the great wine-producing province in France, Oregon's northern Willamette Valley has a cool marine climate, rich soil on the southern slopes of rolling hills, and a long, gentle season with ample sunny days. Now, decades later, Oregon wines hold their own against the best wines in the world.

But don't take our word for it. Taste these remarkable varieties yourself by taking a tour of northwestern Oregon's wine region. It's a delightful drive through some of the state's most bucolic countryside. Many of the wineries are open to visitors; and some are near fine restaurants and inns along one of the most popular tourist loops on the West Coast.

Plan for a journey that starts in the morning, looping out into wine country and back to Portland by evening. Visit the **Oregon Winegrowers' Association,** www .oregonwine.org, (or 1200 Northwest Naito Pkwy., Suite 400, 503-228-8403). We cannot emphasize enough how essential this resource is—it provides a comprehensive listing of all the wineries in the Valley (and in Oregon). You can preorder brochures for the specific appellation you are interested in at www.oregonwinebrochure.org; these have information on winery tasting rooms, maps, and other features. Give yourself time to plan a good route and be sure to designate a driver. It will make your trip much better. (If you are not into a DIY wine tour, then we highly recommend utilizing the resources of the Portland Visitors Association. They have a list of commercial wine tour vendors available at www.travelportland.com/visitors/daytrips/vineyards.html). There are 155 wineries in the northern Willamette Valley alone—but not all of them are open to the public or have tasting rooms. So planning is essential.

Once the planning is out of the way, you can get on the road. Below is an example tour of the northern Willamette Valley that hits three of the founding vineyards as well as samples those of more recent vintage.

Start by visiting **Ponzi Vineyards,** one of the most important winemakers in the valley. Take I-5 to SR 217 and on to SR 210 for 4.5 miles to Vandermost Road. Turn left and head south, following signs to 14665 Southwest Winery Lane. Here, with the exception of January and holidays, visitors are welcome to sample the wines of the pioneering Ponzi family, who have been instrumental to the establishment of Oregon's wine industry and to its continued success. The Ponzis were one of the first to grow grapes in the region, just a little after David Lett. They continue to produce stellar wines, as well as being true community leaders and supporters of young growers. Their tasting room is spacious and attractive, and the grounds offer bocce courts in addition to the views of rolling countryside—bocce being one of the two great games one can play with a wineglass in one hand (boules is the other).

The next leg of the journey, the longest, will take you through about 30 miles of beautiful farmland and vineyards—both large estates and small craft wineries such as WillaKenzie, noted for its Burgundy-style wines—to the **Carlton Winemakers Studio** (www.winemakersstudio.com). This handsome LEED-certified building holds the tasting room for about eight local winemakers, including pinot star **Andrew Rich**. The studio also offers classes and events. To get there from Ponzi, you will follow Southwest Winery Lane back to Southwest Vandermost Road, turn right, and take the first left onto SR 210/Southwest Scholls Ferry Road. You should be heading west. After about two miles, you'll make a left turn to stay on SR 210/Scholls Ferry Road. Stay on this road—it will turn into SR 219/Southwest Hillsboro Highway, and you'll follow SR 219 for nearly 10 miles. You will turn right at East Illinois Street in Newberg, then quickly turn left at North Main Street, and then turn right onto SR 240 West, the Yamhill-Newberg Highway. You'll continue on this road, and then turn left to stay on SR 240 West. When you come to the junction of SR 47, turn left and follow this road south to Carlton. You'll turn right at West Lincoln Street; the Carlton Winemakers Studio is at the intersection of Lincoln and Scott (801 North Scott St.).

After you chat with the winemaker on duty at the Carlton Studio, head south to the tasting room for **Eyrie** (www.eyrievineyards .com/journal), David Lett's visionary winery, in McMinnville, about 7 miles to the south. You'll backtrack on Lincoln Street to SR 47, and follow it to West Main Street. Turn left at Main (still on SR 47—there will be a sign for McMinnville), and then follow SR 47 through the second right onto South Pine Street. This street will turn into the Tualatin Valley Highway, but you will still be on SR 47. Stay on this road until you reach SR 99W; take a slight right, continuing to follow the signs for McMinnville. Stay on 99W, driving southwest, until you reach Northeast Lafayette. Turn left (following the sign for Bayton—Salem), and follow Northeast Lafayette for almost a mile and a half until Northeast 10th Ave. You'll find Eyrie in an unprepossessing building

at 935 Northeast 10th Ave. Eyrie is noted for not only the first pinot noir plantings in the Willamette Valley but also the first pinot gris plantings in the US. David Lett's international-medal-winning pinot noir wines were the catalyst that turned the Valley into the winemaking hub it is today. In 1979, the French winemaker Robert Drouhin was so amazed by Lett's third-place finish in a blind-tasting competition in Paris that he held a new contest the following year. This time, Lett's wine came in second. (The Drouhin family soon set out for Oregon themselves, and now they are one of the top producers in the area.) David's son Jason Lett now runs the family business, still producing elegant pinots and other varietals, and numerous rising winemaker stars have apprenticed with him and his father.

McMinnville is a pretty college town and the home of the International Pinot Noir Festival (see the Festivals and Annual Events chapter). It has good tasting rooms, wine bars, and restaurants featuring local wines and food, as well as some quite good shopping. **Nick's Italian Café** (521 Northeast Third St.; reservations 503-434-4471) would be a pleasant stop for lunch.

Next up is **Erath Vinyards,** which is famous not only for the excellence of its pinot noirs, but also for bringing French grape clones to the Valley, in 1974. Until then, the small grape-growing community had been working almost exclusively with California grapes. If the Oregon climate was more like the Burgundy region of France, why not use French clones? From Eyrie, backtrack onto SR 99W and turn right. (If you are in downtown McMinnville, make your way toward 99W Forest Grove/Portland.) You'll travel about 9 miles east on 99W to the outskirts of Dundee. At Southwest

Niederberger Road you will turn left off the highway (it will say CR 78 on the right). Stay on Southwest Niederberger Road for about half a mile and turn right on Northeast Warren Road. After about .7 mile, take a left on Northeast Worden Hill Road. Erath has a friendly tasting room with a patio that offers gorgeous views across the Willamette Valley.

Complete your tour by heading back onto 99W and into Dundee or nearby Newberg, each of which has several outstanding restaurants. In Dundee, you must choose between **Tina's** (760 SR 99W, 503-538-8880), which is a highly rated place that specializes in local, seasonal dishes; and the charming **Dundee Bistro** (503-554-1650) next to the excellent **Ponzi Wine Bar** (both are at SR 99 and 7th Street). To get to either of these restaurants from Erath, drive southeast onto CR 12/Northeast Worden Hill Road. Stay on CR 12. Turn left at Southwest View Crest Drive and then right at Southwest 7th Street. If you want to go to Tina's, turn right at 99W—the restaurant will be just to the right; if you want to go to the Dundee Bistro, turn left into the parking lot just before the highway.

If you want to head to Newberg from Erath, stay on CR 12 until you reach 99W, and turn left onto the highway. Take 99W north until Newberg. Here, you'll need to make a choice. You can turn right at South College Street and head to the **Painted Lady** (201 South College St.; 503-538-3850). This superb restaurant is in a beautifully restored Victorian house and serves fine seasonal Northwest cuisine. Or you can head to the luscious **Allison Inn and Spa, featuring Jory Restaurant** (2525 Allison Lane; 503 554 2526 for the dining room). Instead of turning on South College, you'll stay on 99W; it will veer to the left, becoming East Portland Road. Turn left at North Springbrook Road. You'll

reach a traffic circle; stay straight to remain on North Springbrook. Turn right to stay on North Springbook (if you don't turn, you will be on East Mountainview, which you don't want to do). Take North Springbook until Allison Lane, on the left.

At this point, your designated driver may wish to stop driving and savor some wine at Jory—or perhaps the luxurious spa treatments and rooms at the Allison. You could stay over and the next morning enjoy an alternative view: **Vista Balloon Adventures** (800-622-2309, www.vistaballoon.com) in Newberg offers aerial tours in hot-air balloons for around $200. This is a lovely way to see wine country—though a little far from the tasting rooms.

In any case, whether you stay the night or head home, to return to Portland from either Dundee or Newberg, take 99W through Sherwood and Tigard, all the way back to I-5.

THE OREGON COAST

About 100 miles west of Portland, you will find some of the most spectacular coastline in the world. The Oregon coast is a favorite destination for Portlanders, offering a complete range of experiences from resorts to rustic. To get there, take US 26 west, following the signs that direct you toward the ocean beaches. Once past town, this road winds through picturesque farmland before it climbs the Coast Range mountains.

When you reach US 101, turn north toward Astoria if you want to visit Fort Clatsop, the site of Lewis and Clark's winter encampment. This historical re-creation is as entertaining as it is educational. Astoria, a few miles north of Fort Clatsop, is a delightful working harbor at the mouth of the Columbia River. Or turn south on US 101 for Cannon Beach. By now you're probably ready for lunch, and Cannon Beach, a lively beach town, has many shops and restaurants, as well as beautiful hotels and spas. Cannon Beach is the home of the famous **Haystack Rock** (at 235 feet high, the third-tallest coastal monolith in the world).

i Astoria is the setting for Steven Spielberg's 1985 movie *The Goonies*—a film that capitalizes on the legends of pirates' treasure buried on Neahkahnie Mountain and other coastal sites.

A bit farther south, you'll encounter **Neahkahnie Mountain,** with a trail leading to its summit and a view that is breathtaking for its scope up and down the coast and back into the Nehalem Valley. Neahkahnie is an excellent viewing area for whales in the spring and fall.

Continuing south, you'll pass through the charming towns of Manzanita, Nehalem, and Wheeler. Manzanita, which lies just west of US 101, has especially good beaches, and all three towns are filled with charming shops. Next you'll reach the fishing villages of Garibaldi and Bayside and on to Tillamook. Just to the west of this friendly blue-collar burg is the **Three Capes Loop,** a 35-mile byway off US 101 between Tillamook and Neskowin. As you cruise through gentle, misty dairy country that has a time-out-of-mind feel, you'll get far enough west to check out Cape Meares to the north, Cape Lookout midway, and Cape Kiwanda at the end of the loop. This last cape is right next to Pacific City, where dory anglers compete each year in a contest to see who can launch their fishing boat into the surf, row around yet another Haystack Rock, and return with a real fish.

Just a short way down the coast is Neskowin, a sweet little town with a pretty beach in the shadow of Cascade Head, a looming monolithic outcrop favored by hikers seeking solace in a genuine rain forest. After beachcombing at Neskowin, drive a few more miles south to the junction of US 101 and SR 18.

Here you have a choice of directions. You can continue south along the coast, past Lincoln City on to Newport with its fascinating Oregon Coast Aquarium, Hatfield Marine Science Center, historic Nye Beach, and scenic Yaquina Head lighthouse and bird-watching station. It's an easy, if long, journey back to Portland from Newport either by backtracking to SR 18 or heading east on US 20 to Corvallis and then on to I-5 and north. But it will make for a long day, so you may want to plan for a stay-over in one of the many hotels and motels along US 101.

Or you can choose to take SR 18 and angle back to Portland, stopping for some great grub at the **Otis Cafe** at Otis Junction, 2 miles east of US 101 (541-994-2813). Just past Otis you'll enter the Van Duzer Corridor, a stretch of ancient firs that frame the road with their verdant grandeur. Beyond the forest, and past the Spirit Mountain Casino and a broad valley dotted with barns and farmhouses, you'll cruise through Yamhill County and on to Portland. Once home, after dumping sand out of your sneakers, you'll start planning another trek to Oregon's wondrous coastline to revisit favorite spots and discover a few more.

Appendix

LIVING HERE

In this section we feature specific information for residents or those planning to relocate here. Topics include real estate, education, health care, and much more.

RELOCATION

Portland is repeatedly honored across the nation as being one of the best places to live. Its setting among mountains, farmland, and rivers contributes to its desirability, and so does its solid economy and unfrenzied style of life. Yet above all, we are a city of neighborhoods. And this may be the true secret of Portland's charm, the source of its community feeling. Government agencies such as Metro, nonprofit organizations such as the Coalition for a Liveable Future, neighborhood associations, far-sighted real estate developers, and plain old unaffiliated citizens keep the neighborhood spirit alive and provide a foundation for its strength to grow. After you've had a look at some of our neighborhoods, we'll turn to the topic of real estate and let you know about ways to find your own place in our beautiful metropolitan area. And we'll tell you other important facts about moving to the area.

NEIGHBORHOODS

Researchers predict that the Portland Metro area will increase to 2.5 million people in the next 50 years, an increase of about 1.5 percent each year. All these new people will have to live somewhere, but we also need to protect forests to clean the air and water (and the spirit), and we need to preserve the farmland to feed all these new residents. Our unique tri-county government, Metro, plays an important role in determining land use policies, and because its officials are elected, these policies ideally reflect the wishes of citizens. This unusual tri-county government helps to protect open spaces, to allow for coordinated transportation management, and to stabilize development by encouraging population density instead of suburban sprawl.

Metro and the kind of planning it embodies is not without its critics from both sides of the political spectrum. Developers rankle under the land-use plans, while

environmentalists worry that the urban growth boundary actually encourages growth by requiring a certain amount of urban space to be dedicated to development. The best hope is that the competing interests will work in fertile tension with each other. For example, Metro's encouragement of affordable housing and mass transportation have sparked some of the most innovative developments in the nation. Orenco Station, which was built in Hillsboro specifically to take advantage of the light-rail line, has been dubbed "America's Best Master Planned Community" by the National Association of Home Builders. This assemblage of cottages, craftsman retros, and row houses reverberates with an old village way of life. Similarly, highly accoladed projects such as the Belmont Dairy, Irvington Place, and Albina Corner, which reclaimed underused urban space and now provide attractive, mixed-use facilities and affordable housing for lower- and middle-class residents, might never have happened without the productive constraints of land-use planning.

Old or new, upscale or downhome, Portland's neighborhoods embody the genius loci of the city. From the friendly, front-porch lifestyles of St. Johns to the funky old Victorian houses of inner Southeast Portland to the stately manors of the Dunthorpe district, Portland is home to a healthy array of diverse and distinct communities. We have 94 formally recognized neighborhoods in the city of Portland alone. This chapter is meant to serve as a broad overview of Portland Metro area neighborhoods. In the first section of this chapter we try to give you a feel for Portland's four distinct areas—Southwest, Northwest, Southeast, and North/Northeast—and also to introduce you to Vancouver and at least some of the communities outside Portland's formal borders.

Southwest Portland

The heart of Southwest Portland is the **downtown area.** Not only is it the home of many businesses, cultural organizations, government agencies, and public spaces, it is also the home of many residents, who like the urbane atmosphere and the proximity to work and nightlife. Portland's downtown is a mecca for shoppers, with department stores such as Nordstrom, Macy's, and Saks Fifth Avenue, as well as the Pioneer Place shopping center, all within several blocks. Pioneer Courthouse Square is a popular meeting place and offers a wide range of free, live entertainment during the noon hour. But despite the tempting stores, the impressive statues, and the well-designed business towers, nothing defines downtown Portland as well as the **Willamette River.**

In the early 1970s the city underwent a huge renewal project, ripping apart a four-lane highway along the west bank of the Willamette and transforming it into beautiful **Tom McCall Waterfront Park.** It is the site of numerous concerts, festivals, and celebrations as well as a showplace for community events. Eight blocks west, Park Blocks, a 25-block boulevard of trees, grass, flowers, fountains, and statues, offers another urban refuge for workers, shoppers, and students. Nearby are many of the city's most important cultural and recreational facilities, including the Portland Art Museum, the Oregon Historical Society, the Performing Arts Center, and the Arlene Schnitzer Concert Hall. Just outside the inner city is Washington Park, home to the Metro Washington Park Zoo, the tranquil Japanese Gardens, the World Forestry Center, and Hoyt Arboretum.

Beyond the park's boundaries to the south and west are several of the most established, picturesque, and tree-lined of all the city's neighborhoods. Collectively referred to as the **"West Hills,"** each of these neighborhoods nonetheless has distinctive features. For example, **Arlington Heights,** one of Portland's most scenic neighborhoods, just west of downtown above the city center, gives residents easy access to the spectacular Portland Rose Test Gardens and all of Washington Park. The houses here tend to be older, and the architecture diverse—one house is a miniature replica of Canterbury Castle in England. Arlington Heights's neighbor, **Portland Heights,** also displays diverse architectural styles. Ranging from Victorian cottages to the latest contemporary dwellings, these houses are noted for their lovely gardens and spectacular views. Nestled amid the Southwest Hills, **Council Crest** affords extraordinary views of both the city and the western valleys. Farther west, on the other side of the hills, you'll find **Multnomah Village,** named by *Money* magazine as one of Portland's best neighborhoods. This charming neighborhood offers the grace of older houses and the vitality of the newer ones; but all houses are tempered by a hint of the rural past—it wasn't formally annexed until 1954, and some of the most desirable houses yet repose on unpaved roads. Multnomah Village itself is a notable shopping and business district that offers a congenial center to village life. (See the Shopping chapter.) The newest neighborhood is the **South Waterfront district.** This glass high-rise village across from Ross Island, reminiscent of Pacific Rim cities such as Vancouver, British Columbia, is defining itself as the leading edge of Portland development. Built on landfill along the Willamette on a parcel that was once used for building ships, the South Waterfront district is anchored by Oregon Health and Science University's Center for Health and Healing and the Portland Aerial Tram. The luxury condominiums and apartments have new shops and restaurants on the ground floors, and along the banks of the river, greenway trails are under construction. The residents, however, are already defining themselves with a strong community voice; they are deeply involved in shaping the character of the neighborhood.

More Southwest Neighborhoods

CORBETT-TERWILLIGER AND LAIR HILL

On a 4-mile-long ribbon of land along the west bank—one of the most scenic segments of the Willamette River—you'll find the Corbett-Terwilliger and Lair Hill neighborhoods, directly south of downtown Portland. Residents here are indirectly responsible for preserving the character of our city. Years ago, when urban renewal crept its way to the north end of these older neighborhoods, a backlash resulted in establishment of the South Portland–Lair Hill Historic Conservation District, the first protected historic district in Portland. This was an appropriate gesture, given that Portland's very first building, a cabin constructed by William Johnson in 1842, was built in what became this neighborhood, near Southwest Gibbs and I-5. Some residents later balked at the construction of the Portland Aerial Tram, which glides above this neighborhood, but the new development on the South Waterfront seems to be a net positive for this neighborhood. The houses in this pretty urban neighborhood are mostly older Victorian-style structures, but there are intriguing modern structures as well.

HILLSDALE NEIGHBORHOOD

Hillsdale is just 3 miles from downtown Portland, but its location atop the Southwest Hills gives it an almost rural feel. Hillsdale's commercial district evolved in the 1940s along old dairy-cow pastures, and after the war, as suburban-style houses were built in the area, the virtues of things such as sidewalks were forgotten. Now Hillsdale residents are guiding developments to foster accessibility and community. Southwest Terwilliger Boulevard, one of Portland's favorite scenic routes for bikers, pedestrians, and cars— and the product of community planning efforts—is a hallmark feature along with Oregon Health and Science University, one of the major employers in the state. This area is very popular with young families, since the neighborhood schools are very good.

Hayhurst Neighborhood

A unique feature of the Hayhurst neighborhood area is the Alpenrose Dairy, which continues to operate as a dairy, as well as serving as a community center offering sports fields, picnic facilities, entertainment, and bicycle racing. In a sense, Portland's most familiar dairy symbolizes the wholesomeness of this middle-class area, which is made up mostly of single-family houses and is creating ways to accommodate growth while preserving its distinctive neighborhood character and livability. Hayhurst School and its nature learning garden and Pendleton Park with its neighborhood planting projects are some of the community-friendly features of this neighborhood. This is another family-friendly area—schools are good, backyards are large.

Goose Hollow

Goose Hollow's name goes back to the 1870s when women who lived there raised flocks of geese. Early residents of the district were the barons who guided the destiny of the region from its raw pioneer days through the prosperity of the 1890s and the following war years. But while Portland boomed between 1970 and 1990, Goose Hollow slumbered. However, since 1991, Westside light rail and high-density planning have spurred unprecedented developments, pumping more than $50 million in improvements into the 3.2-square-mile district. Bordered by downtown, Washington Park, the University District, and Burnside Street, the western end of the district is hilly and residential, while the eastern portion is flat and commercial. Served by the MAX line, this neighborhood has seen handsome new apartments and condominiums in recent years, along with attractive new commercial spaces, infusing the area with new life.

Northwest Portland

Northwest Portland offers panoramic views of the mountains, the Willamette River, and the city. Northwest Portland is a delightful blend of old and new and of classic and Bohemian, and community interaction is extremely high in this area as residents and neighbors strive to create a secure and friendly living environment. Northwest Portlanders find boutique shopping, art galleries, coffee, and culture within easy walking distance. Well-built and beautifully reconditioned Victorian houses, huge fir trees, and lush parks and gardens provide an old-world feel, while above the city, contemporary mansions in the **Arlington Heights** neighborhood demonstrate that American dreams of progress are still alive. The heart of Northwest Portland is the **Nob Hill** neighborhood—the commercial and residential areas north of Burnside along Northwest 21st and 23rd Avenues. Though many of its three-story Victorian estates have been converted into condominiums, this neighborhood has retained its elegance and appeal, and there are many handsome apartment buildings dating from the early twentieth century, with their vintage features intact. The numerous shops on Northwest 21st and 23rd Avenues offer unusual and distinctive wares, though chain stores like Pottery Barn and Gap are slowly encroaching. Still, this is one of the toniest areas of the city—also one of the most densely populated, and popular with young professionals.

Excellent hospital facilities, fine schools, many banks, good grocery stores and restaurants, and a highly efficient public transit system that includes the new streetcar system add to the desirability of Nob Hill. Possessing a wide range of socioeconomic diversity, the area supports an impressive variety of employment, volunteer, and recreation opportunities. And it's moments away from Washington and Forest Parks as well as downtown.

More Northwest Neighborhoods
PEARL DISTRICT

Money magazine designated the Pearl District as one of the best places to live in the best city to live in. This is remarkable because not long ago the area was a grimy, downtown postindustrial wasteland. Today it is one of the most fashionable locations in the close-in city. Extensive renovations and adaptive use of historical and other structures have led to lofts, row houses, new restaurants, theaters, art galleries, and new retail activity. Also, a flurry of important new urban creative-commerce entrepreneurs, ranging from small Internet service providers to internationally known advertising and multimedia companies, are staking out territory here.

In addition, the Pacific Northwest College of Art, PICA, and other arts organizations have chosen the Pearl as their home. Well-clad entrepreneurs sip coffee next to spiky-haired students; art supply stores and antiques shops vie for attention; cool lofts with cityscape views perch above truck-loading ramps. The atmosphere in the Pearl is a heady brew of past and future productively engaging. Important retail and residential developments include the Brewery Blocks (on the site of the old Henry Weinhard Brewery), between Burnside and Northwest Davis, as well as an innovative restoration project by Ecotrust. The latter, the Jean Vollum Natural Capital Center, 907 Northwest Irving, holds a major Patagonia retail shop

in addition to other shops and offices. This restored brick building is constructed with eco-friendly timber and energy-efficient spaces. Its roof is planted with native vegetation that keeps the building cool and filters rainwater.

The Pearl District draws urbanites young and old, and more recently, families with children. Many of the newest shops and cafes are taking advantage of this new demographic trend. The work in progress here should give hope to cities everywhere.

LINNTON

The great documenter of Oregon, Ralph Friedman, writes that the cofounder of Linnton, Peter Burnett, foretold that Linnton would one day "be the great commercial town of the territory." Peter Burnett went on to be elected the first governor not of Oregon but California, which is telling. Linnton was platted in 1843; at the time, its location near forest and river seemed preferable to the flooding swamp of Portland. By the time it incorporated, in 1910, the bustling town had its own train service, two newspapers, and a jail. In 1921 the plywood mills employed more than 1,000 workers, but that prosperity came to a halt during the Depression and then was killed beyond recovery during the 1940s, when fires burned down the mills. Things got worse as the century crept along, when trucks began to replace railroads as the favored means of transportation, and, in a concomitant development, Linnton's business district was demolished to make way for a larger road.

Today, however, Linnton is being rediscovered and its property is among the newly desirable. New houses are being built on the hillside and younger families are moving in, since this neighborhood's children attend some of the best public schools in the city. The neighborhood association has embarked on a master plan to guide the developments along the river and the highway.

OLD TOWN–CHINATOWN NEIGHBORHOOD

As its name implies, Old Town–Chinatown is one of the pioneer neighborhoods of Portland. Besides serving as the Chinese District, the city's early docks and railroad station were teeming with sailors on shore leave and loggers from the nearby woods, creating colorful—if rowdy—city scenes.

This neighborhood, which lies just east of the Pearl District, serves as a gateway to downtown Portland. Art, music, culture, great ethnic food, unique architecture, small businesses, major corporations, and residents of all income levels thrive here. Numerous social service agencies harmoniously coexist with for-profit businesses. The diversity of the residential population is reflected in the housing, which ranges from single-resident hotels to upper-end apartments and lofts. The Chinese and Japanese cultural roots of the area are manifested in old buildings as well as new developments, particularly in the Classical Chinese Garden on Northwest 3rd and Everett.

i Want to know more about Portland's neighborhoods? Check out the useful website sponsored by the Office of Neighborhood Involvement Programs and Services: www.portlandonline.com/oni.

Southeast Portland

The east side of Portland has seen a renaissance during the last decade. Expansive renovation, busy commercial activity, and general vigor have ignited the return to the city of many former suburbanites and the reclamation of the city by confirmed urbanites who always understood the virtues of established neighborhoods with beautiful parks, good schools, and appealing architecture, especially in the close-in neighborhoods. These neighborhoods offer a reduced commute time and greater access to cultural life than the suburbs. The **Hawthorne** and nearby **Belmont Districts,** which are subdivided into many distinctive neighborhoods such as **Richmond, Sunnyside, Buckman,** and **Mt. Tabor,** are filled with single-family houses and mixed-use apartment buildings. Bakeries, coffeehouses, boutiques, music shops and bookstores, pubs, and restaurants are within walking distance of many houses, buses run frequently, and street life is abundant. Similarly, the neighborhoods of **Eastmoreland, Westmoreland, Sellwood,** and **Laurelhurst** have vibrant retail districts along with their single-family houses.

Surprisingly—given its proximity to downtown—inner Southeast Portland has taken longer than other neighborhoods to complete its revival. It might be because its early renewal efforts lost momentum, or it might be because much of it is industrial, but for whatever reason, its renovation seemed to stall. It remained purely industrial.

That is now changing, and there are signs of mixed development. The **Eastbank Esplanade** opened up the east side of the river to pedestrians and cyclists, and they love the subtle promise of the west views of the Willamette and the city skyline. By connecting all the bridges from the Steel Bridge to the Sellwood Bridge, the Esplanade seems to have shaken things up and people are looking at this chicly industrial area once again. For example, more influential restaurants opened in the past several years in inner Southeast Portland than in any other neighborhood—the chef behind nationally acclaimed Le Pigeon chose a renovated storefront in Southeast Portland for his restaurant, and chef Dave Machado opened up not just one but two major restaurants in the area (Lauro and Vindalho). New restaurants seem to open weekly along Southeast Division, and **Southeast Belmont** is is a mecca for coffeehouses—Stumptown Coffee has two of them there. Southeast Portland is more affordable than almost any other place in Portland for both business and houses; if you factor out the high prices of Eastmoreland, the houses in Southeast Portland are probably the best value for the money in town right now.

The trendiest neighborhood in town is **"LoBu"—Lower Burnside**—home of the Doug Fir Lounge, the Jupiter Hotel, and Biwa. The enterprising folks who have started businesses there took advantage of the fact that the area had been stuck in a time warp and used it to their advantage, since everything comes around again eventually. Technically, LoBu straddles both Southeast and Northeast Portland, but in terms of spirit and aesthetic, it is Southeast all the way.

More Southeast Neighborhoods

INNER SOUTHEAST PORTLAND

The core of inner Southeast Portland comprises three commercial streets—Hawthorne, Belmont, and Division—that run from the Willamette east (in the case of Division, all the way to Gresham). These business districts are filled with independent, DIY businesses, from food carts to yoga studios

to high-end design. The neighborhoods that surround these innovative and entrepreneurial districts are likewise independent-minded, and you will find many sustainable organic gardens, ecoroofs, alternative public and private schools, and architect-designed chicken coops, along with young families, old Italian grandparents, urbanites, and professionals living in single-family turn-of-the-century homes and brand-new condominiums all in a glorious mélange.

Hawthorne Boulevard supports high-density housing that meshes with retail activity, fashioning one of the city's premier shopping and living districts. This street intersects the Sunnyside and Richmond neighborhoods. Pedestrian-friendly and lined with gift stores, period clothing shops, and distinctive restaurants, this district is bordered by the Central Eastside Industrial District, home to the Oregon Museum of Science and Industry to the west and the base of Mount Tabor, an extinct volcano and one of the city's most beloved parks, to the east.

The houses on Mt. Tabor's west side are large, older, and upscale. Belmont, which also ends on Mt. Tabor, used to hold the streetcar line, and you will see gorgeous estates at the east end of the street, where well-to-do Portlanders built them at the beginning of the 20th century, taking advantage of the streetcar to get them to their firms in the city. Further west, Belmont, which is the core of the Sunnyside neighborhood, is filled with bustling coffeeshops, bars, and stores.

Division is rapidly refreshing itself, with some of the city's best new restaurants and bars opening along this bustling route and a new master plan for the street in the works. Attractive new live-work spaces are also being built to take advantage of its proximity to downtown. This renewed focus on Division is fitting—in some ways, the neighborhood revolution in Portland began here in the early 1970s, when the state of Oregon proposed, essentially, to turn Division into a freeway. Citizens banded together to stop it, prompting officials to rethink the freeway scheme in general. Eventually, this freeway revolt led to strong neighborhood associations, alternative transportation plans, and a new ethos for the city, including removing the old freeway downtown. These citizens didn't just stop a freeway: they created a revolution.

HOSFORD-ABERNETHY

Also called Ladd's Addition, this neighborhood was settled in the mid-1800s. In the southeast sector, Hosford-Abernethy is one of Portland's oldest neighborhoods. The Ladd tract—one of the nation's first planned communities, with sidewalks, paved streets, electricity, and a streetcar line—began developing early in 1900. After World War II many of the residents abandoned the neighborhood in favor of the suburbs, and the area declined. Beginning in the 1970s hundreds of historic houses have been restored, bringing back its sense of neighborhood, and now it might be considered an exemplar of good planning. One hundred years later, this neighborhood has some of the most valuable property in the city.

Retail storefronts, schools, parks, churches, community gardens, movie houses, live theater, restaurants, and coffee shops are within easy walking distance, but the centerpiece is still Ladd Circle's beautiful garden and the little shops that surround it, which provide the neighborhood with a meeting place and a focus. This neighborhood also hosts one of the liveliest food cart pods, at the corner of Southeast Hawthorne Boulevard and Southeast 12th Avenue (see the Restaurant chapter).

i Each April *Portland Monthly* magazine (www.portlandmonthlymag.com) devotes itself to describing the climate of real estate and emerging trends—and gives their stamp of approval to the 20 top neighborhoods and why they consider them such, including statistics on commute times, crime rates, and other information of interest. This popularity contest—of great interest to homeowners all over town—is not available online, but you can buy back issues from the website.

SELLWOOD–WESTMORELAND

Historic Sellwood is known for its Antique Row, composed of more than 50 antiques stores tucked into the neighborhood of Victorian houses and turn-of-the-20th-century architecture. Where Sellwood meets the river, you'll find Oaks Bottom, home to the Oaks Bottom Wildlife Sanctuary, a refuge for herons, beavers, ducks, and other marsh animals and birds. Here, the neighborhood meets the Willamette, with houseboats docked along the river's edge. Sellwood is also renowned for its strong community spirit. Westmoreland is graced with one of the city's most beautiful parks, as well as its own healthy retail district, including the wonderful Moreland Theater, an independently owned movie theater that is a true community hub. Most of the houses in this neighborhood are single-family dwellings, from small bungalows and old Victorian cottages to some houses that are impressive in their scale and architecture. Many of these can be found along the ridge above Oaks Park. Families like this neighborhood, its good schools and beautiful parks.

EASTMORELAND

Eastmoreland is a lush residential neighborhood. Quiet and tranquil, it is bordered by the Eastmoreland Golf Course, Reed College, Crystal Springs Lake, and the Crystal Springs Rhododendron Gardens. Houses are large, expensive, and handsome. Public schools are top-notch. Eastmoreland claims on city surveys to be the happiest neighborhood in all of Portland.

LAURELHURST

Laurelhurst is a pretty neighborhood with a variety of house styles, most of them well landscaped with mature plantings and offering some of the most desirable property on the east side. The neighborhood is bordered by Belmont to the south, and it has its own charming retail district on Burnside between Southeast 28th Avenue and Southeast 32nd Place. Its anchor, however, is the gorgeous, Olmsted-designed Laurelhurst Park (see the Parks chapter for more information).

North & Northeast Portland

Many Oregonians regard this section of Portland as an area of tremendous opportunity. Here, Portlanders are rightfully proud of their old, well-established neighborhoods featuring lovely houses and elegant, historic mansions. And that pride has been refreshed, since many intense redevelopment activities are pumping new life and vitality into this section of the city, making it a more exciting and appealing place to live, work, and visit.

Beautiful older houses line the tree-shaded streets in the Northeast neighborhoods of **Beaumont, Irvington** and **Alameda.** Some of the houses in the Alameda neighborhood, especially those along the periphery of the ridge, afford good views of the Willamette River and the downtown skyline. Alameda and Irvington share schools and shopping districts, and both are among the most highly prized neighborhoods in town.

Attractive shopping areas draw people from around the region, and so does **Portland's Convention Center,** between the Lloyd District and the river. The MAX train stops outside the center's north entrance and also serves the adjacent **Rose Quarter,** a 43-acre complex featuring the Memorial Coliseum arena, the Rose Garden arena, the One Center Court entertainment complex, and four parking garages. The Rose Quarter hosts a variety of sports events, including the Portland Trailblazers, the Portland Winter Hawks, college basketball, and indoor soccer. Around Lloyd Center, the **Northeast Broadway Business District** is blossoming, and just east, the delightful **Hollywood District** offers a wonderful blend of affordable housing and great small shops. **Grant Park** is another popular neighborhood. With the eponymous park at its center, this tree-lined area of pretty single-family houses, many of which were built in the 1920s and 1930s, has great schools, an incredibly convenient location, and a superfriendly vibe.

Other neighborhoods farther north, such as **Hayden Island, St. Johns,** and **Kenton,** offer their own distinctive charms. These areas, rich in character and history, are blessed with many well-tended parks and green spaces.

More North Portland Neighborhoods

BOISE-ELIOT NEIGHBORHOOD

Formerly the city of Albina, which was established in 1872 and annexed to Portland in 1891, the Boise-Eliot neighborhood in inner Northeast Portland started out as a community of European immigrants. Today it is one of the foremost residential and cultural centers of the African-American community.

From 1960 to 1990 the area lost more than half its housing to urban renewal projects, conversion to business and institutional use, and neglect. This neighborhood is now one of the most vital and popular, especially with first-time home buyers and young families.

No place is this more evident than North Mississippi Avenue. Both historic and innovative, North Mississippi Avenue is undergoing a renaissance. This neighborhood was a vibrant hub in the early 20th century, complete with its own streetcar line. But history passed it by and left it with vacant lots and buildings, crime, and deterioration. After suffering generations of neglect, North Mississippi Avenue is now filled with young entrepreneurs who are bringing the deserted storefronts to life and filling the vacant lots with gardens and new buildings. Cafes, art galleries, bakeries, flower nurseries, antiques stores, food carts, and other indie enterprises are revitalizing the street, and many of these urban pioneers make their homes here as well, living above or next to their businesses. Unlike many neighborhood improvement projects, this one has been specifically designed to protect its longtime residents from the unintended consequences of gentrification—though this is not always as successful a message as planners had hoped—but overall, Portland

views North Mississippi as a model for future urban renewal.

OVERLOOK NEIGHBORHOOD

Nestled along a high bluff above the Swan Island industrial area and Willamette River Overlook in North Portland, the Overlook neighborhood was once the home of many shipyard workers. Today it has drawn a diverse ethnic population, reflected in an elementary school population among whom 22 percent study English as a second language.

This historically rich district is home to Kaiser Town Hall, a cherished neighborhood meeting place; popular Overlook Park; Saint Stanislaus Church and Polish Hall, the site of a yearly festival and repository of cultural heritage; the Interstate Firehouse Cultural Center, a recycled firehouse used for a wide variety of community activities; and the Overlook Community Center. With its beautiful older homes, it is undergoing a major gentrification boom.

PIEDMONT NEIGHBORHOOD

Piedmont was originally developed as Portland's first suburban community—and a bit of a snooty one at that. Renters were discouraged, and no commercial activity was allowed in the district. Lovely Edwardian houses are a feature of the neighborhood.

Piedmont's character changed during World War II, as Kaiser began to employ shipbuilders, who flocked to the pretty, nearby houses in Piedmont and either bought them or rented them. Although this neighborhood was once a popular choice for starter houses, its stability was disrupted by the recession of the 1980s and a wave of crime problems. Thankfully the area is enjoying an unprecedented rejuvenation as a wide range of community development projects are under way. These include foot patrols, landlord training seminars, concerts in Peninsula Park, a first-time homebuyer's club, and other projects that promote property improvements—and first-time home buyers and young families are returning to the neighborhood in droves. The MAX line serves the area, and urban renewal is well along, with upscale grocery stores, restaurants, and other attractions.

ST. JOHNS–CATHEDRAL PARK NEIGHBORHOOD

At the tip of the North Portland peninsula near the confluence of the Columbia and Willamette Rivers lies Cathedral Park and adjacent St. Johns, one of Portland's oldest communities. Once an independent village, it still has the feel of a small community, especially in its bustling retail district. The industrial area surrounding St. Johns is a source of employment for residents but also a point of conflict as the community struggles to protect its livability and adjacent natural resources. The St. Johns Bridge, the jewel of Portland's bridges, is the area's most visible landmark, and the graceful arches of its base give Cathedral Park its name. The popular park represents a 10-year effort by the locals to preserve some of the riverfront for public use. The area is also home to Smith and Bybee Lakes, both unique natural and recreational resources.

More Northeast Portland Neighborhoods

CONCORDIA NEIGHBORHOOD

A large, northeast Portland neighborhood dating back to the turn of the century, Concordia was once considered a suburb. Now indisputably urban, this neighborhood is an exemplar of urban renewal. Thanks to the efforts of the neighborhood association and enterprising entrepreneurs, the commercial spine of this area, Alberta Street, is a vital, thriving artery. Concordia University, for which the neighborhood was named, is just 3 miles from downtown and continues to play an important role in the area's positive changes.

A showcase of these positive developments is the old Kennedy School, a neighborhood landmark since 1915. Declared surplus decades ago by the school district, the building slowly deteriorated over the years as competing interests wondered what to do with it. Portland's McMenamin brothers solved the problem by converting it into a huge attraction, complete with pubs, a bed-and-breakfast inn, and a movie house. (See our Brewpubs and Accommodations chapters.) The beneficial effects of the Kennedy School development have helped to revive the real estate market in the area and have spilled over into nearby neighborhoods.

SABIN NEIGHBORHOOD

Sabin is another highly diverse residential neighborhood comprising mostly older houses that has gentrified mightily since 2000. In recent years the nonprofit Sabin Community Development Corp. has developed more than 100 units of housing for very-low-income families in the area.

In other endeavors, Sabin hosted Portland's first multicultural festival and stages an annual Alberta Street Festival on the revitalized Alberta Corridor. Tree plantings and murals add to the friendliness and attractiveness of the area. Retail activity is starting to take off, and urban pioneers are buying their first houses in this area, where handsome old houses may still be reasonably priced.

2010 Average House Prices by Area

Portland

North	$227,000
Northeast	$295,000
Southeast	$243,000
West	$413,000

Outlying Areas

Gresham/Troutdale	$210,000
Milwaukie/Gladstone	$266,000
Oregon City	$245,000
Lake Oswego/ West Linn	$441,000
Northwest Washington County	$375,000
Beaverton	$256,000
Tigard/Tualatin	$311,000
Hillsboro	$230,000

(Figures are from the Realtors Multiple Listing Service and reflect rounded averages for the period ending June 30, 2010. "West" includes both Northwest and Southwest Portland.)

HAZELWOOD/GATEWAY NEIGHBORHOOD

Saddled atop the old Barlow Trail, one of the earliest pioneer routes across the Cascade Mountains into Portland, is Hazelwood. This neighborhood stretches throughout eastern Portland on both sides of Burnside, and most of the area's housing was built during the post–World War II development boom of 1946 to 1960. Some of these developments include high-quality projects such as Cherry Blossom Park. Hazelwood, like most of the outer east area, remained unincorporated until it was annexed to Portland in the 1980s.

This has been a combined blessing and curse. It allowed the community to acquire new urban services but also forced it to adapt to a new political system and absorb new development at a fast pace. Other distinctive features of Hazelwood include the new East Portland Police Precinct, Midland Branch Library, the Gateway Apartments mixed-use project, Midland Park with plantings by local students, and the blossoming Gateway business area.

i Community newspapers are the glue that holds the neighborhoods together. Neighborhood association meetings, traffic plans, and discussions with local legislators and officials combine with personal essays, advertisements, and advice columns to provide community spirit and critical information for residents. Look for papers locally in stores, coffee shops, and kiosks—and see the Media chapter for more information.

Vancouver

In the blink of an eye, Vancouver increased in size from 26 square miles to more than 44 square miles and nearly doubled its population from 68,000 residents to 128,000. At the stroke of midnight on January 1, 1997, with the Eastside annexation, Vancouver, which sits across the Columbia River directly north of Portland, became the fourth-largest city in the state of Washington and the second-largest city in the Portland Metropolitan region.

The seat of Clark County, Vancouver is one of the fastest-growing regions in the United States. This burgeoning high-tech port and city, with a current population of more than 165,000, was established as a fur-trading center by the Hudson's Bay Company in 1825. The trading post and historic Fort Vancouver, surrounded by a fertile plain, soon became the commercial center for the Pacific Northwest. Although neighboring Portland's superior port facilities made it the leading city of the area, Vancouver's role remained essential to the economy and character of the region.

Outlying Areas

West of Portland

BEAVERTON

Midway between Mount Hood and the Oregon coast, Beaverton is 7 miles west of downtown Portland in Washington County at the crossroads of US 26 and SR 217. With a population of more than 90,000, and its status as the largest city in Washington County (total population of nearly 540,000), this suburb of Portland is coming into its own as a mini-metropolis.

Spread over 15 square miles, the town features many shopping areas, including Beaverton Mall, Beaverton Town Square, and Washington Square. Tree-lined streets highlight the clean neighborhoods, while a 25-mile network of bike paths and trails connect its well-groomed playgrounds and green spaces. Building activity is vigorous.

In the city itself there are 100 parks—one within a half-mile of every house—encompassing 1,000 acres and offering 30 miles of hiking trails. Beaverton is relatively prosperous and its school district is one of the most esteemed in the state. However,

the major traffic artery leading to Beaverton, US 26, or the Sunset Highway, becomes quite congested, particularly during peak traffic hours.

HILLSBORO

Incorporated in 1876, the city of Hillsboro has grown from a tiny farming community into a modern city of nearly 90,000 residents. Originally called Hillsborough, the city was named for David Hill, one of the pioneers who crossed the Oregon Trail and became one of the state's original legislators.

About 20 minutes due west of Portland, Hillsboro is spread out over 19 square miles in the heart of the Tualatin Valley. Today, as the seat of Washington County in the heart of one of Oregon's booming high-tech communities, Hillsboro lies within the 9,000-acre Sunset Corridor, Oregon's fastest-growing economic development region. Many impressive facilities have sprung up in Hillsboro, including one of the highest-quality corporate parks in the United States: 319-acre Dawson Creek Park, which contains seven lakes, fountains, promenades, and more than 5 miles of pedestrian and bicycle trails.

TIGARD AND TUALATIN

Tigard and Tualatin are the southwest outposts of the metro area, both characterized by major new commercial, industrial, high-tech, and residential development. About 50,000 residents live in Tigard; many commute to Portland, but others work in nearby electronics or computer firms. It's a young town—a third of its residents fall in the 20 to 44 age demographic. Tualatin had 750 residents in 1970. It now has more than 25,000. Its gazillion new housing developments are big hits with families—there are more children than 20- to 44-year-old adults here. As with Tigard, many people find work close to home in business services, manufacturing, and other modern forms of employment; there also remains a great deal of agricultural work in the area.

East of Portland

GRESHAM AND TROUTDALE

Once a land of berry fields and farmland, Gresham has blossomed into a bustling city of 100,000 residents while still retaining its small-town appeal. Now the state's fourth-largest city, Gresham sits at the east end of the MAX light-rail system, providing its residents with cheap, efficient transportation into downtown Portland. Situated in eastern Multnomah County and encompassing 22.5 square miles, Gresham is the gateway to the Columbia Gorge and Oregon's year-round playground, Mount Hood National Forest. Its downtown area is particularly appealing and easy to navigate. Colorful, pedestrian-friendly, and well-designed, it offers a wide variety of restaurants, retail shops, and services in a concentrated area. Gresham also maintains an excellent educational system, including its notable Mt. Hood Community College. Troutdale lies just west of the Sandy River, with about 14,000 residents. It is the official gateway to the Mt. Hood recreation area, with an old-fashioned downtown area and pretty riverside houses.

South of Portland

LAKE OSWEGO AND WEST LINN

These two riverside residential cities are pretty and quiet, with reputations for fine schools and well-to-do inhabitants. Lake Oswego, with a population of more than 36,000, is known for its older English cottage- and Tudor-style houses built in the first half of the 20th century, but today most people live in contemporary houses, many of which are in developments. However, you can find the vestiges of its sleepy rural history evident in the properties that still boast horse pastures and chicken coops. The neighborhood associations are busy and active. Lake Oswego is alluring to many people, but there's only so much of it to go around, so its neighbor West Linn has seen much growth in the past decade. In fact it's grown about 40 percent since 1970—but its residents still number only about 24,000 people. Both towns are a short commute from downtown Portland, traffic permitting.

OREGON CITY

This historic city 10 miles south of Portland was founded in 1844. Oregon City was the first incorporated city west of the Rocky Mountains, and when the city of San Francisco was originally platted, its papers had to be filed at the federal courthouse in Oregon City. Because the town awaited at the end of the Oregon Trail, and because Oregon City was the place where pioneers refreshed and restocked before traveling to their new farms south in the Willamette Valley, it became known as Pioneer City.

For decades the city thrived as a mill town, but today its economy is becoming much more diversified, and its population is more than 30,000—and growing. Housing developments seem to be springing up in its outlying areas almost overnight. The downtown area, nestled on the banks of the Willamette River, is still a beehive of commercial, retail, and community activity.

Milwaukie & Gladstone

Small-town charm, life on the waterfront, easy access to big city amenities—all these describe Milwaukie, the City of Dogwoods. Situated between Oregon City and Portland on SRs 99 East and 224 in Clackamas County, Milwaukie, a city with more than 20,000 residents, has been named as one of the 50 best places in the nation to raise a family. Milwaukie and neighboring Gladstone (population 12,000 and counting) provide clean environments, good transportation, excellent schools and health care, and many cultural and recreational opportunities. Many shopping centers, industries, and commercial businesses flourish near this modest-to-upscale area.

REAL ESTATE

If you are new to Oregon and looking to buy a house in the Portland area, you may be in for sticker shock. People really like living in this area, and houses in the Portland Metro area are priced significantly higher than the national average. It is becoming increasingly difficult to find a decent single-family house in the city for less than $200,000—even as the market reflects national trends of price declines.

The market in Portland seems to be returning to historical norms in which real estate was meant to be a long-term investment whose main purpose was not to generate cash but to provide a home. Like most of the rest of the nation, Portland's real estate market has declined since its peak in 2007, an average to date of about 21 percent, and as of this writing it is too early to tell whether these price declines are leveling out—though it appears that they are. Nevertheless, mortgage rates are still comparatively low, making more houses affordable. While this is a glimmer of good news for buyers, houses in the inner core of the city are still desirable, especially in a city that prizes both public transportation and easy commuting. The cost of energy makes houses close to downtown and other centers of employment very attractive, and prices may remain more stable in these areas.

Southwest Portland

With city center as its hub, the Southwest area features every different kind of housing opportunity you could imagine. Downtown has single-family residences, duplexes, and triplex housing, and all kinds of condominiums; many have glorious views and all the amenities you could ask for. You will rarely find anything for less than $300,000, and prices run into the millions of dollars, even now. Outside of downtown, the inner Southwest area in general features woodsier settings than the east side, with lots that tend to be larger than those found across the river. The west side is also more expensive—average prices here are more than $400,000. Perhaps the most prestigious area is **Portland Heights,** featuring large, older houses with spectacular views starting at well over $500,000. **Council Crest,** which borders Portland Heights, is another upscale, established neighborhood with fantastic views.

The **Southwest Hills, Raleigh Hills, Bridlemile, Burlingame,** and **Multnomah Village** areas are some of the other Southwest options, each with a wide variety of old and new construction offering an array of choices for home owners. **Goose Hollow, Lair Hill,** and the **Johns Landing area** feature an eclectic mix of older houses with architectural charm as well as an explosion of condominiums, row houses, and town houses, many with views of the Willamette River. The prices of houses here reflect their architectural diversity.

Other Southwest Portland possibilities include the **Corbett-Terwilliger and Lair Hill neighborhoods,** where fine Victorian houses and modern riverside condos sell at prices that can be quite affordable. Or not—some hilltop houses in the southern end of this area afford magnificent views of the Willamette River and command prices that match. **Hillsdale** and **Hayhurst,** like much of the area, have many fine houses on big lots; prices range from under $100,000 for some small condos to more than $1 million for large estates, but most houses are in the $300–500,000 range. These neighborhoods have a slightly suburban feel to them.

Northwest Portland

No area in the city has seen higher appreciating values than the Northwest District. An urban treasure of wonderful older architecture abounds here—including Old Portland, Victorian, Georgian, colonial, and bungalow styles—but most of the single-family residences are quite expensive. There is also a wide choice of condominiums and row houses available, some newly built, as well as older houses radiating charm and character that have been subdivided into smaller units.

The Northwest neighborhoods also include tony **Forest Heights** and **Kings Heights** with expensive new houses, most of them in developments with "custom" floor plans and other prepackaged features. In general the **West Hills** have most of the seven-digit gated communities. Trees are being felled daily to make room for their mini-mansions, and the forests are toppling like dominos all the way out to the Coast Range. However, the deforestation makes for spectacular views in all directions.

Perhaps the hottest area currently is the **Pearl District** (see the Neighborhoods section for greater detail), with many older industrial sites converted into high-end residential and combined residential-occupational loft spaces.

Southeast Portland

Southeast Portland features many established neighborhoods with a strong sense of community and average sales prices of $243,000. And a lot of people want to live there: The market is busy, with houses remaining on the market for just days or even hours for a well-priced property, even in this challenging market.

Richmond, Belmont, and **Sunnyside** are some of the neighborhoods along or near Hawthorne (see the Neighborhoods section). The desirable **Mt. Tabor area** has a wider variety of houses in price and style, and at its heart is Mt. Tabor Park, which sits on an old dormant volcano and has splendid views of Mount Hood as well as downtown. The architecturally consistent **Eastmoreland** has, perhaps, the most luxurious houses. Home to a lush golf course, Eastmoreland borders the stately brick and ivy Reed College and showcases older, magnificent houses, many on large lots that are priced in the $600,000 range and up. Its large canopy of trees and distinctive street layout add to its appeal. *Money* magazine designated **Sellwood,** the south border of the city, as a top neighborhood in Portland. You will find a mix of housing styles, ranging from modern row houses to pioneer homesteads and stately houses that overlook the river. Prices vary, of course, but you can still find good values. Laurelhurst and Mt. Tabor also have fine houses and the prices that reflect their elegance, but even here you can find fixer-uppers in which to invest some sweat equity.

The **Buckman area, South Tabor, Woodstock, Brooklyn, Montavilla,** and **Mall 205** neighborhoods feature more modest houses with smaller price tags. These areas are near good schools and plenty of shopping areas and are a great option for those on a budget or seeking starter houses. Also, older houses in the Hosford-Abernethy area tend to be below Portland's overall median price (though its immediately adjacent neighbor Ladd's Addition features houses far beyond the median price).

North & Northeast Portland

The Northeast section, where average house prices were $295,000 in mid 2010, is famous for its older, established neighborhoods of friendly, involved communities. Many lavish and expensive houses preserve the features of days gone by. **Alameda, Beaumont,** and **Irvington** are all just minutes from downtown and near the flourishing Lloyd Mall Shopping Center; here you will find some of the most beautiful houses in town, with prices that reflect their desirability. Alameda and Irvington not only have some of the best real estate, but they also have thriving commercial districts—particularly along the prosperous **Northeast Broadway Corridor**—that add character to the neighborhood. You can find some of the city's finest shops and restaurants here; the schools tend to be very good, and the residents cosmopolitan (see the separate listings for more information on these neighborhoods). Alameda and Irvington tend to be more expensive than other Eastside neighborhoods, but within each area you will find a variety of houses, and there are still deals for those handy with a paintbrush and wood stripper.

Bargains are getting scarcer in North Portland as it rapidly gentrifies. You'll most likely find houses at less than $300,000 in **Irvington Heights,** the popular **Boise and Sabin areas, Beaumont and Wilshire,** and **Parkrose.** Rose City, surrounding one of the area's most popular golf courses, has reasonable prices for its charming postwar bungalows. Many great houses in all price ranges surround Glendoveer, another Northeast golf course.

Vancouver & Outlying Areas

North of Portland, across the Columbia River, **Vancouver** is reinventing itself for a new century. Vancouver has 64 neighborhoods, and the housing prices in this oldest city in Washington state are generally lower than in Portland. But the market is booming, with tract houses and mini-mansions bursting forth from the earth seemingly overnight. During noncommute times, Vancouver is about 20 minutes from downtown Portland; Camas, its suburb to the east, just a few minutes more. The whole of Clark County is ripe with big new houses, some with acreage. Your money will definitely go far here, comparatively speaking, though the average house price for mid-2010 was similar to the rest of the area, at about $250,000.

South of Portland are many other livable communities. **Dunthorpe** is an unincorporated bit of Valhalla along the west bank of the Willamette. The large trees, lovely views, top-rated schools, and fine estates draw some of Oregon's most influential residents, among them former governors, senators, and ball players. The housing prices here belong in the "if you have to ask, you can't afford it" category.

Just to the south, and long considered the home of many of the finer neighborhoods in the entire metro area, **Lake Oswego** boasts a quick and scenic commute to downtown Portland as well as many lovely and grand houses. A good number of those houses—especially those commanding the highest price tags—are sprawling lakeside mansions or large, elegant houses with lake views. This postcard-like city is clean and quiet and its school district is considered top-notch. In Lake Oswego and **West Linn,** median house prices are the most expensive in the metro area, and the average price in mid-2010 was $411,000. While some properties are close to the area average, the view, lakeside, and country club properties cost millions of dollars. However, the area also boasts a multitude of condominiums, particularly in the **Mountain Park area,** with one-bedroom condos going for more than $100,000.

The second-largest community outside of Portland's city limits, **Beaverton** features a wide array of housing, from small houses to lavish mansions, as well as many condominiums. An average house in Beaverton sold for around $256,000 in 2010. The western edge of Beaverton, as with all the outer Southwest communities, is undergoing a development boom, with thousands of condominiums and single-family dwellings—and the Home Depots, Targets, and Olive Gardens to support them—erected in the blink of an eye where yesterday the horses were pastured and the strawberries grew.

Situated around Intel and the many newer high-tech industrial parks, **Aloha** and **Hillsboro** are also booming with new construction, and many older, established neighborhoods in these cities are loaded with cute, affordable houses. In the Hillsboro area, an average-price house sold for $230,000 in mid 2010. **Tigard, Tualatin, and Wilsonville** are experiencing similar breathtaking development of entire villages of houses with three-car garages. The average price in these communities is higher, running to about $311,000. Although not far from Portland proper, the commute from all these towns can be a grind, especially if it in anyway involves the Sunset Highway (US 26). Enough development is happening, however, that you might be able to find a job on the west side and obviate the commute problem.

East of Portland, **Gresham** is the largest area outside Portland's city limits, and the once working-class and farm neighborhood has—like everywhere—seen an amazing amount of growth, while still retaining some of its wide-open appeal. Gresham provides a good blend of old and newer housing (average price is $210,000), with many affordable houses.

Houses—New or Used?

The competition between house remodeling and new house construction is a pendulum that swings back and forth, but several factors in Portland are tilting the scales in favor of the fixer-uppers. With the spiraling costs of land and building materials, the expense of constructing a new house has doubled in the last decade. The increased focus on achieving higher urban population densities and maintaining the urban growth boundaries are other important factors. But if you are looking for a fixer-upper, plan on doing some research before making any financial commitments. Check out several neighborhoods and talk to a few different Realtors about promising residential areas. Compare schools, property values, and the quality of the nearby roads. If you like a place in the daytime, go back at night and look around. Problems and noise often come out after respectable people pull their shades. For great inside information, check with longtime residents; they often provide a wealth of information and are good sources because they have no vested interest in a property transaction. Ask lots of questions, never assume anything, and don't be satisfied with a single opinion. The main challenge may be to find a house with no major structural problems, but you'll also want to live in a safe, clean area with decent neighbors. Remember, even if you fall in love with a house, never, never sign anything binding until the property is checked out by a qualified inspector, and make sure your inspector has a license.

While there are plenty of new houses in the suburbs, you can find pristine new construction in the inner core too: the Pearl District and the South Waterfront District are still building new lofts, condominiums, and row houses. And you will find attractive new construction in North Portland in the Boise-Eliot neighborhoods and in Southeast on Hawthorne and Division.

Older Portland Houses

Older sections in many of the charming inner-city neighborhoods feature Victorian, English Tudor, bungalow, or old Portland houses along streets lined with 100-year-old trees. Here we give a description of these typical Portland houses.

CLASSICAL VICTORIANS

These are the "beautiful painted ladies," featuring solid wood trim, hardwood floors, and ornate cedar shingle siding and roofs. The ornate two- or three-story houses, built

mostly between 1875 and 1910, are found all around the Portland Metro area, especially in the inner Northwest and Southeast neighborhoods. The charming and cozy Victorians can present challenges everywhere from their stone foundations to the hand pattern-cut roofs, and complications in these unique houses also frequently arise in plumbing, heating, and electrical upgrades. In addition, many Victorians are framed with 20-foot-long 2x4s so additional studs and fireblocking must be added.

CRAFTSMAN BUNGALOWS

Stone or brick foundations and large porches with battered columns are hallmarks of these houses, which were built from the turn of the 20th century to just before World War II. Low-pitched roofs, wide, overhanging eaves, and exposed roof rafters are distinctive features of these high-quality and sturdy houses. A mix of wood and brick exterior and wood shingle or composition roofs, these structures seldom present serious problems. Still, basement seepage often occurs—it is Oregon, after all—and electrical and plumbing upgrades are commonly required.

PORTLAND FOUR-SQUARE

These two-story, one roofline structures, known as "Old Portland–style" houses, were mostly built between 1910 and 1935. They may retain their original lighting fixtures, molding, and built-in cabinetry, though many of them went through unfortunate "modernization" in the 1970s and 1980s. Usually sitting on a hand-poured concrete foundation, these solid houses feature huge front porches. Though crafted with the best timber money can buy, such houses often require major kitchen renovations, insulation, and weatherization. Check to make sure the electrical system is up to date.

COLONIAL REVIVAL

Elegance and classic lines define Portland's colonial revival houses, built between 1910 and 1955. Concrete foundations, wood frames, and full basements, along with temple entry, stately pillars or columns, and a gabled roof, are their hallmarks. These two-story, wood-frame houses—often located in the city's finer neighborhoods—are also rich with moldings and trim, cornices, and elegant, small, paneled windows. Beware of lead plumbing that must be replaced with copper. Also, the colonial revival house often needs weatherizing, and because of their symmetry, additions are problematic.

WESTERN RANCH

Footings or slab foundations, all-wood frames, and composition roofs are characteristic of this type of sprawling one-level house. Of course, these popular houses are still being built, but their real heyday was between 1950 and 1960. Overall, the ranch houses present few problems; still, windows and roofs often need repairs, and interestingly, basement conversions are a popular improvement. The most flexible of all housing styles, ranches pose few limitations for vertical or horizontal additions.

NORTHWEST CONTEMPORARY

Solid concrete foundations, wood frames, and oversize two- or three-car garages typify these houses, built from the 1960s to the present. Vaulted ceilings, "great rooms," dramatically pitched roofs, heavy beams and timbers, and lots of glass lend character to these versatile two-story structures some critics refer to as "McMansions." Generally, the Northwest-style houses have fewer complications with electrical and plumbing upgrades, but be on the lookout for shoddy construction and materials, especially when it comes to siding. Windows with blown seals are a common headache, and inferior craftsmanship and construction materials can result in warped walls, squeaky floors, and worse. Also, most of these houses have little interior architectural detail; that you'll have to do yourself.

New Portland Houses

If you are interested in building a new house, choose your builder carefully and get plenty of information. You can start by calling the **Home Builders Association** at (503) 684-1880, or visit their really useful and well-linked website, **www.home-buildersportland.org.** Talk to your pickiest neighbors to see who they liked. Ask for written bids, get every detail of the project in writing, and have a lawyer take a look at any contract (and keep the original contract!). Don't make large down payments, and wait until after the inspection to make your final payment. Make sure contracting licenses are up-to-date and contractors are insured. Ask for references, call them, and if possible, have a look at the work itself. And remember, you get what you pay for. Look really carefully at low bids—they might be fine, but they also might reflect a misunderstanding about the work or a lack of experience with your kind of project.

NEIL KELLY CO.
804 North Alberta St.
(503) 288-7461
15573 Southwest Bangy Rd.
www.neilkelly.com

RELOCATION

This top remodeling firm is worth a special mention because of its ability to combine profitable business practices with good ecological thinking and loyal ties to its North Portland neighborhood. The founder, Neil Kelly, had an eighth-grade education and rode the rails during the Depression, but he created a true Horatio Alger story with this company in the heart of North Portland. Today, his son, Tom, is carrying on the family legacy. Their business practices are efficient and responsible and dedicated to accountability. The company is committed to using sustainable woods and other components designed to promote responsible resource consumption. House repair "teams," consisting of a carpenter, sales estimator, and general contractor, run many projects but may be a single person wearing all hats—with one person handling everything, there is less overhead and no one else to blame for delays, cost overruns, and mistakes. Neil Kelly Co. and its employees have received many awards for community involvement and industry leadership, among them the designation as a "Founder of a New Northwest" by the Sustainable Northwest organization, a 2010 Oregon Ethics in Business award, honors as one of the best green businesses to work for, and the Better Business Bureau's 1998 Business Integrity Award. And its philosophy and high-quality work have paid off: Neil Kelly is one of the most successful contracting companies in the Northwest. They have an entire division devoted to assessing and improving your house from a "systems" perspective—light, heat, air, and so on—and they offer many seminars on a variety of topics. One of the few all-union general contractors in the area, for the past several years Neil Kelley has been named one of the best 100 companies to work for by *Oregon Business* magazine.

STREET OF DREAMS
Home Builders Association of
Metropolitan Portland
(503) 684-1880
www.streetofdreamspdx.com/home/
home.php

Builders showcases have proliferated across the land, but ours was the first! The Street of Dreams started in 1976; each year a new development is built to spotlight the latest, most mouthwatering trends in home design. The popular Street of Dreams is the place where home owners learn that two dishwashers are ever so much more convenient than one or that granite floors are not just attractive but absolutely critical. We're waiting for the houses run entirely by fuel cell, and until then, we'll take the yearly tour with covetous pleasure. And we're not alone—the summertime exhibit draws more than 80,000 people. Moreover, the Street of Dreams is a fund-raiser for Doernbecher's Children's Hospital. For several years the particularly generous firm of Wallace Custom Homes has donated time, materials, and labor to create the Miracle House, the proceeds of which benefit the hospital. Who said nothing good ever came from envy?

i If you don't know what your tenant rights are, or if you have questions in general, call the Renter's Rights Hotline at (503) 288-0130 or check them out online at http://oregon-cat.org. This hotline is hosted by the Community Alliance of Tenants, a grass-roots group dedicated to promoting fairness for you, the renter. They have experts who can help you with advice as well as information and referrals.

Condominiums & Row Houses

Portland also offers a wide variety of condominiums and row houses. Although condo living isn't for everyone, many people who can't afford their dream house can still get into a very nice condo for much less and make a great investment. Key assets include what many condo dwellers call easy living: quick access to city shopping and employment, low maintenance, and no grass to mow, trees to prune, or snow to shovel. However, they all have dues associated with them, so be sure you understand what you are getting into.

In some aspects the whole city benefits from the condominium phenomenon, which promotes the concept of the Urban Growth Boundary and higher population density in the city, particularly along the main transportation corridors. Condos increase the number of owner-occupied houses, which many neighborhoods assume is a big plus because they bring stability, so in the long run, condos can increase property values for all.

In Portland, you'll find some condominiums that have been converted from large houses or from older apartment complexes. You will also find modern, upscale developments featuring recreation facilities and health clubs. In downtown areas such as Goose Hollow and the Pearl District, many of the old warehouses are being converted into light, airy, and very stylish lofts.

Apartments

The Portland Metropolitan area offers a wide variety of apartments in diverse areas, designs, and price ranges. Residents can choose large apartment complexes offering security and health clubs or tiny efficiency apartments. Finding the right apartment can be challenging, especially if you are on a tight budget, but there truly is something for everyone. Apartment seekers may find downtown or the Northwest area highly competitive. However, if you are able to live in different areas such as St. Johns or outer Southeast, you increase your options immensely. One tip from Susan Marthens, a relocation expert and Realtor at Windermere, is to look at the ratings for the schools in the neighborhood you're interested in. If the schools are good, the community is probably stable. You can find state report cards for all schools at www.ode.state.or.us/data/reportcard/reports.aspx, and her excellent website at www.movingtoportland.net/index.html.

As of this writing, the rental market is in flux. Many luxury condominium complexes that were started during the real estate boom have been converted to apartments as the boom has gone bust, increasing supply. Yet at the same time, more people are looking to rent, not wanting to—or unable to—buy. Thus, move-in expenses for a single person, including rent and damage deposits, can easily total $1,000. On the east side, a simple studio may range in cost from $500 to $700, and a two-bedroom apartment may cost anywhere from $550 to $1,500. On the west side, a similar studio ranges from $600 to $800, and a two-bedroom apartment, from $650 to $2,000. Still, the rental market is not as tight as it is in some other cities.

The Sunday *Oregonian* is a good place to start an apartment search because the information is so current. *Willamette Week*, which is published every Wednesday, also has a very good rental section. *For Rent* magazine is another resource; it's available for free at many local supermarkets and in little kiosks in urban neighborhoods. Even just thumbing through the pages will help you get a feel for what is available in the Portland area, but be forewarned—most of the listings are really advertisements taken out by developers, so if you rely too heavily on this publication, you will not get a complete picture of the rental scene. Still, it can be useful for comparison purposes, and you may find a perfectly lovely apartment. But your best bet is to search Craig's List (www .portland.craigslist.org) and buy a copy of the *Oregonian*. You can also walk around in neighborhoods you'd like to live in and look for for rent signs and moving vans.

Other Kinds of Housing

Alternative and Co-Housing

In addition to conventional housing, the Portland scene has several communities of houseboats nestled along the Willamette and Columbia Rivers. These floating houses, for rent and for sale, are ideal for avid water enthusiasts and for people who want to simplify. You can even fish out of, and tie your boat to, your front door. And there are no lawns to mow. Co-housing is a national movement in which people form intentional communities that reflect their values, and as such, they are very Portland. Several communities have formed in the area in the past decade. Ask your Realtor about houseboats and check out the co-housing information at www.cohousing.org.

Temporary Housing

Temporary housing facilities vary from elegant suites to family units with kitchens to bed-and-breakfasts in historic mansions to bare-but-clean motel rooms. Craigslist and Vacation-Rental-By-Owner are good places to start (see the Accommodations chapter), or you can try the old standbys of the Marriott Residence Inn (www.marriott.com/ residence-inn/travel.mi) or the Oakwood. (www.oakwood.com/corporate-apartments/ US/OR/Portland.html). Of course, if you are already in contact with a real estate agent, the firm's relocation department may be able to provide a list of temporary lodging facilities.

Student Housing

The state's largest college, Portland Community College, offers no student housing. Portland State University, the University of Portland, Marylhurst College, Reed College, and Lewis & Clark College all encourage full-time students to take advantage of dormitories. The student housing tends to fill up fast, and if you are planning to attend college in Portland, you should get on the housing list as soon as possible. In most cases you must register for classes first. The housing, for the most part, is first come, first serve, and the nicer accommodations go fast. There is a tremendous amount of development activity around Portland State University's blossoming University District, so more housing is available. Some students who prefer to live off campus team up with their peers and share two- or three-bedroom apartments or houses. Many families or property owners who rent out rooms or efficiency apartment to students advertise on bulletin boards near the student unions or other popular meeting places. Wherever you decide to live, keep in mind that automobile parking is a huge hassle for students, so bicycles, buses, and light rail are popular options.

Buying a House

Help for First-Time Buyers
PORTLAND HOUSING CENTER
3233 Northeast Sandy Blvd.
(503) 282-7744
www.portlandhousingcenter.org
Buying a house is the biggest, most important investment that most people make in their lives, and jumping through all those hoops can be a complicated and frustrating process. If you are a first-time house buyer, you may be eligible for help. Through the combined efforts of the federal government, Multnomah County, and the city of Portland, the Portland Housing Center offers counseling and first-time-buyer programs that can help you overcome such barriers as financing and credit problems. This program also offers classes in first-time house buying, and as many as 600 individuals each year benefit from the services. If you qualify financially, it doesn't matter whether you are new to the area or have lived here all your life. Give the Portland Housing Center a call. Their well-trained, informed, and courteous staff can often do a preliminary screening over the telephone, and they also offer comprehensive information and referral services.

Realtors
For people relocating to a new area, one of the first and most important contacts is their real estate agent. Most of the larger real estate companies have relocation departments dedicated to making your move easier. These specialists have a good working knowledge of the area, neighborhoods, schools, and commute routes. It is important that you get along with your agent and establish a good working relationship. Be sure to ask about his or her experience with the kind of house you are looking for—and especially with the neighborhood you are interested in. Agents tend to specialize in neighborhoods, so look for an agent with the right expertise. Be prepared to answer lots of questions about your lifestyle, the type and size of house you want, and your price range. Armed with the right information, these professional house and apartment finders can start the hunt for you before you arrive and can sometimes help arrange temporary housing. You can also ask them to help you get preapproved financing, but you may be better off seeking an independent source. For more information on selecting a real estate agent, contact the **Portland Board of Realtors** at (503) 228-6595. Listed below are some of the area's agencies; many of them have offices citywide, in addition to the branches we have included here.

SOUTHWEST PORTLAND

THE HASSON COMPANY
10960 Southwest Barnes Rd.
(503) 643-9898
www.hasson.com

JOHN L. SCOTT REALTY
5457 Southwest Canyon Court
West Hills
(503) 291-1900

OREGON REALTY
8552 Southwest Apple Way
(503) 297-2523
oregonrealty.com

RE/MAX—EQUITY GROUP
8405 Southwest Nimbus Ave., Suite C
(503) 670-3000

1260 Northwest Waterhouse Ave.
Beaverton
(503) 680-1221
www.equitygroup.com

WINDERMERE CRONIN & CAPLAN REALTY GROUP, INC.
6443 Southwest Beaverton–Hillsdale Hwy.
(Raleigh Hills)
(503) 297-1033
www.windermereportland.com

NORTHWEST PORTLAND

COLDWELL BANKER BARBARA SUE SEAL
2275 West Burnside St.
(503) 224-7325
www.cbseal.com

HASSON
22 Northwest 23rd Place
(503) 228-9801
www.hasson.com

HOYT STREET REALTY
1130 Northwest 10th Ave.
(503) 227-2000
www.hoytliving.com

REALTY TRUST
1220 Northwest Lovejoy St., Suite 130
(503) 294-1101
www.realtytrust.com

WINDERMERE CRONIN & CAPLAN REALTY
733 Northwest 20th Ave.
(503) 220-1144
www.windermere.com

SOUTHEAST PORTLAND

HANNA REALTY
9415 Southeast Stark
(503) 774-8893
www.hannanetwork.com

JOHN L. SCOTT REAL ESTATE
4111 Southeast Woodstock Blvd.
(503) 775-4699
www.johnlscott.com

MT. TABOR REALTY
6838 Southeast Belmont St.
(503) 252-9653
www.mttaborrealty.com

PORTLAND'S ALTERNATIVE REALTORS
3144 Southeast Belmont St.
(503) 234-3456
www.climbatree.com

REALTY TRUST
5012 Southeast Hawthorne Blvd.
(503) 232-4763
www.realtytrust.com/jancaplener

SOCOLOFSKY/GMAC
3828 Southeast Division St.
(503) 234-1502
www.socolofskygmac.com

WINDERMERE REAL ESTATE, MORELAND
1610 Southeast Bybee Blvd.
(503) 233-7777
www.windermereportland.com

NORTH & NORTHEAST PORTLAND

DAVID D. JONES—RE/MAX EQUITY GROUP
237 Northeast Broadway
(503) 287-8989
www.equitygroup.com

ERA FREEMAN & ASSOCIATES REALTORS
1122 Northeast 122nd St.
(503) 256-0220
www.eraglobal.com

LAURELHURST REALTY
3046 Northeast Glisan St.
(503) 232-6750
www.laurelhurstrealty.com

REALTY TRUST
3902 Northeast Sandy Blvd.
(503) 416-2000
www.realtytrust.com

TOWNSHIP PROPERTIES INC.
4122 Northeast Broadway
(503) 281-8891

WINDERMERE CRONIN & CAPLAN
   REALTY
825 Northeast Multnomah Blvd.
(503) 284-7755
www.windermereportland.com

VANCOUVER & OUTLYING AREAS

COLDWELL BANKER
14201 Northeast 20th Ave.,
Vancouver, WA
(360) 574-4600

8101 Northeast Pkwy.,
Vancouver, WA
(360) 892-7325

HASSON
15400 Southwest Boones Ferry Rd.,
Lake Oswego
(503) 635-9801
www.hasson.com

OREGON REALTY
12901 Southeast 97th Ave., Clackamas
(503) 652-2260

1124 Northeast Burnside St., Gresham
(503) 661-7344
www.oregonrealty.com

PRUDENTIAL NORTHWEST
   PROPERTIES
5 Centerpointe Dr., Suite 150,
Lake Oswego
(503) 624-9660
www.homejones.net

10002 Northeast 13th Ave.,
Vancouver, WA
(360) 256-1120
www.pru-nw.com

WESTLAKE PROPERTIES
21420 Willamette Dr., West Linn
(503) 656-0323
www.westlakepropertiesonline.com

CHILD CARE & EDUCATION

Portland's solid sense of community, reinforced by consistently high marks for its quality of life, makes it a fine place to raise a family. But even here, child care can be difficult to find, especially for infants and toddlers, and choosing a school causes much soul-searching among parents of future kindergarteners and of families moving into the area. Parents are often bewildered by the number of decisions they must make in choosing the nature and scope of their children's care and education. To make those decisions easier, we survey the territory for you. And you may also be interested in other local resources. Two free publications, Metro Parent and Portland Family, offer regular updates on child-care facilities in the area and on local schools. Another good source is Portland Monthly, which compiles extensive data from the state on local public and private schools. And informal networks through community centers, libraries, religious organizations, and word of mouth can put parents in touch with good caregivers and schools.

CHILD CARE

State Programs & Initiatives

The Oregon Commission for Child Care; OCCC; www.oregon.gov/employ/ccc, an advisory board to the governor, studies the issues concerning the development of accessible, affordable, and high-quality child care and makes legislative recommendations based on its findings. The OCCC has become a major player on these issues since its inception in 1985, and one of its major successes has been the creation of a program for child-care resource and referral, the Child Care Division of the Oregon Employment Department. This division certifies child-care centers through criminal history checks and inspections of facilities. It also registers family child-care businesses, though it does not inspect them. (Family child-care providers are still required to undergo criminal background checks and a certain amount of training.) The division sponsors mentoring and training programs for providers, working closely with the Center for Career Development in Childhood Care and Education at Portland State University.

Child Care Resource & Referral Network

The Child Care Division of the Oregon Employment Department has also developed the Child Care Resource and Referral (CCR&R) agencies (www.oregonchildcare .org). These community-based agencies strive to provide all parents with as much information and as many options for quality child care as possible. The CCR&R agencies direct parents toward resources for child-care screening as well as to other community resources, including child-care provider support groups. Although the CCR&R programs are extremely busy, and you must leave a message on a recording, they generally return calls within a reasonable amount of time and are quite helpful. CCR&R staff are knowledgeable and will answer questions about a wide range of topics and dispense information about child-care accreditation, local workshops for providers, and information about scholarships to help cover training and accreditation fees. Your local CCR&R representative can also meet with you and provide a personal consultation to address concerns about your child-care situation, health and safety matters, child development issues, activities for children, and even technical information regarding business development, taxes, and zoning. CCR&R resources are considerable, including a lending library of videos, books, toys, and equipment, so don't be afraid to ask for help or advice. Check the website to find the one nearest you.

Work and school may help you with your child-care needs. Since Oregon gives employers good tax breaks when they subsidize child care, many employers keep their workers happy by offering this benefit. If you're still working on your degree, Portland Community College (www.pcc.edu/resources/child-care) and Portland State University (www.hgcdc.pdx.edu) campuses have lovely, though limited, child-care programs for students and staff. Likewise, some employers offer some childcare subsidies or discounts. Check with your benefits office to see your options.

Child Care Providers

Finding someone to care for your child can be remarkably stressful, but surveying the territory will make things a little easier. Regardless of what option seems to best suit your needs, you should start your search for child care early. A range of care is available, but a lot of other parents are looking for qualified help for their child-care needs, and waiting lists are not unusual. It takes time to find the right person or center for your child and your family.

Doulas & Early Care

Child care begins early for some of us. Many Portland parents find the transition to their new roles goes more smoothly with the help of a doula, a professional family helper who provides nonmedical assistance to new parents at home. Doulas may show anxious parents how to hold, bathe, dress, and feed the new little one; they may take care of the house or older siblings; they may aid with nursing; in general, they help to keep things peaceful and calm. Since hospital stays for postpartum women are notoriously abbreviated, a doula could be just the person to ease you through the surprise of new parenthood. You can find doulas in a variety of places. Your ob-gyn may have some contacts, and midwives are very good sources; often midwifery practices include them on staff.

Sometimes all you need is the support of other parents. Hospitals and health-care organizations will often run programs for new parents and their infants. Hosted by nurses or other health-care professionals, these free or low-cost forums allow you to ask questions about breast-feeding, child development, and other issues. Just hanging out with the other parents is comforting, especially when you find out they all feel the same way that you do. Check with your hospital or HMO to see whether they offer such programs, and on the web look in the Craig's List community section under Child Care, where parent support groups may be listed as well as discussion forums for parents (http://portland.craigslist.org/). And don't forget the power of the spoken word: Most of the people we know found their groups informally, through their childbirth education classes, friends of friends, story time at the library, the baby swings at the park, the Baby Gap store at the mall, or interesting conversations about baby acne at the local Starbucks. Later, when the babies get bigger, these groups are invaluable resources for setting up casual babysitting co-ops.

Nannies

If you read the *New York Times,* you might worry that hiring a nanny will require you to sign away not just your first-born child but his or her entire inheritance. However, this is still Oregon, and while nannies are expensive, they are still affordable for many families. In fact, nanny care is growing in popularity, for it may be the least disruptive to the family. Nannies can be full- or part-time; they can live in your house or in their own; they can be temporary or long-term. Nannies have widely varying responsibilities and duties, such as housework, meal preparation, and picking the children up from school and driving them to sports or extra-curricular functions. You should make it clear what duties the job entails and spell them out in a contract.

Two good sources for nannies are Northwest Nannies and Care Givers Placement Agency. Contact Northwest Nannies at (503) 245-5288 or www.nwnanny.com. You can reach Care Givers Placement Agency at (503) 244-6370 or online at www.cgpa.com. Both agencies can find you temporary or permanent full- or part-time help. Care Givers will also help you find temporary emergency child care; contact them in advance, if you think you might be subject to emergencies, to see how their system works. While the nannies we have known have been trustworthy, reliable, and resourceful, nannies are not licensed in Oregon; going through an agency may afford you some protection since the agency screens the applicants and expects them to have some training. If you want to take on the job of performing background checks yourself, however, Craig's List (www.portland.craigslist.org) can be a fantastic resource for finding child-care help.

Day-Care Centers & Family Care

Day-care centers are open 52 weeks a year, are licensed by the state, and are usually staffed with a number of teachers who are supervised by a director. They can charge up to several thousand dollars per month for full-time care, depending on the scope and number of children you enroll. Care-giver–child ratios are strict and vary with the age of the child. Day-care centers are becoming increasingly specialized and are more competitive than ever. These centers, which according to state law must provide at least 35 square feet of space per child, can be quite large and usually offer lots of recreational and educational activities to help children acquire new skills as they burn off their seemingly endless supply of energy. There are hundreds of day-care facilities in the area. Many families choose one close to either home or work, but wherever you live and work, you'll have to sort through the facilities to find one that coheres with your outlook on things. As you might expect, the kind of care and theory behind it varies widely; we have pretty much everything here, from Waldorf-based philosophies to Montessori philosophies to Piaget's philosophies, and everything in between. Many day cares incorporate religious themes. Some of the nationally known chains that operate in Portland are the Learning Tree, Kindercare, La Petite Academy, and Children's World, but there are many locally grown centers for you to probe.

i Saturday Academy (503-725-2330; www.saturdayacademy.pdx.edu) is an award-winning, innovative enrichment program for kids in grades 4 through 12. Area professionals share their labs, equipment, and expertise to teach hands-on experimentation and critical thinking in science, math, writing, and other subjects. Saturday Academy has won seven National Science Foundation grants among other honors. Scholarships are available.

In-home, or, as the state refers to it, "family" day care, is ubiquitous throughout Oregon and involves taking your child to someone's home for care. In-home day-care operations must be registered with the state and can provide care for up to 10 children at a time. Be sure that you check the qualifications of anyone you hire to care for your children in his or her home and ask to see the paperwork. As with day-care centers, strict requirements for ratios of caregivers to children apply. Also, operators and employees must undergo criminal background checks, and new training requirements demand that they have an overview session, are trained in CPR, maintain a food handler's certification, and are trained to prevent child abuse and neglect. They must also carry household insurance. The Child Care Resource and Referral network listed above can refer you to providers.

Extended-Care & Summer Programs

Many Portland schools, both public and private, offer extended-care programs after and before school for children whose parents have incompatible work schedules, and these programs often run during school breaks as well. The public schools have contracts with 18 state-certified, nonprofit providers, who run programs in 62 elementary schools. Two additional schools have child care within a safe walking distance (that is, a distance that could be covered by a child in kindergarten). Your child's school can give you information about these programs, or you can call the Portland Public Schools Child Care coordinator at (503) 916-3230.

In addition to extended care within the schools, you'll find other weekday programs that take care of children until their parents can. Boys and Girls Clubs are helpful in this regard; they have four clubs in the area and run summer programs in addition to their extended-care programs. Their administrative office in Southeast Portland, at 7119 Southeast Milwaukie, (503) 232-0077, is a well-equipped facility that keeps kids busy with all kinds of wholesome activity, from basketball to photography. The number for the club is (503) 238-6868. Other locations include the Wattles Club, 9330 Harold St., (503) 775-1549; the Blazers' Boys and Girls Club, 5250 Northeast Martin Luther King Jr. Blvd., (503) 282-8480; and in Hillsboro, at 560 Southeast 3rd Ave., (503) 640-4558. You can find them online at www.bgcportland.org.

The YMCA of Columbia-Willamette has 10 regional centers and a number of in-school programs for child care, education, and extended care. The YMCA offers flexible and affordable day care and does a great job of keeping youngsters involved in stimulating and challenging activities. These fully licensed and well-staffed centers are conveniently located on both sides of the river and offer full- or part-time options for busy parents. In addition, the YMCA manages a half-dozen Child Development Centers for six-week old infants up to five-year-old children. As an added bonus, members of their child-care programs receive a 25 to 75 percent reduction in monthly membership dues at any YMCA Fitness Facility with the joining fee waived. You can reach them at (503) 327-0007 or www.ymca-portland.org.

Portland Parks and Recreation and summer day camps, both covered in the Kidstuff chapter, can also help you take care of your child. Summer day camps are a popular form of "child care." Devoted to activities such as basketball, dance, computer or language training, art lessons, theater, monitoring baby animals at the Oregon Zoo, or an array of other things, they provide care for the kids and peace of mind for their parents. *Metro Family* publishes a multipart guide to camps, and camps themselves sponsor a big exhibition, the Summer Camp and Vacation Show, at the Convention Center in the spring. Finally, Portland Parks and Rec sponsors many after-school and school-break programs throughout the city. These offerings change regularly and vary according to the season; they range from acrobatics to Zen flower arrangement. Download a catalog at www.portlandonline.com/parks.

EDUCATION

Philosophers tell us that there is no education without growth. Oregonians have seen a lot of growth in the past decade—and

that has influenced education and been an education in itself. The institutions devoted to education have also had to contend with growth. As a result they are multifaceted and diverse—they include state and private universities, community colleges, and public and private elementary, middle, and high schools.

The metro area has more than 200 public schools and a robust selection of private institutions. In both public and private schools, you may find a selection of special-needs facilities as well as experimental settings where students are challenged in different ways, from learning other languages to designing business plans. The schools in Oregon are generally well regarded, despite recent and ongoing fiscal trials. It's a testament to parents and teachers alike that the public schools remain strong in spite of the financial turmoil. Portland is also the home of Portland State University, one of seven universities run by the Oregon University System, as well as the site of a commendable list of private colleges. Among these are Reed College, Lewis & Clark, Marylhurst College, and the University of Portland. And Oregon Health and Science University holds a significant place in the Portland skyline. It is devoted to teaching and training medical professionals and research scientists, and it is responsible for innovative research in the fight against cancer and other diseases.

Community colleges play a major role in the area's educational scene. Indeed, Portland Community College has more students than any other college in the state. All the community colleges offer a broad range of programs for a broader range of students, whose reasons for attending are various and idiosyncratic. You will find newly graduated high school students who plan to transfer to a four-year college, students wishing to earn their high school diplomas, students returning to college after a number of years, students who are pursuing some kind of professional training, and students who just want to take a sculpture class or two. Besides Portland Community College, which has satellite campus sites around the area, you will also find Mount Hood Community College in Gresham, Clackamas Community College in Southeast Portland, and Clark College in Vancouver.

This section presents a snapshot of schools and colleges in the area, divided into two further sections, K–12 and Higher Education. The K–12 section is organized alphabetically into elementary, middle, and high schools, and multigrade schools in the Portland area and beyond. The Higher Education section begins with universities and four-year colleges then covers community colleges and vocational training.

K–12 Education

Ninety percent of area residents send their children to public schools, making Portland Public Schools one of the few remaining intact urban school systems, despite constant budget pressures. Changing demographic information also places pressure on the schools, for even as the area balloons in population, many families moving into the area choose the suburbs, and current projections predict enrollment declines for city schools. Although Portland's population is increasing, many new urban residents are young and childless or retired with grown children. Thus, the state legislature has pushed Portland Public Schools to cut costs, and Portland Public Schools have suffered budget cuts. These have resulted in fewer teachers, librarians, and counselors, fewer

electives, ailing physical plants, and pressure to increase the student-to-teacher ratio.

Across Oregon, school budgets have been hit hard by recent economic trends. The Portland Public School system in particular has gained national notoriety for its budget troubles, especially after it looked as though more than a month would have to be cut from the school year. Attracting less notice, however, was the way that the citizens of Portland came together to support the schools. Teachers worked for free for 10 days, while local businesses accepted a small tax increase and voters in the county agreed to a temporary tax raise to protect the schools, restore the school year, and leave programs intact. Our troubles are not over, but the faith that we have in our schools creates hope and sends the message that a creative response to problems is possible.

Like all urban school districts, Portland has its share of challenges, especially as the national debate about No Child Left Behind and other benchmarking and testing rages on. Nevertheless, Portland schools have many strengths. They are sometimes less crowded than suburban schools. A number of schools have become the nexus for dynamic neighborhood and community development. In 1999 Multnomah County introduced a program called SUN Schools. "SUN" is an acronym for Schools Uniting Neighborhoods, and the idea behind it is to use the schools, which are natural gathering places for families, to serve their communities even more thoroughly. In this program buildings open early and stay open late to act as neighborhood centers that provide health clinics, computer labs, entertainment, or other activities for residents. They have become important neighborhood centers, points of contact that total more than the sum of their parts.

The SUN Schools program is just one of the innovative programs designed to solve persistent school-funding and other education-related troubles. Another is the charter school law, passed in 1999. This bill allows Oregon to apply for federal charter school development funds. Charter schools are independently run public schools that are taxpayer funded. They are free to set their own curricula and rules of operation. If the charter school produces students whose performances don't meet academic standards, the school's charter can be revoked and the school could be closed. There are a number of charter schools in Portland. Three established programs are the Opal School at CM2 (503-471-9917, www.opalschool .org), which opened in 2001 and has an arts-centered curriculum; Trillium (503-285-3833, www.trilliumcharterschool.org), which opened in 2002 and focuses on a curriculum of urban and global studies, serving K–12 students; and the Emerson School (503-525-6124, www.emersonschool.org), which focuses on project-based learning in real-world settings. Charter schools in Oregon have had a bit of a rocky start, but their founders remain undaunted and new ones are being added every year. For a complete list of Portland charter schools, look online at www.pps.k12.or.us/departments/education-options/index.htm .

The number of Portland-area schools is high enough to demand numerous school districts (see listing in this chapter). The largest is Portland Public Schools (School District 1J), a prekindergarten through twelfth-grade district with about 100 schools and 50 special-needs sites. Listed here are a few selected public and private schools in the Portland Metro area. We're highlighting schools with distinctive approaches to education such as arts or science programs or language immersion schools where students speak to each other and their teachers in a foreign language for half of their time at school. We've grouped the schools into elementary, middle, high, and multigrade schools, and we've sorted them further by whether they're public or private. Since parents may choose to send their children across town, schools are listed alphabetically rather than geographically.

i Those schooled at home have many resources available in the Portland area. City parks and recreation programs give supervised instruction in sports and other activities just for homeschoolers—even prom. Call them at (503) 823-7529 for more information. And check out Homeschoolers in Portland, a Yahoo group for pooling resources and bolstering you with moral support: http://groups.yahoo .com/group/HIP_list.

Elementary Schools
PUBLIC ELEMENTARY SCHOOL PROGRAMS

Portland does have a flexible school choice policy, but unless you live within the boundaries for your chosen school, you'll have to apply for an administrative transfer. You can get the paperwork from the school that you are designated to attend. Special programs within schools may have their own application processes; contact the schools for more information. The Portland Public Schools website will let you know your designated neighborhood school, as well as link you to the websites of neighborhoods and others schools and programs: www.pps.k12.or.us.

BUCKMAN ELEMENTARY SCHOOL: ARTS MAGNET PROGRAM

320 Southeast 16th Ave.
(503) 916-6230

Buckman has an award-winning arts program that incorporates dance, drama, visual arts, and music into the regular curriculum. Students are encouraged to use their artistic gifts to devise interdisciplinary approaches to research projects and other academic work. The student body is astonishingly diverse, with about 10 different languages heard in the halls. The teachers are also diverse, and make use of the "multiple intelligences" approach to learning. Families are deeply involved in this beloved school.

Language Immersion Programs

In a modern world of global awareness, the Portland School System gives its students a chance to learn about cultures through immersion in their languages. Immensely successful, these language immersion elementary schools are taught half in English and half in a foreign language. The special schooling gives students not only second language competency, but also a greater cultural understanding and proficiency by grade five. These programs operate as separate schools within schools, and students must apply to get into all of them. Requirements and activities may vary in each program. For instance, children who wish to attend the immersion program at Richmond Elementary must start as kindergartners, unless they are from Japan or have lived in Japan up to the time of registration. Immersion programs include Spanish, Mandarin, Russian, and Japanese. Check the Portland Public School website for a list of all the immersion programs: www.pps.k12.or.us/schools-c/find_your_school.php.

PRIVATE ELEMENTARY SCHOOL PROGRAMS

CEDARWOOD WALDORF SCHOOL

3030 Southwest 2nd Ave.
(503) 245-1477
www.cedarwoodschool.org

Cedarwood School, with 125 students, is based on the Waldorf philosophy; it is in the process of acquiring full Waldorf accreditation. They provide prekindergarten through eighth grade education, with much attention to the arts, as well as Spanish and Japanese. The school is just south of downtown, in the Lair Hill neighborhood, making it convenient for commuting parents.

FRENCH AMERICAN SCHOOL

8500 Northwest Johnson St.
(503) 292-7776
www.faispdx.org

Since 1979 the French American School has been immersing students in the language of diplomats, and its graduates have gone on to great successes in Portland and far beyond. The school is devoted to academic rigor, a nurturing environment, and small class sizes. There are 440 students in the school, but this number includes Gilkey Middle School. The elementary school serves prekindergarten through fifth-grade students.

THE INTERNATIONAL SCHOOL

25 Southwest Sherman St.
(503) 226-2496
http://intlschool.org

The International School, which teaches 235 children ages three through grade five, offers full-immersion programs that nurture as well as challenge students. The school focuses on traditional academic areas in its small classes (the average student-to-teacher ratio is nine to two). Languages taught at the

International School include Chinese, Japanese, and Spanish.

WHOLE CHILD MONTESSORI CENTER
5904 Southeast 40th Ave.
(503) 771-6366
www.wholechildmontessori.org
One of a number of Montessori schools in the Portland area, Whole Child is distinguished by its excellent teachers and its beautiful children's garden. Whole Child teaches preschoolers through kindergartners; their graduates are remarkably well prepared for the first grade. Children are encouraged to follow their intellectual paths on their own, but in an atmosphere of supportive preparation that enables the children to effectively teach themselves. The well designed garden, with its evergreens, flowers, bridges, paths, and perennials, makes a wonderful place for children to roam safely and freely, reconnecting their modern little minds to their bodies.

Middle Schools
PUBLIC MIDDLE SCHOOL PROGRAMS

DA VINCI ARTS MIDDLE SCHOOL
2508 Northeast Everett St.
(503) 916-5356
This public middle school, founded by a group of parents in 1996, serves 300 students who come from the entire metropolitan area. It's an arts magnet, and students must apply to get in; classes are a mix of age groups. Besides special instruction in visual arts, dance, music, theater, and writing, the school requires rigorous academic classes infused with aesthetic principles.

HARRIET TUBMAN MIDDLE SCHOOL
2231 North Flint Ave.
(503) 916-5630

Harriet Tubman Middle School has a special, interdisciplinary focus on the health sciences and biotechnology. It has formed community partnerships with, among others, Legacy Emanuel Hospital, Oregon Health and Science University, and the American Lung Association. Tubman students can work alongside research scientists and others from these organizations. Many electives, such as marine biology, are not available to middle school students elsewhere in the district.

PRIVATE MIDDLE SCHOOL PROGRAMS

GILKEY MIDDLE SCHOOL
8500 Northwest Johnson St.
(503) 292-9111
www.faispdx.org
Part of the French American School, this school provides bilingual education in German, French, and Spanish, but it also offers an international track in which no previous foreign language experience is required to attend. Small class sizes and an academically rigorous program are added features. (See the French American School, under Private Elementary School Programs, for more information.)

High Schools
PUBLIC HIGH SCHOOL PROGRAMS

Public high schools in the Portland area have been quietly developing innovative programs to ensure that students receive high-quality educations in a variety of modes and settings—perhaps another reason that the SAT scores of Oregonians are so good. Many of these programs accept students from other schools and even other districts, if they can meet the requirements and manage the bureaucracy of transfer.

BENSON HIGH SCHOOL
546 Northeast 12th Ave.
(503) 916-5100

Benson is highly regarded in Oregon for its professional and technical programs that take kids from school to work. After their sophomore year, students at Benson choose a major and supplement it with real-world experience in jobs and internships. It has been honored as a New Century School by the US Department of Education.

INTERNATIONAL BACCALAUREATE PROGRAM

The International Baccalaureate (IB) program is a demanding international college-prep program that tests students in six areas: language, second language, experimental sciences, social sciences and humanities, mathematics, and the arts. This program is more rigorous than programs based on multiple-choice tests; its graduates are skilled in higher-order reasoning and research, and their writing skills are highly prized by the colleges that accept them.

Schools that participate in the IB program are Cleveland High School (3400 Southeast 26th Ave.; 503-916-5120) and Lincoln High School (1600 Southwest Salmon; 503-916-5200) in the Portland School District. In Beaverton three schools participate: Beaverton (13000 Southwest 2nd St.; 503-259-5000), Sunset (13840 Northwest Cornell Rd.; 503-259-5050), and Southridge (9625 Southwest 125th Ave.; 503-259-5400). Suburban participants include Gresham High School (1200 North Main; 503-674-5500); Tigard High School (9000 Southwest Durham Rd.; 503-431-5400), and Tualatin High School (22300 Southwest Boones Ferry Rd.; 503-431-5600).

MERLO STATION HIGH SCHOOL– SCHOOL OF SCIENCE AND TECHNOLOGY
1841 Southwest Merlo Dr., Beaverton
(503) 259-5575

The School of Science and Technology (SST) routinely has the highest test scores in the state. This small special-focus program offers an outstanding and stimulating program that incorporates fieldwork and projects in its curriculum. It also has close alliances with businesses and colleges in the area. The program is built around the sciences, but it expects its graduates to be well rounded and therefore also has vigorous humanities requirements.

RIVERDALE HIGH SCHOOL
9727 Southwest Terwilliger St.
(503) 892-0722

Riverdale High School is a public school in a tiny district in Portland, but this small school's reputation is formidable, with always-outstanding test scores. Its challenging curriculum emphasizes preparing for college and almost every Riverdale graduate is also a college graduate. (Riverdale is also unusual in that it charges tuition—quite a lot of it.)

PRIVATE HIGH SCHOOL PROGRAMS

CENTRAL CATHOLIC HIGH SCHOOL
2401 Southeast Stark St.
(503) 235-3138
www.centralcatholichigh.org

Central Catholic High School, teaching grades 9 through 12, is a college-prep school that emphasizes moral and ethical training in addition to its academically challenging program. About 800 students attend.

NORTHWEST ACADEMY
1130 Southwest Main St.
(503) 223-3367
www.nwacademy.org

This independent, accredited school for grades 8 to 12 takes advantage of its downtown location to integrate the visual arts (painting, printmaking, and photography), the performing arts (jazz, dance, and theater), and media arts (film, video, sound design, and audio engineering) into its curriculum. Of course, all the traditional subjects are taught as well. The school has 60 students, who enjoy small classes (the average number of students is 15).

ST. MARY'S ACADEMY
1615 Southwest 5th Ave.
(503) 228-7181
www.stmaryspdx.org

Catholic nuns established St. Mary's in 1859, and since then it has educated more than 7,000 young women. Its long history has served it well—three times, it has received the US Department of Education's Blue Ribbon award for schools of excellence, the only school in the region to be so honored. Its curriculum is academically rigorous but also imaginative, flexible, and interesting; graduating from St. Mary's is shorthand in Oregon for being well educated. And don't let the old-fashioned brick façade fool you—it is thoroughly wired, one of the most technologically advanced schools in the city. Enrollment at St. Mary's is about 550, and the average class size is 13.

Multigrade Schools

Most people like their children's elementary schools; it's what happens afterward that they worry about. Many people feel that public middle schools are just not working,

and so quite a number of schools, both public and private, are returning to a multigrade plan. Of course, some multigrade schools have always been that way: Portland has a strong network of Catholic schools such as St. Thomas More in Southwest Portland, (503) 222-6105; St. Ignatius, (503) 774-5533, in Southeast Portland; and Cathedral Catholic School, (503) 275-9370, in Northwest Portland. All offer solid academic programs and traditional values for grades K–8. But in the private schools that are not religiously affiliated, parents have responded so positively to their children's elementary education that many of the private schools have added higher grades. A fine example is the Gilkey Middle School (see separate entry), but Waldorf initiative schools such as Cedarwood (see Elementary Schools) are also adding grades. Parents and teachers find that mixing the ages together seems to work better for everyone. Not only does it help the students academically, but it fosters a sense of connection and responsibility for all.

PUBLIC MULTIGRADE SCHOOLS

Portland Public Schools maintains a number of multigrade schools or programs within schools, and the district is returning to a more widespread use of the K–8 model. Here are just a few of the notable ones; for more information visit the PPS website, www.pps.k12.or.us.

BEAVERTON ARTS & COMMUNICATION MAGNET
11375 Southwest Center St.,
Beaverton
(503) 672-3700
www.beaverton.k12.or.us/acma

This school is the only stand-alone arts magnet in the state, and its students must be gifted in one or more of the visual, written, performing, or other arts; a written essay and portfolio are requirements of admission. Students must also be able to work independently and in groups. And no one is getting out of math: The academic requirements are tough. Students also declare a career pathway (sort of like a major) after 8th grade, which enables them to direct their educations in a useful direction. This program focuses on all forms of the arts for students in the 6th through 12th grades.

CREATIVE SCIENCE SCHOOL
1231 Southeast 92nd Ave.
(503) 916-6431
www.pps.k12.or.us/schools/
creativescience
This constructivist program for grades K–8 is based on the research of psychologist Jean Piaget. Its curriculum is fashioned to educate through activities such as observation, interaction, experimentation, and theorizing; independent thinking and problem-solving are prized very highly here. Subject periods are longer than at most elementary schools; an individual lesson might last an hour, and the particular unit may be incorporated throughout many lessons during the day. Children are encouraged to combine scientific reasoning with play. This program encourages a seamless transition between school and family life by involving parents deeply in the school.

METROPOLITAN LEARNING CENTER
2033 Northwest Glisan St.
(503) 916-5737
Portland Public School District's only K–12 school, the Metropolitan Learning Center provides a noncompetitive atmosphere with written evaluations (instead of letter grades),

cooperative learning, cross-age experiences, and off-campus activities. A particular focus of the school is a healthy environment, and many lessons are devoted to this. Former governor John Kitzhaber recognized it as the first "green" school in the state. But the students and teachers at MLC are imaginative enough to understand that the "environment" is the place we live; thus, a major focus of the school is the urban community that surrounds MLC, and it's an essential part of the curriculum.

SUNNYSIDE ENVIRONMENTAL SCHOOL
3421 Southeast Salmon St.
(503) 916-6226
www.sesptsa.com

The Sunnyside Environmental School, or SES, as it's known around here, is a special-focus program of Portland Public Schools in which students in mixed-age classes study the traditional subjects but with an emphasis on the natural environment. For example, a basic question throughout many courses is "How does history influence the environment and how does the environment influence history?" The environmental core curriculum, studied by all students at the same time, consists of three-year rotations focusing on rivers, mountains, and forests. SES is a small program, and its nurturing size and low ratio of students to teachers makes it very desirable. Accelerated math and Spanish are also available; community service is a key component of the curriculum as well.

WINTERHAVEN
3830 Southeast 14th Ave.
(503) 916-6200
www.winterhavenschool.org

Winterhaven is a wonderful K–8 public school magnet program that makes use of mixed-age classrooms, interdisciplinary intellectual approaches, and positive discipline techniques to foster personal responsibility. Winterhaven has attracted a high number of talented and gifted students who respond well to these approaches, which allow them to bloom in their own way while still being academically challenged, particularly through its focus on math, science, and technology. Community involvement is prized, and families are asked to volunteer 50 hours per year.

PRIVATE MULTIGRADE SCHOOLS

THE CATLIN GABEL SCHOOL
8825 Southwest Barnes Rd.
(503) 297-1894
www.catlin.edu

This distinguished coeducational school is well known for its dedication to individuality, rigorous academics, and liberal arts training. Courses educate the total person, incorporating academic excellence along with the visual and performing arts, physical education, and a strong sense of community service. Students are encouraged to devote service hours to the school and to the community; in fact one of the requirements for upper-school students is to dedicate 12 hours of service to local agencies. Catlin Gabel has an enrollment of about 680 students in preschool through grade 12. The average class size is 17.

FRANCISCAN MONTESSORI EARTH SCHOOL & ST. FRANCIS ACADEMY
14750 Southeast Clinton St.
(503) 760-8220
www.fmes.org

Parents who send their children to Montessori preschools grow misty-eyed when they later recall the wonderful experiences their children had there. Now they can extend this effective learning atmosphere all the way through middle school. Founded in 1977, the school serves about 350 students from the Portland Metro area, including Vancouver (it's right off I-205). This environmentally and globally focused school is run by an order of Franciscan nuns. Students grow gardens and are even prepared for travel abroad. If we're lucky, they'll start a graduate school for the rest of us.

THE GARDNER SCHOOL
16413 Northeast 50th Ave.,
Vancouver, WA
(360) 574-5752
www.gardnerschool.org/home.html

The Gardner School is dedicated to developing the potential of its 100 students. Howard Gardner's Multiple Intelligences model serves as a framework for individualized skill development and interdisciplinary, thematic studies. Community partnerships provide students with real-life experiences that help them become productive, responsible, compassionate citizens. Classes are held for preschoolers through grade eight. The student-to-teacher ratio is nine to one.

OREGON EPISCOPAL SCHOOL
6300 Southwest Nicol Rd.
(503) 246-7771
www.oes.edu
Oregon Episcopal School (OES) is a coeducational, independent, college preparatory school where teachers challenge students in small, demanding classes. Active parent involvement is encouraged. OES holds its students to rigorous academic standards, while encouraging a free spirit as part of the joy of learning. Modern dormitories staffed by resident-faculty families provide a safe home away from home for students coming from far away rather than commuting every day. OES serves 720 students, 50 of whom are boarders. Half of these are international students, mostly from China, Japan, and other Asian countries. Most of the other boarders are from eastern and southern Oregon, California, and Washington. The schoolwide student-teacher ratio is seven to one.

PORTLAND LUTHERAN SCHOOL
740 Southeast 182nd Ave.
(503) 667-3199
www.portlandlutheran.org
Founded in 1905, this school began its life as a training school for Lutheran ministers, but over the years, its focus changed. By 1989 it was a K–12 school, and it's now the fastest-growing parochial school in the east part of the city. It offers prekindergarten through 12th grade. The elementary program is centered on traditional single-grade classrooms through the eighth grade, while the high school's main focus is a college-prep curriculum in both liberal arts and the sciences. Ninety-five percent of its graduates attend college. PLS is owned and operated by the Portland Lutheran Association for Christian Education (PLACE), a pan-Lutheran association of churches dedicated to providing quality Christian education to the young people of the Portland Metropolitan area. PLS enrollment is 440. Classes usually have 25 to 27 students, except for prekindergarten through kindergarten classes, which usually consist of 10 to 12 students.

PORTLAND WALDORF SCHOOL
2300 Southeast Harrison, Milwaukie
(503) 654-2200
www.portlandwaldorf.org
The Waldorf School ethos is very Portland; in fact, there are other Waldorf-based schools in the area, two of which have started up recently—Cedarwood (see Private Elementary School Programs) and Swallowtail in Hillsboro, (503) 846-0336. But the Portland Waldorf School is the original one in the area, established in 1982. Known for fostering creativity by nurturing the "head, heart, and hands" of the whole child, the Waldorf School challenges its students to develop their intellect and compassion. Kindergarten focuses on storytelling, music, movement, and artistic activity. The academic program is culturally enriched with Spanish and German, needlework, drama, drawing and painting, gardening, folk dancing, orchestra, and woodworking. Portland Waldorf has an

enrollment of about 300 students and a faculty and staff of about 50 persons. The Portland Waldorf School serves students through 12th grade.

Higher Education

Higher education in Oregon has a long history—longer than anywhere else in the western United States. The Rev. Jason Lee established the Oregon Institute in his parlor in 1842; that event is now honored as the founding of what would eventually become Willamette University in Salem. Willamette also established the first western medical school, in 1866, and the first western law school, in 1883. Ever since 1842, Oregonians have been creating and nurturing high-quality independent colleges and universities.

Excellent higher education that is also affordable is a struggle for most Americans; here in Oregon we have made some progress in achieving this combination. A number of fine private and public universities, as well as a variety of smaller colleges, inhabit the region. Together this network allows students access to many academic programs. Because Portland is the state's major population center, several state universities have continuing education programs here, particularly Oregon State University and the University of Oregon, both of which offer certificate programs, for-credit classes, and graduate classes in Portland through satellites and extension programs. The University of Oregon's extension program can be reached at http://pdx.uoregon.edu; Oregon State's can be found at http://oregonstate .edu/dept/portlandmetro.

Oregon's network of public community colleges stretches across the state, and in the metropolitan area, students may choose among Clackamas Community College in Oregon City, Mt. Hood Community College in Gresham, or the state's largest school, Portland Community College with its campuses in Southwest Portland, Washington County, North Portland, and Southeast Portland. These schools offer an array of educational opportunities, ranging from traditional undergraduate academics to noncredit classes in sailing, kayaking, Chinese cooking, or dog training.

The diversity of Oregon's people is clearly reflected in its high-caliber institutions, which provide undergraduate liberal arts and sciences curricula, specialized two- and four-year professional and technical training, and a wide range of graduate studies. Enrolling more than 90,000 students in the Oregon University System (OUS) alone, and employing thousands of tax-paying Oregonians, these schools add billions of dollars to the state's economy. They keep thousands of Oregonians from leaving the state for specialized college experiences elsewhere and also attract out-of-state students drawn to Oregon for a variety of reasons.

Whether you are just out of high school, returning to school after some time off, or looking for a new way of being in the world, Portland's colleges and universities offer excellent choices and opportunities. They also offer good values, and whatever your hopes for your higher education, you are likely to find a program that suits you.

Colleges and Universities
CONCORDIA UNIVERSITY
2811 Northeast Holman St.
(503) 288-9371
www.cu-portland.edu
A Christian liberal arts school and part of the Concordia University System, Concordia University is a small college that draws about

1,100 students from all over the world to its campus in Northeast Portland. Courses of study include psychology, biology, theology, health and fitness management, humanities, and education. Graduate degree programs within the College of Education were established in 1996. Concordia is accredited by the Northwest Association of Schools and Colleges, and it offers small classes and an opportunity to work closely with professors.

GEORGE FOX UNIVERSITY
414 North Meridian St., Newberg
(503) 538-8383
www.georgefox.edu
Originally founded in 1891 by Quaker pioneers, this liberal arts college has been named one of America's best colleges numerous times by *U.S. News & World Report*. It includes Herbert Hoover among its alumni, though when he attended, the college was known as Friends Pacific Academy. Some things have stayed the same since President Hoover's time: The pretty residential campus is still in the town of Newberg, about a half-hour southwest of downtown Portland. It still emphasizes moral and religious as well as intellectual development. But George Fox is in every way a modern college too, with a new mission that includes working adults in its graduate, seminary, and degree-completion programs. Classes for the George Fox MBA program, which are held in Portland, are offered one night a week and occasionally on weekends at the Newberg campus. The students, faculty, and staff number about 2,700 persons.

LEWIS & CLARK COLLEGE
615 Southwest Palatine Hill Rd.
(503) 768-7000
www.lclark.edu

Lewis & Clark College, which sits on a lush site overlooking the Willamette River, is distinguished by its nurturing ambience, its fine and accessible faculty, and the demanding academic standards of its undergraduate, graduate, and law schools. Lewis & Clark can trace its history to 1858, when Presbyterian pioneers established Albany Academy. Then it was a tiny neighborhood school, but it moved to its present location in 1942 and changed its name to Lewis & Clark, and now it is the largest independent college in the state, with a total enrollment of around 3,000. (The undergraduate program has about 1,800 students; the Northwest College of Law, about 700; and the other graduate programs, another 500 or so.) In 1965 Northwestern School of Law was merged with Lewis & Clark College, and in 1984, graduate programs in education, special education, and counseling psychology were consolidated into the Graduate School of Professional Studies. All programs of the college have excellent national reputations.

MARYLHURST UNIVERSITY
17600 Pacific Hwy. (SR 43)
(503) 636-8141, (800) 634-9982
www.marylhurst.edu
Marylhurst, a Catholic liberal arts university, is nationally noted for being an excellent value, especially considering that no class has more than 50 students. Accredited by the Northwest Association of Schools and Colleges, Marylhurst offers its students a great deal of flexibility, with bachelor's or master's degree programs that can be completed during the weekdays, evenings, or weekends. Many returning students have completed their degrees here. If you're the type of person who never likes to leave the computer screen, Marylhurst's classes,

programs, and degrees that use web-based learning might be for you. There are, of course, regular on-site classes as well. The university also sponsors some absorbing graduate programs, such as a Master's in Art Therapy or in Interdisciplinary Studies. They have very generous life-experience credits. Though it was originally founded by Catholic sisters, Marylhurst is coeducational and accepts persons of all faiths.

NATIONAL COLLEGE OF
NATUROPATHIC MEDICINE
49 Southwest Porter St.
(503) 552-1555
www.ncnm.edu
National College of Naturopathic Medicine (NCNM) has been in continual operation since 1956, making it the oldest accredited naturopathic medical school on the continent. This extremely rigorous and competitive medical school offers two postgraduate degree programs, the Doctor of Naturopathic Medicine and the Master of Science in Oriental Medicine. Applicants are expected to have a strong background in science. Graduates are eligible to take board exams in their fields. In addition to lab and lecture courses, students are expected to devote 1,500 hours to clinical work. Students come from all over the United States and from other countries to study at NCNM, where enrollment has doubled in recent years. Each entering class is kept to 120 students, and currently only one out of every three applicants is accepted. Perhaps that's because academic worth is not the only criterion: NCNM college admissions literature states that "in addition to the educational prerequisites, candidates for admission must demonstrate to the college that they possess outstanding moral character, maturity,

academic aptitude, and commitment to naturopathic medicine."

OREGON COLLEGE OF ART AND CRAFT
8245 Southwest Barnes Rd.
(503) 297-5544
www.ocac.edu
Oregon College of Art and Craft was born in 1907 during an international movement to preserve and revive the arts and crafts that humans had practiced for a thousand years. Since then the Oregon College of Art and Craft has been training students in fiber art, metalworking, ceramics, and the production of many other useful and beautiful objects. Their book arts program is renowned the world over. The college, which rests on the grounds of an old filbert orchard, grants a Bachelor of Fine Arts degree; the training for that includes liberal arts, professional practices, and writing. The college also grants certificates in individual specialties. And there are numerous courses and programs available for those who want to simply take a pottery course or learn how to bind books. (See The Arts chapter for more information.)

OREGON HEALTH AND SCIENCE
UNIVERSITY
3181 Southwest Sam Jackson Park Rd.
(503) 494-8311
Oregon Health and Science University (OHSU) has roots that reach back to the 1800s, but its modern history began in 1974, when the Oregon State Board of Higher Education combined extant schools of nursing, dentistry, and medicine with the Medical School Hospital, Doernbecher Children's Hospital, and various clinics to form Oregon Health Sciences Center. In 1995 the center, now called OHSU, extracted itself from the Oregon State Board of Higher Education to

form a nonprofit public corporation governed by a state-appointed board. The result has been a major expansion of services and an even larger infusion of research grant money. Today OHSU educates health professionals and biomedical researchers in a variety of fields, and it provides excellent, state-of-the-art health care and research. It also devotes many resources to community service and education, including caring for the neediest patients in Oregon. And, finally, it is the largest corporate employer in the city. All things considered, few institutions have such a direct and indirect influence on the life of Portland citizens.

The main campus overlooks the city that it serves, poised atop Marquam Hill, with stunning views of the Cascades, the Willamette, and the city. The central campus is a maze of buildings connected by bridges, tunnels, stairs, and skyways, but the relatively compact nature of the hospital complex makes a visitor forget that there is another 260-acre campus west of Portland as well as many other clinics and facilities throughout the city and beyond. OHSU's programs and services extend across the state's entire 96,000 square miles, reaching into neighboring states.

The main components of OHSU are the School of Dentistry, the School of Medicine, the School of Nursing, and a number of signature research institutes. One of America's first-rate academic health care and medical research centers, OHSU attracts top-ranking students from throughout the country. Graduates of the School of Dentistry regularly maintain a 97 percent first-time pass rate when they take their board exams, and no dental students in the nation have more clinical hours upon graduation. The School of Medicine has equally impressive numbers;

not only do graduates attain nearly a 100 percent first-time pass rate, but the primary care education program ranks among the top 2 percent in the nation. Similar numbers are available for the School of Nursing graduates, whose master's programs also ranked in the top 2 percent. OHSU's research units are also distinguished; they include, but are not limited to, the Center for Research on Occupational and Environmental Toxicology, the Vollum Institute for Advanced Biomedical Research, the Knight Cancer Center, and the Oregon Regional Primate Research Center. OHSU offers both Masters and PhD programs in a variety of disciplines, from neuroscience to biochemistry to nursing to healthcare administration. Research funding at OHSU has almost tripled since 1995, and discoveries by its scientists are in the news daily. In fact, OHSU brings in $300 million in research funding every year, making it one of the top biomedical research sites in the nation.

OREGON INSTITUTE OF TECHNOLOGY
7726 Southeast Harmony Rd.,
Beaverton
(503) 725-3066
www.oit.edu
The Oregon Institute of Technology (OIT) offers four-year degrees, degree-completion programs, and a number of workshops and seminars on its campuses in Klamath Falls in southern Oregon, where OIT was founded, and on its campuses in Portland and Beaverton. Its degrees are granted in a broad spectrum of different engineering, science, and technological disciplines, including—but not at all limited to—health technologies, applied sciences of various kinds, communications, and environmental engineering.

PACIFIC NORTHWEST COLLEGE OF ART
1241 Northwest Johnson St.
(503) 226-4391
www.pnca.edu

The Pacific Northwest College of Art (PNCA) has been training students in the visual arts since 1909, when it was an arm of the Portland Art Museum, but by 1994, PNCA was a separate institution that granted Bachelor of Fine Arts degrees in addition to its community education classes. Over the years PNCA grew so much that it had to move from its lovely Pietro Belluschi–designed building next to the museum to a large, visually stunning converted warehouse in the Pearl District. This has allowed the college to add two times the space devoted to photography, as well as providing state-of-the-art computer capability. Public galleries showcase the work of students, and the Swiggert Commons, a large space for exhibitions, installations, lectures, and other events, provides an exciting hub for aesthetic activity in the already-happening Pearl. Students here receive careful, attentive training in their specialties and are regarded for their imaginative design. They are also trained in useful and practical skills like writing, math, and professional concerns. (See The Arts chapter for more information.)

PORTLAND STATE UNIVERSITY
1721 Southwest Broadway
(503) 725-9800
www.pdx.edu

One of the seven universities and colleges of the Oregon University System, Portland State (PSU) is Oregon's urban university, responding to the needs and interests of the greater Portland area. PSU offers more than 100 undergraduate and graduate degrees in the humanities, sciences, social sciences, and professions, including doctoral degrees in education, electrical and computer engineering, environmental sciences and resources, public administration and policy, social work and social research, systems science, and urban studies and planning. PSU grants more graduate degrees than any other university in the state.

The 36 acres of the university, which straddles the southern Park Blocks downtown, are replete with big trees, fountains, ivy-covered buildings, hip students in coffee bars, and other accoutrements of a modern urban campus. Visitors will also find beautiful new buildings that house some of the most prestigious programs (such as the College of Urban and Public Affairs, which is appropriately found at the southern terminus of the new streetcar system). About 15,000 students are enrolled at Portland State, including more than 4,200 graduate students. Continuing education programs add thousands more students to the total numbers. Most students commute, but there are some dormitories and the university can assist students in finding housing, applying for financial aid, acquiring a campus job, and other staples of student life.

Like all decent universities, the programs at PSU extend beyond the tree-lined campus to serve all citizens. PSU is the epicenter of a variety of cutting-edge research and public service programs, including the Center for Black Studies, the Center for Science Education, the Center for Population Research and Census, the Center for Software Quality Research, the Center for Urban Studies, the Institute on Aging, the Institute of Portland Metropolitan Studies, and the Portland Educational Network.

REED COLLEGE
3203 Southeast Woodstock Blvd.
(503) 771-1112
www.reed.edu

Reed College looks like the cinematic version of a private college, all ivy and brick, with grassy playing fields and a picturesque stream. However, appearances can deceive: Reed College, founded in 1908, is much less traditional than it looks. One way Reed is different is that conventional letter grades for each course are recorded but not distributed. As long as you're doing satisfactory work, you don't have to worry about grades. This frees students to actually learn something, a freedom that pays off for everybody. Writer Loren Pope describes it as "the most intellectual college in the nation," one at which faculty are thrilled to teach because the students are genuinely interested in learning. A measure of the success of this approach is the rate at which Reed students win awards like Watson Fellowships and Rhodes Scholarships.

Reed is a four-year liberal arts school (though the college does offer a master's degree in liberal studies as well). The standard liberal arts majors are available, but in addition, the college offers a number of interdisciplinary majors in subjects such as theater-dance and biochemistry. Its annual enrollment is about 1,400, small enough to provide an intimate environment for learning, but large enough so that everyone isn't exactly like everyone else. All Reed students take a one-year course in humanities their freshman year, and all write a senior thesis. Many departments hold weekly seminars by faculty, students, and visiting scholars, and frequent lectures and seminars further expand the opportunities for intellectual exchange. The Hauser library, a depository for US government publications, also maintains special collections of rare books, manuscripts, and archival materials.

UNIVERSITY OF PORTLAND
5000 North Willamette Blvd.
(503) 943-8000
www.up.edu

The University of Portland has been consistently ranked by *U.S. News and World Report* as a top-10 university in its class. Its 2,600 students pursue 75 undergraduate and graduate degrees, notably in the liberal arts, business, education, nursing, and engineering. Founded in 1901, the University of Portland is affiliated with the Congregation of Holy Cross, the Catholic order that also runs its sister school, the University of Notre Dame; its dedication is to the heart and spirit as well as the mind. Its reputation increases daily—with a faculty that garners substantial awards and grants (from the National Science Foundation and the National Endowment for the Arts, among others) and a 14 to 1 student-faculty ratio allowing personal contact, it's no wonder. The University of Portland sits on a dramatic bluff overlooking the Willamette; its 125-acre campus is in a pretty, residential neighborhood of North Portland. Plus, they have a phenomenal women's soccer team that's a contender for the national title nearly every year—including 2006, when they won.

WARNER PACIFIC COLLEGE
2219 Southeast 68th Ave.
(503) 517-1000
www.warnerpacific.edu

A Christian liberal arts college founded in 1937, Warner Pacific College, which serves 650 students, is in Southeast Portland near Mt. Tabor Park. Accredited by the Northwest

Association of Schools and Colleges, Warner Pacific has trained students in a Christian-centered curriculum of liberal arts for more than 60 years. Warner Pacific offers a number of education programs, including early childhood education, teacher education, and English as a second language (ESL), in addition to its four-year degrees. Warner Pacific also has an imaginative degree-completion program that is ideal for many returning students who work full-time.

Community Colleges

The Portland Metro area is blessed with no fewer than three top-notch community colleges, and they all offer state-of-the-art facilities and a wide range of academic, technical, and vocational learning opportunities. Besides the savings in tuition, the easy access, excellent instruction, and desirable teacher-to-student ratios make community colleges an attractive option.

CLACKAMAS COMMUNITY COLLEGE
19600 South Molalla Ave.,
Oregon City
(503) 657-6958
www.clackamas.cc.or.us

Serving about 28,000 students annually, almost 8,000 of them full-time, Clackamas Community College (CCC) may have a lot of students, but it feels like a small college. CCC students take advantage of a variety of programs, from basic literacy and study skills to college-prep courses. Popular programs include the two-year Associate of Science degrees or the Certificates of Completion; these are granted in more than 30 areas of study. Students also may pursue the Oregon Transfer degree, an Associate of Arts degree that guarantees junior standing at any Oregon University System school (and

which many non-Oregon University System schools will also honor). Transfer-degree students have more than 70 options for major study.

Because many students lack the basic skills to obtain even a high school diploma, CCC also offers personal tutoring and courses that cover fundamental academic and life skills. Some of these programs cover GED preparation and English for nonnative speakers in addition to courses in career possibilities and parenting. CCC also offers credit and noncredit courses that cover dozens of areas of personal interest at more than 100 locations.

MT. HOOD COMMUNITY COLLEGE
26000 Southeast Stark St., Gresham
(503) 491-6422
www.mhcc.cc.or.us

Mt. Hood Community College (MHCC) enrolls approximately 27,000 students each year at its campuses. MHCC's services cover the spectrum from providing adult literacy classes to preparing students for transfer to a university or entry into highly technical fields such as microelectronics, and the college provides one- and two-year degrees and certificates in more than 100 professional, technical, and transfer programs. Academic opportunities are, naturally, also available, including the Oregon Transfer Degree, the Honors College, and the MHCC–Portland State University Co-Admission program. In addition, continuing education classes are offered to the community at locations throughout MHCC's district with topics ranging from art to aerobics, cooking to computing, investing to woodworking. Classes are offered at the 200-acre main campus, as well as at satellite campuses throughout the district.

PORTLAND COMMUNITY COLLEGE
12000 Southwest 49th Ave.
(503) 244-6111
www.pcc.edu

Portland Community College enrolls more students than any other college in Oregon—97,000 annually, full- or part-time. PCC is a two-year college that offers myriad educational opportunities. Three main campuses provide lower-division college transfer courses, two-year associate degree programs, professional and technical career-training programs, and adult basic education courses. Several other locations offer workforce training, literacy training, and other training courses in addition to their basic academic services. And an open campus offers programs in a variety of places throughout the district. Moreover PCC also offers many community outreach services available to students and nonstudents alike. If you do decide to enroll, you may take courses at any of the campuses—it all depends on what is offered at what times. And anyone may attend PCC, even those who haven't yet finished high school.

PCC's Cascade campus sits in an urban area off North Killingsworth Street, and more than 9,000 students each year attend this city campus. It has become a focal point for rebirth in the neighborhood, for many area residents have turned to the Cascade campus for job training, college transfer, and self-improvement courses. Many community services such as child care, legal aid, neighborhood associations, and job referral services are found on the campus. Cascade also hosts the Festival of African Films each year as well as a Mardi Gras celebration; these events draw visitors from all over the area.

About 10,000 students attend the Rock Creek campus, which lies 12 miles west of town and draws many of its students from Beaverton-Hillsboro. As with all community college campuses, a multiplicity of programs is available here. One draw is the Aviation Technology Hangar, where students can have direct experience working on airplanes and helicopters.

The Sylvania Campus, PCC's administrative center, in Southwest Portland, has the largest campus. More than 26,000 students attend the programs here each year. In addition to its well-regarded basic programs, Sylvania has three specialized programs with admirable reputations: the nursing, dental, and developmental education programs.

Specialized Schools
INTERNATIONAL AIR AND
HOSPITALITY ACADEMY
2901 East Mill Plain Blvd.,
Vancouver, WA
(360) 695-2500
www.airacademy.com

The International Air Academy has placed 17,000 graduates in airline careers, and they can get you started in a travel career through their 20-week Airline Travel Specialist diploma program. For many students this is the first step toward becoming a certified travel consultant. Graduates of the program are qualified for a broad range of positions, including travel and tour agent and customer service agent, and for a variety of jobs in transportation, travel, and hospitality marketing. Another diploma program, the 10-week airline reservations and airport services, provides entry to jobs in reservation sales, ticket agents, and gate and ramp agent positions. Many alumni of International Air Academy are hired by major airlines as flight attendants, in customer service positions, and as schedulers or reservation agents.

They also offer a hospitality program for those who want training as event planners and similar careers. Founded in 1980 this school is accredited by the Accrediting Commission of Career Schools and Colleges of Technology. The majority of students qualify for financial aid, and dormitory housing is available for out-of-towners.

LE CORDON BLEU COLLEGE OF CULINARY ARTS
600 Southwest 10th Ave., Suite 400
www.chefs.edu/Portland

Every year aspiring chefs take their first step toward becoming artists in the kitchen at Le Cordon Bleu, formerly Western Culinary Institute. The 12-month course is full-time and culminates in a diploma, certification, or both. Notable chefs from around the world teach classes Mon through Fri; the curriculum emphasizes fine dining, hotel and resort cooking, and catering. Students learn hands-on at two on-site restaurants as well as through off-campus internships. Le Cordon Bleu offers financial aid to most students and assists with housing needs and part-time employment; the school claims a very high job placement rate.

OREGON CULINARY INSTITUTE
1701 Southwest Jefferson St.
(503) 961-6200
www.oregonculinaryinstitute.com

The Oregon Culinary Institute not only trains students to be expert in the culinary arts, but they also do it in a way that is affordable and focused, providing plenty of hands-on training for real-world experiences. This gives their graduates top-notch foundational skills, and not just in the back of the house— their restaurant management program gives would-be chef-owners tangible practice in the business side of the restaurant. Also offered are professional degree and diploma programs in culinary arts, baking and pastry, and restaurant management. See the close-up in the Restaurant chapter for more information.

WESTERN STATES CHIROPRACTIC COLLEGE
2900 Northeast 132nd Ave.
(503) 256-3180
www.wschiro.edu

Western States Chiropractic College (WSCC) is a private, nonprofit, professional school that educates students in the art, science, and philosophy of chiropractic self-healing, and its graduates are prepared to work within an interdisciplinary medical framework. Its reputation is outstanding: its graduates test very well on their board exams, and the college was the first chiropractic college ever, in 1994, to receive federal research money—nearly $1 million in grant funds from the Department of Health and Human Services. The WSCC student population numbers between 400 and 500 and comes from all parts of the United States and from several foreign countries; about one third of the students have earned a bachelor's degree before they arrive, and many are already working professionals in some other field. Originally founded as the Pacific Chiropractic College, the school was reorganized and became Western States Chiropractic College in 1932. In 1986 the college opened its 9,000-square-foot Outpatient Clinic on campus, making it the largest chiropractic facility in the Northwest.

HEALTH CARE

Portland's healing community is at the heart of a state known for innovation in healthcare delivery, biomedical breakthroughs, and rigorous exploration of alternative therapies. It began with the Sisters of Providence in the days before statehood. Portland was an early adopter of the Kaiser model during its shipbuilding heyday in the 1940s, and Kaiser Permanente Northwest—as well as its Center for Health Research—continues to be a trendsetter in health care. This spirit of experimentation paved the way for the exciting advances in health reform and cutting-edge legislation that comprised the Oregon Health Plan. Initiated through a series of laws enacted from 1989 to 1995, this program provides health insurance to low-income residents, including the working poor, seniors, people with disabilities, children, and pregnant women. While, like most states, budget shortfalls have recently strained the Oregon Health Plan, Oregon is well prepared to meet the challenges of national health care reform because of this important public health experience.

Another notable trend suggests that Portland is in the forefront of a worldwide movement to integrate health-care modalities: a growing number of health plans offer coverage of visits to chiropractors and acupuncturists. The Western States Chiropractic College, Oriental College of Oriental Medicine, National College of Naturopathic Medicine, and East-West College of Healing Arts, which train these practitioners, are thus important features of the health-care landscape; these institutions offer, in addition to their training programs, clinical services for a variety of conditions (see the Child Care and Education chapter for more information).

Portland is also the home of influential medical research. Notably, Oregon Health and Science University's (OHSU) Brian Druker and his laboratory developed the first chemotherapy drug that specifically targets cancer cells and leaves healthy cells alone. This drug, called Gleevec, works by preventing the proteins in chronic myeloid leukemia cells from binding together—and therefore from multiplying. This drug proved for the first time that targeted therapy was feasible and effective—the shot heard round the world in the war on cancer.

OVERVIEW

The Portland healthcare landscape is defined by a number of major health systems: Kaiser Permanente, Legacy, Providence, Oregon Health & Science University, and Adventist health systems are the anchors of the healthcare system, especially if you have health insurance. The hospitals associated with these systems are listed below, but each of these hospitals also has associated clinics and other services for routine care.

Close-up

What If You Don't Have Insurance?

If you don't have health insurance, Portland offers some unique resources: the state of Oregon offers a special high-risk plan if your employer doesn't offer insurance and you need it. You can find out more information on their website: **www.omip .state.or.us.** You can also try the Multnomah County Health Department (www .mchealth.org/appointments.shtml) for help with access to primary care services if you are low-income.

A new company, **ZoomCare,** offers healthcare services that you pay for directly, without the need for insurance at all. If you need a sprained ankle examined and bandaged or an abcess drained, you can call them and get a same-day appointment, get treated, pay the bill, and be done with it. They post a price list on their website so you know what you are in for. This is a new model of healthcare delivery, one based on extended hours and same-day service—and meeting the needs of Portlanders. For example, if you don't have insurance, you can still get a complete physical for less than $100. These clinics are thus ideal not only for people who don't have health insurance but also for people who might have, for example, catastrophic coverage because they're self-employed. This might also be a good option if you are visiting Portland and you are uncertain if your healthcare plan covers out-of-area coverage. You can find out more about ZoomCare and its citywide clinics at www .zoomcare.com.

State of Oregon tax law requires hospitals to report on their benefits to the community, and each of these systems produces a comprehensive report detailing these benefits; these are available on the health systems websites and are invaluable resources detailing their activities and priorities.

i No matter what your health plan, the number for emergency services is 911.

HOSPITALS

Southwest Portland

OREGON HEALTH AND SCIENCE UNIVERSITY
3181 Southwest Sam Jackson Park Rd.
(503) 494-8311
www.ohsu.edu

OHSU is an internationally renowned center for research and education, as well as a complex of hospitals and clinics, that traces its beginnings to the turn of the 20th century. It is the region's only academic health center, which means that it not only teaches the next generation of physicians, nurses, and other providers, but it also engages in cutting-edge biomedical research. It is also a level-one trauma center, with Life Flight helicopters making all-too-frequent landings. Most of Oregon's state-of-the-art biomedical research and treatment goes on here, bringing hundreds of millions of dollars to Oregon's economy. It is also a level-one trauma center that participates in the Life-Flight program.

But OHSU provides other important health services to Oregon. For example, it runs Oregon's Poison Control Center (800-222-1222 or www.ohsu.edu/poison), a hotline of information and instructions about what to do in the event that dangerous substances are ingested. It conducts rural outreach programs to bring the latest in research and treatments to people across Oregon, and its Biomedical Information Communication Center (BICC) holds hundreds of thousands of biomedical journals, books, and other materials that make the latest research available to the general public—electronically or in dead-tree format. In addition, OHSU researchers and clinicians give frequent talks to the public, including series such as the award-winning Brain Awareness events in February and March.

PROVIDENCE ST. VINCENT MEDICAL CENTER
9205 Southwest Barnes Rd.
(503) 216-1234
www.providence.org/oregon
Providence St. Vincent has a history in Portland dating from 1856, when five nuns arrived from Montreal to care for the natives. The Providence Health System has grown to a regional service that has more than 3,500 clinicians in 40 specialties and more than 16,000 employees statewide. In this particular hospital there are 523 beds, nearly 1800 medical staff, and 4,200 employees. Its specialties include, among other things, a notable cardiac and vascular program, good services for women and children, and the Oregon Medical Laser Center, where lasers rather than scalpels are used in surgery. (For information on another of Providence's hospitals in Portland, see the entry for Providence Portland Medical Center in the section on North/Northeast Portland.)

Northwest Portland

LEGACY GOOD SAMARITAN HOSPITAL & MEDICAL CENTER
1015 Northwest 22nd Ave.
(503) 413-7711
www.legacyhealth.org
This full-service hospital is a part of the Legacy Health group. Known as "Good Sam," this popular organization features a community health education center in addition to its hospitals and clinics, in which staff provide information on a variety of health and wellness topics and treatment options. Legacy is also home to a noted Breast Health Center, (503) 413-811, where diagnostic, educational, and support services allow women to get mammograms, receive results quickly, and obtain follow-up tests, counseling, and care. And its Family Birth Center is beloved by new parents across the region for its beautiful facilities and excellent staff.

Southeast Portland

ADVENTIST MEDICAL CENTER
10123 Southeast Market St.
(503) 257-2500
www.adventisthealthnw.com
Adventist Medical Center is a 302-bed hospital with a medical staff of 500 and 2,000 employees. It is part of Adventist Health, a not-for-profit health-care system of hospitals throughout the western United States, all open to the general public. The hospitals and clinics are operated by the Seventh-day Adventist Church, with headquarters in Roseville, California. The Adventist Health System also offers numerous clinics in the metro area. To make an appointment or find out more about available medical professionals, call the Physicians Referral Line at (503) 256-4000.

KAISER SUNNYSIDE MEDICAL CENTER
10180 Southeast Sunnyside Rd.,
Clackamas
(503) 652-2880
www.kaiserpermanente.org
While Kaiser has lovely facilities throughout the Portland Metro area, this facility is a gorgeously remodeled, full-service hospital, including a responsive emergency department for pediatric and adult patients, as well as a hub for most kinds of surgery. In addition, it is a regional center for infectious disease, kidney issues, and cancer care, as well as for spine and neurosurgery. Kaiser's clinical services are found throughout the region in centers easily located on their website. These services not only include routine physician care but also urgent care clinics, healthy living classes, and a variety of other resources.

North & Northeast Portland

LEGACY EMANUEL HOSPITAL & HEALTH CENTER
2801 North Gantenbein Ave.
(503) 413-2200
www.legacyhealth.org
Besides being the largest hospital in the local Legacy Health System, this health center is also the site of one of the two level-one trauma centers in Portland. It is also the home of Legacy Emanuel Children's Hospital. To promote safety and health for children, Emanuel sponsors an annual Healthy Kids' Fair in the spring, highlighted with sales of bike helmets and car safety checks. The Children's Hospital has its own Emergency and After Hours Care. Call (503) 413-2200 for both information and physician referral. Legacy Emanuel is also the home of the Oregon Burn Center, which specializes in treating those who have endured serious burns.

PROVIDENCE PORTLAND MEDICAL CENTER
4805 Northeast Glisan St.
(503) 215-1111
www.providence.org/oregon
Not only is Providence a full-service community hospital, but it also has fine research centers such as the Earle A. Chiles Institute, a multidisciplinary center devoted to the research of heart disease, cancer, diabetes, and infectious diseases; the Robert W. Franz Cancer Research Center, which focuses on the immune system in treating breast cancer; and the Albert Starr Academic Center for Cardiac Surgery, where Dr. Starr, coinventor of the artificial heart valve, and his colleagues continue to explore the field of cardiac surgery, now including heart transplants.

The campus of the Providence Portland Medical Center is also home to the Child Center at 830 Northeast 47th Ave., (503) 215-2400. This pediatric outpatient clinic serves children with autism, seizure disorders, and mental health difficulties. The Gamma Knife Center is the newest addition to Providence. The gamma knife is a highly advanced technological tool that uses beams of gamma radiation to treat a variety of brain lesions and disorders. The Providence Resource Line is (503) 574-6595. This line will help callers select physicians and health education classes and obtain access to various programs.

Vancouver

SOUTHWEST WASHINGTON MEDICAL CENTER
400 Northeast Mother Joseph Place
3400 Main St., Vancouver
(503) 972-3000, (360) 256-2000
www.swmedctr.com

Southwest Washington Medical Center comprises a number of urgent-care clinics, physicians' offices, and other health-care facilities in Clark County. But its heart is the Medical Center, the first hospital in the Pacific Northwest. It has 360 beds and a level-two trauma center. The latest development at this medical complex is the Family Birth Center with 49 beds, many in private rooms with Jacuzzis.

The main medical campus is thoroughly modern, with a state-of-the-art Cancer Center, a well-designed Physician's Pavilion, and updated patient facilities. Its other clinics and centers scattered throughout Clark County offer laser eye surgery, specialized care for mothers and children, and urgent care. A second location is at 3400 Main St. also in Vancouver.

SPECIALIZED HOSPITALS & OTHER MEDICAL FACILITIES

DOERNBECHER CHILDREN'S HOSPITAL
3181 Sam Jackson Park Rd.
(503) 494-8311
www.ohsu.edu/health/
clinics-and-services/doernbecher/

CHILD DEVELOPMENT AND REHABILITATION CENTER
(503) 494-8095
Since its founding in 1926, Doernbecher has provided the best available medical care to children in Oregon and southwest Washington, including children from families with limited incomes. Financial assistance, through the Oregon Health Plan or Oregon's Children's Health Insurance Program, assures that services here are available to all of Oregon's youth. About 30,000 children visit Doernbecher every year, some from as far away as northern California, Idaho, Alaska,

Hawaii, and Montana.

The current Doernbecher Children's Hospital opened its doors on July 14, 1998. It's a gorgeous building, and families can have private rooms with showers. Parents' lounges and a research library make stays easier for family members, and large playrooms, courtyards, and an in-house art therapy program help youngsters take their minds off their illnesses.

Doctors here not only do research but also provide a wide range of medical services from bone marrow, stem cell, and organ transplants to treating cancer, cystic fibrosis, and rare genetic diseases. The Child Research and Rehabilitation Center focuses on children with developmental disabilities, providing cutting-edge research and providing the multidisciplinary care that these children and their families require.

PORTLAND VA MEDICAL CENTER
3710 Southwest US Veterans
Hospital Rd.
(503) 273-5289
www.visn20.med.va.gov/portland
This VA hospital is good news for regional vets. Rather than dodge "Big Nurse," these men and women who served their country receive excellent care from cheerful, nurturing doctors and nurses. Many of the clinicians at the VA hospital also have faculty appointments at OHSU, and clinical, research, and education partnerships are common, enhancing resources available for patients. To get from one hospital to the other, patients and staff walk across a Sky Bridge with a beautiful view of Portland, the Willamette River, and Mount Hood. This VA facility is a national center of excellence for hearing research.

RETIREMENT

Portland is a particularly agreeable place for retirement whether you are moving here specifically for that purpose or you have lived here your whole life. And that's because civic life is still celebrated here. We have a sophisticated, affordable, and reliable mass-transit system that is sympathetic to the needs of seniors, an outstanding public library, world-class health care, a fine public parks system, and most of the other amenities that make life worth living. The temperate climate ensures that there usually won't be too many very hot or very cold days. In the interest of full disclosure, however, we should let you know that many seniors in the area spend part of the year in warmer climates such as Palm Springs and save their Portland time for the months from June through Oct, when the weather is especially good. However, we have noticed more and more seniors retiring to Portland permanently and choosing to live downtown, with its convenient access to the streetcar and other transportation, as well as outstanding restaurants, shopping, and the arts.

Portland seniors will find many different housing options in many different parts of the city. (Currently Washington County has the fastest-growing senior population.) You will find communities devoted solely to seniors, as well as neighborhoods that have a balance of all ages, whichever you prefer. If you live independently but are ready to give up such tasks as mowing the lawn and maintaining a house, you'll have a wide variety of choices available. And this is also true if you need more help than just having the lawn mowed. One word of caution: Portland is comparatively expensive when it comes to real estate, especially in the heart of the city, which has the most accessible services. However, if you look hard you can usually find something well priced, especially if you're looking for a row house or condominium. Many charming, well-planned, affordable housing communities are being built all across the region; some of these are close to the MAX line.

CHOOSING A RETIREMENT COMMUNITY

Our retirement communities offer independent apartment, house, or condominium living, along with support services such as weekly housekeeping. Some locations offer one or more meals per day. Many of these places contract with private home health agencies to provide extra assistance to residents for which there are additional fees. In general these retirement communities are not licensed as care facilities, but some locations offer floors or sections that are licensed to provide a higher level of care. There is no financial assistance available to help cover the cost of housing in nonlicensed retirement communities.

In the Portland area alone, there are more than 100 retirement communities—one for every taste and budget. Some have buy-in fees and long-term leases, some rent apartments by the month. Some have swimming pools, health spas, and tennis courts; others focus on providing activities such as bridge clubs, group outings, and community meals. Many offer different levels of care should you ever need them. We've listed a representative sample of housing styles here to get you started, but you can ask your Realtor, the State Office of Senior and Disabled Services, or an online service such as Senior .com for more comprehensive information. Most retirement centers will be delighted to send you a brochure and arrange a guided tour.

While many of the retirement communities are designed for seniors without serious medical problems, many of them do provide continuing care when needed. Some of the following communities are designed to meet the increasing care needs of an aging resident by providing independent apartment living supplemented with an on-site health-care facility, usually licensed by the State of Oregon Senior and Disabled Services office. The residency agreement includes a contract, and tenants pay a large entrance fee (or buy-in) in addition to monthly rates. Before making a decision on any retirement community, check with Senior and Disabled Services at (800) 282-8096. They can tell you about any complaints made against the place you are considering. If you are in the market for Alzheimer's care or other intensive, continuing-care facilities, we suggest you also check the Oregon Department of Human Services website—it has a comprehensive guide to long-term care and provides a list of local offices that can help you find placement (www.oregon.gov/DHS/spwpd/ltc/inhome.shtml#overview).

Home Ownership in Senior Communities

Home ownership in a senior retirement setting is available in the following communities, which are primarily intended for independent living for persons over 55 years of age. Except for the retirement setting, the arrangements are not very different from home ownership in the community at large, and assistance in the home is the responsibility of the resident.

Portland
CLAREMONT ADULT RESORT LIVING
15800 Northwest Country Club Dr.
(503) 629-5614
www.claremontgolfclub.com
Does the idea of living on the edge of a beautiful golf course sound appealing? Ten miles from Portland's city center, Claremont is one of the most exclusive adult communities in the state, with beautifully built homes selling at the higher end of the real estate market. While one doesn't have to be retired to live here (it just doesn't allow children younger than 18), most residents are 55 or older. Many are retired professionals who have active, vigorous lifestyles. The custom-planned houses have fireplaces, private outdoor terraces, spacious island kitchens, big master suites, studies, and oversize garages. There are at least 10 distinctive styles of homes to choose from. Claremont's grounds are meticulously maintained; ponds, waterfalls, streams, and fountains are everywhere; and the golf and putting course

are excellent. Two elegant and comfortable clubhouses are available only to residents and guests, and a pro shop, two outdoor swimming pools, tennis and croquet courts, lawn bowling, and a fitness center are on-site. The town of Cedar Mills, which offers all the shopping opportunities one could ask for, is just a mile away.

SUMMERPLACE
2020 Northeast 150th Ave.
(503) 257-0733
http://summerplacehoa.com
Summerplace offers a combination of housing styles and apartments. There is a wide selection of houses with two bedrooms and two baths. Many seniors here pursue a variety of activities from ballroom dancing to golf, to attending the numerous spaghetti dinners and crab feeds that Summerplace holds. Besides the outdoor swimming pool, there are tennis courts and a well-equipped exercise and weight room to help residents stay in shape. Summerplace also offers its residents a variety of fun classes, ranging from woodcarving to flower arranging. Although there isn't a golf course on-site, one of the area's most popular golf clubs, Glendoveer (see the Golf chapter), is only a stone's throw away. Summerplace is located in a fairly quiet area of outer Northeast Portland off 148th Avenue, but it is close to major arterials such as Marine Drive and Glisan Street. There are numerous medical and shopping facilities and plenty of restaurants in the vicinity. Summerplace also has extensive assisted living facilities, including Alzheimer's disease care, so that families have many options for housing. The assisted living facilities can be found at 15727 Northeast Russell St. (503-252-9361 or www.prestigecare.com/assisted).

Upscale Retirement

A unique senior facility is emerging in the South Waterfront district: **Mirabella** in Portland. This innovative continuing care retirement community is designed to allow residents to "age in place"— in chic condominiums with amenities such as a penthouse dining room atop the 30-story building. A major component is its relationship with Oregon Health and Science University, which will use its world-class researchers and caregivers to address every dimension of the aging experience in order to improve care. To learn more, call Mirabella at (503) 245-4742 or visit their website at www.mirabellaretirement.org/portland/index.htm

Home Sharing

SHARED HOUSING
1819 Northwest Everett St.
(503) 225-9924
www.emoregon.org
An Ecumenical Ministries of Oregon program, Shared Housing has proven to be invaluable to many seniors, enabling them to stay in their homes despite financial or physical limitations. This referral and matching service brings together those who need affordable housing with those who can provide it and has arranged more than 2,000 home-sharing agreements since 1982. Through the program, housing is provided in exchange for vital services such as cooking, cleaning, and yard work. Agreements

can include rent only, services and reduced rent, room and board, and room and board plus salary. Shared Housing staff checks references, arranges initial meetings, and provides periodic follow-ups. There is an application fee of $10 to $30, depending on the homeowner's income.

RESOURCES FOR SENIORS
Home Repair & Weatherization

COMMUNITY ENERGY PROJECT
422 Northeast Alberta St.
(503) 284-6827
www.communityenergyproject.org
The Community Energy Project (CEP) helps seniors on a fixed income enjoy a warmer home and lower utility bills during the winter months. They install vinyl storm windows that roll up and down easily, weather-strip doors, caulk and eliminate drafts throughout the home, and save money and energy by insulating water heaters and pipes. The CEP also helps seniors with minor repairs and adjustments such as installing safety bars, repairing stairs, installing carbon monoxide and smoke detectors, and other services that will improve quality of life and safety. Home owners as well as renters are welcome to call, and all services and materials are provided free of cost.

HOME ACCESS AND REPAIR FOR THE DISABLED AND ELDERLY (HARDE)
Washington County
Aging Services Department
328 West Main St., Hillsboro
(503) 846-8897
www.co.washington.or.us/Community Development/HousingRehabilitation/ senior-and-disabled.cfm

The HARDE program for low- to moderate-income seniors can provide a $3,500 grant for accessibility improvements such as ramps, wider doorways, grab bars, lower counters, and security devices. Other improvements for home owners may include heating, plumbing or electrical repairs, and roof and siding upkeep. Low-interest loans up to $25,000 are also available for qualifying residents to make needed home improvements. In some cases the repayment may be deferred as long as the senior owns and occupies the home. Renters are also eligible for help with improvements for accessibility.

Elders in Action

Elders in Action advocates for seniors in large ways and small. Not only do they help individuals find resources in their community, but they also provide workshops on how best to use these resources, advocate for policy changes that benefit seniors, and guide businesses and local governments in making senior-friendly services and products. You can find them at 1411 Southwest Morrison, Suite 290, (503) 235-5474, or online at www.eldersinaction .org.

HUMAN SOLUTIONS ENERGY ASSISTANCE PROGRAMS
12350 Southeast Powell Blvd.
(503) 548-0200
www.humansolutions.org

This program, similar to the project listed above, helps low-income families and seniors stay cozy while reducing their utility bills during winter months.

REBUILDING TOGETHER
5000 North Willamette Blvd.
(503) 943-7515
www.rebuildingtogetherportland.org
This nonprofit agency donates material and labor to do extensive remodeling on homes owned by low-income seniors. They accept referrals in the fall and winter and do the work in the spring, investing more than $1 million in the repair of 50 to 60 homes each year.

Legal Help

Before you call your attorney, you may want to check *Legal Issues for Older Adults,* published by the Oregon State Bar Association. It is a fine reference guide, providing legal information on issues ranging from Medicare to age discrimination, and it includes valuable insights on safety, insurance, and landlord-tenant rights. To order, call (800) 452-8260, ext. 413, or check it out online at www.osbar .org. A printed copy costs $10, but you can download it for free.

Meals & Grocery Delivery

LOAVES AND FISHES/MEALS ON WHEELS
7710 Southwest 31st Ave.
(503) 736-6325
www.loavesandfishesonline.org

Since 1969, Loaves and Fishes and their army of caring volunteers have carried out their mission "to enrich the lives of seniors and assist them in maintaining independence by making nutritious food, social contacts, and other resources easily available." In addition to wellness and community programs, Loaves and Fishes provides more than one million low-cost, nutritious meals to senior citizens in the Portland Metro area each year. In addition, each day Meals on Wheels delivers thousands of hot meals throughout the metro area to homebound seniors who are at least 60 years of age or have a spouse 60 or older. They have 35 sites, and you can have meals delivered or eat at the sites themselves, with transportation provided. Although the suggested donation for a meal is $3, no one is turned away. Besides offering balanced and carefully planned meals and fellowship, Loaves and Fishes sponsors numerous activities and parties throughout the year, especially on the holidays. Loaves and Fishes centers offer a lot more than hot meals—companionship, spiritual fellowship, and ethnic meals and celebrations make the centers a hub of activities for a wide range of elderly clients. To find your nearest Loaves and Fishes, call the central line, listed above, or take advantage of their comprehensive website.

SENIOR CITIZENS COUNCIL OF CLACKAMAS COUNTY
(503) 657-1366
www.seniorcouncilofclackamasco.org
The Senior Citizens Council offers a variety of services, including grocery delivery, home care, help with medical equipment and oxygen tanks, and information and referral assistance. They also provide guardian and conservatorship services for elderly citizens who may be vulnerable.

STORE TO DOOR OF OREGON
2145 Northwest Overton St.
(503) 200-3333
www.storetodooroforegon.org
This volunteer agency shops for and delivers groceries to the disabled and senior citizens throughout most of Multnomah and Washington Counties.

Recreation & Education

Portland Area Senior Centers

Senior centers around the Portland metro area are oases of hospitality, compassion, and fun for many senior citizens. Besides offering such wide-ranging activities as ballroom dancing, bingo nights, Bible classes, and knitting and crocheting sessions, they are a place for seniors to meet longtime companions as well as to make new friends and learn about different cultures.

In addition to providing recreational and educational activities, the centers also function as information and referral sites, and periodically provide health and cholesterol screenings, tax and legal assistance, flu shots, and referrals for medical and mental health needs. At many senior centers, volunteers are available to help with a variety of in-home services, shopping and transportation, and other needs.

PORTLAND PARKS AND RECREATION COMMUNITY CENTERS
1120 Southwest 5th Ave.
(503) 823-7529
www.portlandonline.com/parks
Portland Park Bureau's community centers offer a variety of programs and a good number of them are designed specifically for senior citizens. Many of the centers have swimming pools; most have fitness centers and basketball and volleyball courts. It would

---

Elder Care Resources

What if you're a healthy senior but your spouse needs substantial care? Life can be difficult for those whose family members have chronic and debilitating diseases—but help is close at hand. **Expressions,** (503) 252-9361, which cares for Alzheimer's patients, is right next door to Summerplace (see the Home Ownership in Senior Communities section). It's part of a growing trend that places continuing care facilities adjacent to facilities for independent seniors, permitting families to stay together.

Adult day-care centers are another way for seniors and their families to find respite and care. **Providence ElderPlace** is one of a number of interdisciplinary health-care programs set up to provide comprehensive care for both body and soul to frail seniors who are still living at home. They may be reached at (503) 215-6556. You also can check with your local office of the Oregon Senior & Disabled Services Division (SDSD) to find out about similar programs.

---

be impossible to list all the courses that Portland Parks offers—even classifying them takes several pages in the seasonal Portland Parks and Recreation catalog. However, to give you an idea, recent offerings included line dancing, drawing and watercolor painting classes, guitar and piano lessons, birdhouse building, stained glass, sculpting, origami, and flower arranging. Community centers provide more than instruction and classes—they are hubs of social activity. Contact the Parks office to have a complete catalog sent to you.

SENIOR RECREATION PROGRAM
Portland Parks and Recreation
426 Northeast 12th Ave.
(503) 823-4328
www.portlandonline.com/parks
Activities ranging from piano lessons and ceramics classes to Native American pow-wows and hikes on Mount Hood are available at low cost through the Portland Parks and Recreation's Senior Recreation Program. There are also a variety of excursions and day trips planned throughout all seasons of the year. Some are close, such as trips to see the Swan Island dahlias and to ride the Canby Ferry; others are all-day affairs at the Oregon coast or treks up to Silver Star Mountain in Washington. The year-round seniors program provides many great opportunities to meet new friends while staying in good physical condition. Wilderness hikes—to destinations such as Lewis River Falls, Blue Lake, Mount Adams, and Devil Rest Trail in the Columbia Gorge—are offered every weekend during spring and summer months. The program is progressive, giving novices a chance to build up stamina and strength. Other activities include dances to big band orchestras, visits to area golf courses, art classes, yoga training, and computer classes. Activities are held at park sites throughout the city. The service will also help golfers obtain an identification card for reduced greens fees at city of Portland courses. The one-time cost for the card is $10. A handy seasonal catalogue is available online and in print. (Be sure to check out the Portland's Parks chapter for

more information on the vast offerings of this wonderful park system.)

Transportation

The senior centers in the Portland Metro area provide a wide variety of services, including help with transportation needs in their area. But they can only do so much, so many other agencies and volunteer groups have stepped up to fill the gaps in transportation services for seniors.

AMERICAN RED CROSS
3131 North Vancouver Ave.
(503) 284-1234
www.oregonredcross.org
Providing nonemergency transportation to seniors throughout Multnomah and Washington Counties, the American Red Cross will gladly help with almost any request in return for a modest $1.50 donation. This helpful service is available on weekdays from 9 a.m. until 4 p.m., but they stay very busy and it is best to schedule your ride up to two weeks in advance.

**NEIGHBORHOOD HOUSE AGING
SERVICES**
7780 Southwest Capitol Hwy.
(503) 246-1663
www.nhpdx.org/WhatWeDo/seniors
.html
Neighborhood House offers many programs for seniors, but among the most important are the services that help coordinate transportation to medical and dental appointments in southwestern Multnomah County.

PROJECT LINKAGE
2200 Northeast 24th Ave.
(503) 249-0471
www.metfamily.org

Oregon State Services for Seniors

The **Oregon Department of Human Services** (DHS) is the state agency that assists older adults, persons with disabilities, and their caregivers, and they are dedicated to helping people live dignified and independent lives. The division **"Seniors and People with Disabilities"** (SPD) serves as a clearinghouse for all kinds of information, from how to find a nursing home to how to find discounts on travel. You can reach the state office of SPD at 500 Summer St. NE, Salem, OR 97301, (503) 945-5921, (800) 282-8096 (voice/TTY). Their website, http://oregon.gov/DHS/spwpd/index.shtml, is easy to use, comprehensive, and features many links to local, state, and national organizations.

Through its 175 volunteers, this agency assists elderly people living in Northeast and Southeast Portland with a wide range of transportation needs, as well as yard work, housekeeping, minor bookkeeping and bill paying, shopping, and home maintenance.

RIDE CONNECTION
3030 Southwest Moody Ave.
(503) 528-1720 (office),
(503) 226-0700 (transportation services)
www.rideconnection.org

The mission of the nonprofit Ride Connection is to keep seniors mobile for as long as possible. They coordinate a network of more than 30 transportation providers so the elderly and disabled can get where they need to go. This innovative program has won many accolades for its approach to service.

Volunteer Opportunities

If you have the time, many agencies, services, and hospitals in the Portland Metro area would be grateful for your volunteer services. Check with your professional organizations too. But here are just a few places to get you started.

ELDERS IN ACTION
1411 Southwest Morrison St.
(503) 235-5474
www.eldersinaction.org

FOSTER GRANDPARENTS PROGRAM
Metro Family Services
2200 Northeast 24th Ave.
(503) 249-8215
www.metfamily.org

RETIRED AND SENIOR VOLUNTEER PROGRAM OF MULTNOMAH COUNTY
2145 Northwest Overton St.
(503) 413-7787

MEDIA

The media landscape in Portland, like everywhere, is transforming before our eyes. The city's major daily newspaper, the *Oregonian,* is losing subscribers to the dead-tree edition but has a large online following. Local television stations have active, high-traffic websites. Weekly newspapers and monthly glossy magazines continue to have loyal readership; online magazines start and fold—but new ones keep coming. In the face of this experimental churn, it's too early to tell where we are headed.

One notable characteristic, however, is Portland radio. Though Portland's independent music scene could be better represented on the local airwaves, other forms of radio are robust. Oregon Public Broadcasting's radio audience is at the top of the market for National Public Radio programs such as All Things Considered. Local conservative commentator Lars Larson is syndicated nationally. Classical music fans have the outstanding KQAC, one of the few remaining stations that broadcasts nothing but classical music—this time, to an international audience, thanks to the livestream on the Internet.

Ad firm Weiden + Kennedy also deserves a mention—they influence the local media scene but they also have a big national effect, from its iconic ads for Nike to its Old Spice commercials. They have launched the careers of many a copy writer, graphic artist, and web designer, the kind of people who have gone on to influence the look and feel of Portland's media scene.

This chapter takes you through the major and minor players in Portland's news and entertainment media circus. Don't overlook the smaller publications—they are excellent windows into the soul of the city and its microregions.

NEWSPAPERS
Daily Publications

THE COLUMBIAN
701 West 8th St., Vancouver, WA
(360) 694-3391
www.columbian.com
By far the biggest daily newspaper in southwestern Washington, the *Columbian* started out as a weekly newspaper in 1890. In 1908 it became a daily and in 1972 grew to include a Sunday morning paper. Herbert Campbell bought the newspaper in 1921,

and it has been owned by the Campbell family ever since. The *Columbian* is one of the few family-owned and -operated dailies left in the nation and is the fourth-largest newspaper in Washington, with a current daily circulation of 56,000 and a Sunday circulation of 66,000. An afternoon newspaper, the *Columbian* is published every day of the week except Saturday. It prints *TV Times* on Thurs, an entertainment guide titled *Weekend and Beyond* on Fri, a monthly real estate magazine, *Home Book,* and a weekly nonsubscriber product, *Cover Story*, as well as numerous special sections throughout the year. The *Columbian* is available at all newstands and many library branches. You can also look for it online.

THE DAILY JOURNAL OF COMMERCE
2840 Northwest 35th Ave.
(503) 226-1311
http://djcoregon.com

This small paper covers everything from local small businesses to venture capital dealings around the Pacific Northwest. Founded in 1872, the *DJC* is a five-day court and commercial newspaper that is the official publisher for the city of Portland. In addition to general business news, the *DJC* publishes extensive construction industry news and data, mostly for readers in Oregon and Washington. The *DJC* is an essential resource for the business and legal community in Portland.

THE OREGONIAN
1320 Southwest Broadway
(503) 221-8327
www.oregonlive.com

Owned by the New York-based giant media conglomerate Advance Publications, the *Oregonian* casts a long shadow—not just extending over Portland but over the entire state. Loved by some, intensely disliked by others, it seems everyone has an opinion about "the Big O." It is charged with being too conservative and pro big-business on one hand, while on the other, it is accused of leaning too far to the left. Even its critics would agree, however, that as the only major daily newspaper in Oregon, the *Oregonian*, with the largest daily circulation in state (upwards of 250,000), dominates the print media scene. That said, like many daily newspapers, it faces major circulation challenges as the landscape for the newspaper business shifts.

The Sunday *Oregonian* (circulation about 350,000) is still filled with auto, real estate, and other advertisements. The Friday *Oregonian* is also noteworthy for the special *Arts and Entertainment Guide*, information about everything from unique places to go hiking, biking, and bird-watching to classical music performances and public lectures. The guide also features comprehensive coverage of clubs, restaurants, movies, and Portland's live music and fine arts and literary scene. Also, the listing of restaurants and the 10-day planner—an A&E special fold-out calendar—are particularly useful.

Nondailies

THE ASIAN REPORTER
922 North Killingsworth St., Suite 1-A
(503) 283-4440
www.asianreporter.com

This weekly newspaper carries a unique blend of local, regional, national, and international news that impacts or is of interest to the area's Asian community. The *Asian Reporter* features at least three regular opinion columns and frequently profiles notable Asian personalities, including local and visiting artists, writers, and political activists. Besides featuring a variety of carefully selected wire stories, the newspaper provides in-depth coverage of issues related to schools, family, human rights, and culture. The "Arts, Culture, and Entertainment Calendar" lists and describes almost every noteworthy Asian event.

BEAVERTON VALLEY TIMES
6975 Southwest Sandburg Rd.
2nd Floor, Tigard
(503) 684-0360
www.beavertonvalleytimes.com

This community newspaper, dating to the early 1950s, has a circulation of approximately 18,000. It covers news, sports, and livability issues affecting Beaverton and its surrounding environs. It is distributed on Thurs.

THE BUSINESS JOURNAL OF PORTLAND
851 Southwest 6th Ave.
(503) 274-8733
www.bizjournals.com/portland
Part of the nationwide *Business Journal* chain that includes 39 newspapers, the weekly *Business Journal of Portland* was founded in 1984 and is owned by Advance Publications Inc., which also owns the *Oregonian*.

CATHOLIC SENTINEL
5536 Northeast Hassalo St.
(503) 281-1191
www.catholicsentinel.org
Founded in 1870, the *Catholic Sentinel* is the oldest Catholic publication on the entire West Coast. A weekly tabloid with a circulation of approximately 16,200, it covers the local, regional, and national news of interest to the region's Catholic community. The *Catholic Sentinel* is the official publication for the Archdiocese of Portland, which encompasses 29,717 square miles and extends from the summit of the Cascade Mountains in western Oregon to the Pacific Ocean. It's owned and operated by the Oregon Catholic Press of Portland, which is a large publisher of religious books and liturgical materials.

GRESHAM OUTLOOK
1190 Northeast Division St., Gresham
(503) 665-2181
www.theoutlookonline.com

Published Wednesday and Saturday, the *Outlook* reports on all the goings-on in the Gresham area and is particularly noted for its education and sports coverage. Founded in 1911, the *Gresham Outlook* is owned by the Pamplin Corporation, which has also snapped up many community newspapers and the *Portland Tribune*.

THE HOLLYWOOD STAR
3939 Northeast Hancock St., #3
(503) 282-9392
www.thehollywoodstar.com
One of the older and better-established community newspapers in town, the *Hollywood Star* does a solid job of covering the news happenings and people of central Northeast Portland, including the Hollywood, Alameda, Grant Park, Rose City Park, and Madison neighborhoods. This paper has a circulation of about 50,000, and it is distributed by mail and newsstands. The focus is on community news, new businesses, and neighborhood livability issues.

THE JEWISH REVIEW
6680 Southwest Capitol Hwy.
(503) 245-4340
www.jewishreview.org
Serving Oregon and southwest Washington since 1959, this twice-a-month tabloid is published by the Jewish Federation of Portland and features a wide range of national, international, regional, and local news articles and features. The *Review* covers political and sociological issues, features a number of syndicated columns, and regularly reviews adult and children's books. Its calendar provides a good overview of the seminars, concerts, plays, and other events that are of special interest to the Jewish community.

JUST OUT
6234 North Greeley Ave.
(503) 236-1252
www.justout.com
This free, monthly tabloid covers current events and social-political issues affecting the area's gay and lesbian community. The staff regularly reports on the Oregon State Legislature as well as on national issues. The publication also features sections containing news briefs gathered from other states and from around the globe. In each issue *Just Out* runs a comprehensive calendar, including everything from theater and chamber music events to gay roller-skating parties and discussion groups.

THE MID-COUNTY MEMO
4052 Northeast 22nd Ave.
(503) 287-8904
www.midcountymemo.com
This monthly tabloid reports on the news, events, and personalities in outer Northeast Portland, from 82nd Avenue west to 155th Avenue and from Stark Street north to Sandy Boulevard. The *Memo,* with a circulation of about 15,000, focuses on neighborhood concerns and on livability issues, like education and crime, and also features profiles of small businesses and people who are making a difference in the Gateway and Parkrose Districts as well as covering several other smaller midcounty neighborhoods.

THE NORTHWEST EXAMINER
2066 Northwest Irving St.
(503) 241-2353
www.nwexaminer.com
As far as monthly community newspapers go, the *Northwest Examiner,* founded in 1986, is in a class by itself. It tackles controversial issues and isn't afraid of offending advertisers or business interests. Instead of the typical puff pieces about cronies and business supporters, it is full of hard news and unusual feature articles and offers a well-thought-out editorial column that addresses current neighborhood issues. The newspaper includes a section covering the bustling Pearl District. The *Examiner* also does a nice job of describing the restaurants, pubs, bistros, and other businesses on lively 21st and 23rd Avenues. The *Examiner's* 28,000 circulation is distributed throughout the Northwest District and nearby surrounding areas.

THE PORTLAND ALLIANCE
2807 Southeast Stark St.
(503) 239-4991
www.theportlandalliance.org
Founded in 1981 and published by the Northwest Alliance for Alternative Media and Education, the *Alliance* focuses on social, political, and environmental advocacy and reports on a wide spectrum of human rights issues. This progressive, alternative, local news monthly also features a comprehensive calendar of events ranging from peace rallies to union-organizing sessions. It is an articulate venue for progressive causes in Oregon. The newspaper's 21,000 copies are distributed throughout the Portland Metro area by the small but hardworking and versatile group of volunteers that make the *Alliance* tick.

i If you hike or bike to the summit of Mount Tabor at the east end of Southeast Hawthorne, you'll see a statue of Harvey Scott, editor of the *Oregonian* from 1865 to 1910. Scott, with his arm outstretched and finger pointed accusingly at the objects of his editorial wrath, once said, "Write so the hod carrier will understand you."

PORTLAND MERCURY
605 Northeast 21st Ave.
(503) 294-0840
www.portlandmercury.com
In addition to a sizable investigatory article in each issue, knowledgeable coverage of the local music scene, fashion advice, and pithy film reviews, this weekly paper offers columns by staffers on books, television, and restaurants, as well as hilarious advice to the lovelorn by Dan Savage. The *Mercury* offers an irreverent take on all things Portland, including the other weekly.

PORTLAND OBSERVER
4747 Northeast Martin Luther King Jr. Blvd.
(503) 288-0033
www.portlandobserver.com
Portland's oldest and largest newspaper serving the African-American community, the *Observer* was founded in 1971 and covers a broad range of issues and offers features and opinions from Portland and beyond. It's distributed on Wednesday throughout the Portland and Vancouver Metro areas.

PORTLAND TRIBUNE
629 Southwest 5th Ave., Suite 400
(503) 226-6397
www.portlandtribune.com
This weekly newspaper with a daily online edition provides objective news writing, features, and columns. The *Tribune's* expertise at providing follow-up, in-depth coverage to local headlines has brought it national and regional awards. The *Portland Tribune* is an excellent introduction to what's going on in town.

THE SELLWOOD BEE
P.O. Box 82127, Portland, OR 97282
(503) 232-2326
www.readthebee.com
One of Portland's oldest community newspapers, the *Sellwood Bee* serves the Eastmoreland, Westmoreland, Sellwood, Brooklyn, and Reed neighborhoods in inner Southeast Portland. The focus of this monthly publication is news coverage of the events and people that affect the local community.

THE SKANNER
415 North Killingsworth St.
(503) 285-3400
www.theskanner.com
Founded in 1975, the *Skanner* covers the news, politics, and events affecting Portland's African-American community, with a good amount of ink devoted to the family, education, and livability issues of North and Northeast Portlanders. The *Skanner* has won a host of regional and national journalism awards and in 1996 received the Northwest Family Business Award for the small family business of the year. In 1987 The Skanner News Group published its first Seattle edition; today the combined papers have 15 employees and a readership of approximately 75,000. In addition to its regular publication, the *Skanner* prints a half-dozen special issues each year, including a black history edition in Feb, a career guide in June, a minority business enterprise edition in Oct, and a holiday issue in Dec.

THE SOUTHEAST EXAMINER
P.O. Box 33663, Portland, OR 97292
(503) 254-7550
www.southeastexaminer.com
Founded as the *Sunnyside Up News* in 1990 and once a sister publication to the

Northwest Examiner, this monthly tabloid is now independently owned. The *Examiner* covers news from inner Southeast Portland, including the Industrial District, the booming Hawthorne District, and the emerging Belmont and Division Streets all the way out to 82nd Avenue. With a circulation of 24,000, of which 20,000 are home delivered, its coverage area extends roughly from Burnside Street south to Foster Road. The *Southeast Examiner* reports on a wide range of topics with a focus on neighborhood issues, arts and music, food, and history.

STREET ROOTS
211 Northwest Davis St.
(503) 228-5657
www.streetroots.org
This small, lively monthly newspaper gives voice to the homeless while addressing issues relating to homelessness, including health and survival. *Street Roots*, which is published the first of every month, contains news stories, columns, and editorials, and 14,000 copies are distributed throughout downtown Portland.

WILLAMETTE WEEK
2220 Northwest Quimby St.
(503) 243-2122
www.wweek.com
Founded in 1974 by Ron Buel as an alternative newspaper, *Willamette Week (WW)* has grown in size to a circulation of 80,000 and is distributed on Wed throughout the Portland Metro area (and well beyond) at stores, restaurants, coffee shops, and microbrew pubs. This free weekly tabloid has evolved into an upscale publication geared toward a sophisticated audience; it covers local politics, business, and other important issues as well as the cultural scene. Watch for *WW*'s "Best of

Portland" issue in July; it covers everything from the best drinking fountain to the best elevator in town. Willamette Week also publishes an extensive voter's guide in election years as well as annual guides describing the area's best restaurants and brewpubs, which are lively, well written, and informative.

> **i** Portland is a city of neighborhoods, and reading the neighborhood newspapers is indispensable for finding out the scoop on local businesses and events—as well as the political issues that might affect you directly. Find them at coffeeshops, grocery stores, restaurants, and sidewalk kiosks wherever you are.

MAGAZINES

1859
550 SW Industrial Way, Suite 24, Bend
(541) 550-7081 (office)
www.1859magazine.com
This beautiful glossy is notable for its Oregon-wide perspective on lifestyles, history, and culture. 1859 was the year that Oregon became a state; this quarterly magazine is filled with intelligent writing, great photographs, and unusual features, in addition to the expected spreads on stylish houses and people.

METRO PARENT
P.O. Box 13660, Portland, OR 97213
(503) 460-2774
www.metro-parent.com
This user-friendly guide for parents offers a variety of thoughtful articles pertaining to the overall well-being of children. Besides offering an extensive calendar of events, *Metro Parent* regularly features a directory for new parents that includes a wide assortment

of support groups and resources for special-needs children. The monthly calendar is jam-packed with all kinds of stuff, ranging from children's theater to carnivals, concerts, and special exhibits that are geared toward the whole family.

NORTHWEST PALATE
P.O. Box 10860, Portland, OR 97296
(503) 224-6039
www.nwpalate.com
This bimonthly, glossy, consumer magazine focuses on gourmet food, wine, entertainment, and travel in the Pacific Northwest. *Northwest Palate,* which was started as a wine newsletter nearly 20 years ago by owner/publisher/editor Cameron Nagel, is still independently owned and has now built its circulation to 45,000 with readers in all 50 states and Europe—most concentrated in Washington and Oregon. It is a well-written, indispensable guide to the local food, farm, and wine scene.

OPEN SPACES
www.open-spaces.com
Open Spaces quarterly provides intelligent commentary on the major issues facing the Pacific Northwest, giving voice to a variety of perspectives and opinions. This thoughtful magazine offers respite from the cacophony of unsubstantiated opinion that too often passes for debate in our 24/7 connected world. You should read it, even if you don't live in Portland. It also features good fiction, poetry, and other kinds of writing.

OREGON BUSINESS MAGAZINE
610 Southwest Broadway, Suite 200
(503) 223-0304
www.oregonbusiness.com

Founded in 1981, owned by MEDIAmerica Inc., and with a circulation of 20,200, this highly polished publication covers the business scene all over Oregon and southwestern Washington. Issues regularly contain investigative business reporting, small business articles, profiles of unique people and their companies, and section pieces ranging from transportation issues and electronic commerce to education. The continuing focus of the magazine is helping large and small businesses identify and solve problems. Each year *Oregon Business* publishes special editions, which cover the fastest-growing companies in Oregon and the 100 best companies to work for.

OREGON HOME
MediAmerica Inc.
610 Southwest Broadway, Suite 200,
Portland
www.oregonhomemagazine.com
Oregon Home is a glossy magazine published bimonthly that is devoted to houses in Oregon—how they are decorated and lived in. Their company mantra is "real people, real homes," and it's true. One of the pleasures of this publication is reading it to see if anyone you know is featured in it. It happens more than you might think. You can find it by looking at supermarket checkout stands and other newsstand spots, or contact the publisher online to subscribe.

PORTLAND FAMILY MAGAZINE
12725 SW Millikan Way, #300, Beaverton
(503) 906-7952
www.portlandfamily.com
This slender and wholesome-as-apple-pie magazine offers useful information for all concerned parents. Besides tackling serious issues such as education, health and

wellness, and child development, *Portland Family Magazine (PFM)* keeps a calendar of events listing and describes events and fun activities that parents and their kids can enjoy together. A handsomely designed monthly with short readable stories and blurbs, *PFM* includes a column, "School Notes," with the latest info on education, and *The Spirit of Giving*, a guide for families, organizations, and individuals in need. A good resource for families, *PFM* is distributed throughout the Portland and Vancouver areas.

PORTLAND MONTHLY
623 Southwest Oak St. Suite 300
(503) 222-5144
www.portlandmonthlymag.com
This monthly magazine provides outstanding coverage of all things Portland, from real estate and restaurants to fashion and fundraisers. Established in 2003, it has quickly become a must-read magazine for Portlanders. They present annual issues dedicated to health care, vacations, and other themes. But they also can take on the serious issues of the day. Find it at newsstands all through town, or subscribe online.

i Blogging is very Portland—it's the essence of the do-it-yourself spirit. Some of our favorite Portland blogs are *Overheard in PDX* (http://overheardinpdx.blogspot.com), a report of the funny, the odd, and the witty things that strangers say; *Good Stuff Northwest* (www.goodstuffnw.com), a compendium of delightful Oregon things; and *Silicon Florist* (http://siliconflorist.com), which usefully covers the start-up scene.

TELEVISION

KATU-TV CHANNEL 2 (ABC)
2153 Northeast Sandy Blvd.
(503) 231-4222
www.katu.com
The ABC affiliate is noted for refers to its number on the dial and to a pair of weather and traffic choppers hovering over the town like two dragonflies. Not only does KATU deliver crisp and clear news reports, it also hosts a Town Hall roughly every quarter in which citizens can sound off about issues making headlines.

KGW-TV CHANNEL 8 (NBC)
1501 Southwest Jefferson St.
(503) 226-5000
www.kgw.com
Perhaps the most flamboyant of all the local stations, KGW seems to have the biggest news staff. Maff Zaffino, an affable weather guy, is noted for his briefings on snow conditions up in the Cascade Mountains. Another popular feature is KGW's Unit 8, a consumer hotline that sends investigators out to find out who's scamming seniors, adding bogus charges to your phone bill, or charging the government big bucks for substandard housing.

KOIN-TV CHANNEL 6 (CBS)
222 Southwest Columbia Dr.
(503) 464-0600
www.koin.com
This pioneer broadcasting operation began as a radio station in 1925, sending out a signal from a single room in the Portland Hotel. By 1930 KOIN was Portland's CBS affiliate, and on October 15, 1953, KOIN-TV signed on as Portland's first VHF television station and as an affiliate of the CBS Television Network. KOIN was the first station in

Portland to broadcast a one-hour newscast at 5 p.m. Currently KOIN is in the KOIN Tower, an easily recognizable landmark in downtown Portland.

KOPB-TV CHANNEL 10 (PBS)
7140 Southwest Macadam Ave.
(503) 244-9900
www.opb.org
The Oregon Public Broadcasting station started in 1922 as an engineering professor's 50-watt transmitter. KOPB now serves the entire state and a portion of southwest Washington as the affiliate for PBS and a venue for local issue-driven and cultural programs.

KPDX-TV CHANNEL 49 (FOX)
14975 Northwest Greenbrier Pkwy.,
Beaverton
(503) 906-1249
www.kpdx.com
The only local programming on KPDX, a local FOX affiliate, is a news program at 10 p.m. But those who watch FOX's "tabloid television" to catch the goofy pratfalls and dangerous dangles broadcast by the network don't seem disappointed at the lack of local shows.

KPTV-TV CHANNEL 12 (FOX)
14975 Northwest Greenbrier Pkwy.,
Beaverton
(503) 906-1249
www.kptv.com
This TV station in Portland was launched in 1952. It is a local affiliate for the Fox Network and the nation's first laboratory for digital-to-air technology. It's also known for its independent, quirky broadcasting like the popular *Good Day, Oregon,* which might feature taking your dog on a hike through the snow, how to braise chicken legs, or what's

the latest hot exhibit for kids at the Oregon Museum of Science and Industry (OMSI). KPTV also gets viewer points for airing the 10 o'clock news an hour earlier than most late-night newscasts.

i For a really useful guide to Portland Metro arear radio, check out www.pdxradio.com/Home.html—you'll find information on the format, call letters, and other tips on the local airwaves, including historical notes and details on finding good Internet radio.

RADIO STATIONS

KBOO/90.7 FM
20 Southeast 8th Ave.
(503) 231-8032
www.kboo.org
The call letters KBOO were chosen because the gang organizing the station decided to go for it on Halloween 1963; they were on the air the following June. The local Pacifica affiliate, it is dedicated to innovative programming, including classical, rock, and folk. In the early 1980s, KBOO broadened its commitment to multicultural programming by adding Spanish, Asian-American, and African-American musical shows.

KBPS/89.9 FM AND 1450 AM
515 Northeast 15th Ave.
(503) 916-5828
www.allclassical.org
KBPS is Portland's classical music station. Wonderfully commercial free, the station began in the early 1980s as a project of students at Benson High School. Budget cuts to the program led to its eventual independence, and the station is now building an endowment to ensure that the works of the great composers, as well as their less famous

peers, are heard throughout western Oregon forever. KBPS also broadcasts headline news from the BBC. Plus, they organize interesting concerts, contests, and other events—even music-focused tours of Europe.

KINK/102 FM
1501 Southwest Jefferson St.
(503) 241-1020
www.kink102.com
A popular station for more than 30 years, KINK is home base for local baby boomers who enjoy aging rockers, folksingers, and jazz artists as well as new releases by contemporary popsters.

KKRZ/100 FM
4949 Southwest Macadam Ave.
(503) 226-0100
www.z100portland.com
This station, known as Z-100, has been No. 1 in the local ratings competition for the past few years because of the wide appeal of its contemporary hits format.

KMHD/89.1 FM
26000 Southeast Stark St., Gresham
(503) 661-8900

"The Jazz Station" since its start in 1984, KMHD is operated by Mt. Hood Community College in nearby Gresham. With an extensive library of more than 6,000 LPs and CDs, KMHD plays a full spectrum of jazz artists ranging from Ella Fitzgerald to Miles Davis to Horace Silver.

KNRK/94.7 FM
700 Southwest Bancroft St.
(503) 733-5470
www.947.fm
Portland's boldest champion of new rock stretches the envelope of alternative music with live broadcasts from local rock venues as well as a steady bill of edgy tunes.

KOPB/91.5 FM
7140 Southwest Macadam Ave.
(503) 293-1905
www.opb.org
The local spot on the dial for National Public Broadcasting, KOPB will connect you to *A Prairie Home Companion, Thistle and Shamrock,* and *Alternative Radio,* as well as local talk shows and lectures.

INDEX

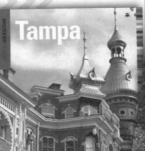

INSIDERS' GUIDE®

The acclaimed travel series that has sold more than 2 million copies!

Discover: Your Travel Destination.
Your Home. Your Home-to-Be.

Albuquerque

Anchorage &
  Southcentral
  Alaska

Atlanta

Austin

Baltimore

Baton Rouge

Boulder & Rocky Mountain
  National Park

Branson & the Ozark
  Mountains

California's Wine Country

Cape Cod & the Islands

Charleston

Charlotte

Chicago

Cincinnati

Civil War Sites in
  the Eastern Theater

Civil War Sites in the South

Colorado's Mountains

Dallas & Fort Worth

Denver

El Paso

Florida Keys & Key West

Gettysburg

Glacier National Park

Great Smoky Mountains

Greater Fort Lauderdale

Greater Tampa Bay Area

Hampton Roads

Houston

Hudson River Valley

Indianapolis

Jacksonville

Kansas City

Long Island

Louisville

Madison

Maine Coast

Memphis

Myrtle Beach &
  the Grand Strand

Nashville

New Orleans

New York City

North Carolina's
  Mountains

North Carolina's
  Outer Banks

North Carolina's
  Piedmont Triad

Oklahoma City

Orange County, CA

Oregon Coast

Palm Beach County

Palm Springs

Philadelphia &
  Pennsylvania Dutch
  Country

Phoenix

Portland, Maine

Portland, Oregon

Raleigh, Durham &
  Chapel Hill

Richmond, VA

Reno and Lake Tahoe

St. Louis

San Antonio

Santa Fe

Savannah & Hilton Head

Seattle

Shreveport

South Dakota's
  Black Hills Badlands

Southwest Florida

Tucson

Tulsa

Twin Cities

Washington, D.C.

Williamsburg & Virginia's
  Historic Triangle

Yellowstone
  & Grand Teton

Yosemite

To order call 800-243-0495
or visit www.Insiders.com